American Battle Monuments
Commission
WWI and WWII Cemeteries
and Memorials
Europe and North Africa

✝ American Cemetery
✚ American Cemetery and Memorial

Berlin ✪

GERMANY

Prague ✪

CZECHIA

SLOVAKIA
Bratislava ✪

Budapest ✪

HUNGARY

Ljubljana ✪     Zagreb ✪
SLOVENIA     CROATIA

BOSNIA AND
HERZEGOVINA
Sarajevo ✪

ITALY

✚ Florence

Adriatic
Sea

Rome ✪
Sicily-Rome ✝

To Tunis,
Tunisia,
315 miles

Gene Thorp

T0356121

# REMEMBER
## US

## Also by Robert M. Edsel

*Rescuing da Vinci: Hitler and the Nazis Stole Europe's
Great Art, America and Her Allies Recovered It*

*The Monuments Men: Allied Heroes, Nazi Thieves, and the
Greatest Treasure Hunt in History* (with Bret Witter)

*Saving Italy: The Race to Rescue a Nation's Treasures from the Nazis*

*The Greatest Treasure Hunt in History: The Story of the Monuments Men*

# REMEMBER
# US

★ ★ ★

American Sacrifice, Dutch Freedom, and a
Forever Promise Forged in World War II

### ROBERT M. EDSEL

#1 *New York Times* bestselling author of
*The Monuments Men*

**WITH BRET WITTER**

HARPER HORIZON

*Interior design: Kait Lamphere*

ISBN 978-1-4003-3782-8 (eBook)
ISBN 978-1-4003-3781-1 (HC)

**Library of Congress Control Number: 9781400337811**

*Printed in the United States of America*
25 26 27 28 29  LBC  5 4 3 2 1

*To the men and women in uniform who defend freedom.*
*To the Dutch adopters who continue to honor the*
*sacrifice of their American liberators.*

*And to my boys, Rodney, Francesco, and Diego:*
*always remember that service to others is the*
*path to a meaningful and joyful life.*

# CONTENTS

Author's Note.............................................xi
Major Characters ....................................... xiii
Prologue: A Journey of Discovery and Gratitude .... xix

### Part I: Freedom Lost

1.  "It's War!"......................................... 3
2.  Rising Stars...................................... 8
3.  Mr. and Mrs. Kippenburgemeester ........... 14
4.  A Way Out....................................... 23
5.  "Willie"............................................. 28
6.  The Caves ........................................ 32
7.  Hostages........................................... 38
8.  Pig Paths.......................................... 44
9.  Risks ............................................... 49
10. Most Popular Boy ........................... 54

### Part II: To the Wall

11. Hardships and Happier Times ............... 65
12. A New Arrival................................... 74
13. Basic.............................................. 75
14. The Library...................................... 80
15. Floating Objects .............................. 83
16. A Welcome Surprise........................ 84
17. Memory Books............................... 88
18. Hope Overhead ............................... 90
19. The Message.................................... 95
20. Peasants and the Powerful ................... 97

# CONTENTS

21. An Egg ..................................... 101
22. A Miracle ................................. 104
23. Faith........................................ 110
24. Mother ..................................... 111
25. Pain ........................................ 116
26. D-Day ...................................... 119
27. News ....................................... 126
28. Purple Heart Lane......................... 127
29. Homecoming .............................. 132
30. Trust ....................................... 136
31. Exodus ..................................... 139
32. Liberation ................................. 144
33. Hell's Highway............................. 153

## Part III: Homefront Limburg

34. The Process................................ 165
35. Lending a Hand ........................... 175
36. Trouble .................................... 183
37. Transitions................................. 188
38. The Stripping Line ........................ 190
39. A Necessary Task.......................... 194
40. Entertainment ............................ 199
41. New Faces ................................. 205
42. Papa........................................ 210
43. Courage ................................... 213
44. The Worst Job............................. 215
45. Christmas ................................. 221
46. Special Friends............................ 227
47. The Honeymoon Ends .................... 231

## Part IV: Over the Rhine

48. Curley...................................... 239
49. Ritchie Boy ............................... 247

# CONTENTS

50. The Cathedral .............................255
51. "It Will Be Done" ..........................257
52. The Civilian Committee.....................264
53. A Ragged Bunch ..........................267
54. The Dance ...............................270
55. Promise Kept ............................274
56. Respite ..................................275
57. First Jump ...............................280
58. Frantic Days .............................284
59. River Crossing ...........................288
60. Lost .....................................290
61. Man Behind .............................292
62. O-910847................................295
63. The Letter ...............................297
64. Slaughter ...............................298
65. The End .................................303
66. The Photos ..............................306
67. Memorial Day............................309
68. A Sign ..................................316

### Part V: Love and Remembrance

69. Going Home..............................321
70. Mail.....................................330
71. Tour Guide ..............................337
72. Family Affair.............................341
73. Haarlem .................................346
74. Reinforcements ..........................351
75. Relocations and Beautification..............356
76. A New Approach .........................362
77. Planning.................................365
78. Approvals................................371
79. The Trip.................................374
80. A Special Good-bye .......................387
81. Closure..................................389

# CONTENTS

Epilogue: Eighty Years . . . . . . . . . . . . . . . . . . . . . . . . . 393

The Forever Promise Project . . . . . . . . . . . . . . . . . . . . . 421

Acknowledgments . . . . . . . . . . . . . . . . . . . . . . . . . . . . . 423

What's in Your Attic? . . . . . . . . . . . . . . . . . . . . . . . . . . . 431

Endnotes . . . . . . . . . . . . . . . . . . . . . . . . . . . . . . . . . . . . 432

Bibliography . . . . . . . . . . . . . . . . . . . . . . . . . . . . . . . . . . 477

Photo Captions and Credits . . . . . . . . . . . . . . . . . . . . . 486

Index . . . . . . . . . . . . . . . . . . . . . . . . . . . . . . . . . . . . . . . 490

# AUTHOR'S NOTE

The photo on the front cover is of an American paratrooper from the 82nd Airborne Division playing with two Dutch children, near the village of Malden, south of Nijmegen, the Netherlands, on September 18, 1944, the day after the commencement of Operation Market Garden. Please contact the author at *info@robertedsel.com* if you are able to identify the soldier or children in this photograph.

*The battle for the preservation of decency and of freedom and of justice is a battle that never begins and never ends; it just always is. This makes of life, your life and my life, a kind of warfare in which we are ever constantly engaged. . . . Peace, therefore, is never mere absence of war. True peace is that knowledge that . . . in the midst of the warfare we are doing our duty.*

First Lieutenant Paschal D. Fowlkes,
Chaplain, 507th Parachute Infantry

— ★ —

# MAJOR CHARACTERS

As they were on May 10, 1940, the day of Nazi Germany's invasion of Western Europe:

**Robert G. Cole**, a twenty-five-year-old professional soldier from San Antonio, Texas. He is one month from marrying his high school sweetheart, Allie Mae, and is serving as commander of an anti-tank company at Fort Lewis, Washington. He will become a lieutenant colonel in the 502nd Parachute Infantry, 101st Airborne Division.

**Paschal "Pat" D. Fowlkes**, a twenty-four-year-old Episcopalian minister from Burkeville, Virginia. He has recently graduated from the seminary and is one month from marrying Elizabeth, whom he has known since high school. He will become a U.S. Army chaplain.

**Jacob T. Herman Jr.**, a fourteen-year-old member of the Oglala Lakota Nation living with his family in the Badlands of South Dakota. He will become a paratrooper in the 505th Parachute Infantry, 82nd Airborne Division.

# MAJOR CHARACTERS

**Walter J. Huchthausen**, an accomplished thirty-five-year-old architect and son of German immigrants who is teaching at his alma mater, the University of Minnesota. He will become a Monuments, Fine Arts, and Archives officer (a Monuments Man).

**Bill M. Hughes**, a seventeen-year-old high school student who dreams of escaping the racism of his hometown of Indianapolis, Indiana. He will become a radioman in the segregated 784th Tank Battalion.

**Emilie Michiels van Kessenich**, a thirty-three-year-old Dutch mother of eight and the wife of the mayor of Maastricht, the capital of the southernmost province of the Netherlands, Limburg. She will have three more children during the war and find new purpose working with and for American soldiers.

**John L. Low (pronounced like "how") Jr.**, a twenty-year-old graduate of Bowling Green Business School and an office manager at the family business in Laurel, Mississippi. He will become the group bombardier of the 467th Bombardment Group.

**Bill F. Moore**, a nineteen-year-old who has recently dropped out of the University of Georgia and taken a job at an engineering firm in Atlanta, Georgia. Moore and Low will end up in a bomber over Germany together.

## MAJOR CHARACTERS

**Sigmund (Stephen) Mosbacher**, a sixteen-year-old German Jew who immigrated to the United States with his family in 1938. They are settling into their new home in Toledo, Ohio, where Stephen is studying chemical engineering at a local university. He will become an interpreter and member of a military intelligence team in the 8th Armored Division.

**James A.** and **Edward R. Norton**, nineteen-year-old twin brothers who are roommates at Clemson College. They are the sons and grandsons of the town doctors in Conway, South Carolina. Never apart, The Twins (as they are known) will fly together as pilot and copilot in a B-26 Marauder.

**Frieda van Schaïk**, a fifteen-year-old Dutch schoolgirl living in the village of Heer, about four miles east of Maastricht. The youngest of six children, she will shoulder many of the burdens of her family's home life during the German occupation.

**Jefferson Wiggins**, a fifteen-year-old delivery boy from a poor but proud sharecropping family near Dothan, Alabama. He will become a staff sergeant in the Army's Quartermaster Corps.

**Margraten**, a quiet, unassuming Dutch village of about 1,500 people until the morning of May 10, 1940, when German tanks roll across the border just ten miles away.

## *At Margraten*

**Father Johannes Heuschen,** an energetic young Catholic priest in his early thirties assigned to the parish in the village of Margraten in fall 1944.

**Father Pierre Heynen**, a local Dutch priest who administers to the American soldiers at Margraten.

**Joseph Ronckers,** the mayor of Margraten.

**Joseph van Laar,** the Margraten village clerk and Shomon's primary interpreter.

**Captain Joseph J. Shomon,** a forester from Connecticut, who, as the commanding officer of the 611th Quartermaster Graves Registration Company, is responsible for siting, building, and overseeing what would become the Netherlands American Cemetery at Margraten.

# The Young Dead Soldiers
## Do Not Speak

— ★ —

*Nevertheless they are heard in the still houses:*
*who has not heard them?*

*They have a silence that speaks for them at*
*night and when the clock counts.*

*They say, We were young. We have died.*
*Remember us.*

*They say, We have done what we could but*
*until it is finished it is not done.*

*They say, We have given our lives but until it is*
*finished no one can know what our lives gave.*

*They say, Our deaths are not ours: they are yours:*
*they will mean what you make them.*

*They say, Whether our lives and our deaths were for peace*
*and a new hope or for nothing we cannot say: it is you who*
*must say this.*

*They say, We leave you our deaths: give them their meaning:*
*give them an end to the war and a true peace: give them a*
*victory that ends the war and a peace afterwards: give them*
*their meaning*

*We were young, they say. We have died.*
*Remember us.*

Archibald MacLeish

# PROLOGUE

— ★ —

*A Journey of Discovery and Gratitude*

The snow is six or seven inches deep on the graves at the Netherlands American Cemetery outside the small village of Margraten. It was not this deep in the harsh winter of 1944, when these graves were dug by hand, but it was cold and rainy, and the steam poured off the backs of the diggers as they descended into the mud. It rose from the shoulders of the men who lugged the corpses, from the engines of the trucks that idled at the mortuary tents, and from the bloodied bodies piled high beneath their canvas tops.

It's quieter now. Silent, almost, where hundreds of men once toiled. The snow coats the crosses and the Stars of David. It covers the grass that blankets the graves. It frosts the cherry trees—symbols of rebirth that remind us life is fleeting—lining the central walkway and the frozen reflection pools that lead the visitor up a gentle slope to the memorial tower. Along the edges, the Walls of the Missing. Beyond the tower and chapel, the curving fan of graves, where fifty rows away schoolchildren follow an older man, a cemetery volunteer. Small groups are gathered at several graves; at other graves a single person stands, hunched against the cold, but whatever they are saying is lost in the wind whistling through the immaculate white headstones doubling, tripling, and repeating down eighty-five nearly identical rows.

Every graveyard tells a story. This one is relatively straightforward. The Netherlands American Cemetery is the final resting place of more than 8,200 American soldiers, airmen, and support personnel killed in the liberation of a portion of the Netherlands and in the assault on Germany in late 1944 and 1945. It was here, in the winter of 1944, that the United States Armed Forces began to bury their fallen, even as thousands of soldiers took rest from the front in nearby towns and billeted in houses within sight and sound of the graveyard. And it was here, in May 1946, on the second postwar Memorial Day, that more than 40,000 Dutch mourners came to honor the American men and women who had died to restore their freedom at what was, at the time, the largest American military cemetery in Europe.

Beginning in 1947, the United States government offered to bring its 280,000 sons and daughters home for reburial. Many families accepted the government's offer, but 39 percent did not. Since 1949, when the 8,200 or so remaining bodies at Margraten were reburied in the permanent layout, the Netherlands American Cemetery has been their final home. The Walls of the Missing, fronted by the beautiful cherry trees, are carved with the names of 1,700 more. They are the Americans, mostly young, many volunteers, who gave everything. They rest here now through the rains of spring, the heat of summer, the leaves of autumn, and the snow of winter.

Almost 10,000 stories—too many to tell.

They include Major General Maurice Rose, the highest-ranking American officer killed by enemy fire in the European Theater of Operations. Staff Sergeant George Peterson, a recipient of the nation's highest award for valor, the Medal of Honor, who fought his way from North Africa and Sicily to France and Germany and was killed on the same day as General Rose. Private First Class Jack Cook, an orphan, lied about his age: he was just fourteen years old when he enlisted. Staff Sergeant Itsumu Sasaoka, a Japanese American who fought with the fabled "Go For Broke" 442nd Regimental Combat Team of Nisei warriors, killed by the Soviet Red Army while escaping from a German POW camp. Private Henry E. "Rickey" Marquez, son of a Mexican immigrant, who went missing in action during the Battle of Hürtgen Forest. His remains were found in 2007. And First Lieutenant Wilma R. "Dolly" Vinsant—one of four women at Margraten—a newly married combat nurse who volunteered to fly one last mission of mercy as a favor to a friend, only to have her plane shot down. All their sacrifices are worth celebrating. All their stories are worth hearing. Every story in Margraten is worth the time to sit, listen, and learn.

The American service members chosen for this book are no better or worthier than the men and women they lie beside. They are airmen who flew on small raids or within enormous bomber armadas, infantry officers who saw combat as the organizing principle of their existence, and volunteers who fell to their knees at the prospect of facing the enemy but rose again to fight on. They are doctors' sons from the Deep South and poor kids from the Northeast; citizen soldiers and Army lifers; Native Americans and Jewish refugees. Six members of the Band of Brothers (Easy Company, 506th Parachute Infantry) are buried at Margraten, along with forty sets of biological brothers buried side by side. There are women killed in combat support; quartermaster troops killed by a bomb while doing laundry; chaplains who died with Bibles in their pockets; and Black tank crews who fought so bravely and so well that even the most hardened white soldiers learned to respect them, if not love them, for their prowess on the battlefield. With a fallen soldier from all fifty states, plus the District of Columbia, the cemetery is a snapshot of mid-century America.

Together, these sons and daughters tell a larger narrative with a narrow sweep: how Western Allied forces rolled into the Netherlands on the backs of thousands of brave young men and women, why their advance faltered there, and of the effort and sacrifice it took to carry the offensive across the German border and through the final march on Berlin.

This book is not a collection of personal stories. It is the story of World War II as seen from one small province in one small country, an epicenter for four of the war's most famous battles: Operation Market Garden, the Battle of Aachen, the Battle of Hürtgen Forest, and the Battle of the Bulge. The first province in Western Europe conquered by the Nazis, the headquarters for the Ninth United States Army, the graveyard of thousands. A rural province only 850 miles square (smaller than the state of Rhode Island) that nonetheless highlights a fundamental truth that lies at the heart of the Netherlands American Cemetery at Margraten: The heroes buried here were part of something larger than themselves, but it was the collective strength of their individual actions and sacrifices that turned back the tide of totalitarianism and turned mankind away from bitterness and hate. Not forever. Not even for a generation. But this time.

Eighty years later, the bloodshed and deprivation in Western Europe is gone. Damaged cities have been rebuilt. Pockmarked countryside has returned to its natural state. Former enemies are now allies. But America's overseas military cemeteries remain, filled with service members who, as Supreme Allied Commander General Dwight D. Eisenhower noted after the war, stormed the beaches and dropped from the skies "not to gain anything for ourselves, not to fulfill any ambitions that America had for conquest, but just to preserve freedom."

Freedom is, in the final analysis, worth dying for, and the Netherlands American Cemetery represents its cost—as measured in children not born, lives not lived, careers not pursued, art and beauty not created.

The dead, these dead, are the heart of this story. And yet, they are only a part of it. The Netherlands American Cemetery is also the story of the leaders who created this burial ground; the officers who planned it; the army that built it; the soldiers who scoured every inch of the Netherlands and Germany to find the missing; and the men who transported, autopsied, cataloged, and buried the remains—every piece of the apparatus dedicated to fulfilling the unique promise of Lieutenant General William Hood Simpson, commanding general of the Ninth Army, to bury no American on enemy soil.

It is the story of the men who dug thousands of graves by hand in the drenching rains of 1944; who placed a dog tag in the mouth of each fallen man and woman, lowered them into the ground with respect, but placed in nothing more than a mattress cover. It is a reminder that this quiet vale of snow, with its mature trees and marble tombstones, was once a sucking field of mud, its edges stacked with bodies, its silence shattered by the dull thud of shovels, its dark and choppy surface marked with white wooden crosses and Stars of David nailed with the second dog tag of the young dead American buried underneath.

It is the story of the commissioners and staff of the American Battle Monuments Commission (ABMC), who today, with unfailing dedication, operate and maintain twenty-six military cemeteries and thirty-two federal memorials, monuments, and markers in seventeen countries. It is the story of the Defense POW/MIA Accounting Agency (DPAA), the office within the Department of Defense whose teams of experts carry on the mission to locate the remains of service members still missing.

And it is the story of the Dutch, because the Netherlands American Cemetery is not *anyplace* but is in a specific place: outside the village of Margraten, eight miles southeast of the city of Maastricht, in the province of Limburg, at the southern tip of the Netherlands. It was the Dutch who drew me to this story, or more specifically, a letter from a young Dutch woman seeking the address of a soldier's mother.

"He is buried at the large U.S. Military Cemetery in Margraten, Holland," she wrote in fall 1945, "a place 6 miles from where I live. *I am taking care of his grave.*"

On May 30, 2016, I met the Dutch woman who wrote that letter. By chance, it was Memorial Day. I thought of my visit as a social call; we had a shared interest in, and affection for, the same soldier. But by the time she showed me photographs of American tanks parked in front of her home, and an American soldier holding her toddler niece, I knew it was more. This wasn't just his story. It was her story too.

Then she showed me photos of the Netherlands American Cemetery. "Have you heard of the Margraten grave adoption program?" she asked.

Embarrassed, I said that I had not. But I promised to do my homework and return.

"We were young. We have died. Remember us." Archibald MacLeish wrote in his masterful poem "The Young Dead Soldiers Do Not Speak":

> *They say, Our deaths are not ours: they are yours:*
> *they will mean what you make them.*

What I've learned since that Memorial Day in 2016 is this: How we remember and honor those who died in war matters. It comforts those left behind. It gives their sacrifice meaning. It reminds all of us that freedom is not free. The Dutch of the South Limburg region understand this. They have, since 1944, been going to extraordinary lengths to honor and remember the young, dead Americans buried in their midst. Since spring 1946, when a committee of caring citizens in the small town of Margraten completed its work matching a local adopter with every grave in the cemetery, no fallen American has been left without a mourner. No life has been forgotten. This work is not a duty to these thousands of adopters; it is an honor. Partial payment on a debt that can never be repaid. A thank-you from the Dutch to the men and women who liberated them from evil. A forever promise, now in its eightieth year.

It has been my honor to spend eight years in the presence of the soldiers, aircrews, tankers, and nurses buried in the Netherlands American

Cemetery and with the Dutch citizens, especially those involved with the Foundation for Adopting Graves American Cemetery Margraten, who watch over them as their own: researching, interviewing, working, reworking, and walking the sacred ground of Margraten, trying to feel as best I can the terror, the fortitude, the faith, and the love. Not trying to *make* a meaning, as MacLeish wrote, but to *uncover* the meaning that has always rested here.

It is hard to know where to start a story. Any story. I tried many different places with this one. Too many to count. But in the end, I realized, this story starts where all stories of triumph must: with defeat.

Because how can you truly cherish the priceless things—freedom, love, friendship, even life itself—if you've never had them taken away?

*Robert M. Edsel*
*On my eighth return from Margraten*
*January 2023*

# PART I

# FREEDOM LOST

— ★ —

## May 1940–May 1943

*In the future days, which we seek to make secure, we look forward to a world founded upon four essential human freedoms. The first is freedom of speech and expression—everywhere in the world. The second is freedom of every person to worship God in his own way—everywhere in the world. The third is freedom from want . . . everywhere in the world. The fourth is freedom from fear . . . anywhere in the world. That is no vision of a distant millennium. It is a definite basis for a kind of world attainable in our own time and generation.*

President Franklin D. Roosevelt

German Invasion
of the Netherlands
May 10-17, 1940

# CHAPTER 1

# "IT'S WAR!"

— ★ —

*Emilie Michiels van Kessenich*
May 10, 1940

Emilie Michiels van Kessenich snapped awake just after 2:30 a.m. The night was dark and full of crackling, set against a heavy droning sound. At first, she didn't know what she was hearing. Then she realized: gunfire and aircraft.

"Manka," she said, her pet name for her husband, Willem, "little man" in Dutch, but he was already up.

"I know," he said. "Get the children."

Jenneke, their eldest daughter, lay awake, barely breathing, listening as the warplanes passed overhead. She was eight and convinced that if she didn't move, if she didn't make a sound, everything would be alright. And then her nanny was at her shoulder, shaking her firmly, tossing her clothes on the bed and almost shouting: "Hurry, child. It's war!"

By the time the nanny, Agnes, had woken Jenneke's younger sisters, Emilie was hurrying the four boys down the stairs, with the baby in her arms. One, two, three . . . she counted all eight children. "To the basement," she said, much more calmly than she felt.

By then, Willem was dressed. He kissed Emilie good-bye, turned back at the door to hug her once more, then rushed out to city hall. He was the mayor of Maastricht, the capital of the Dutch province of Limburg, and he was off to fulfill, as Emilie wrote in her journal, "his gritty job."

The German warplanes had crossed into Dutch airspace at 1:30 a.m. A massive, lightning-fast ground assault, a blitzkrieg, followed close behind.

3

This was more than an assault on a country, it was a hinge of history: Hitler had turned his war machine toward Western Europe. Within two months, Paris would fall, France would surrender, and all of continental Europe between the Soviet Union and Spain would lie in the Nazi shadow. But that morning, May 10, 1940, in the southern Dutch province of Limburg, the main concern was the left flank of Germany's Army Group B. They were speeding up the Rijksweg Maastricht-Aken, the main road connecting Maastricht with the German city of Aachen, shouting through megaphones, "Nicht schießen, Holländer, nicht schießen!" ("Don't shoot, Dutchmen, don't shoot!")

The Netherlands had declared neutrality in 1939, after Germany invaded Poland. It had maintained its neutrality in every European conflict for four generations, including World War I. The last attack on Maastricht was during the Napoleonic Wars. Nonetheless, the Dutch had prepared, mobilizing and positioning their army for defense the year before. But the first two defensive lines in Limburg collapsed so quickly the Dutch troops were captured before they could retreat. The third line held, but for less than an hour. By 4:00 a.m., Emilie could hear explosions across the Maas River, which divided Maastricht from its eastern neighborhood of Wyck. She could feel the thunder of the antiaircraft emplacements firing at the warplanes overhead.

Last spring, her daughter Jenneke had celebrated her First Communion. Last summer, she and Willem had taken the children on a long hike across the country. The day before, they had attended a wedding full of love and grace, a promise like every wedding of happy times ahead. Now, Emilie worried about her family surviving the hour. She worried she'd never see her husband again. Now Jenneke was on her knees, praying the Rosary over and over, loud enough for God to hear.

And little Mathilda, somehow asleep in Emilie's arms, only six weeks old.

"The Prussians! The Prussians!" two men on bicycles shouted, tearing down the Wycker Brugstraat, the street connecting the train station in Wyck to the Sint Servaas Bridge. Seconds later came the tanks, the armored cars, the infantrymen with their drab gray uniforms and distinctive coal scuttle helmets, their rifles and "potato mashers," the infamous German hand grenades on wooden handles that made them easier to throw.

*Calm, my little ones*, Emilie thought in her basement across the river. *We are in God's hands.*

On Akerstraat, a Dutch ambush destroyed two tanks. Gunshots echoed off the buildings as the Germans leapt into doorways, seeking cover. At 5:45 a.m., the first Germans to reach the Maas River watched as the 650-year-old Sint Servaas Bridge collapsed in front of them. The explosion was so powerful it shattered windows on both sides of the river, sending flying glass into the streets. Fifteen minutes later, still hoping to slow the enemy advance, the Dutch blew up the Wilhelmina Bridge. They blasted the third and final bridge, the railroad trestle, five minutes later, along with a company of German soldiers halfway across it.

On the far side of the river, Emilie prayed.

In the basement of the hospital in Wyck, doctors treated Dutch soldiers burned by German flamethrowers. They bound gunshot wounds. They attended to a delirious German soldier clutching a crumpled photo of his recent bride, his testicles blown off by shrapnel, muttering, "Ich war gerade verheiratet. Und nun werde ich nie Kinder bekommen." ("I was just married. And now I will never have children.") Nearby, an elderly nun fingered her rosary and countered each explosion with a whispered prayer, "Hail Mary, full of grace . . ."

On the street, a German tank crew lay dead, their hobnail boots sticking out from under a tarp.

It was too little resistance, against too much. At 9:30 a.m., the territorial commander, with more than half his force captured, wounded, or killed, marched to the fallen section of the Sint Servaas Bridge under a white flag and surrendered the city of Maastricht. Within an hour, the Germans forded the river and swarmed through the streets and into city hall, issuing orders, demanding hostages. Elsewhere, they crossed the Maas and raced their tanks (panzer in German) toward France.

"The same fate as Poland, Denmark, Norway, Belgium!" a Dutch teen lamented in his diary. "Neutral! I'll be damned!"

In Washington and London, senior officials read the cables, stunned by Hitler's assault on the West. In The Hague, the Dutch royal family and national government rushed to evacuate across the English Channel. The rest of the Netherlands would hang on for four more days until the Germans made good on their threat to bomb Rotterdam, killing 711 people, leaving another 80,000 homeless, and flattening the historic city center. Then the Netherlands surrendered. But in Limburg, the battle was already over, and the terrified citizens were burning patriotic items, anti-Nazi pamphlets, and anything else that might give away their sympathies.

"Remarkable," wrote a resident of the village of Vaals, "so many chimneys that beautiful sunny morning of the red May were smoking."

Emilie knelt at the makeshift altar beside her bed, the one Manka had set up because she was so often pregnant or sick. A terrible day. A terrifying day. But her trust in divine Providence was unwavering. *God spare our beloved country,* she prayed, *our royal family, our region, our city, our family, our love.*

The next morning, a Dutch teenager watched from her bedroom window as a long line of German tanks rumbled past her house four miles east of Maastricht, on the far edge of the village of Heer. German soldiers marched alongside them, easy, free, triumphant. One stopped and banged the butt of his rifle against their door, demanding water. Her Moekie (Dutch for mommy) gave the man a cup. What else could she do? But her hand was steady, and she looked him in the eyes. The Dutch were broken, but unbowed.

"We'll get you for this!" Frieda van Schaïk yelled in German, as the soldier turned away. "Sooner or later, we'll get you!"

6

"Danke schön," the soldier laughed. "So ein Witz." ("Thank you, what a joke.")

Frieda was fifteen years old, and her world was shattered. The freedom she had always known, and taken for granted, was marching into the past.

# CHAPTER 2

# RISING STARS

— ★ —

*Robert Cole*

July 1940–February 1941

"I've been with this regiment about five months, and am having the time of my life," Lieutenant Colonel Dwight D. Eisenhower wrote to Lieutenant Colonel Omar N. Bradley, a friend from the United States Military Academy at West Point, on July 1, 1940, one month after the dramatic rescue of the battered British army at Dunkirk and three weeks after the fall of Paris. "Like everyone else in the Army, we're up to our necks in work, but this work is fun. I could not conceive of a better job; except, of course, having one's own regiment, which is out of the question because of rank."

Ike had reported to the 15th Infantry, garrisoned at Fort Lewis in Tacoma, Washington, in February 1940 as the regimental executive officer (XO). He was the liaison between the brass and the soldiers, responsible for organizing the regiment's training and daily tasks. The 15th Infantry had been one of the most sought-after assignments in the Army when it was stationed in China from 1912 to 1938, protecting American commercial interests. But by 1940, after a decade of complacency and Depression-era budget cuts, it was far below full strength, short of rifles, machine guns, mortars, and about 400 men. It was without two majors and seven captains. There were so few officers, Eisenhower also served as the commander of the regiment's 1st Battalion. This was the job he really wanted. Holding command and leading soldiers in combat was what he had trained for, and it was pivotal to those who dreamed of the next promotion.

There was plenty of work. For Eisenhower, Fort Lewis in the spring of 1940 was stuck in an "apathy that had its roots in comfort, blindness, and wishful thinking." Officers cared more about the inconvenience of long training exercises that might keep them from their social rounds, he believed, than in preparing their soldiers. It was an isolationist mindset that had infected much of the Army, and much of the United States. The officers at Fort Lewis did not believe, despite Germany's blitzkrieg of Norway and Denmark in April 1940, that war was coming.

Eisenhower made things clear to his lieutenants that, under his command, things were going to change. "If any of you think we are not going to war," he told them, "I do not want you in my battalion. We are going to war. This country is going to war, and I want people who are prepared to fight this war."

The 15th Infantry, and especially Eisenhower's 1st Battalion, spent spring 1940 in the field, from shooting at the range to conducting field exercises. It's one thing for soldiers to learn in a classroom; it's another for them to be put through the paces, advancing twenty miles over rough terrain with tanks, keeping the vehicles fueled, keeping everyone fed, reading maps, getting the artillery to coordinate with infantry, fixing broken radios, trucks, rifles, and ankles. The exercises were punishing, often lasting all night in bad weather, since hunger, exhaustion, and pouring rain were not possibilities in battle but inevitabilities. The old guard mocked him as "Alarmist Ike," but Eisenhower loved grunt work. He bragged to visiting officers that he was running on two hours of sleep and "frequently caked with dirt and sweat."

He was not only training but evaluating, and one soldier who impressed him was a young company commander named Robert George Cole. The son of an army doctor, Cole had been born in the base hospital at Fort Sam Houston in San Antonio. Briefly, he had sought a different path, attending junior college after high school. But a year later, he enlisted in the U.S. Army as an infantryman. A year after that, he received an appointment to the United States Military Academy at West Point.

Few exemplify the West Point cadet of 1939 as fully as the young man in Robert Cole's senior photograph. He is white, like all but a handful of cadets to that point, his dark hair cropped short but parted and styled, his face smooth and clean. His eyes stare into the distance intensely, his mouth set, but with a slight upturn at the corner, the hint of a cocky smirk.

Looking again at his eyes, they aren't so much intense as eager. He is a young man looking toward a future he can't wait to begin.

Cole personified the hard-driving young officers Ike loved. If Ike was caked in dirt and sweat, Cole came back buried in mud. If Ike got two hours of sleep, Cole got one, or none at all. Even those who can lead men in battle don't always lead them on a twenty-mile run neck-deep in the muck and mire, but Cole *always* led from the front, whether doing KP (kitchen police) duty or out in the field. He had a natural exuberance for every part of soldiering, which meant he never stopped working when something more could be done, and he did everything with that same wry smile, that same eagerness in his eye. Many men came back from an overnight exhausted, dragging their feet with their heads down. Cole came back with the kind of shit-eating grin on his mud-caked face that made it clear he hadn't just endured a night of deprivation, he'd enjoyed the hell out of it.

He could be harsh, like his mentor. Ike once tore a commander to the studs over a recordkeeping error by one of his soldiers. Cole once chewed a sentry to the nub for forgetting a password. Quick-witted, with a South Texas drawl, he was renowned for his use of expletives, which he could unwind into flamboyantly ingenious chew-downs of filth and insult. That night, Cole let the invective fly, because sentry duty was vital. Sentry duty kept soldiers safe. Attention to detail, every detail, kept men alive. By the time he was through with the sidewinder, the young man was in tears. In the Army! A soldier in tears!

In response, Robert Cole reached over his shoulder and gave that soldier the poncho off his back. It was a blisteringly cold night, but Cole spent it without his poncho, so his sentry could stay warm. Cole had, as one of his men summarized, that "rare combination of courage, integrity, a sense of humor, and lastly, a deep understanding and concern for the men under his command." He could "care and swear," as the saying goes, at the same time.

He shared that trait with Eisenhower, who, after dressing down the officer over the clerical error, went out of his way to assure him the lecture was over, the failure forgotten. But Cole did not learn that from Ike. It came naturally to him. You must be made of the right kind of mettle to hone both edges—the strength and the tenderness—without warping or dulling the blade.

On May 10, 1940, the Germans launched the attack that officers like

Eisenhower and Colonel George S. Patton, a battle-hungry armor officer at Fort Benning, had anticipated. They watched the Netherlands surrender five days later. Then Belgium on May 28. On June 22, one month after German tanks had rolled down the Rijksweg into Maastricht, France followed. In Washington, reformist leaders in Army Headquarters like General George C. Marshall and Brigadier General Lesley J. McNair, who shared Ike's sentiments about the coming war, swung into action. It would take time to transform a military that had grown complacent, but it was clear by fall 1940—even as most Americans continued to insist on isolationism—that men like Dwight D. Eisenhower had a future in this new, forward-thinking Army. And company commander Robert Cole, having caught his commander's eye, was perfectly positioned to rise with him.

It wasn't enough.

While most officers studied German armor doctrine, a few were focused on a smaller aspect of the Wehrmacht's lightning-fast invasion: the thousands of Germans troops who had parachuted out of airplanes behind enemy lines.

The Soviet Red Army was the first to employ airplanes to drop men into combat, or at least the first to consider it something other than suicidal. They tested the technique in the mid-1930s but lost the initiative when a paranoid Joseph Stalin began purging 30,000 officers from his military in 1937. The Germans experimented with small parachute drops in Poland in 1939, and Denmark and Norway in April 1940, but the first full-scale airborne operation was on May 10, 1940, when, before dawn, thousands of German paratroopers dropped near key targets far beyond the Dutch border, including air bases near Rotterdam and The Hague.

The most successful drop was in the Limburg line of advance, where the primary objective wasn't Maastricht, or even the Netherlands, but Belgium's Fort Eben-Emael. The fortress, tunneled out of a large hill four miles south of Maastricht, had been built in the 1930s as the impenetrable anchor of the Belgian defensive line. Its thick concrete walls were designed to withstand a frontal assault, an encirclement, or a months-long siege. So at the start of their advance, ten German planes towed ten fabric-covered gliders to the Dutch border, then released them and turned back. Guided by signal flares set by German spies on the ground, the motorless, silent gliders passed over Dutch territory unobserved and landed on the unprotected grass roof of Eben-Emael. Inside each glider were eight men, with rifles, machine guns, explosives, and equipment. By the time German panzers crossed the Maas River at Maastricht, the "impenetrable" fortress at Eben-Emael had already fallen—to seventy-eight German glider troops.

One month later, in June 1940, the U.S. Army formed its first airborne test platoon.

In September, it decided to stand up a battalion.

Soon after, Robert Cole began considering a transfer to this provisional parachute battalion. He was a rising star in one of the most respected front-line infantry units in the Army, and a favorite of the man who would in a few years become the supreme commander of Allied forces in Europe. But this new paratrooper concept was something else: a leap beyond the forefront of war, developed around a hard core of volunteers, career soldiers like Robert Cole who sought the greatest advantage and most difficult challenge.

The transfer wasn't a sure thing, since the paratroopers didn't want married men in their ranks. The concept was too risky, the expected casualty rate too high. A married man had too much tying him to home, too much to live for, and that was certainly true of Robert Cole. He had married his high school sweetheart, Allie Mae, in June, on the one-year anniversary of his graduation from West Point. They had begun to build a life together in the married officers' quarters, where Allie Mae often played piano for Ike and his wife, Mamie, especially Ike's favorite, "The Beer Barrel Polka." The airborne meant not only a dangerous future, but a move away from Fort Lewis to Fort Benning, Georgia.

Allie Mae endorsed the transfer. Her husband was charming, yes, impossible to say no to, sure, but she took no convincing. She was an Army wife. She knew what that meant. And she understood the man she had married. She knew what fired the spark in his eye, the smirk in his smile, and it wasn't honors or medals, and it wasn't the quiet life of a husband safe at home. Robert Cole wanted to be the man in the arena, as Teddy Roosevelt famously described it, the man who risked his life for a cause when others only watched—or trembled at the thought. He wanted to prove himself under the harshest circumstances. He wanted to serve with men dedicated to being the best; men who, when their country called, would willingly throw themselves into the abyss beyond thousands of dug-in enemy soldiers and bring them death from above.

In November 1940, Robert Cole officially requested his transfer. In February 1941, despite being married, and despite the open path before him in the 15th Infantry, he received it. Soon after, he reported for duty with the U.S. Army's first parachute unit, the 501st Parachute Infantry Battalion.

# CHAPTER 3

# MR. AND MRS. KIPPENBURGEMEESTER

— ★ —

*Emilie Michiels van Kessenich*

Summer 1940–August 1941

The Michiels van Kessenich family owned half of their duplex villa on Sint Lambertuslaan, one of the nicer residential streets in Maastricht. Named Villa Maya—naming houses was common in the Netherlands at the time—the house was large and well-built, with patterned brickwork and an attic tower. It was so lovely, it was featured in a postcard series of Maastricht buildings in 1930. Perhaps that's why, a few days after the invasion, it was occupied by forty German soldiers and two officers. The Germans had ordered every front door in Maastricht kept open during the day, ostensibly so citizens could get inside quickly in case of British bombers. But really, Emilie knew, it was a message. *We are in control. We have our eyes on you.* So the Germans simply walked through the open door of Villa Maya and commandeered it.

At first, Emilie and her eight children slept on the dining room floor. Then they moved to the basement, which Willem had outfitted as a bomb shelter in 1939. They had a cache of canned food and sleeping pallets, although a shortage of space—or a surplus of family members, plus several friends the family took in and the three young women who served as household staff—forced the smaller children to sleep on the ping-pong table. What Emilie really wanted was Manka at her side, but he was rarely with them.

The German occupiers were the gravest danger to the citizens of Maastricht in at least a hundred years, and Willem's days and nights were spent with the city council making difficult decisions under intense pressure—and under the watchful eye of the German Feldkommandant and the leaders of the Nationaal-Socialistische Beweging in Nederland, the Dutch Nazi party, known as the NSB. For the entire month of May, either Willem or his deputy mayor was always present at city hall, meaning Manka was away from his family many nights, and exhausted whenever he was home.

"Don't bother your father with your problems," Emilie told the children. "He is very busy. Bring them to me."

In the end, the city was fortunate. Maastricht's defenses had collapsed so quickly that damage was minimal. Fifteen civilians died in the invasion. A few buildings were destroyed. And while the German soldiers who commandeered some other homes stole family heirlooms and pulled down curtains for bedding, the soldiers at Villa Maya didn't steal or destroy anything. They allowed the children into the backyard for an hour or two every day, for fresh air. After the Belgian surrender on May 28, when the last hope of a quick return to freedom in Maastricht flickered out, they moved on, without threats, allowing the family to begin their new lives under the thumb of German occupation.

The news was relentlessly awful. Mass casualties and destruction in Rotterdam. German victories in Belgium, Luxembourg, and France. The near destruction of the British army at Dunkirk, followed by the declaration of war against Great Britain by Fascist Italy. Thousands of prisoners of war were being marched through Maastricht toward Germany. Thousands of flak guns and other weapons were passing the other way to the front. The Catholic Church in the Netherlands, Emilie's church, had a clear moral vision. It had forbidden Catholics from joining the Dutch Nazi party in 1936. After the invasion, NSB members were excommunicated. Father Robert Regout, the Jesuit priest and university professor, insisted on the right to peaceful resistance and preached it on the radio. In June, he disappeared. His colleague, Father Titus Brandsma, took up the message. He disappeared too.

On July 6, a friend's wedding was called off. Not for lack of love. For lack of hope.

There was nothing to do, Emilie knew, but to press on. To remain positive. To be strong. She feared for her children's health and happiness if their world was thrown too far off-balance, if they truly comprehended how much their lives had changed, and how much danger everyone faced.

To her surprise, it was Willem, her love, her rock, who collapsed under the strain. One Sunday in August, the family took an afternoon canoe trip on the Maas. The next morning, Willem could barely rise. His doctor diagnosed exhaustion. He prescribed bed rest. Emilie, who knew him so well, suspected it was also sadness, a sickness on his soul for what the Germans were doing to the city.

Emilie and Willem had met in college, at a chaperoned dance. That was how couples met in the 1920s, at chaperoned events. Willem was tall and thin, with a regal bearing that could come across as cold, but Emilie broke through his shell by asking about his plans.

"I want to be an ambassador," he told her proudly. Willem was from an aristocratic family, but his father was a zwermer—a wanderer. He wore a robe and had a long beard, rejected religion and society, and tramped around the continent with his wife and son in tow, all their worldly possessions in a single trunk. Willem, who by chance was born while his parents were passing through Germany, had rebelled by becoming a sturdy, studious, unemotional rule-follower, a rock in an ever-churning sea. Most importantly to Emilie, the young man had devoted himself to Catholicism.

"What about you?" he asked. "What do you want from life?"

Emilie smiled. "I want to be the wife of a kippenburgemeester."

A "chicken mayor," Dutch slang for the leader of a small town. Emilie wanted a husband she could talk with—mayors in the Netherlands were appointed, not elected, and came from the educated class—a man who cared about public service. A man with a meaningful job, but who had time to be home with his family. Emilie was an only child, until her father remarried in her teens and gave her half-siblings. More than anything, she told Willem, she wanted many children.

"I've changed my mind," Willem said the next time he saw her, in the first sign this gregarious, high-spirited woman would utterly change his life. "I want to be a kippenburgemeester."

They were married in 1929, when Emilie was twenty-three. Not long after, Willem was appointed the municipal mayor of Beek, north of Maastricht, and Emilie became pregnant. She miscarried. She knew God was present in all things, even a tragedy, but the sadness hit her hard, especially because Emilie's mother had died giving birth to her.

Later that year, Emilie became pregnant with twins. She took to her bed to rest, and the boys were born healthy. She had five more children in the next seven years, all born "the natural way," as Willem liked to say.

By then, Queen Wilhelmina had appointed him mayor of Maastricht. At 68,000 citizens, Maastricht was no "chickenburg," but the largest city in Limburg Province. The Michiels van Kessenich family bought half a duplex—the other half of Villa Maya was owned by a bachelor doctor—a short bicycle ride from city hall. They hired live-in help, not uncommon in those days. They joined the parish of Onze-Lieve-Vrouwebasiliek— the Basilica of Our Lady—an imposing, eleventh-century Romanesque church a short walk from their home. On his first day in office, Willem pulled a chair into the Market Square and checked his watch every time an employee arrived at city hall. This was controversial. The locals loved their Maastricht Quarter, the practice of arriving everywhere at least fifteen minutes (okay, thirty minutes) late, but Willem was a man of order.

We will be on time. We will stay until the end. We will work. These were Willem's values. The citizens of Maastricht, in his opinion, deserved nothing less.

"Being born into a noble family," Emilie often told her children, "means nothing more than an obligation to serve others."

"Your father may seem important to the city," she told her daughter

Jenneke, "but the men who collect the waste each week are more important. When they go on strike, there will be a disaster. When your father is away, there is always someone else at city hall to take his place."

Duty. Service. Love and charity. It was what her Catholic faith asked of her and her social position demanded. Bonus Simplicitas. Latin for "good simplicity." It was the name she had given her guardian angel, whom she had learned about at four years old, before her First Communion. A guardian angel protects you, she was told. A guardian angel is your advocate, interceding for you with God. Emilie's guardian angel was the closest friend, the most trusted confidante, of her lonely, motherless childhood. Bonus Simplicitas, she named him, and it was more than a name. It defined how she tried to live each day: To be good and to live simply. To love others, strangers and family alike.

These values she shared with Willem. She knew that because she knew him, body and soul. Their shared devotion to family, to kindness and propriety, was one reason they remained so passionately in love, even after twelve years and eight children.

But this invasion. This occupation. This unprecedented rupture of the social order that left the citizens of Maastricht demoralized, impoverished, and afraid. There was no plan, no prior experience, for handling an invasion of your city. Willem wanted to be a rock of stability in a raging sea, but even a rock can be worn down.

His doctor advised a few days of bed rest. It didn't take. Willem's breakdown stretched into a second week. He was sent to recuperate with out-of-town friends. That didn't work either. So Emilie went to him, and they took a three-day bicycle ride. It rained every day. Perhaps that cleansed him. Perhaps the fun they had, laughing about the rain, revived his spirits. Emilie was the only person ever able to lift the burden of his self-imposed propriety.

After his return, Willem told his officials to enforce the German order to register the race of all government employees, the first openly Nazi edict imposed on the city. The registry included everyone from Willem and his forty-person staff at city hall—all men except for Willem's eighteen-year-old secretary, Else Hanöver, whom he had recently hired because she spoke German fluently—to teachers, policemen, municipal clerks, and garbage collectors.

Emilie worked to keep her family safe and, as much as possible, comfortable in their old routines. She rose each morning, early, to pray and give Mathilda her bath. The other seven children bathed only on Saturday, in a stand-alone tub refilled once, after the four boys were finished. For Mathilda, who was only a few months old, Emilie filled a little zinc bath on wooden legs from the tap in the sink. She had done the same for her last several babies. There was no better way to start the day than with a giggling infant and a warm bath.

Her mornings were devoted to letters, cards, and correspondence. Like many prosperous women, she had a wide social circle and numerous charitable activities. Else Hanöver was Willem's secretary, but Emilie was an important aide. She handled his personal mail, wrote many of his letters, acted on his behalf in small matters. Their whole life together, in everything, they had been partners.

Afternoons were for schoolwork and lessons: French, German, English, art, literature, and the Bible. Emilie taught the older children piano, with a weekly visit from a teacher. The piano teacher was an older woman, unmarried. She had lost her job at the conservatory for refusing to pledge her loyalty to the Nazis. She wanted no charity, but Emilie helped her, as she helped so many, in this case by recommending her to wealthy friends. Soon, the woman had enough private pupils to support herself.

By then, the sale of tea and coffee had been prohibited. The sale of cloth, including clothing, had also been prohibited. Silver coupons were issued in place of Dutch guilders, which were in short supply because the Germans were confiscating bank accounts and charging the Dutch for the occupation. The list of items available only with the Nazi-issued ration coupons called "bons" was growing: butter, coal, bread, coffee, tea, rice, peas, beans, flour. Nazi-issued passes were required to cross the repaired bridges between Maastricht and the neighborhood of Wyck.

In November, the Nazis confiscated Willem's convertible Chevrolet "for the war effort." He loved that car, but it barely mattered. There was hardly any gasoline in the country.

The same month, the Nazis ordered all Jewish government employees fired. The remaining employees were forced to sign a registry and publicly declare they were not Jews. Those who refused were also fired. Willem and the forty public servants at city hall were responsible for carrying out these policies. They all signed the registry.

The husband of a friend, Anne van Royen, was arrested and sentenced to sixteen weeks in a prison camp. Father René, Emilie's parish priest, was arrested. After his release, he was banned from holding official positions. The Catholic Scouts, of which the Michiels van Kessenich twins, Willem and Eduard, were proud members, was disbanded. At the direction of German occupation authorities, Willem issued an ordinance removing Dr. Charles Mendes de Leon from his position as head of the Calvariënberg Hospital because he was of "Jewish blood."

In February 1941, there was an uprising in the Amsterdam ghettos, where Dutch Jews from all over the Netherlands were being rounded up and forced to live. The Dutch police were overwhelmed, but when the Schutzstaffel (SS), the elite guard of the Third Reich, arrived a few days later, they responded with deadly force. Nine men were killed. Dutch Communists went on strike in solidarity with the Jews, and hundreds of thousands of ordinary citizens joined them. For a moment, it seemed that good might come of it, until the SS started shooting strikers. The mayor of Amsterdam imposed a curfew and ordered the city's employees back to work, ending the uprising. Some cursed the mayor's weakness. Others cursed his betrayal.

But what was the man supposed to do? His people were being murdered. What could a public servant like Willem do, Emilie wondered, under this intolerable regime?

By then, teachers were required to sign a pledge of loyalty to the Nazi Party. Those who didn't were fired. Doctors were imprisoned for refusing to follow the Nazi rules of practice. Engineers lost their licenses. Artists were blackballed for defying the German guild's strict adherence to the heroic and romantic. Businesses were shuttered. Jewish businesses confiscated. Priests disappeared. Some Limburgers, driven by poverty and hunger, left to work in the German war factories. Others openly supported the Nazis, not many, maybe 5,000 of the 68,000 citizens of Maastricht. Many, many more forfeited their livelihoods for their principles. Some even joined a nascent movement, the Valkenburg Resistance.

The Dutch government-in-exile exhorted its mayors to remain in office. If they quit, the government-in-exile reasoned, their replacements would be worse. They would be true believers.

Willem understood. He stayed. But for how much longer? Emilie wondered. For how much longer could someone so religious, so proper in his heart, reconcile his moral convictions with what was being demanded of him?

"Are you doing good, Manka?" she asked him gently on the nights she felt him tossing in their bed. "Is there still good, my Willem, to be done?"

They listened to Radio Orange at 9:00 p.m., like all the good Dutch did. Queen Wilhelmina, in exile in London, would sometimes speak to her people. Or members of her cabinet would report news of the war and the resistance. *Have courage.* That was the message. *Help is coming. Stay strong. Carry on.*

*For how long?* Emilie wondered. She touched her belly tenderly. She was pregnant again. Ten times in eleven years, including two miscarriages. Ten times pregnant, thank God, when her mother had not survived even one.

The child would be born under occupation, without the freedoms the Dutch had always known and taken for granted. She couldn't help but worry. Would their homeland still be occupied when the child was grown?

Bicycle tires were rationed, in a nation where almost everyone rode bicycles. Only those who lived fifteen miles or more from work could get them. Manka's father died and his mother, financially unstable, was forced to leave the home where the old society-shunning zwermer had finally settled down. The coffee distribution ended, even for those with ration bons. There would be only ersatz coffee made of chicory or other bitter substitutes. It had been a year since Maastricht fell, and every day, it seemed, conditions worsened. Perhaps there would never be coffee again.

Signs appeared in city parks, including in the tree-filled roundabout outside the Michiels van Kessenich home: "No Jews." Emilie knew that Willem had been forced to issue this and other German occupation ordinances.

"If Jews can't enter the parks," she told her children, "then neither will we."

"I'm sorry," she told the children, when they protested. Some of them were, after all, only three and four years old. "We cannot enter. You will just have to walk around."

In August 1941, Count Max de Marchant et d'Ansembourg, the radical Dutch Nazi who served as the link between the German occupiers and the citizens of Limburg, insisted on meeting with Willem and the province's other mayors. As soon as her husband returned, Emilie knew something was wrong.

They were not doing their duty, D'Ansembourg had scolded the mayors. They were not . . . *enthusiastic* for the new order. They were lagging on implementation. They needed, D'Ansembourg said, or rather shouted in the style of the Führer, to undertake a course of "personal Nazification." To study Hitler's writings. To embrace the philosophy. They needed to govern "without reservations," according to National Socialist principles. He was dissolving the town councils. He was ending their limited independence. The mayors would work directly under the Nazi regime.

Emilie-Hélène, their ninth child, had been born on July 30, 1941. The baby was only a few weeks old. Emilie was still in her nursing bed, resting and recovering. But she knew there was only so much her husband could tolerate. There would be no "personal Nazification." He would not enthusiastically enforce D'Ansembourg's orders. Willem Michiels van Kessenich resigned, along with thirteen other Limburg mayors. One of his last acts, eight days after his resignation and a few days before leaving office, was to sign a memo instructing city officials to enforce the German ordinance expelling Jewish students from their current schools.

"You did all that you could," Emilie assured her husband.

"We'll have no money," he said. Willem would inherit the title of baron one day, but it came with little more than a piece of property. They depended on his salary, and the Nazis had stripped him of his severance and pension when he resigned. A serious situation for a man with nine children under the age of eleven.

"We will survive."

"Of course we will, Lietje. I'm just not sure how."

The next morning, there was a knock at the back door. It was well known that on two Wednesday afternoons a month, Emilie Michiels van Kessenich opened her home to those in need, to see if there was anything she or the city of Maastricht could provide. Often, especially on Sundays after church, people would knock on the back door, hoping she could meet them then too. This time, when Agnes answered, there was nothing outside but a sausage and a loaf of bread.

A gift from God, Emilie believed. A sign from Bonus Simplicitas that she and Manka were doing what was right, delivered straight from the heart and hand of the thankful citizen who left it.

# CHAPTER 4

# A WAY OUT

— ★ —

*Jefferson Wiggins*
January 1942

Jefferson Wiggins was born in a wooden shack outside the small farming community of Columbia, Alabama, in 1925. His family settled on a birth date of February 22, but it was an estimate, by his own admission. It might take a doctor four or five months to get around to checking on a baby born in rural Alabama in the 1920s, and the midwife usually didn't register the birth much faster. This was especially true when the baby was Black. Houston County, Alabama, didn't much care if its Black midwives registered its Black babies or not.

Jefferson's parents, Clemon "Clem" and Essie Mae Wiggins (née Dawson), were sharecroppers on a cotton plantation. They lived in a world almost completely divorced from the white world around them. They could enter only some white establishments, and those only by the back door. Essie Mae took in sewing from white customers, but otherwise was not allowed to touch clothing that might be worn by white women. Black people were discouraged from making eye contact with the white people in town, much less speak to them unless spoken to first. Every Black person knew to step from the sidewalk into the street, not just to let a white person pass but if they saw a white person on any part of the sidewalk at all. There was nothing truly shared between whites and Blacks in Houston County— not even the ground.

These were not suggestions, they were rules of survival that Clem and Essie Mae drilled into Jefferson and his six brothers and sisters every

Saturday before the family took the wagon to Dothan for their weekly shopping trip. Keep your eyes down, keep your thoughts to yourself, and good Lord, keep your hands in your pockets. Jefferson and his siblings whispered among themselves at the cabin or down along the nearby creek, daring each other to take chances and break their parents' rules. But they never tested the boundaries of the white world, because Clem and Essie Mae took those boundaries seriously. They spoke of whippings in hushed whispers over supper. They gossiped about night riders at church. Even the minister spoke of the Ku Klux Klan in quiet tones, because the repercussions of a forceful rebuke would almost certainly be severe.

You never know who *they* are, Essie Mae warned Jefferson. They might be the butcher, the store owner, the man on the sidewalk. So you never speak of them out loud, and you never act the fool.

When he was nine, Jefferson's sister Othel suddenly fell ill. She was taken to a hospital, but the operation was unsuccessful. The next day, Othel died. It was appendicitis, a common childhood danger in those days. Jefferson put his fingers over the edge of her rough wood coffin and stared until his mother dragged him away. His sister's face was smooth, unmarked. Softer than it had seemed in life. Softer than sleep. But Jefferson remembered how, at first, the doctor had refused to come to their cabin. How when the man finally arrived, he prescribed castor oil, which made his sister vomit all over the kitchen floor. If they had operated sooner, he was convinced, his sister would have lived. Of course she would have. She was only eleven years old.

A few months after the funeral, Jefferson bolted upright in bed. He had been so sound asleep he was unsure where he was, but he heard voices in the darkness, the stamping of feet, so he rushed to the window with his brother and sisters. Light jerked shadows across the walls. A cross was burning in the yard. Grandma Dawson, his mother's mother, whose father had been born enslaved, opened the cabin door. Calm. Formidable. The fire was reflecting off her skin, but not touching her. She was barely five feet tall, but she barred the way of the four hooded men on the porch.

"Where's that n\*gger Clem?" the leader demanded.

"I don't know. But if I find him, he's a dead n\*gger, don't you worry about that."

"When did you last see him?"

"About first night, drunk and heading into town." Jefferson, watching from the window, knew this wasn't true.

"Well, if he comes back, you let us know."

"Yes, sir. Where will I find you, sir?"

"Just tell any white man and we'll come on out. Do you understand, Aunt Clara?"

"Yes, sir."

"Then go on back to bed now, Aunt Clara. Ain't no harm will come to you."

The leader turned to the twenty or so men walking a circle around the cross in full Klan robes, shotguns clutched in their hands. The fire was crackling. The flames jumping at the sky.

"Let's go, boys," he said.

Jefferson didn't notice the small one until he heard him cry out, "I don't wanna go home, Daddy. You broke your promise. You said you'd let me help to kill a n*gger."

He might have been nine, the same age as Jefferson. The firelight flashed off the shotgun in his hands.

"Ah, you'll get your chance, son. But this one here tonight got away."

Jefferson only found out later what his father had done to deserve a lynching: he had sold a bale of cotton without the landowner's permission because the family was starving. That night, all he knew was that his father had been inside the cabin, and he had escaped out the back while Grandma Dawson faced the white men down.

"If you ever get a chance to get away from here," she told Jefferson soon after, and not for the first time, "you take it." Jefferson knew that was what Essie Mae, his mother, wanted for him as well.

You're better than them, Grandma Dawson often told him. All you need is a chance.

It was several years later when a white man on the third floor above the post office in Dothan, Alabama, stopped Jefferson as he was turning to leave. Grandma Dawson had gotten her grandson a job as a delivery boy for the drugstore, and he had just delivered the man a package.

"How much is it, boy?" the man asked.

"The price is on the package, sir."

"I know that, boy. That wasn't my question. I want to know if you can read it."

Poor but proud, the Wiggins children had worked the fields almost as soon as they could walk from one end of a row to another. During the season, they worked from sunup to sundown, with barely a break for lunch. Jefferson had only a sixth-grade education, and even that had been intermittent. Grandma Dawson and his mother had taught him to read the Bible, though. He told the man the price.

The man looked Jefferson over. "You're a big boy," he said.

"Yes, sir."

"Do you know that your country is at war?"

It was January 1942, a few weeks after the Japanese surprise attack on the U.S. naval base at Pearl Harbor. Everyone was talking about Doris "Dorie" Miller, mess attendant second class on the battleship USS *West Virginia*. Dorie had raced to the deck and, with no training, began firing one of the ship's .50 caliber antiaircraft machine guns at the attacking Japanese planes. The newspaper, the preacher, even the Klan went on and on about Dorie Miller. A Black man who (they always pointed out) couldn't read or write but who risked his life for his country. For *this* country! Jefferson Wiggins thought Dorie Miller sounded like a fool.

"Yes, sir," he said. "I do."

"You're skinny, son. Did you know you can get three meals a day in the United States Army?"

Jefferson didn't like the conversation. He felt threatened. He always felt threatened when talking to a white man.

"You have to be eighteen to enlist. How old are you, boy?"

"Eighteen, sir."

"All right, then, tomorrow, you bring your parents here. We'll get their signatures or marks, and you will be a United States soldier."

The encounter stayed in Jefferson's mind the rest of the day, as he made his round of deliveries. He couldn't shake the thought of that damn fool Dorie Miller. But he also couldn't shake the thought of three square meals a day, health care if he got sick, and $21 a week. The sergeant had promised $21 pay *every week*, seven times the amount he was making as a delivery boy and more money than anyone in his family had ever made. They would treat him better too. That's what the sergeant had promised, and the sergeant would know. The sergeant wasn't from Houston County, Alabama.

*Never lie. No matter what you do, tell the truth.* That was Grandma Dawson's rule, and Jefferson couldn't shake that thought either. It ate at him, that rule, because he'd told the sergeant a lie. He wasn't eighteen. He was only sixteen.

But hadn't Grandma Dawson told a lie when she told the Klan his father wasn't home? Was his lie any worse than that?

And then he thought of Grandma Dawson's other admonishment, the one he had heard from her more times than he could remember: *If you ever get a chance to get away from here, you take it.*

The next day, January 13, 1942, Jefferson Wiggins forged his mother's signature on his enlistment papers. He placed a large *X* next to his father's name, since Clemon couldn't write.

*At least I'll know my enemy,* he thought. *He'll see my face, but I'll see his too. He'll have a weapon, but this time, so will I. And that's a fairer chance than I'll ever get if I stay here.*

CHAPTER 5

# "WILLIE"

— ★ —

*Bill Hughes*
January–August 1942

Bill Hughes shook his head in disbelief when he read the telegram from the War Department offering him a job in Washington, D.C., as a clerk/messenger: "Report date 28 January 1942. Written permission of parents required." Bill Hughes was eighteen, and he'd wanted to get out of Indianapolis, Indiana, for as long as he could remember. And then, out of the blue, here it was: an offer. In a telegram.

His first love was music. Duke Ellington, Count Basie, Jimmie Lunceford: Bill Hughes loved swing bands, with their elaborate instrumentation and improvised interplay, the sounds of cool men in tuxedos making sophistication feel effortlessly smooth. He was a saxophonist, loved Andy Kirk, the leader of the Twelve Clouds of Joy, the epitome of the Kansas City sound. He dreamed of going to college to study music, but it was the Depression. His father had a steady job at American Foundry making engine blocks, but Bill was living with his mother, who had remarried, and times were tough. It was 1940. Times had been tough for Black families in Indianapolis for a long, long time.

It was the segregation and discrimination he really hated, even more than the lack of opportunity. The schools were segregated. The stores were segregated. So were the theaters, clubs, and churches. Every block he walked, every door he entered, was a reminder of his second-class status. Every side-eye or flinch a reminder that his fellow citizens feared him for no reason and resented his right to walk these streets. There were parks with signs hanging on their fences: "Whites only." "No Negroes allowed."

It hadn't always been that way. As early as 1878, as its factories became engines for the migration of Black workers, Indianapolis integrated. Bill's ancestors had come from Missouri and Kentucky, not the Delta or the Deep South. For them, Indianapolis was a short journey to opportunity. Black neighborhoods were prosperous. Black businesses thriving. In the factories, Black worked alongside white, making less, being passed over for promotions, but on the same line.

Then, in the 1920s, the Ku Klux Klan all but seized the state government. The movement exploded in popularity after World War I, when "traditional" Americans accused immigrants of making their country poorer, dirtier, and taking their jobs. In Indiana, the Klan's membership rolls were said to top 250,000. Half the state legislature was rumored to be members, and Edward L. Jackson, elected governor in 1924, was associated with Klan leadership. That year, the United States government, itself in the grip of a nativist fever, limited each country's immigrants to 2 percent of that ethnic group's existing U.S. population. The Indiana legislature went further, passing a raft of laws that cemented white Protestants at the top of the economic pyramid.

The power of the Klan in Indiana began to wane soon after. The state's grand dragon, nothing more than a con man who happened to blow up in the right place at the right time, was convicted of rape and murder, undermining their law-and-order message. Governor Jackson was ensnared in a bribery scandal. And the passion abated of its own volition, since the Klan had already accomplished its primary objective of demonizing Catholics, Blacks, and Jews.

Bill Hughes was one year old when the Jim Crow laws were passed in Indiana; four when the city resegregated its school system and established Crispus Attucks High School in 1927. The city had several all-white high schools, but every Black student in Indianapolis attended Crispus Attucks, with its secondhand textbooks and worn-out desks. The heat didn't work, the cafeteria ran low on food, the classrooms were overcrowded. Unlike the white schools, Crispus Attucks didn't have a gym until 1938. But the teachers were a treasure, proud Black men and women, many with master's degrees and PhDs, since colleges wouldn't hire Black faculty.

Many of them were known to take into their own home students with nothing to their names.

The Black community pooled its pennies to buy instruments for the school band. And that band was good, maybe great. Wes Montgomery and Bill's good friend J.J. Johnson were destined for the stage. But playing past high school was just a dream for Hughes. He took a night job at Indiana Bell Telephone. All phone calls, local and long-distance, were pay-by-the-minute. Bill's job was to sort the daytime tolls to make sure the correct customers were charged. He was making less than the white employees doing the same work, and he knew it, but he didn't let it bother him too much. He had a new goal: he was going to work the night shift at Indiana Bell for three years until he had enough money to get the heck out of Indianapolis.

It couldn't be like this the world over. He had pondered it, and that was his conclusion: There was no way the whole world was like Indianapolis. There were places where a Black man had a fair chance. There had to be. And he was going to find one of those places as soon as he had the fare.

He had taken the civil service examination as a senior in high school. There was a gambling pool among his friends for the best score. The test was free, so why not? Bill Hughes got the highest score and won a cool $25. Then he forgot all about it. Until the telegram. He had scored so high that, nine months and one devastating attack on Pearl Harbor later, the U.S. Army wanted him in Washington, D.C. It took him three days to convince his mother to let him go, but then, suddenly, unexpectedly, Bill Hughes was out of Indianapolis and on his way.

He arrived to find a capital city frantic with activity, an anthill that had just been kicked. The year before, officers at Fort Lewis had been making fun of "Alarmist Ike." Now, Eisenhower was in Washington working for Army Chief of Staff General George C. Marshall. He was a deputy in the War Plans Division, responsible for standing up in a small amount of time a large force skilled enough to fight two powerful enemies on opposite sides of the globe. There was so much work and so little time that Hughes spent his first few days in an enormous waiting room with hundreds of other civil servants, waiting for someone to choose him for a task.

He eventually interviewed with and was chosen for the Armored Force Liaison Office, which was responsible for evaluating and organizing tank units. Bill Hughes was a low-level employee, a courier with some administrative responsibilities, yet he was handling tasks that would have a direct relation on the way hundreds of thousands of tankers were trained, assigned, and provisioned. He was working beside men and women, white and Black, who treated him as just another hand at the wheel. The office was so busy, there wasn't time for distractions and inefficiencies like segregation.

High-ranking officers, including generals, were frequently in and out. The old system of promotion had collapsed under the pressing need for action, and the most talented—or the most talented at self-promotion—were being thrown up the chain of command.

One visitor in particular commanded Bill Hughes's attention. His tailor-made riding breeches, brown shining leather boots, and oversized stars made him stand out from other generals who visited the office, including Devers, Chaffee, Crittenberger, Walker, Woods, Daniels, and Dean. The only thing missing was the ivory-handled revolver. And then, of course, there was the flippancy, the arrogance, the high-pitched voice, the tough talk laced with profanity.

*He knows he's somebody special*, Hughes thought, *and he carries himself that way.*

Three days passed before a secretary introduced him to Major General George S. Patton, who had recently received command of the newly formed I Armored Corps. He was in Washington to ram through a few of his more unorthodox ideas, and to secure his son a coveted spot at West Point.

"This is Billy," the secretary said. "Billy Hughes."

"I'll just call you Willie," Patton barked.

Patton thought of himself as a straight talker and a hard-ass who judged a man by his actions, but like many of his generation, he had a blind spot. "A colored soldier cannot think fast enough to fight in armor," he had written to his wife, as if his bigotry were a scientific fact.

"That's fine, sir," Bill Hughes replied. "Willie it is."

He didn't like his new nickname. In fact, he hated it. But he knew there was no point in complaining, especially if he wanted to stay in the system. And Bill Hughes wanted to stay in any system that distanced him from the racism and lack of opportunity that had defined his life in Indianapolis.

# CHAPTER 6

# THE CAVES

— ★ —

*Frieda van Schaïk*
March 1942

D avid "Dave" van Schaïk was an electrical engineer. He arrived in Limburg in 1927 from Arnhem, a prosperous city farther north, to consult on a cable-cart tunnel through Sint Pietersberg, the farm-covered mountain (a large hill, really, but huge compared to the rest of the flat Netherlands) on the southern edge of Maastricht. The cement company chewing into the west side of the mountain wanted a cost-effective way to transport its marlstone, a type of crushed limestone used in cement and fertilizer, to the Maas River on the eastern side.

In 1930, Van Schaïk moved his wife and children to Limburg, eventually settling in a rented red-brick duplex named Huize Dennenzight (House Pine View) in the village of Heer, four miles east of Maastricht. The tunnel was completed in 1932, along with Dave van Schaïk's contract, but by then, it was too late. He was obsessed with Sint Pietersberg. The cement operation was strip mining for marl, but for most of the previous 2,000 years—since the Romans—miners had entered the mountain to hand-cut limestone slabs. They left behind a labyrinth of interconnected chambers and passageways that had slowly, down the centuries, accreted into fantastical forms. Sint Pietersberg was two and a half miles long, and a half mile wide, but inside were more than 190 miles of hand-dug passages and chambers.

Pappie lost his heart to the caves, his daughter Frieda said. They took over his life, and the life of their family. Dave had few paying contracts after the cart tunnel project because he pursued few paying contracts. He was a gregarious man, at least about the subjects he liked: local plants, biology, soil erosion, electricity. He was a naturalist at heart. He spent nearly every day in the caves: studying, exploring, photographing, mapping. The locals called him, with both affection and bewilderment, the Pioneer of Sint Pietersberg. But he was deeply, almost pathologically, impractical at business.

Frieda was the youngest of his six children, five girls and a boy. She was five years old when Pappie uprooted the family. By ten, she was regularly hiking with her father and brother Wim, the second youngest, deep into the underground world of Sint Pietersberg. They carried little more than ropes, measuring tools, and kerosene lanterns called Tilley lamps. The passageways were sharp and rectangular, with corner columns and smooth walls, but they followed no pattern. They turned, doubled-back, and dead-ended. A huge chamber might follow a thin hallway, or a passage might lead away into darkness. Some routes were blocked by rockfalls; some ceilings eaten through by seeping water. All outside light was extinguished at the first turn, and soon, all outside noise. The soft limestone absorbed their voices, the absolute darkness their lantern light. Only the striking of their hammers rang clearly. Dave had learned to recognize which walls were load-bearing, and which were cracked or compromised, by the quality of the sound.

It was a peculiar darkness, mysterious and powerful. There were moments when Frieda felt the danger, even loneliness, of this black and quiet world. Who knew what was around the next turn? Who knew how deep into the history of the mountain they had passed? These caves had produced the massive skull of mosasaur, the "giant lizard of the Maas River," one of the first marine reptile fossils. They were decorated with house marks, the precursors of coats of arms, signifying ancient ownership. They hid human skeletons, the unfortunate lost.

Mostly, though, she was excited by the darkness and silence, awed by the natural wonder, and safe, even warm, in her father's circle of light. She loved how the scoring in the limestone dated each passage, since mining tools had changed down the millennia; how cart wheels had worn ruts into the floors; how the fossilized remains of ancient fish pocked the walls. She read the graffiti like cherished books: drawings of pompous judges from

1801; the last writings of four doomed monks lost in the caves in the 1700s; a declaration that "Silvius and Chrystens [in] the year 1630, 5th April, 2 o'clock in the afternoon" had beaten a man named Bolgi in this chamber despite his offer of "two golden Charles-coins" for their mercy.

Of course the Nazis wanted to exploit her family treasure. Of course they planned to corrupt this sacred place. In late 1941, in consultation with the Reich Commissariat Netherlands, the Dutch National Service for the Protection of Monuments identified Sint Pietersberg as an ideal bombproof location for the storage of hundreds of the nation's most important works of art. Since no one knew the mountain better than Dave, he consulted on the design and construction of the vault. Dave had refused to sign the Nazi registry after they fired the Jews. He swore he would never again work for the State Supervision of Mines. But this was not a request from the Germans or their collaborators. It was a request from the Dutch government to help safeguard its national treasures, and Dave considered it an honor. So he helped site it within the eastern flank of the cave system and provided technical assistance on the power and water supply.

That work was why Frieda, along with her father and brother Wim, was present at the vault on the night of March 24, 1942, when trucks began arriving under heavy German guard. Frieda watched as the drivers pulled to a stop at the edge of Sint Pietersberg. They began to unload. It was a crisp, dark coldness Frieda felt as she thought of that parade of dying flowers, lush skyscapes, half-eaten meals, and fat, rich Dutch burgers in high ruffed collars. Paintings by Frans Hals, Jan Steen, Jacob van Ruisdael, Johannes Vermeer, and Rembrandt—the greatest artists of the Dutch Golden Age, all national treasures of the Netherlands—were passing into the mountain, down a well-lit tunnel to a large steel door painted yellow.

The Van Schaïks followed them into the vault. Frieda saw the priceless paintings, leaning in long rows, waiting to be hung on sliding steel frames. She heard grunts and shouting in the distance and turned away, wondering what was coming.

And then, it appeared: a huge rolled canvas almost fifteen feet long and as thick as a palace rug, carried on a spindle by a group of twelve or more men. It was Rembrandt's monumental painting, *The Night Watch*, which had covered an entire wall in their national art museum, the Rijksmuseum in Amsterdam. Frieda had never been to the Rijksmuseum.

She had never been to Amsterdam. But every Dutch citizen knew *The Night Watch* and Rembrandt's masterful depiction of Captain Frans Banninck Cocq, proudly in charge of his troop of civic guards patrolling the streets. It was one of the world's great masterpieces. A snapshot of life in seventeenth-century Holland. The country's symbol and pride.

Now, as the painting was pushed into a special niche built for added protection, a mover doffed his cap and put it to his heart, almost in jest. But then more men doffed their caps. They bowed their heads. The vault was the property of the Dutch government, but many suspected that it was only a matter of time before the Germans decided to relocate the art treasures a final time—to the Fatherland.

Thus, the doffed caps. Thus, the sadness Frieda felt when she too bowed her head at the passing of *The Night Watch*. There was more than one way, after all, to steal a nation's soul.

A few days later, Dave and Wim stood at the entrance as a large black Mercedes staff car flying swastika pennants pulled up to the caves. The Kommandant of the German armed forces in the Netherlands, General Friedrich Christiansen—the highest-ranking German military officer in the country—stepped out, and after much heel-clicking and heiling with various officials, was introduced to "Die Herren Spezialisten"—the specialists. Once again, their presence had been a requirement, not a request.

They went first to the art vault, where the Dutch guard refused to admit them because Christiansen was wearing his pistol.

The Kommandant was furious. This was *his* vault.

No, it was the property of the Netherlands, the guard insisted—*Good man*, Frieda thought when she heard the story, *brave fellow*—and no firearms were allowed.

The Kommandant refused to give up his pistol. The guard refused to admit him. There was a long silence. Then Christiansen turned on his heel and snapped, "Ich will ja diese Scheiss Bilder überhaupt nicht mehr sehen." ("I do not want to look at these shitty paintings any longer.")

He demanded, instead, that Dave lead him into the mountain. Wim sat with Frieda that night, around their kitchen table, and told her how he had followed with a Tilley lamp as their father gave the Kommandant and his entourage a special tour. At the first turn, Wim was confused. At the second, he was worried. Their father was taking the Nazis through the worst chambers, with their wet floors, rubble-filled entryways, and collapsing walls.

Then it struck him: Pappie was deliberately taking the Nazis through the most unstable chambers. He led them around dangerous corners, appeared to lose his way, backtracked into caverns with dark crevasses in their ceilings and bats hanging in great hairy mounds. He was taking them down another seemingly endless corridor, the light of the Tilley lamps dying a few feet ahead and retreating behind, when the angry Christiansen finally snapped, "Nein, nein."

Inspired by the art vault, "The Kommandant" had hoped to turn the caverns into a military industrial complex and ammunition dump. "Pappie's ingenious tour convinced him otherwise," Wim said, laughing and shaking his head.

Frieda thought of her father. His quiet, almost downcast aspect. On his return, he had said only, "They will not be using Sint Pietersberg."

Frieda had rebelled as much as a fifteen (now sixteen)-year-old could. She wore the orange bands that marked the legs of the family chickens as rings, since orange was the color of the Dutch royal family and thus forbidden. She dropped a suitcase on a German soldier's foot when she took the train to visit her sister. She tried to walk through and disrupt their stupid formation when a group of them marched down the Bemelerweg, although that one backfired when she slipped on some ice and went down face-first in the street. A German soldier—with kindness, she had to admit, though she hated the thought—helped her up. All while her father, her Pappie whom she loved and admired, had seemed too worried, *or too afraid*, to face what their lives had become.

She had thought of him as passive, unresponsive. And yet, she saw now, there was intelligence, even bravery, in his quiet ways. There was more than one way, after all, to defeat the enemy.

# CHAPTER 7

# HOSTAGES

— ★ —

*Emilie Michiels van Kessenich*
June 1942

O ne of the first things the Germans did when they occupied Maastricht on May 10, 1940, was take over city hall and demand ten hostages, to be harmed or even killed if the Dutch resisted. Willem, a conscientious public servant, gathered all the officials in the municipal building that day—about eight of the more than fifty workers on an ordinary day, including the vice mayor, the police chief, and several members of the city council. The men discussed the German demand and created a list of hostages. None of their names appeared on that list. Instead, half the hostages were citizens from Wyck, and the other half were members of Sociëteit Momus in Maastricht, a gentleman's social and philanthropic club. The two groups were rounded up by German troops and held in separate hotels.

Those in Maastricht were released twenty-four hours later; those in Wyck were held another day and a half. Their plight had troubled Willem immensely. In the first two weeks of occupation, when he worked around the clock, he left Emilie only one note. It was impressed with the seal of the burgemeester of Maastricht and read:

*Mevrouw: Het wordt laat. Alles wel. Men heeft mij bericht dat de gijzelaars vrij komen. (Madame: It is getting late. All is well. I have been informed the hostages will be freed.)*

The Germans continued to take hostages throughout that summer: priests, doctors, prominent businessmen. It was their preferred method of intimidation. Many weren't as fortunate as the original hostages, who endured a terrifying but short-lived ordeal. Some were sent to camps in Germany. Some disappeared. Some were executed, including several Catholic priests. When the Germans arrested Léon Lhoest, the popular director of the Royal Dutch Paper Factory, a local paper mill, Willem warned the Feldkommandant they had gone too far. The workers were on the verge of a strike.

"In Ordnung, fein," the Feldkommandant sighed. "Okay, fine."

Lhoest was among the fortunate. He was released after less than a day. Willem met him outside the rowhouse near the railway station the Gestapo had commandeered for a detention and torture center.

"Give you a ride?" Willem asked, indicating his bicycle. It was six miles to Lhoest's home outside Maastricht; he rode on Willem's luggage rack.

A year later, as Willem Michiels van Kessenich prepared to leave office as mayor of Maastricht in September 1941, he was confronted by Max de Marchant et d'Ansembourg. The NSB leader had told Nazi colleagues he considered the mass resignation of the Limburg mayors a "well-considered political action, mainly directed at myself." He swore revenge. Dozens of prominent Maastricht citizens were being detained at Camp Haaren, a German prison camp in the neighboring province of North Brabant. Willem's friend and fellow mayor, Sybrand Marinus van Haersma Buma, was removed from office and taken into custody. He had not been heard from since. That was a much different situation. Buma was active in the Resistance, Willem was not. But those distinctions were sometimes lost on people like D'Ansembourg. Willem judged the Dutch Nazi's promise of revenge to be more than an idle threat.

He decided to go into hiding. Lhoest took him in. After a few weeks, Willem began to move frequently between the homes of friends who, like Lhoest, lived in outlying villages. He met every two weeks with his former secretary, Else Hanöver, to keep abreast of what was happening in city hall.

It would do no good to fret, Emilie knew. Everyone had hardships, and she had nine children to take care of. The newest, Emilie-Hélène, was just a few months old.

Since the "No Jews" signs, the children had not gone to the city parks. Instead, on occasion, Emilie took them to a small paved area a few blocks from their home. The younger children complained bitterly about having to play in such a boring square, but Jenneke took them by the hand and started a game.

"Thank you, darling," Emilie said wearily, smiling at her sad, responsible oldest daughter. Jenneke was only nine, but already a second mother to the younger girls.

The truth was, one of the rowhouses across the street was owned by a friend, and Willem sometimes snuck into town to stay there. Emilie couldn't meet with him—too dangerous, they had decided—but she brought the children to this grubby square so he could watch them from the window.

She felt bad, keeping such a secret from her oldest daughter, but Emilie barely trusted herself not to stare at the window on the second floor, where she assumed her husband was hidden in the dark. It was dangerous even to glance. German officers had commandeered and were living on the ground floor of that very house.

Even after D'Ansembourg moved on to other hatreds (he had many) and Willem returned home, times were tough. Without his salary, they had no income. The ration bons were barely enough to feed a family of eleven and three servants, even with Mathilda and Emilie-Hélène under two years old, and thus eligible for an extra half bottle of milk a week. Still, it was with a sad heart that Willem admitted, finally, that they had to let Agnes and the other two girls go. They simply didn't have any money to pay them.

The young women asked if they could stay on for room and board, without salary, until things improved. Emilie accepted, thankfully. All three were as close as family members. The children adored their Agnes, and they loved making skits for and singing songs with all three of the girls. But Emilie knew their decision was as much about practicality as loyalty. Maastricht was suffering terribly. There weren't many jobs, and even necessities were scarce and tightly controlled. Agnes was giving most of her ration bons to her parents, Emilie knew, so they could live in at least a little bit of comfort.

Which is why it was so extraordinary that Emilie and Willem received so many gifts of food and other basics, much of it anonymous, from those who appreciated what Willem had tried to do for the city.

"I do not know if my dear children—and grandchildren perhaps—will ever read this diary . . ." Emilie wrote shortly before Christmas, after the family had received anonymous gifts of pork liver sausage, cooking fat, soap, cloths, and, wonder of wonders, fifteen pork chops, enough for every member of the family and household. "[But] I would like to give them something for their whole life: 'Be brave and trust in God and you will not be ashamed.' For four months now we have been unemployed and from day to day we experience how we are carried, and strengthened, protected and blessed. Nothing has been lacking, we live like the lilies of the field, food, clothing, and everything else are thrown at us. Do not be faltering, do not doubt, ask God for a miracle and He will deliver one to you, as He did them for us in His overwhelming goodness . . . because we put all our hope in Him alone."

"A difficult year lies behind us," she wrote on January 1, 1942; "much has happened, much still awaits us. [But] with fresh courage we seek the sun again in our potbellied stove with flame!"

Finally, in March, Manka found a job. Léon Lhoest, the man he had urged German authorities to release, hired him as a comanager of the paper mill. Emilie was so excited, she served a luxury that night for dinner: fresh spinach.

"Jhr. Mr. W. Michiels van Kessenich Director of the N.V. Koninklijke Nederlandsche Papierfabriek sends me beautiful roses," she noted cheekily on April 16, "as I used to get from the mayor of Beek and Maastricht."

It had been nine brutal months. Emilie was optimistic throughout, especially in front of the children, but in private, the stress wore her down. She was often sick or simply tired, laid up in bed with a "quiet please" sign on the dining room door, since the children were prone to slamming it and disturbing her rest. Now, with their financial situation stabilized, and Agnes and the other servants paid, she craved a reminder of ordinary times. June 1942 was her and Manka's twelve-and-a-half-year wedding anniversary, the copper anniversary. A traditional celebration in Dutch culture. The situation in Maastricht might be lousy and getting worse, but wasn't that, perhaps, the most important time to throw a party? To remind everyone that they still possessed the most valuable things in life—marriage, friends, and family?

The big day, June 30, began with Holy Mass at 8:00 a.m. Manka, the children, and Agnes attended with Emilie. Afterward, the family had a wonderful breakfast provided by their friends: bread, butter, meat, cocoa for the children, and real tea with milk, all things they no longer ate in their daily lives.

The guests began to arrive at Villa Maya an hour later: neighbors, coworkers, friends from across the city, the province, even the country. Everyone was "Aunt" this or "Uncle" that, Emilie and Willem's favorite terms of affection. Two close friends couldn't come; they had been arrested by the Germans. General J.C.J. Bongers, a retired officer who had served in Indochina, had been held in Camp Haaren for six months. Willem's father had died the year before and his mother, sadly, was too frail to attend. Ninety invitees sent cards of congratulations. But dozens upon dozens came. There were so few days of celebration by 1942, no one wanted to miss one.

In the afternoon, after the greeting and chatting, the Michiels van Kessenich family served the anniversary feast. Emilie had economized her ration bons for months so the cook would have basics like eggs and flour, and luxuries like meats and vegetables were still available, if you didn't mind searching and paying exorbitant prices. Emilie had found mushrooms for soup, sole to serve with spinach and potatoes, strawberries for a pie. Some of the guests brought wine, Willem provided champagne and something close to coffee, and everyone went off so happy that the 5:00 p.m. train out of Maastricht was a raucous party from the first-class carriage to the third.

They left behind a house full of gifts. A few traditional items, like a porcelain cachepot and silver asparagus tongs. Baskets of food: chocolate, cherries, strawberries, cookies, a drum of water crackers, and a handful of potatoes from Mrs. van Grotenhuis. The most common offering, though, was flowers, which grew in abundance in Limburg in the spring. Bushels of carnations, blue irises, gladioluses, larkspur, hydrangeas, and begonias filled the rooms with riotous color, tickling the air with their fragrances. Walking the first floor, the dirty dishes still out on the table (reminders of the impermanence of life, the Dutch Old Master artists would no doubt say), Emilie felt as if she were in a garden, a hope-filled spring, a monument to the beautiful life she and Willem had built together.

Then she realized she had forgotten to bring down the children.

They were upset to have missed their moment at the party. Emilie felt guilty. But the delicious strawberries and cherries soothed them a bit.

*Taste*, she thought, *and see the goodness of the Lord.*

One week later, Emilie and Willem took the children by train to the nearby town of Valkenburg. This was the family celebration, long planned. By chance, there was a carnival, with autoscooters and a merry-go-round. (Thank you, Bonus Simplicitas.) They hiked to the top of a mountain (a hill, really, but they were Dutch) and looked out at the green fields of Limburg, at a Dutch sky and its low horizon punctured three times by thin church steeples.

*What will life be like*, Emilie wondered, *in another twelve and a half years? God grant that we will all be here, together.*

On July 13, the Germans rounded up dozens of Limburgers. Five were executed. The others were sent to the prison camps. All items made of copper, tin, nickel, lead, and other metals were confiscated for the war effort. On July 23, Professor Johannes Hoogveld, a priest and leading light for Dutch Catholic intellectuals, died. He had been arrested and imprisoned in Germany. He returned, but his health never recovered. He was killed by the brutality of the Germans.

Soon after, an article appeared in a local newspaper: "Hostages from Limburg." It listed eighty-four names. Emilie put a red mark beside thirty. The names of her friends and acquaintances.

# CHAPTER 8

# PIG PATHS

— ★ —

*Paschal Fowlkes*
July 1942

Late spring in the rolling hills of northern Virginia brought out the flowers. The dogwoods white on hillsides, the bluebells purple in the meadows, the bleeding hearts dripping red from their long, drooping stems. The hills slid down to hidden creeks, and Paschal Fowlkes—Pat, as he was known—knew in his heart the soft murmur of those clear waters, even if he couldn't hear it from the ridge. Ahead of him, a pig trail traced a path to a modest farmhouse tucked over the edge of the hill. He knew from experience the yard would be muddy from the trampling of hooves, the rusty furrows leaning against the mossy rock walls of the pens.

What a day the Lord had made, with the hills overlapping in soft green varieties, and the farmhouse sitting low among the waves, and no clouds in the sky. He wished he could sit for a moment under a tree—a black walnut, perhaps, or a white oak—and enjoy the wild seclusion of this land he'd loved for twenty-six years, but he was here for the farmer, not the hills, so he climbed back into his car and carried on. Not sadly. Gladly. With joy in his heart, for the stranger he might soon call friend.

Virginia was rich with such old hills, old farms, this older way of life. The Civil War had been fought here three-quarters of a century earlier, and Pat's ancestors had fought in it. He was raised beneath their photographs, hard faces in Confederate uniforms staring down from the wall. His great-grandmother kept a handwritten note from General Robert E. Lee, thanking her for the blankets she had provided. As a boy, his parents had opened a trunk and showed him not only the letter but one of the blankets. There was history here, pride and a sense of duty.

It unsettled him. It had for years, long before his time at the University of Virginia, where he was editor of the school yearbook and wrote for the school paper, *College Topics*. When he was a boy, his family had moved from the countryside to Richmond. There he saw Baptist churches with white columns and porticos like antebellum plantation houses, and he knew they had been built by slaves. During the Depression, when unemployed men stood a hundred deep in breadlines, rich men had donated to those same churches to build them even higher. That work was done by desperate men for near-slave wages, while others went hungry six blocks away. And none of it, neither the hoarding of wealth nor the way it was distributed, seemed right to him.

He considered journalism, since he loved writing for *College Topics*. He thought of becoming a lawyer. Instead, he switched from Baptist, the religion of his conservative family, to Episcopalian and became a minister. He was not raised to the calling. His father was a physician who worked for the nutrition company that made Pablum, a processed baby food. His mother was a housewife. There were no ministers in either of their family trees. But Pat was an outstanding public speaker, renowned for a speech he delivered to his college classmates in 1936 urging peace. He was singled out by deans for both his tenderness and his strength. He was called a teacher by his fellow students. A listener and a leader. Perhaps, instead of writing about others, or arguing for others, he chose the ministry so he could speak his own beliefs.

He married Elizabeth Rives Williams, whom he met in Richmond as a teenager, on June 22, 1940, a month after his graduation from Virginia Theological Seminary and less than six weeks after the Netherlands surrendered to Nazi Germany. He was assigned to St. John's Episcopal Church in McLean, Virginia. It was a small church in a mostly rural area, and Pat set out to meet the congregants. He was especially keen on those who had fallen away, "travel[ing] every dirt track and pig path in the entire section," as the senior warden of St. John's remarked, visiting members and "bringing them back into the active work of the church."

He and Elizabeth—called Lib—had a child. A boy. Frank. Born in September 1941, a few weeks after Willem Michiels van Kessenich resigned his position as mayor of Maastricht.

By then, Pat was ministering to a second congregation, Church of the Holy Comforter in Vienna, Virginia, a small-town church (Vienna had 1,237 citizens in the 1940 census, while McLean had been too small that year to even register) in an area that would in the coming decades become part of greater Washington, D.C. Pat's congregants were mostly gentleman farmers and the professional class, and he enjoyed their company. He was an ambitious young man. He wanted to make a difference, and the well-connected needed the gospel too. But a pig farm was a welcome respite, a place of history and memory. He saw the smoke rising silently from the chimney, a cooking fire, and knew it was a simple house of simple people, where a young rector could rest his legs and speak his simple truth.

He was careful with his parents. He loved them, but he knew that he had broken in some fundamental way from people who glorified the Confederacy and what it represented. He confided in Lib, his advisor and confessor. He did not have to go to war. He was a husband, deeply in love with his wife. He was a new father, devoted to his son, Frank, whom he referred to as his little frog. He was a rising rector, known for his aspirational sermons, and clergy were exempt from the draft. His congregations were growing, not only in number but as his superiors at Holy Comforter wrote, "in unity with Christ." Robert Jackson, a justice of the Supreme Court, had been coming to hear him preach. Paschal Fowlkes was feeding the spiritually hungry, from the pig paths of Vienna to the epicenter of his nation's power.

But Nazi Germany's invasion of Western Europe and its bombing of Britain ... the tide of racism and antisemitism ... the rise of Italian Fascism and Imperial Japan ... this was a battle he could not turn away from. It was, he told his congregation from the pulpit in May 1942, "one of the greatest struggles against the massed forces of darkness the world has ever known."

A few weeks later, Pat Fowlkes joined the Army. In July 1942, he was accepted into the Army Chaplain Corps. He wrapped up his ministry, moved his family to Lib's mother's house in Richmond, and reported to Chaplain School at Fort Benjamin Harrison in Indianapolis, Indiana.

July 1942 was the month of the first American air raid on Europe, a daylight mission across the northern coast of the Netherlands. A raid not tactical but political. The British had been bombing the continent since May 1940, and Commanding General of the U.S. Army Air Forces

(USAAF) Lieutenant General Henry H. "Hap" Arnold had promised Prime Minister Winston Churchill the Americans would join the fight by Independence Day. They reached that goal, but barely. The six American crews flying alongside six British crews in the twelve-plane formation on the morning of July 4, 1942, had been trained by the British, outside the usual U.S. military structure. They had to "borrow" their Douglas DB-7 Boston III light bombers from the Royal Air Force.

A daylight raid compelled the mission's pilots to bring their formation in low and fast, under German radar. They were so low that one pilot claimed to have dodged church spires and waved at two astonished Dutch girls eating breakfast in an apartment in The Hague. Another plane was so low that it skidded along the ground as it pressed forward for the attack. The pilot, Captain Charles C. Kegelman, was able to firewall the throttle on his one good engine, fire his nose guns at German crews in a flak tower directly in front of him, then narrowly avoid flying into it. When he landed the damaged bomber back at base in England, Dutch dirt fell out of the bomb bay.

Eisenhower—now Lieutenant General Eisenhower, commanding general, European Theater of Operations, U.S. Army—was so impressed that he wrote across the squadron commander's after-action report, "This Officer [Kegelman] is hereby awarded the Distinguished Service Cross," second only to the Medal of Honor.

Then he turned and asked his aide, "Are all of the reports going to be like this one?" Three of the twelve aircraft were lost (two American, one British), with most of the six-man crews killed. Four of the six American bombers hadn't even dropped their bombs. Nothing of value was destroyed.

But the message had been sent: The Americans are here at last. Or, at the very least, they are in the process of coming.

Later that month, the trains began running east from the ghettos of Amsterdam, carrying Jews and others the Germans deemed undesirable to the concentration camps.

Soon after, Pat Fowlkes wrote his first letter home to Lib. It was July 26, 1942, his twenty-seventh birthday: "My darling, there is so much I want to tell you that I do not know where to start.... The men are put through a very strenuous program, beginning with calisthenics at six in the morning, and I find I am terrifically behind." Pat was one of 120 chaplains in training at Fort Benjamin Harrison. "Mostly R.C.'s [Roman Catholics]. Four Negroes. Two rabbis, who eat with their hats on—and almost don't eat, the meat not being kosher! I have a very nice room on the east side of my building. It is approximately 150 feet long by 60 wide, so I have lots of room and only seventy roommates."

In December 1941, on the eve of Pearl Harbor, there were 140 chaplains in the regular U.S. Army, the vast majority Catholic. By July 1942, that number had reached nearly 3,000, including those in training. "[But] the Army will need 6,000 by January 1st!" Pat wrote Lib, "[and] I am beginning to hope I go in with an air unit or an armored unit. I have volunteered for the parachute troops but feel there's little chance. They need one Protestant and two [Roman Catholics], but I was very late volunteering and am taller than they prefer."

That was his strength, his courage. And then came his tenderness, always.

"I do not need to tell you how much I have missed you and Frank and how constantly you have been on my mind." Please, he asked his beloved Lib, "Write me all about yourself and about my little fat frog."

CHAPTER 9

# RISKS

— ★ —

*Frieda van Schaïk*
October 1942

When it came to parenting, Frieda's Pappie was predictable. As soon as an argument began, he scuttled out of the room. "I'm sorry, I can't, I'm busy now," he muttered whenever Frieda asked for advice, then pedaled furiously away on his bicycle, even though she knew he had nowhere to go.

Discipline. Lessons. Sacrifice. All those fell to Margareta van Schaïk, Frieda's beloved Moekie. She was the pillar who held aloft the family's life. Moekie was the parent who commandeered and comforted, ran the household, did the chores, planted and harvested and canned and scrimped to make ends meet. And never complained.

If you wanted to talk about nature and science, though? That's when Dave van Schaïk came alive. He was, in the parlance of the early twentieth century, homo universalis: a universal man. He read and was published in gentleman's quarterlies and scientific journals. His articles covered not only his discoveries under Sint Pietersberg but his thoughts on the world around him, since Dave was knowledgeable about the local flora and fauna, conversant in topography and soil, a keen observer of erosion, a master of electricity, a self-taught expert on rock pressure and tunneling, and a lover of trains. His door was always open to another homo universalis who wanted to discuss his many areas of expertise. And no matter how late the hour or short the notice, Moekie managed to find these visitors food but never alcohol, since the Van Schaïks didn't drink.

"We were never entirely sure where we were going to sleep," Wim wrote, since Moekie also offered these visitors her children's beds.

*And there was nothing better,* Frieda might have added. She loved eaves-dropping on the lively chatter from the staircase landing, dreaming of the day she would be invited down, with her father and his guests, to discuss her own fascinations.

Her favorite since ten years old, and still at seventeen, was the bats.

It started in 1937, when a college student down from Haarlem asked if there were any bats in Sint Pietersberg.

"Oh yes," Pappie told them. "Thousands." They clung like hairy black growths to the white walls and in enormous mounds inside the crumbling ceilings.

In fact, as the student discovered, Sint Pietersberg housed millions of bats, since it was the hibernation habitat for twelve of the fifteen bat species in the Netherlands. That winter, at the student's urging, a handful of enthu-siasts descended on the Van Schaïk house, eager for the Pioneer of Sint Pietersberg to lead them to the bats. The next year there must have been a couple dozen. Excitedly, enthusiastically, Frieda accompanied them into the labyrinth. She used bags on the ends of long bamboo poles to detach the bats, hung them on her shirt while she collected more specimens, then measured and tagged them before returning them to the walls. Posing for photos, she spread a bat's wings wider than her shoulders, then smiled.

She loved the camaraderie of these scientific expeditioners. The Van Schaïk household had always been a riot of activity, with six children,

a cousin from the Dutch colonies, two Belgian lodgers, the local pastor, the milk delivery boy, the greengrocer, and other frequent visitors. And yet, Frieda loved the dozen or so winter nights, after long hours of exploring, when the amateur scientists crowded around their kitchen table, with Pappie smoking his ever-present cigarettes, and left no topic untouched, from plants to politics, geology to art.

To her great disappointment, the middle-aged couple sitting across the dinner table from her on this particular night was not like that. Not at all. They kept their eyes down, their lips set. Moekie had slaughtered a chicken, a sacrifice as the food rations dwindled, but the couple barely ate. They ignored their chicory coffee. They had come from Berlin. They carried hiking packs and nature guides, but there was no conversation as with the other naturalists who knocked on their door, and the candles were quickly snuffed. The next morning, Pappie headed to the caves, walking his bicycle packed with exploring gear while the couple walked beside him. After they left, Moekie took a canning jar and buried it in the garden.

"If you ever see your father walking his bicycle with someone you don't recognize," she told Frieda, "pretend you don't know him."

Nothing else was said, because it didn't need to be. Frieda knew that

51

her father was part of a network stretching through many universities and intellectual circles. Someone, maybe Pappie himself, had realized the valuable service the Pioneer of Sint Pietersberg could provide. The caves had dozens of openings on the east-west access, including Pappie's cable-cart tunnel. Those entrances and exits were all in the Netherlands. But if you passed through the mountain from north to south, it could take you from the Netherlands to Belgium.

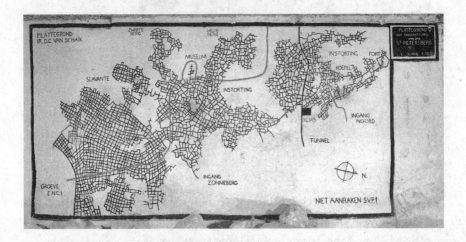

The problem, as clearly shown on the maps Pappie made of his explorations, was that the north half of the tunnels did not connect with the south. But as Frieda knew, a connection did exist. In a deep chamber, at the top of a wall, was a smuggler's hole. It was rough-hewn, a couple feet wide and a few dozen feet long, and it led to a chamber in the southern labyrinth. It was so straight that a lantern held at the end could be seen on the other side.

Frieda could barely imagine the trust, or fear, that would drive strangers to climb into that hole, deep in a mountain, and crawl until the passage narrowed so much that they had to pull themselves through and then drop ten feet to the floor. But she knew the hole, and the caves, were only part of the couple's journey. She did not know about the secret rooms behind panels, the sub-basements hollowed out of coal cellars and the cobwebbed, claustrophobic crawl spaces where Jews and other "undesirables" hid in cities like Amsterdam, but she knew the refugees were part of a network, because they had arrived with code words and false papers. It was their real identities Moekie buried in canning jars in the garden, at random, without a map. The Germans searched homes, confiscating medicine, linens, metals, and anything else of value. If they found a map and dug up a jar, it was death for them all.

Frieda never knew if her mother had agreed to be part of the Resistance. Moekie was a devout Christian; she never turned away a soul in need. But she barely slept after burying that first jar in the garden. Had she given her blessing, or had Pappie, as usual, simply done whatever he wanted to do?

There were collaborators, and informers called quislings, and German spies. The NSB. The Gestapo and its sycophants. There were eyes and tongues and rotten brains, you never knew who they were, or where they were, which is why Moekie told Frieda never to acknowledge her father when he was walking with a stranger. People informed. People disappeared. If she knew him, she was part of it, and everyone had heard stories, many of them true. Limburg was safer than the industrial cities of the North, where the Nazis infiltrated daily life at every level, but even in Heer, it only took one slip.

That's what terrified Margareta van Schaïk, Frieda's beloved Moekie. It only took one misstep, one word, one suspicion, one person out for profit or power or gain. There wasn't anyone, outside of her family, she could trust.

And Frieda? She smiled the next morning, as she crouched in her wooden clogs to tend the first pea shoots of spring and feed potato peels to the family's chickens. She wasn't afraid. Not yet. She was proud.

# CHAPTER 10

# MOST POPULAR BOY

— ★ —

*Edward and James Norton*
May 1943

D r. Jamie and his wife, Miss Ed Norton—yes, her given name was Edward—were well known in the small coastal town of Conway, South Carolina. Miss Ed was the daughter of the Presbyterian minister (who seems to have been hoping for a son). Dr. Jamie was the son of the town's doctor, and he became, in his turn, the town's new doctor. He was said to have performed the first appendectomy in Horry County in a farmhouse kitchen under a kerosene lamp (a few claimed using only a spoon), and even in the 1930s he was known to carry his black leather doctor's bag and drive his horse and buggy to late-night calls, often with Miss Ed to accompany him.

The Nortons had five children, three of whom survived childhood, before Dr. Jamie left to serve as a captain in the Army Medical Corps in World War I. They assumed they would have no more. Dr. Jamie was over forty when he returned from the war, Miss Ed in her late thirties.

But here they came in 1920, two blond-haired, blue-eyed identical twin boys, inseparable from the moment of their birth. Miss Ed named one James, after his father, and the other Edward, after herself, because she knew they would be her last. Dr. Jamie and Miss Ed were pillars of stability in their community, but their twins were agents of chaos, always running at top speed through their sleepy little town. A stranger might wonder at their adventures and how they always seemed to get away with it, no matter what *it* happened to be, but the locals just shook their heads. "Miss Ed's boys," they said with a smile, as if that explained it.

The boys were six when Charles Lindbergh became a national hero by flying solo across the Atlantic Ocean. Not long after, they began building model airplanes. As teens, they assembled and flew gas-powered models, a few feet long with radio controls. At sixteen, they tried to talk their mother into letting them buy a secondhand motorcycle they found for sale in a nearby town.

Too dangerous, she said. Too fast.

So, of course they talked her into letting them buy an airplane.

Miss Ed could never say no to The Twins, not for long anyway, and what was the use? If anyone had ever been born to fly, it was her twins.

Dr. Jamie bought a piece of sandy scrubland outside town. Together, the three of them cleared and leveled it for a runway. People in Conway had seen crop dusters, but they were no doubt delighted to see the 40-horsepower Taylor Cub circling overhead, no brakes and a skid for a tail wheel. Everyone knew Hoggy and Wack, as The Twins were known. They copiloted the Pepsi van, making deliveries and cheerful conversation all over town. Those were their favorite sons, their hometown boys up there in their bright red Cub, circling the town, skidding wildly across their sandy, weedy runway.

The Twins were flying home from watching the Citadel-Newberry football game in Charleston when they buzzed the town flagpole for the first time. The pilot—no one would say which boy was flying that day—and did it really matter?—came in so fast and low that the flag snapped at its grommets, homburgs bolted from heads, and aprons clutched desperately at the store clerks' calves. Not many could have gotten away with that, but the downtown witnesses had to laugh when they heard it was Hoggy and Wack. Who else would it have been but Dr. Jamie and Miss Ed's wildly loved, and wildly indulged, youngest boys? By the time they finished high school, The Twins had more than fifty hours of flight time and at least a flagpole run apiece.

They were chosen "Most Popular Boy" their senior year of high school. Not one of them, but both, as if they were one person. Edward's senior quote was by the poet John Gay: "The brave love mercy and delight to save." James chose a quote by Cicero: "Whoever is brave, should be a man of great soul."

They were roommates at Clemson College in fall 1938, taking the same courses in civil engineering. They played football for the Tigers.

Somehow, they each wore the number four. They both signed every hand-written letter home, and even their parents weren't sure which boy had written which words. They had never, it was said, spent an evening apart.

When they withdrew from college to volunteer for the U.S. Army Air Forces in November 1941, the story appeared in the *Horry Herald*, the local newspaper founded by their grandfather, the old town doctor. By volunteering, they could serve together, a privilege the Army denied those drafted, and a must for two boys inseparable since before birth. They were accepted into pilot training on November 19, 1941, a few weeks before Pearl Harbor. This triumph was also announced in the *Horry Herald*.

In a way, they were typical American boys. Many small towns had newspapers in 1941, and many of those newspapers were celebrating the local boys who were volunteering their futures to Uncle Sam. Many of those boys wanted to be fighter pilots. Like the Nortons, most found themselves diverted to bombers, which were more numerous and required two pilots per aircraft. Bomber commanders trained as both pilot and copilot, a system that allowed The Twins to fly together.

They trained on B-26 Marauders, a medium-sized bomber, at MacDill Field near Tampa, Florida, with hundreds of others. Most were like the

Nortons: in their late teens or early twenties, with a partial college education or none at all. Most had spent their whole lives within a hundred miles of where they were born. Now they were eating, sleeping, and training with men from all over the United States. And while they knew a fair number of them wouldn't live to see twenty-five, each believed he would be one of the heroes who survived.

Or, in the Norton twins' case, they believed they would both survive. Even at MacDill, Hoggy and Wack roomed together. Flew together. Ate meals and exercised and had fun together. Neither boy could imagine living without the other.

"Double trouble is in store for the Japs and Nazis when [The Twins] begin doing their stuff from Uncle Sam's bombers," *The State* declared, when Hoggy and Wack received their wings on September 6, 1942.

Now, after almost two years of training, it was finally time: May 17, 1943, early morning, European Theater of Operations. The nervous energy crackled, the cigarette smoke hung heavy as Lieutenant Colonel Robert M. "Moose" Stillman, commander of the 322nd Bomb Group, walked into the Quonset hut that served as the briefing shack at Bury St. Edmunds Airfield, near Suffolk, England. Crammed into the room, shoulder-to-shoulder like a football huddle, were the thirty-five pilots, copilots, and navigators Stillman had chosen for that morning's mission.

This was only the 322nd's second mission in the war, so most, like the Norton twins, had never flown in combat.

The anticipation grew as Colonel Stillman went over the particulars: weather, altitude, speed, landmarks, rendezvous points. This was their moment, the high point of their young lives, but a few faces dropped as the mission objective sunk in. Three days earlier, the 322nd, on their first mission of the war, had targeted a power plant at Velsen, near the Dutch coastal city of IJmuiden, that supplied electricity to fortified German submarine pens. Most American bombing runs came in high with air cover, but the 322nd had come in low and fast, with no fighter escort. The mission had initially been deemed a success: all bombs dropped on target, only one casualty, the pilot of a crippled B-26 that crashed on landing. But reconnaissance photographs the next day showed the power plant in working condition.

Now, the airmen were being tasked with flying that same stealth mission, to the same target, only three days later.

"That's stupid, sir," Stillman had said to his wing commander when he was briefed the evening before. "I won't send them out."

The wing commander, Brigadier General Francis M. Brady, agreed, but the orders came from above. "You will send them out," Brady said, "or the next group commander will."

Late that night, as Stillman tossed on his cot, his senior intelligence officer typed out a memo titled "Extreme danger in contemplated mission." It anticipated *violent enemy action* from the *skilled and experienced* ground defenses and begged command to reconsider. In a postscript, the staff officer typed a message to his commanding officer and good friend Moose: "Col: You were asleep and I did not want to wake you up—for God's sake get fighter cover."

There would be no fighter cover, Stillman told the boys in the briefing. There would be only speed, low-level flying, and the element of surprise. It was an invitation to be mauled, and everyone knew it, but if any of the boys had misgivings, they kept them to themselves. They were airmen. It was not their place to question, or to merely follow orders, but to believe in the men who issued those orders.

And the 322nd believed in Moose Stillman. They *would* follow him. Literally. Stillman could have chosen to sit out such a dangerous mission. Instead, he was piloting the lead plane.

"Questions?" Stillman asked the thirty-five young men, barely older than boys, he had come to know better than any others in the world.

"No, sir."

"We fly at 1100 hours."

"Yes, sir."

"Ready, sir." They were bomber pilots; there was room for fear in their world but not for doubt. This was what they had trained for. This was why they had volunteered.

Stillman watched them depart. "Good luck," his senior intelligence officer said.

"No," Stillman snapped, "it's good-bye."

The staff officer knew the odds. He had written the memo urging fighter cover. But there was no point in defeatism. "I'll see you at one o'clock," he said, the scheduled time for the planes to return.

"No, Fritz," Stillman said sadly, "it's good-bye."

Only eleven B-26 Marauders proved airworthy, a consequence of the previous raid, so sixty-six men crowded into the planes that morning: two in the back, one behind the pilot and copilot, and the bombardier/ navigator in the plexiglass nose. This was only the second mission for the

Marauders in Northern Europe—the first being the same route three days before—but the bombers were well known. In the Pacific Theater of Operations, they were called "widow-makers" because their small wing area made them difficult to maneuver for inexperienced pilots, and they stalled if flown at under 120 miles per hour, especially on landing. "One a day in Tampa Bay" had been a common quip at MacDill Field, referring to the number of widow-makers that had gone into the water during training.

Nonetheless, Hoggy and Wack were confident, excited, as their B-26 passed over the English coast and leveled off at fifty feet above the frigid North Sea, beneath the German radar. The planes flew in two tight V formations, Stillman at the front and the Nortons on the far left, with an unobstructed view across the sea. The waves were small, the wind down, the skies clear and quiet, but this was no flyby of the Conway, South Carolina, flagpole. At a cruising speed of 250 miles per hour, covering 366 feet per second flying wingtip to wingtip, the margin between life and death was about one-seventh of a second.

And somewhere out there, the enemy was waiting.

Forty minutes after takeoff, at 11:40 a.m., a bomber developed electrical problems and aborted the mission. Moments later, Stillman spotted enemy ships. He turned the formation south, hoping to create a feint. No shots fired. No warning on their monitored German radio frequencies. At 11:51 a.m., as they crossed the sand dunes that protected the Dutch lowlands from the sea, the Norton brothers turned to each other in the cockpit and smiled, sure they had made it to Europe undetected.

And then the sky exploded with cannon fire. Flame-colored blasts smashed into Stillman's plane, severing the flight controls and killing his copilot. In an instant, Stillman's bomber inverted. Strapped in upside down, with no ability to control the aircraft, Stillman watched as the ground sped toward him. Moments before they hit the ground, a second bomber burst into flames.

The formation had flown into a wall of German antiaircraft emplacements embedded along the Dutch coast, but nobody was sure where. The flight plan didn't call for concentrated enemy fire at this point. Had the diversion taken them too far south? Were they off course? Sitting behind the Norton brothers, the navigator desperately tried to figure out their location, while James kept his eye on the gauges and made adjustments to the engines and propellers. Edward, the pilot, tipped the short-winged bomber to the right, then to the left, to avoid the flak barrage.

There was a sudden flash, as one Marauder slammed into another during evasive maneuvers. James could see the propellers chewing through the aluminum fuselage, creating a shrapnel field flying backward at hundreds of miles an hour, critically damaging the Marauder flying behind. He watched all three planes head down as Edward banked, ripping through a cannonade that seemed sure to send them down, until suddenly, miraculously, it was over, they were through, and the skies were quiet again.

With the North Sea off their left wing, the five remaining pilots formed up, still hoping to bomb the power plant, or at least a target of value. Ten minutes passed as the Dutch countryside slipped beneath them, the calm of the square green fields and straight dikes fighting the adrenaline of young men who had just seen half their comrades go down. They talked continuously on their headsets, trying to assess flight routes and damage, attempting to figure out where they were. Small villages and farms slipped beneath them, but no recognizable landmarks.

"Hold it a minute, I think I see the target," the lead navigator yelled, just as his pilot was about to abort the mission. "Yes. Yes, there it is."

The five planes accelerated into position, dropped their bombs, then banked west for the crossing home. Their bomber felt light after dropping its 5,800-pound load, as if it were floating. The German antiaircraft flak was near silent, almost pretty, just black puffs in the sky as Edward Norton crossed the bright white line of the northern Dutch coast.

And then the murderous shrapnel slammed into the squadron like a swarm of locusts. The flying metal ripped through the aluminum skin of the bombers, tearing through wiring and flesh. The Nortons could hear the metal puncture their cockpit, could see the holes where the jagged, hurtling pieces punched through the fuselage, but there was nothing to do but continue on, to accelerate through the barrage and out the other side. Smoke poured out of the two lead bombers, blinding them, but then their Marauder raced past the smoke as the two bombers sputtered, tilted, lost altitude, then crashed into the sea.

They were losing speed; James could see it in his gauges. He pushed the engines, the propellers, searching for power. Edward firewalled the throttles, hoping to gain altitude, but the yoke pulled in his hand and the plane vibrated wildly. They were over the North Sea, out of the range of the German guns, but against the horizon the other two surviving bombers were pulling farther and farther ahead, and there was nothing more they could coax from their crippled B-26, no more procedures or counter-maneuvers a pilot or his copilot could do.

They were hurtling forward but inevitably downward, and as the future fell away, Edward looked over at James, who looked back sadly at his twin. For brothers who had been inseparable for twenty-two years, a glance was a language. It was a lifetime. Maybe they said, "I love you, brother," as their plane slid toward the sea. Or maybe they said nothing at all, because there was nothing left unsaid between them as their speed slowed below 120 miles per hour and their bomber began to stall.

Two days later, May 19, 1943, Dr. Jamie and Miss Ed Norton received an official notice from the U.S. Army Air Forces. Their twin boys were missing in action.

# PART II

# TO THE
# WALL

— ★ —

May 1943–September 1944

*Freedom. No word was ever spoken that has held out greater hope, demanded greater sacrifice, needed more to be nurtured, blessed more the giver, damned more its destroyer, or came closer to being God's will on Earth. May Americans ever be its protector!*
General Omar N. Bradley,
Commanding General, Twelfth United States Army Group

# CHAPTER 11

# HARDSHIPS AND HAPPIER TIMES

— ★ —

*Frieda van Schaïk*
May–July 1943

The Americans entered ground combat in the European Theater on November 8, 1942, with the largest amphibious assault in history to that point. Three Anglo-American task forces landed at points across 900 miles of North African coastline. Of the 107,000 Allied troops involved, 84,000 were American—nearly half the number of active-duty soldiers in the entire U.S. Army three years before. Operation Torch was designed to ease American troops into the fighting by having them aid the British, who had been fighting German Field Marshal Erwin Rommel's Afrika Korps since 1941. The landings went well, but an airborne assault that was to support the center task force got off to a poor start. On the trip from England, the transport planes flew into a storm. Several crashed in the African desert. Others were blown so far off course that only one group of paratroopers reached their initial objective, where they discovered it had been captured by British troops the day before. The first paratrooper combat drop in U.S. Army history, and it could reasonably be called a disaster. Nonetheless, by February 1943, British General Bernard Law Montgomery had driven Rommel back to his former position at the Mareth Line in Tunisia.

Around the same time, on January 27, 1943, ninety-one American B-17s and B-24s bombed the German naval base at Wilhelmshaven. It was the first American bombing mission over Germany, and it was a relative success, with three planes lost out of fifty-five. Again, the raid was mostly in support of the British, whose bombers had been running the gauntlet to Berlin since August 1940.

The biggest battles, though, and the bloodiest fighting, were happening on the Eastern Front. The Germans had attacked the Soviet Union on June 22, 1941. By December, they were at the gates of Leningrad and Moscow. When the Soviet Red Army managed to push back the Nazis, the Germans pivoted and launched a southern campaign. On August 23, 1942, its 6th Army reached Stalingrad. Hitler had ordered the male population of the city executed and the women and children deported; Stalin had sealed the city and burned the crops, trapping 400,000 Soviet civilians inside. The fighting was ferocious, street-to-street in the rubble of the destroyed city, for almost two months.

In November, the Soviets counterattacked. Within days, the German 6th Army was surrounded. On February 2, 1943, they surrendered. The Germans had suffered between 150,000 and 250,000 killed, and 91,000 German soldiers were captured. Only 6,000 German 6th Army soldiers ever returned home. The Soviets had lost more than a million, including most of Stalingrad's civilian population, many of whom starved to death.

On February 5, on Hitler's orders, the German occupiers closed all the theaters and restaurants, including those in Maastricht, in honor of its 6th Army, destroyed at Stalingrad. This was the same German field army that had barreled up the Rijksweg to Maastricht almost three years before. Perhaps there were some in Limburg who mourned German friends, but most quietly celebrated. Death to the occupiers. And who cared about the restaurants? The streetlights had been turned off for years to keep British pilots from using them as landmarks, and only collaborators went out for entertainment anymore.

Then a string of high-profile assassinations rocked the NSB, the work of the Dutch Resistance.

The Germans had assumed the "Nazification" of the Netherlands would be easy because the two countries shared a cultural heritage and genetic roots. They referred to the Netherlands, along with Luxembourg and Belgium, as their "Germanic brother people" and the "Nordic Reich," and they expected the population to become eager followers of National

Socialism. But most of the Dutch hated their German occupiers. They rebelled, some as part of the Resistance, most by passively undermining orders and refusing to cooperate. An angry Joseph Goebbels, the chief propagandist of the Nazi Party, called them "the most insolent and obstreperous people in the entire West."

By spring 1943, with the war turning against them, the Germans had had enough. They began to seize public property, including a convent in Maastricht. They dissolved Limburg's technical training school for girls. They melted down most of the church bells in Maastricht, though not the bells of Sint Jans (the Van Schaïks' Protestant family church) and the "grandmother" of them all, the 400-year-old bell at Sint Servaas. They seized the Maastricht history museum and ransacked its contents. They even stole a world-famous ant collection.

They looted houses, taking furniture, paintings, tea sets, and rugs. For weeks, long freight trains left the country packed with stolen loot. Huge signs on their sides declared, "THIS IS THE WAY HOLLAND THANKS THE FÜHRER."

On April 30, they announced a labor conscription program, the Arbeitseinsatz. A smaller effort, in April 1942, had failed because of massive resistance—most Dutch men simply didn't sign up. This time, the German occupiers promised violent implementation, beginning with the arrest and deportation to Germany of the 300,000 Dutch soldiers on active duty at the time of the country's surrender in 1940.

Again, as with the Amsterdam ghetto uprisings in early 1941, the Dutch went on strike. This time, the Germans didn't hesitate before shooting strikers, ending the uprising everywhere but in Limburg Province, where 10,000 striking miners stood strong. The State Supervision of Mines—Dave van Schaïk's old friends, now enemies since the signing of the Nazi pledge—had bent to the occupiers, but the Catholic clergy of Limburg were dedicated to resistance, and the miners along the Bemelerweg packed their churches, spilling out beyond their doors.

By the time the strike was suppressed, more than 180 people were dead, 900 had been sent to concentration camps, and Frieda was gone, because her mother feared the Arbeitseinsatz would begin to round up young Dutch women too. Frieda graduated from high school in May 1943, the same month the Norton twins—only four years older than her, twenty-two years to her eighteen—plunged into the North Sea. It was rumored the Nazis were using graduation rolls as conscription lists. They needed workers on the assembly lines to build their newest weapon, the V-2 rocket, the world's first long-range ballistic missile, which could be launched from the Netherlands or France to reach London.

Frieda's mother, Moekie, was adamant that wouldn't happen to her youngest daughter. In her youth, Moekie had studied piano in a conservatory. She had given concerts. Then her husband had gotten that wild hair and moved the family to Limburg, where she lived modestly on a rural street and bent her back every day to take care of the family, alone, with no recognition or thanks, while Dave tinkered in his attic or pursued whatever wild, unpaying passion caught his fancy. It was her piano lessons for farmers' and miners' children that paid most of the bills, not her husband's dreams.

Now her oldest daughter, Jacoba, was a Red Cross nurse in Belgium. Helen, the next, worked at a chemical laboratory in Nijmegen and was rarely granted a travel pass by the occupation authorities. Margaret was married and pregnant and working at a bookstore in Maastricht, God bless her, but that did only so much to alleviate the weight of the occupation. Moekie was not—and here she put her foot down, as she almost never had before—giving up her Frieda to the enemy's war factories.

So Dave worked his contacts for false papers, and Moekie sent her youngest daughter 100 miles northeast to her hometown of Arnhem to pose as a dental assistant.

"Pull up your socks . . ." she started, as Frieda stood on the train platform. It was one of Moekie's favorite sayings whenever someone complained: *Pull up your socks and get on with it*. Frieda had found it annoying, but since the occupation she found it almost comforting. *This, too, can be endured. It is up to us to find and make the good.*

"Pull up your socks . . ." Moekie tried a second time, but she couldn't finish the thought, she was so overcome with emotion. Moekie had pulled up her own socks so many times, for so many years, they were wearing thin. And she never complained. Never broke down. But sending away her youngest daughter, under a false name, to escape the Nazis—how much did God expect her to silently endure?

In Arnhem, Frieda lived with a roommate. She had a salary. She visited with her mother's childhood friends. She held her breath, at first, every time she passed a German soldier, but after a week she relaxed into a quiet, unnoticed life. Peter, a boy she had gone to school with since she was six years old, was also hiding in Arnhem. He had always been sweet on her, and she had always liked him. He stood up for her when her family first moved to the south and she was bullied by some older kids. Soon, they were going out for chicory coffee and evening walks by the river. Her neighbor, a war widow, accompanied them at Frieda's request. She was not the kind of girl to walk alone with a young man.

It was . . . well, not adulthood, exactly, but progress. She was eighteen. For three years, she had been trapped short of womanhood, living in the same small loop she had lived in at fifteen, when the occupation descended on her. Three years of social deprivation. Three years of lost chances to go to college or work, to meet a boy, to explore the world. Three years, and no end in sight. The occupation might go on for a decade. It might go on forever. At least in Arnhem, she could imagine a future, a free world, and a fair chance.

Peter assumed they would marry. It was a war promise. A hope to hold on to in desperate times, so Frieda did little to discourage him.

A month later, Moekie had a stroke. The Arbeitseinsatz was floundering because of massive Dutch resistance. The immediate danger had passed. And her mother, her poor Moekie, needed her. Frieda went home.

It was summer, the season to put away food against the winter. Their large garden, once full of Pappie's experiments and Moekie's flowers, was now entirely used for growing food (and burying canning jars). Frieda secured a small allotment across the road, near the orchard, to grow even more. Even Pappie helped, using chambers under Sint Pietersberg to grow mushrooms and white cardoons, an edible thistle too odd and finicky to bother with before the war.

Some days, Frieda rode her bicycle alongside her Pappie to tend the crops in the caves. Other days, she worked in her garden allotment, or with Moekie on the metal sewing machine (too useful and heavy to hide from the Germans), mending clothes and blankets. She spent mornings cleaning and evenings in a quiet corner with her books. Frieda had taken Department A in high school: languages and bookkeeping, instead of math and science. She spoke French, German, English, and, of course, Dutch. And she loved reading, which, on occasion, exasperated her hardworking mother.

*Pull up your socks,* she admonished when she saw her daughter reading, *and get back to work.*

Before the occupation, evenings had meant nature walks with her father and siblings. She remembered one mild summer day, when she was seven or eight, and her older sisters were still at home, and Pappie had suddenly announced an outing.

"Every hour's sleep before midnight is worth two after," Moekie reminded her children as they scampered out the door in their waterproof boots, but everyone knew the walk would last as long as Pappie wanted, and not a minute less.

He led the children past the nearby houses, waving good night to the miners as they finished their chores. They passed the communal water pump at the intersection of two roads, under the shadow of a small Catholic church too poor for bells. Instead, the parish priest played recordings of bells from a speaker he had rigged in the steeple. Occasionally, he would forget to disconnect this makeshift sound system before playing his personal jazz records—inappropriate records, according to Moekie—and Frieda would have to run to the church, shouting, "Father, Father, you left the speakers on again! We can hear everything!"

It was in the narrow gap alongside the church, as the last light left the sky, that Dave van Schaïk heard what he was after: the mating call of the toads under the flat rocks of the drainageway, first one, then another, then a chorus rising as the sun disappeared.

"Listen," he whispered with a smile. "They each have their own pitch."

He led the children through a hedgerow and across a pasture to a thicket of bushes and trees, a nightingale nesting ground. Frieda crouched transfixed, listening to the songs of the birds. She ambled across the hills and through the fields, Pappie in his suit and tie with his ever-present cigarette, collecting seeds and identifying the sounds of the night until, finally, well past midnight, the crickets serenaded the tired children home along the old tramline. The yellow clover was waist-high, and the bats in the old cow barn were flitting so fast that Frieda swore she could feel the wind of their wings against her bare red cheeks.

All dwellings were in darkness, except one. Moekie was up, awaiting their return.

But now the world was dark, and there were no more toad-nightingale walks with Pappie, no languid strolls alone in the forest. Even Pappie's after-dinner amble with Moekie, a daily habit for years, was lost to the war.

So Frieda and her mother spent long hours in the kitchen together, cleaning and cutting vegetables from the garden, scraping Pappie's mushrooms, making soup. There were often others in the house. Her sister Helen on a rare travel pass from Nijmegen. Her sister Margaret, with her infant daughter. Her brother Wim back from a day at his technical college in Heerlen. Pappie back from his caves. The local priest, Moekie's friend despite their religious differences. But in the kitchen, scrounging eggs and flour for bread, Frieda and Moekie were in a world of their own. The butter came in a block in brown paper, and they would scrape the paper as clean as possible, then heat it over the stove until the last butter remnants dripped into the waiting dough. Nothing was wasted, not even the paper, which was neatly folded and taken back to the ration stand when butter was available again.

Late summer meant apples in the orchards, the only food the hungry people of Limburg had in abundance. The owner of the orchard across the street hired Frieda to sort his crop. For every four baskets of good apples, she was paid one basket of bruised. Her evenings were full of peeling and canning, with pickling and packing away for the winter. But also apple tarts hot from the oven, their brown edges almost burning her mouth. Frieda smiled every time she saved the last drips of butter, thinking of those tarts.

At night, she climbed to the attic window to watch the skies. The house was shut tight: the doors locked, the blackout shutters pulled, as required by the occupiers. The yellow light of the kitchen's single bare bulb dimmed below her, where the brooms and baking sheets rested, the shelf of cans waited. It was black in the attic, but not pitch-black, because of the moon and stars. And not completely quiet. She heard the crickets and toads, a nightingale in the distance. She watched the bats flitting against the moon and searched for stiffer wings, hoping to hear the growling and whistling of the British four-engine bombers. As always, the sound rose like a murmur, far away, growing louder but never arriving until, suddenly, a swarm of planes was overhead, hundreds of tiny crosses like black birds in a black sky, the rumble of their engines nearly shaking the foundations of the house.

It was a message from a distant world, tearing through the shroud of the occupation. The sound of freedom. A sliver of hope.

From the west, a warning flare. From the east, the rattle and flash of antiaircraft guns. Searchlights slashed the darkness like long fingers, their beams sweeping across the clouds until suddenly, a flash of wing, a bomber lumbering east toward the German border. From the south, the antiaircraft guns of the German emplacement at Gronsveld started to rattle. Then a roar, like a chugging train, the distinctive sound of the German 20mm cannons.

"Night fighters!" Wim whispered in Frieda's ear, sneaking up behind her in the darkness.

Suddenly, the sky lit up with a bright yellow flame. A British bomber was hit, the smudge of its wing on fire circling downward until it winked out, extinguished by the rush of wind.

Frieda thought of the pilot: some brave young man, some boy her age. A volunteer from a better, freer world, come to tell them not to despair, the fight was on, the flame had not gone out.

The air raid siren blew, and Frieda was down the stairs. In her bedroom, her clothes were neatly folded on a stool: shirt, then pants, then socks, with her shoes tucked beneath. She placed them there every evening, in the same order, so she would know exactly where they were in the dark.

She pulled them on as the droning overhead became a roar. She heard bombs exploding near Aachen, or dropped by a crippled bomber trying to lighten its load before turning toward home.

She stepped outside. The black sky was full of shadows.

She grabbed her bicycle. She was a volunteer for the International Red Cross, trained in emergency first aid. At the air raid siren, it was her duty to ride to her assigned post and await instructions. A terrifying ride. Her papers designated her a nurse, but the British flew late, after the 10:00 p.m. curfew, so Germans—or worse, collaborators—might stop her. No matter how she tried to avoid it, the thought always came to her on the pitch-black roads: shot because of a German's nerves, or worse.

"They got him," Wim whispered a few hours later, over the meager breakfast of watery porridge Frieda had prepared without milk or butter or . . .

"Who?"

"The RAF pilot. The one who went down. He's alive and at a farm in Heugem."

She swallowed her excitement. It was another thing the occupation had taught her, to be careful of her emotions. "How do you know?"

"My friend Fernand. He said the man will be taken to a neighborhood near the Maas this morning. It will be easier to hide him there. Tonight, they'll row him across the river. That's where Fernand and I take over. We're going to guide him through the caves."

Frieda imagined a brave boy lurching through alleys, a tiny boat on a black river, the long and winding route through the caves she had walked with her father, mapping chambers, studying bats.

She sighed. She hoped for the best. Then placed a bowl of porridge and a glass of water on a tray and went in to see her mother.

# CHAPTER 12

# A NEW ARRIVAL

— ★ —

*Paschal Fowlkes*
May 1943

"I know how hard your lot is in many ways," Chaplain Paschal Fowlkes wrote his wife, Lib, as his deployment date neared. He had not been assigned to the paratroopers, as he had hoped, but to the 314th Troop Carrier Group (TCG), whose primary duty was to fly paratroopers to their drop zones.

> *Not that missing me is an unbearable burden but just that keeping our little family together as a family will be lonesome, I know, without someone phys-ically beside you to share your problems and your hopes and dreams. I hope you will always remember that I am sharing them wherever I am and though many miles separate us. And you must have the pleasure of remembering always that I go off with as easy a mind as ever a soldier went off with, know-ing that in all the world over there is no lovelier mother than the one to whose care I entrust my children and no lovelier wife to return to.*

Lib was pregnant with their second child.

"All I think about now is post-War days," he wrote her, "you and me and our little family. I don't believe I will accept any bishoprics—all I want is a moderate sized, moderate-incomed parish where we can all be together, free and happy. I have so much to live for in you and them that I just never think of not getting back."

"I know I will."

# CHAPTER 13

# BASIC

— ★ —

*Bill Hughes*
June 1943

B ill Hughes's draft number came up in June 1943. He'd received three deferments while with the Armored Force Liaison Office. This time, he knew he was going in. He also knew that, as a Black man, he would almost surely end up in a service outfit—supply, maintenance, transportation, laundry. Many in the U.S. Army thought Black soldiers weren't fit for combat or command. From his desk in Washington, Hughes had seen them shunted by the thousands into peeling potatoes and cleaning latrines.

He wanted to fight.

Fortunately, he was well-liked and well-positioned. His boss, Brigadier General Gilbert X. Cheves, saw to it that he was assigned to the 758th Tank Battalion.

While the U.S. Army was cold to the idea of Black infantrymen, it was positively frigid to the idea of Black tankers. Patton's declaration that "a colored soldier cannot think fast enough to fight in armor" echoed the thinking of the majority of the military brass.

Still, there was a push to form one segregated armored division, about 230 tanks and 10,900 men. The Army had created the all-Black 92nd Infantry Division. The Army Air Forces had the 332nd Fighter Group and 477th Bombardment Group, later known as the Tuskegee Airmen. So a single segregated tank division was within its cramped racial biases. Someone balked, though, at devoting that much armor to "inferior" soldiers.

Instead, the Army formed three segregated, separate armored battalions, each containing a headquarters and four companies of about 70 tanks and 680 Black men, under the command of 40 white officers. This gave the Black tankers about the same number of tanks and men as they would have had as an armored division, but with a crucial difference: An armored division retained control of its tanks and was assigned infantry to support it in battle. It was in command of a fully functioning combat force. Separate armored battalions had no control or command; they were loaned to infantry units and supported the foot soldiers.

The 758th was the first of the three Black separate armored battalions, activated in May 1941. Bill Hughes received his assignment in June 1943 and headed immediately to Camp Claiborne, Louisiana, where the Black tank battalions trained. He arrived in the evening, wearing civilian clothes and carrying a duffel bag. The white military police immediately challenged him for not wearing a uniform.

"I haven't been trained to wear a uniform," he told them.

An exasperated MP picked up the phone. "We have one of your boys down here at the front gate out of uniform," he snapped. "Come get him."

A mistake had been made. Bill Hughes hadn't been through basic training. The executive officer (XO) of the 761st Tank Battalion (not the 758th) who came to retrieve him was apoplectic, cursing Bill Hughes a blue streak, white officer to Black GI. He left the young man to sleep on a concrete floor and buy candy bars from a vending machine if he wanted dinner. In the morning, Hughes called General Cheves, who asked the XO if Bill could receive his basic training in the 761st. The XO, unhappy, transferred the green recruit to the 784th, the third Black separate tank battalion, where the senior enlisted leader of Company D, First Sergeant George Daniels, took in the young man, only twenty, and, as Bill Hughes himself described it, "taught me how to wear a uniform, salute, and march."

Life in the Jim Crow Deep South proved the greater challenge, especially after the relative freedom of Washington, D.C. Camp Claiborne was strictly segregated. The camp was established in 1930 and greatly expanded in 1939. Most of the soldiers, including the Black tankers, lived in canvas tents and huts. Trampled to dirt, the grounds were choking dust when dry, sloppy mud when wet, and the amenities were little more than a movie shed with wooden benches and no air conditioning. Another section of the camp had a movie theater with chairs, a nice mess hall, and air-conditioning, but those areas were white-only. Many of the young Black men in the 784th were from Mississippi. They were used to the thick, suffocating heat of the Delta. They had lived their whole lives here without air-conditioning. But Bill Hughes sweltered in the airless tents. The only thing an open flap did was let in the mosquitos and flies.

This was acceptable, or at least endurable. No Black man, including Bill Hughes, thought life as a soldier in the U.S. Army would be luxurious, much less racially just. He had lived with this separate-and-unequal treatment in Indianapolis.

The nearby town of Alexandria, Louisiana, though, beggared his belief. The hatred was so close to the surface, the town seemed scarred with its perpetual scowl. White Southerners had vehemently opposed Black men serving in the armed forces, and the white citizens of Alexandria despised having Black soldiers nearby. It was a threat to their way of life, these dangerously empowered, "uppity" Northern Negroes, and they feared it, fought it, then loathed it even more.

Making matters worse, the Army's all-white military police sided with the locals, even though most of the MPs were from states like Wisconsin, Pennsylvania, and Michigan. If this was the Army's attempt to quell unrest by bending to local norms, it backfired. Instead of easing tension, it empowered the racists and left the Black soldiers feeling angry and betrayed.

The tension had exploded in January 1942, a year before Hughes's arrival and a few weeks after the Japanese attack on Pearl Harbor. Early on a Saturday evening, with the town swollen with soldiers on liberty, a white MP tried to arrest a Black soldier outside the Ritz Theater. For reasons unclear, the incident escalated, and a race riot ensued, as white MPs, policemen, state troopers, and armed citizens battled hundreds of unarmed Black soldiers along four or five blocks of Lee Street. When word reached the Black side of Camp Claiborne, the tankers stormed the motor pool. Live ammunition was lifted from the armory, and the only thing that stopped the soldiers from driving their tanks into town was the arrival of one of the buses.

The buses that transported soldiers, both white and Black, into town were one of the most hated aspects of life in Camp Claiborne. The drivers were virulent racists, known to be armed. They forced Black soldiers to ride in the back, using insults and racist epithets. With only eleven seats designated to them, Black soldiers often had to wait hours for buses that white soldiers boarded with little or no lines, and if anyone spoke up, stood up, or stepped out of the designated zone, the driver took the bus straight to the sheriff's department, where the soldier was arrested.

When the Black soldiers saw the bus arriving, they rushed it, pelting it with bottles and rocking it almost off its wheels. By the time the riot at the camp was over, the riot in town was winding down. It was the worst in a series of racist incidents near Southern military camps: white patrons attacking Black soldiers at a YMCA in South Carolina, state troopers assaulting Black troops in Arkansas, a hanging at Fort Benning, two killed by MPs at Fort Bragg. The Army investigated quickly when word of the Camp Claiborne riot started to spread in Black newspapers. The official military report accused several white policemen and MPs of "indiscriminate and unnecessary shooting" and counted twenty-nine Black soldiers wounded (later amended to thirty), three critically. One Black woman was shot in the hip. Injuries ran the gamut, from gunshot wounds to the trauma inflicted by brickbats, billy clubs, and bottles.

The report only heightened the frustration and suspicion on the Black side of Camp Claiborne. By the time Bill Hughes arrived, it was widely accepted among the Black soldiers that as many as a dozen Black men had been killed in Alexandria that evening and the Army had covered it up. Many believed in other uncounted deaths. "They would always find one or two dead right out from the post," one soldier reported, while admitting he didn't personally know anyone who was killed.

This wasn't about the local population; the Black soldiers at Camp Claiborne no longer trusted their Army.

Many refused to take their leave off-post, despite the heat and bleak conditions. Others went on Mondays or Tuesdays, when Alexandria was quieter. Few ever went alone. Hughes went to town only once, and he hated the place. The townspeople were unfriendly, the liquor cheap, the drunks aggressive and loud. Grifters accosted him in the streets, and prostitutes, bussed into town by the dozens, openly hawked their wares. He couldn't walk a block without being harassed by hair-trigger MPs or having to step around a puddle of vomit. The place was offensive to everything that he, as a working-class kid from a solid family, as a young Black man who had known all his life that any misstep or infraction would be held against him, held dear.

Bill Hughes was discovering, in other words, that he had been right. Every place in the world was not like Indianapolis. Some places were worse.

Fortunately, he wasn't at Camp Claiborne long. After mastering the basics of military life, he was sent to the radio communications "schoolhouse" at Fort Knox, home of the Army's Armor School, for specialized training. By the time he was a trained radioman, the 784th was in the process of being transferred to Camp Hood, Texas.

But the lesson of Claiborne stayed with him: as a Black soldier in this man's Army, all he could truly rely on were his fellow tankers in the 784th.

# CHAPTER 14

# THE LIBRARY

— ★ —

*Jefferson Wiggins*

July 1943

In summer 1943, as Bill Hughes struggled with Deep South segregation, Jeff Wiggins, who had come from Deep South segregation, found himself on Staten Island. He had been promoted to staff sergeant, and he was kicking around Fort Wadsworth awaiting transfer to his duty station. He was in the quartermaster, which handled supplies and other "back office" operations like cooking, cleaning, driving, and warehousing. He wasn't excited about that. This was the kind of work Bill Hughes had pulled strings to avoid. But there had been no Black combat units at Fort Benning, where Jeff Wiggins had been inducted into the Army.

He sensed, though, that the limits on a Black man's options were not as rigid in Staten Island as they had been in Alabama. He decided to test that theory a few weeks in by walking into a place that had intrigued him since the first time he saw it: the library in the nearby town of Stapleton.

Sergeant Wiggins had never been inside a library. Those in Alabama and North Carolina were white-only. He had only read two books cover to cover: the Bible and the Army's Uniform Code of Military Justice. The Army's rule book scared the hell out of him, because it spelled out in plain language the consequences of lying on your enlistment papers: five years in the brig at Fort Leavenworth, Kansas. He lay with that weight, fearing the consequences of his lie about his age. Afraid he was going to lose what Grandma Dawson and his mother had always wanted for him: his chance at a better life.

The fact was, Jeff Wiggins liked it in the Army. Was it racist? Sure. He realized that when he had to ride in the back of the bus to Fort Benning. Black soldiers, like civilians, still had to know "their place." Was spending the war cleaning toilets the worst duty he could think of? Well, he didn't want to be Dorie Miller, running into enemy fire with no training. That was worse. But he wanted his service to be meaningful, not menial. He wanted to do work he could be proud of.

Still, he had his $28.50 a week in staff sergeant's pay. And his three squares a day. And, at least for now, a decent chance at a proper duty assignment.

He touched his sergeant stripes. The library was a new space for him. A forbidden space, because of the power held in its books. He was in awe, as he walked from room to room, past walls of books and down corridors of books. There were more books than any person could ever hope to read.

Eventually, a woman stopped him. "May I help you?"

"I'm sorry," he said. It was an instinct.

"What are you looking for?" the librarian asked.

Jefferson eyed the small white woman. She seemed sincere. And he was in his uniform with his sergeant chevrons. An Army uniform, even on a Black man, meant something.

"A book of great knowledge," he said.

"You'll need a library card."

She took him to the circulation desk. She took down his information. And she gave him a library card!

Then she recommended a book. Five minutes later, Sergeant Jeff Wiggins walked out of the library with that book in his hand.

A few days later, he was back, and Mrs. Merrill, the librarian, introduced him to the kinds of books she thought would prove to a smart Black teenager that he was a person of value, not a nobody, as the world he'd grown up in had wanted him to believe.

It wouldn't have mattered what she recommended: Jeff Wiggins had read the Army's Uniform Code of Military Justice cover to cover, and anyone who could do that could learn from any book. It was her kindness that impacted him. This white woman saw him—not as a Black teenager, not as Black, but as a man like any other man, and worthy of her respect.

Whenever Sergeant Wiggins thought of his schooling, he thought of a song he had been forced to sing: *My country, 'tis of thee, Sweet land of liberty . . . land where my fathers died . . . land of the pilgrims' pride.*

That song made him angry, because it made him think, *It's not my liberty. It's not my pride. White people wanted to kill my father, and for what? Selling a bale of cotton?*

Mrs. Merrill's kindness poked a hole in that anger, which was really a kind of sadness: for himself, and for a society that would harbor such hatred. Mrs. Merrill almost made Jeff Wiggins believe Grandma Dawson had been right: a hardworking Black man could make more of his life than all those hateful bigots back in Alabama would ever make of theirs.

CHAPTER 15

# FLOATING OBJECTS

— ★ —

*James and Edward Norton*
July 1943

On July 26, 1943, German sentries spotted several objects in the water off the northern coast of the Netherlands. No Dutch citizens were allowed within 150 yards of any beach or dune, so it was German soldiers who pulled the bodies ashore. Two of the bodies, a junior officer and an enlisted man, were buried at nearby cemeteries. The Germans were, among many less savory things, sticklers for bureaucracy. They always documented these discoveries.

The Germans sent the third body, an officer, to the military cemetery at Huisduinen. The young man had been identified as a British pilot, but at Huisduinen, they realized he was an American. They recorded that fact, then buried him there on July 28, 1943, with full military honors.

CHAPTER 16

# A WELCOME SURPRISE

— ★ —

*Paschal Fowlkes*
July 1943

Chaplain Paschal Fowlkes arrived at the airfield outside Kairouan, Tunisia, in the waning days of June 1943. It was Army life at its finest. The men slept on the ground in tents, as the temperature topped 125 degrees. The rains overflowed the drainage trenches, soaking their gear. The tarantulas, scorpions, and snakes loved the shade of their boots and bedrolls.

"We have to stand in line to get rationed water," Pat wrote his mother, "a helmet-full at a time, and it takes about fifteen helmets to do an average-size wash. We also bathe by pouring helmets-full (two in number) on each other. This dust is almost impossible to remove, though. We're still living on C rations: per day, that means a can of vegetables and beef stew, of beans and meat, and of vegetable hash—three in all, plus dog biscuits [their dessert] and beverage."

He traveled to hospitals and troop stations by foot, jeep, and truck, offering prayers and Sunday services. "You have never seen such a human melting pot as the place is," he marveled. "French, Continental Jewish refugees, Arabs, soldiers from everywhere." He offered spiritual guidance to all, with the help of chaplains from other denominations and religions. He helped officers censor their men's letters, scrubbing anything that could be useful to the enemy, as the Army required. He scratched a baseball diamond out of the dust, using his helmet to dig the baselines.

They were training for Operation Husky, the American, British, and Canadian assault on Sicily. The drop into North Africa for Operation

Torch had been a disaster, with more dead men than objectives met, and the 314th Troop Carrier Group was determined not to repeat the mistakes of the past. But it was hard going in the heat. Ground personnel usually stopped working at 10:30 a.m., and didn't start again until 2:30 p.m. As soon as the cots arrived, many of the men gave up their tents and took to sleeping under the wings of the planes.

And then, suddenly, it was here, the day of action, July 9, 1943, and Pat was asked to give the boys a few words of encouragement. A few words to put into context the importance of this first step onto European soil. When he was finished, the troopers "clawed off their greasy caps" and bowed their heads in prayer. Farm boys, city kids, the support troops on the flight line and fuel depots, the crew chiefs and mechanics who kept the thin unarmored transport aircraft aloft.

*Oh, Lord, watch over these your humble servants, on this day and every day.*

After his prayer for the airmen, Fowlkes visited the paratroopers of the 82nd Airborne Division. They were sprawling in the shade under the wings of their transport planes, smoking cigarettes and sweating out their last few hours on terra firma. None said more than a few words to him, most barely looked up. Their packs were hung with the tools of their trade: knives, saws, wire cutters, hammers. Their weapons were strapped across their chests and at their belts. Some had their girls' pictures glued inside their helmets. Others had them tucked away for safekeeping. A few had the New Testament passed out by the chaplains in their breast pockets, which they tapped with a grin when Fowlkes walked past. He studied their chaplains and medical officers: their quiet intensity, the stubby cigarettes burning down in their lips. They had no guns. They were wearing large, clearly visible Red Cross bands on their upper arms. But otherwise, they looked like their men, with similar packs and helmets and photos of those they loved. They were jumping not to kill, but to give comfort and care to the wounded and dying.

"I have never," Pat wrote Lib of the paratroopers, "admired anyone more."

A few hours later, the 314th lumbered out over the Mediterranean, carrying the 504th and 505th Parachute Infantry, 82nd Airborne Division. A storm blew in, and the crossing grew rough. The stripped down, unarmed aluminum transports bucked in the high winds, struggling to stay on course. The jumps went off on time, a few minutes before midnight, but some of the planes were pushed out of position by the storm, and the high winds scattered the paratroopers as they fell. Many missed their rally points by miles, but Fowlkes, apprised of the mission by his airmen after their planes landed back in Tunisia, was proud of the 314th TCG.

"We were the first craft of any kind to land invading troops on the island. We did so, under extremely difficult circumstances, in spite of bad weather, and we did it well—not us alone, but all those who do our kind of work, and [the 314th] had as many in the air as anybody. Moreover, we dropped our troops 1½ hours before the 3 a.m. landing that the newspaper makes you feel was the first landing."

His heart, though, was with the paratroopers who stood in the open door of the plane, holding tight against the whipping wind as they hooked their static lines to the anchor line, the airborne chaplain among them. Then, as the jump lights flashed, they "[dove] out into darkness, over enemy-held territory, the first to do so—having no real idea what awaits them below."

"That is the easiest part," he wrote Lib. "Down below they have their jobs—and they know that much of the success of the initial landings depends on them . . . to knock out pill-boxes, hold bridges, cut communications, cut the barbed wire snarls along the coast designed to check landing troops just long enough to be mowed down."

The paratroopers did their job, Pat assured her, and the Seventh United States Army's and British Eighth Army's landings on the beaches of Sicily were a success. But four transport planes from the 314th went down, two with no survivors. One of the aircraft that crashed without casualties was flown by the group's commander.

Two days later, on July 11, Lieutenant General Patton, who commanded the Seventh Army, ordered the 504th Parachute Infantry, 82nd Airborne Division, to reinforce his ground troops, who were facing a German counterattack. The lead flight had already dropped their paratroopers when, despite several notices, an Allied ship fired on the trailing formation. The Allied fleet and Army antiaircraft batteries ashore, mistaking the transport planes for the Luftwaffe, started firing. Twenty-three planes were hit and crashed into the sea, wounding more than 200 and killing 81, including the 82nd Airborne's assistant division commander. It was the grimmest day in the history of the troop carrier group. But it was a temporary setback. By August 17, the fighting in Sicily was over. The Allies had suffered

25,000 killed, wounded, or captured; the Germans and Italians 28,000. But 100,000 Axis troops had slipped away to mainland Italy.

On September 1, Pat Fowlkes and the 314th were transferred to Sicily to prepare for the invasion of the Italian mainland, Operation Avalanche. His son Frank, his "little fat frog," turned two on September 9. That same day, as the Allied landing craft approached the coastal town of Salerno, a voice called out in English over a loudspeaker, "Come on in and give up. We have you covered."

The shooting started soon after, and it wouldn't stop until the Allies reached Rome nine months later.

It was at some point during those busy early September days that a letter arrived from Lib. It was dated August 24, 1943, and addressed to Pat in Tunisia. His unit must have left for Sicily just before it arrived.

*My Darling—*

*This is another date for us to remember and cherish. Betsy arrived at 2 a.m. Everything went powerfully slowly for a while and then zip! I surprised everyone by doing everything in about an hour. I feel fine but am flat on my back so excuse the writing. Betsy is real cute but not exactly pretty. Her hair is so coal black it would be pretty if it stayed that way. She has fair complexion and dark blue eyes. Her ears are close to her head like F[rank]'s were but not flat at the top like his. They are folded over very delicately. McCoy brought her in twice to practice nursing, and like F, she acted like she'd done it all her life. . . . Yesterday rec'd two letters [from you] and today a V-mail addressed here. And your beautiful red roses greeted me this morning. I love you and thank you a million times for being so good to me. All three of us send love.*

*Always, Lib*

Chaplain Paschal Fowlkes read the letter once, twice . . . how many hundreds of times must he have read it, this beautiful birth announcement for his almost-pretty child? A girl! He hadn't known the sex. Named Betsy! He had not expected that, since he and Lib had been writing back and forth about names. But such was the life of a soldier: away, on the outside of his old life, but always connected to those he loved.

He folded the letter carefully, kissed it softly, then slipped it into the breast pocket of his uniform.

# CHAPTER 17

# MEMORY BOOKS

— ★ —

*Emilie Michiels van Kessenich*
July 1943

On May 13, 1943, two months before the Allied landing in Sicily, German occupation authorities had ordered the Dutch to hand over their radios. Many people, including the Michiels van Kessenich family, complied. But, like most, they had a second, secret radio. It was hidden under a small table covered with a long white tablecloth in Willem and Emilie's bedroom. Two candleholders were always on top. It was the table the priest used to give Emilie Communion, when she was in bed resting for or recovering from another birth. She was doing that now. Her tenth child, Octavie, had been born in June. Still, Emilie brought out the radio at 9:00 p.m. to listen to Radio Orange, the daily report from the Dutch government-in-exile.

They also received a secret written report once a week. Someone clandestinely listened to broadcasts from England, summarized them, then circulated copies into trusted hands. The report for the week of July 9–15, 1943, focused for a full page, single-spaced, on the Allied invasion of Sicily.

Emilie read the report. The unfamiliar names: Licata, Gela, Cape Passero, Syracuse, Palazzolo, Ragusa, Comiso. "The battle on Sicily is going perfectly well. . . . An early capture of Catania, the second city of Sicily. . . . The English troops are halfway to the port of Messina. . . . Sicily practically cut off from all access."

She had always kept a pile of the children's old shoes in a room at the top of Villa Maya. Whenever a child outgrew their current shoes, the old shoes went into the pile and the child found a "new" pair that fit. It was the only practical way to raise ten children. In the first days of the occupation, Manka had procured a large shipment of klompen (traditional Dutch wooden shoes) for the city's citizens. He forced his oldest children to wear them, so that those in need would not feel ashamed. It was part of their duty, he told them, as the mayor's children. Now, after three years of occupation, there were no leather shoes to be had at any price, and Emilie's pile had been worn through. Manka had been right—the klompen were vital. That's how bad it had gotten. In Maastricht, everything was scarce. Even worn-out old shoes.

But this report, this invasion of Sicily: it felt like hope. The Allies had reached Europe. Their liberators might be fourteen hundred miles away, but at least they were on the way.

She went down to the first floor and took her Memory Book, where she hid the letters and articles she didn't want the Gestapo to find, from the secret recess under the stairs. Her daughter Jenneke had been born with a growth on her neck. Dr. Klinkenbergh, the surgeon who removed it, refused their money, saying, "Keep a book of your family's life, and show it to me from time to time. That will be my payment." That was in 1932. Emilie had kept a Memory Book of diary entries, clippings, and personal mementos ever since.

She tipped the report on Sicily into her latest book. It was an important moment in the war, in her family's life, and she wanted to keep it. Underneath it she wrote, so her children would understand if they ever looked back later, "This is how we got our news."

# CHAPTER 18

# HOPE OVERHEAD

— ★ —

*Frieda van Schaïk*
October 1943

The first major daylight raid over Limburg took place on August 17, 1943, when close to 400 U.S. aircraft passed overhead on their way to bomb the ball-bearing factory at Schweinfurt and a Messerschmitt aircraft manufacturing plant at Regensburg. Americans had been flying bombing raids for eight months over northern Germany, but this southern route took them over the country's industrial heartland. The bombers flew at 25,000 feet, too high for Frieda and the others on the ground to hear more than the drone of their engines, but like many she watched them, a swarm of birds migrating eastward, where the Luftwaffe and the German antiaircraft guns were waiting. In the air battle, *Elmer's Tune*, an American P-47 Thunderbolt, went screeching across the sky before smashing into a field on the southwest edge of Maastricht, barely missing a church and killing the pilot. Three more planes, Luftwaffe Fw 190 fighters, spiraled and smashed to bits in the eastern suburbs, two miles from Frieda's home. No survivors.

An hour later, the American bombers limped back, some flying low, trailing smoke across the sky. Their fighter escort, low on fuel, had long since turned back, and the Luftwaffe swooped through the vulnerable planes like bats on moths. The raid was costly, 60 planes and nearly 600 men lost, but to Frieda and the others watching from the ground in Limburg, it was the most hopeful development in three years.

A thousand planes, they guessed in awed whispers. Maybe two thousand. Maybe more. The Allies are coming.

Two months later, on October 14, 1943, the Americans returned with 291 bombers and hundreds of fighter escorts. Frieda, racing to her attic window, saw the white contrails against the blue sky, and despite the American bombers—first one, then two, then four—dropping out of formation in flames, she felt a rush of optimism.

*They came here from a free place*, she thought. *They came to free us.*

The air raid siren sounded, and she sprinted down the stairs as her parents clattered to the basement for cover. She grabbed her bicycle and churned at the pedals, putting the familiar orchards and farmland behind her. She had ridden these roads many times on the way to her Red Cross post, but never in the daylight. She thought of the pilots up there in their tin cans, fighting for her freedom. She thought of the men hanging from their parachutes, at the mercy of German fighter pilots and ground gunners. She counted seven, no eight, white spots in the distance.

Five Kübelwagen appeared, careening past on the narrow road, the soldiers shouting in German. They didn't look at her, or any of the other Dutch cyclists, several of whom had pulled off the road to watch the skies.

The German spotters in the backs of the vehicles were pointing, their eyes on the smoke trail of a bomber falling from the sky. How many men were on that bomber, Frieda wondered? How many parachutes should have appeared?

Ten miles away, eight-year-old Eduard Foitzik, standing in the doorway of his house in a small village near the German border, stared up at that same sky. To him, it was a monolith: less hundreds of individual planes than one great lumbering beast, wending its way toward Germany.

And then one bomber seemed to come alive, to wriggle out of the formation. Eight-year-old Eduard thought it was only a stutter, a trick of his eyes, but then the bomber dropped clear of its brothers and began to drift downward, smoke trailing behind. Five parachutes, and then the left wing folded and fluttered away, like a leaf.

Heinz Michels, ten years old, sitting in his favorite fruit tree, watched the wing float away and the fuselage begin to spin. *What a birthday present*, he thought, too young to grasp anything more than how neat it was to watch centrifugal force pull apart the airplane behind its central bomb bay. The two sections slid in opposite directions, dropping at sharp angles, and it wasn't until it was too late that Heinz realized the rear section, minus the tail, was heading straight toward his favorite tree—and him. He wanted to jump, but he was too high, so he turned and hid his face. He felt the heat wave like an inferno. Small branches caught fire around him. He heard them crackling as the remains of the flaming plane passed so close overhead that later he knew, just knew, that he could have reached up and touched it, if only he'd had the nerve.

Klara Wauters, thirteen years old, heard the same howling and dove for a ditch. Seconds later, the ground shook as the front half of the B-17 crashed to earth and its payload and fuel exploded. She lay still until she could stand the tension no more, then looked up. The crater was thirteen feet deep and thirty feet wide. An American B-17 had a crew of ten, but only half had made it out. Two had died in the plane during the aerial battle, meaning three had been alive, but hadn't been able to make the jump before the plane began to break apart and spin.

Heinz Michels, running up in the aftermath, couldn't believe his luck—a flight cap with goggles, on the ground for the taking! He dropped it, in terror, when he saw what was inside.

"Don't look," Eduard Foitzik's father shouted, when they arrived and saw a body in a ditch. "For God's sake, son, don't look."

"Ride?" a Dutch coal dealer asked the pilot, who was lying half a mile away, beside the dark retention pond of a small, open-pit coal mine.

"No, sir," Second Lieutenant Dennis McDarby replied, kicking out of his parachute and trying to rise. "I'll stay with the boys."

The old man shook his head sadly, then nickered to his horse as McDarby scrambled for cover. He'd lost a boot. His foot was badly injured. He pulled himself along the ground, aiming for a dusty clump of bushes as, a half mile to the east, a group of local citizens surrounded an American tangled in his parachute, blood pouring from a deep cut in his head.

The German authorities had declared that any Dutch man or woman found near a crash site would be shot. Any Dutch man or woman racing in the direction of a parachute would be shot. Any Dutch . . . could be shot, because the Germans knew the Dutch Resistance was rescuing airmen. But the people who crowded around the wounded airman were villagers and farmers, not Resistance. Ordinary citizens inspired and encouraged, drawn out by the awesome might of an American bomber fleet. They wanted to help this young man who had risked so much.

He was tail gunner Dominic Lepore, twenty years old, from New Jersey, injured when a 20mm cannon shell exploded inside his cramped position. He had crawled toward the center of the plane and been pushed out of the bomb bay by a fellow airman just before the plane began to spin. He was too weak from his wound to get up and too foggy to understand a word of Dutch, even if he had spoken the language. When two other survivors appeared, the citizens offered them assistance, but the language barrier was too high. Finally, a man pushed forward his bicycle, and the crewmen rolled away with their injured tail gunner propped between them on the seat. Within an hour, they were captured, along with McDarby and one of the gunners, who had been thrown from the plane and regained consciousness as he barreled toward the Netherlands in an uncontrolled fall. He pulled his rip cord on instinct. His parachute blossomed above him, it seemed, at the exact same moment he smashed into the ground. But it must have been sooner, because he hit hard and rolled to a stop, miraculously unharmed.

The next morning, the five surviving crewmen were transferred to a church in Maastricht that had been converted into a holding pen for prisoners of war, then into the back of an open truck with thirty-five other captives from the battle over Limburg. As the truck pulled away, the airmen noticed several Dutch citizens on the sidewalk who were watching them pass. Word must have gone out, because the next block held more Dutch, and the one after that even more, until finally there were 150 or more Dutch well-wishers, standing two or three deep, cheering for the Americans as their prison truck chugged past.

A few weeks later, Sergeant Robert Wells's parents in Kentucky received a letter. Wells was the first casualty on the McDarby bomber, killed when a German Messerschmitt raked the waist of the plane. He had written home two days before his final mission. He was his parents' only child, barely twenty, and he wanted to reassure them.

"Above all," he wrote, "I don't want any of you to worry about me, for I am only doing what thousands of others are trying to do, make this world a better place."

# CHAPTER 19

# THE MESSAGE

— ★ —

*James and Edward Norton*
November 1943

The news that your child is missing in action is a thunderclap. It is a sudden darkness. It is incomprehensible. Impossible to accept. Impossible to ignore, even for a second. Nothing will take those words away.

And yet, there is a hope, a chance your child might be alive. Even on the darkest days, that spark lives in your heart: He is not confirmed dead. He is *missing*. I might see him again. One day, he might walk through that door. Hug me, smile, and tell me, "Mother, it's me. I'm fine. I'm home."

How much greater the anguish when it is two missing children, not one. When the mission they flew was a disaster, without a single plane returning. One morning, they left to bomb a power plant. No one came back. Who could say what happened between the beginning and the end? Who could know for sure that they crashed? If they bailed out before a crash? If, somehow, they survived?

The plane piloted by The Twins' commander, Moose Stillman, had been decimated, turned upside down, and crashed at speed into deep mud. And yet, Stillman survived. Dutch farmers dug him out just before he suffocated, only to have the Germans capture him soon after. By November 1943, he was in a camp for downed flyers, Stalag Luft III, inside Germany. More than thirty of the sixty airmen on the raid survived and became prisoners of war.

Was it wrong, then, for Miss Ed Norton to hope for her twins' return? Was it foolish?

Of course not. How could a mother not hope? But neither was it help-ful, nor healthy. Miss Ed stopped living, the family said. Her daughter Eugenia had to take over the management of her home. Eugenia was more than a decade older than her twin brothers; Hoggy and Wack had once taken her young son Jim flying over Conway. The boy was in sixth grade grammar class when the school principal told him to go home, his parents needed him. That's how he learned his uncles were missing in action.

The town reacted to the news as a collective tragedy. Hoggy and Wack were so young. They had been among the first to leave. The first to earn their wings. It was their first mission. How could this have happened? How could the boys who flew circles over the town, who buzzed the flagpole, have gone down?

There was no peace for Dr. Jamie and Miss Ed. No closure. Miss Ed could not move on. She could grieve, but only partially, and even that seemed a betrayal. It felt like turning her back on her sons. Her two brave sons who were only *missing* and might be alive.

That chance—that hope—came crashing down on November 2, 1943, as Dr. Jamie watched a soldier in uniform take the long, slow walk up the sidewalk. He knew what that walk meant, even before he was handed the War Department casualty message:

*Report received from German Government through the International Red Cross that your son Second Lieutenant James A. Norton Jr. who was previously miss-ing in action killed in action on seventeen May in European area. The Secretary of War extends deep sympathy.*

The body that had washed ashore and been buried by the Germans at Huisduinen in July was James. There was no mention of Edward, but Dr. Jamie, hugging Miss Ed and crying on her shoulder, knew in his heart that two boys so inseparable from the moment of birth had gone down together, and that Edward's body must be at the bottom of the sea.

CHAPTER 20

# PEASANTS AND
# THE POWERFUL

— ★ —

*Paschal Fowlkes*
November–December 1943

In late October, Chaplain Paschal Fowlkes returned to Sicily from Naples. Italy had surrendered, but the Germans had taken over and were fighting the Allies for every mile. In Naples, he had seen the destruction. "The town is badly bombed out," he wrote Lib. "The people just beginning to come back. Many have the stunned look I've seen on so many faces, too pitiful for words. Some of it, we did. Most of it, the Germans did. . . . Six months ago, one might have felt great hatred for the Italians, but when you look in the faces of some of these old, half-starved people and the undernourished children, you can't be mad with them. . . . [I]t is the Fascist leaders who we must blame."

He was frustrated with what he considered the indolence of the officer corps. In Palermo and other large Sicilian cities, the Army had requisitioned sumptuous buildings for Red Cross officers' clubs. Furnished them with luxurious furniture, magazines and record players, carpets and curtains. When Pat visited, he saw officers being served refreshments, with alcohol from well-stocked bars. All of it, the Army claimed, was for the building of morale.

The Soviets, he wrote Lib, had a million dead, and they didn't need luxuries to keep up morale. Our allies, the Chinese, had resisted the Japanese on their own soil for ten years without setting up $10,000 clubs. Pat worried that America, too rich and new at war, had already lost sight of the hardships ahead and the common people it was fighting for.

"I am afraid that all my life," he confessed to Lib, "I will have to fight being impatient with people who get no pleasure out of simple things. I could so gladly and easily give up all such stuff as the [luxuries of the Red Cross Club] in order to have the same money put in the hands of the hungry Sicilians who beg, with tears in their eyes, on the streets."

The 314th TCG was stationed at Castelvetrano, a small city in western Sicily surrounded by rugged hills. Often, Chaplain Pat took a jeep out alone along the dusty goat tracks of that dry country, where the gullies were full of wildflowers after a rain and the hillside spotted with thick-leaved succulents and tough green gorse. It was an ancient land, with its tumbled rock walls and stained stucco farmhouses, its rutted sheep runs cutting deep furrows through rocky crests, its gnarled and twisted olive trees. He was searching out the lower echelons, as Pat called them, the support units bivouacked in the rocky quarries, or strung out among the orange groves, or resting in the slender shade of the olive trees. A gift, the young privates thought, before trying the hard, impossibly bitter olives fresh from the branch.

They were far from home, and many found this a harsh and unfriendly land, full of quiet strangers and lean goats. But Pat saw the wonder of God's creation, and he saw in the people not an enemy conquered, but the pig farmers and laborers he had ministered to in Virginia. The tough bushes and rock-strewn slags were nothing like the grassy green hills and crystalline brooks of home, but the flinty ruggedness of the rural Sicilians and their close-knit families reminded him of the values he had gleaned there: duty, goodness, fairness, respect, and love. It was an honor to be among them, ministering to the soldiers who performed the simple, necessary tasks.

What would the officers in Palermo do, he wondered, if they had to sleep one night on rocks like the men in their command? What would their morale be then?

In late November, Pat and a sergeant drove to a tiny village to meet the parents of a Sicilian teenager accidentally killed by American forces. The village was like many in the region: a small central square and a few buildings perched on the crown of the hill, with sight lines for miles. Ancient olive groves, rock walls, goats but no fields, because the ground was too rocky for crops—these people lived as their ancestors had. A curl of smoke rose from a small farmhouse set amid the succulents and rocks, a fire against the desert chill, a cooking stove, a simple hearth for simple folks.

There were no cars in the village, so Pat and the sergeant drove the grieving couple to the funeral. Twenty-five mourners, practically the whole village, were at the graveside when they arrived: the women in black funeral wraps that covered their shoulders and heads, the men with their hats in their hands, the young man's friends kneeling in the dust after the walk with the casket. There was hugging, praying, consoling. Pat was used to solemn Protestant ceremonies, where emotion was subsumed. He had never heard, he wrote Lib, such wailing and crying. When he placed a wreath on the grave, an apology from the U.S. Army, it felt both small against that grief and important because of it. Another act of kindness from a man who always kept the small farmers, the simple laborers, the pig paths of the world close to his heart, but for Paschal Fowlkes, it was also a thank-you.

A few weeks before, he had met a Graves Registration Service (GRS) officer whose job it was to search for missing soldiers and bring their remains back for burial. The GRS officer had been tasked with finding the pilot of a single-seat plane that had crashed during the invasion. He searched for three days before finding the plane forty miles from where everyone assumed it had gone down. The pilot, though, was missing. The GRS man tracked him down to an isolated mountain village.

"They had built a coffin for him," Pat wrote Lib, "buried him near their cemetery, and the little children had made a plot of stones around him and a little stone outline on the grave, with a cross; and they brought flowers every day."

Honoring the Sicilian teenager, and helping his family, Pat wrote, "was repaying [that] debt."

On December 8, Chaplain Fowlkes and his troops stood in review for visiting dignitaries: President Franklin D. Roosevelt; General Eisenhower, the commander in chief of Allied forces in the North African Theater of Operations; Lieutenant General Mark W. Clark, commander of Fifth United States Army; and commander of Seventh United States Army, Lieutenant General George S. Patton, among others. President Roosevelt had traveled to Sicily from the Tehran Conference, after conferring with Churchill and Stalin, to award the Distinguished Service Cross to General Clark for his leadership in the Allied invasion of Italy.

"It really was quite a show," Pat wrote, "to hear 'Ike' and Mark and George all calling each other by their first names. Nothing but small talk went on."

As always, though, his thoughts soon turned to more important things. "I'd kinda like the youngsters to have a taste of country life," he wrote Lib. "You mightn't think it, but I profited from mine. I believe in the long run I find a solid piety and dependability among the country boys in the army that I don't find among the city boys. I think you are more apt to be godly when you feel your dependence on Him as much as you do in the country, whereas the city cave-dwellers feel little but dependence on machines. We wouldn't have to teach them the facts of life, with much throat-clearing, if we were within sight of a few cows and chickens."

He put down his pen. It was late. He was tired. But before he turned off his lamp, he took the letter from his pocket and read it for the hundredth time:

> *Betsy arrived at 2 a.m. . . . Betsy is real cute. . . . She has fair complexion and dark blue eyes. . . . McCoy brought her in twice to practice nursing. . . . I love you and thank you a million times for being so good to me. All three of us send love.*
>
> *Always, Lib.*

# CHAPTER 21

# AN EGG

— ★ —

*Emilie Michiels van Kessenich*
Spring 1944

Jenneke stood in the doorway, listening to the creaking of the rickety cart holding the two big pots that her mother took to the central kitchen for her daily allotment of soup. Willem had opened the free kitchen while mayor in spring 1941. It had four man-sized pots and a riser so the "cooks" could stir the giant pots. She was proud that Willem and other city leaders had the foresight to implement this program. She never imagined her own family would rely on it.

But it was March 1944, almost four years into the occupation, and food was scarce. Dinner was almost always stamppot, a traditional Dutch dish of potatoes mashed with cabbage and, when available, a bit of meat for flavor. Louis, six years old and the family comedian, would dig around in his stamppot until he found a speck of bacon or chicken and lift it up with his fork.

"I got one!" he'd yell, as if he'd won a prize.

They had bread twice a week, carefully cut and divided, no grabbing or eating your fill. No butter. Each child was given a small pot of rendered fat with their name on it to flavor their bread. They lined the pots on the mantle above the fireplace, where the heat kept the fat soft. Each pot had to last a week. If you ran out, too bad. Even the youngest were expected to ration.

It was like the wooden shoes. Everyone had to make do. There were even people bicycling on wooden tires, since the rubber ones were impossible to buy.

*The Lord is my shepherd,* Emilie thought, *there is nothing I shall want.*

But at the market where she redeemed their ration bons, there was a notice: no eggs. The woman behind the counter slipped her an egg—one single egg, so odd and brown when seen alone—and then shook her head, as if to say, *The last. We won't be getting any more.*

It crushed her. As she pulled her rickety cart of soup through the streets of Maastricht, she felt the weight of this latest deprivation, and it crushed her. She could not have said why, if anyone had asked. What was so important about eggs? Why now, after everything they had lost over the last four years? She feared that she would never be able to explain this tiredness, this sudden hopelessness, to anyone who had not experienced it with her.

"No, Lietje," Willem said that night, when Emilie mentioned dividing the egg among the children. "It's for you." For two years, she had been hoarding eggs, giving one to a child whenever they were sick. The sickness was usually malnutrition, because there was never enough to eat, and it was impossible to monitor the diets of ten children. One was always falling behind.

"We should play a game then," Emilie said. "The children will choose numbers, and whoever is closest gets to eat the egg."

"No."

"Or share it. Not the younger ones, maybe, but the older four will share with their siblings, I know."

"No, Lietje," Willem said, grabbing her hand. "You have to eat it."

She was pregnant again, and perilously thin. She had been short-changing herself for years so her family could eat.

"But Manka . . ."

"Lietje . . ." he said softly.

She was almost in tears. The loss of the eggs. Would anyone understand, in the years to come, how much the loss of something as simple as an egg had terrified her?

"Manka, I can't."

"One egg won't matter to their health," Willem said, pulling her close. "Let them see their mother taking care of herself."

They made a big production of it, in the end. The delicate egg. Its golden yoke. Emilie snipped off a bit of the white top with her spoon and gave it to . . . who wants it? Who is hungry? . . . Little Mathilda, born a few weeks before the invasion and now almost four. She laughed as the children used their fingers to scrape the last of the runny yoke from the plate, happily elbowing and complaining, although Jenneke could see the pain in her eyes, and understood how much her mother had sacrificed for them.

CHAPTER 22

# A MIRACLE

— ★ —

*John Low and Bill Moore*
April 1944

At 7:14 a.m. on April 29, 1944, a Consolidated B-24G Liberator heavy bomber, serial number 42-52506, took off from Rackheath Airfield near Norwich, England, with a crew of eleven including the pilot, First Lieutenant Bill F. Moore. They were the lead crew of a twenty-two-aircraft group flying as part of a 751-bomber task force on a mission to destroy the Friedrichstrasse railway station in Berlin.

The Luftwaffe was hunting that morning. They attacked the group of bombers ahead of Moore's formation, and the one behind, leaving Moore's mostly untouched. They reached Berlin at noon, where as one crewman said, "The German flak boys opened up with I think everything they had—I'm not absolutely sure, but I thought I saw the kitchen sink." The first hit started a small fire. The second knocked out the bombardier's oxygen supply. The third took out the left outboard engine. Their airspeed started to drop and, two minutes after bombs away, the ship began to fall back. Moore increased the power to the other engines and joined a formation of B-24 Liberators returning to England, ensuring they wouldn't have to fend off German fighters alone. As they neared the edge of the Netherlands, the North Sea was clearly visible, and England felt tantalizingly close.

But then another engine blew, and an alarm bell started blaring. A line had been severed, and they were running out of fuel. Lieutenant Moore calmly checked his military-issue watch and noted the time: 2:03 p.m.

He confirmed their position with the navigator, then told the radioman to send a mayday message to any aircraft within range: Five-Oh-Six had feathered two propellers, and the crew was bailing out near the town of Uddel.

"We are over Holland," the navigator announced on the interphone. "It is occupied but pro-Allies, the citizens will probably help."

The ship had dropped from 25,000 to 13,000 feet by the time First Lieutenant John L. Low Jr., the group bombardier for the 467th Bombardment Group, reached the forward hatch and willed himself through the hole. They told flyers in training not to hesitate, not to look down, that it was no use thinking about hurling yourself into the emptiness three miles above the earth, because your mind would never find it a sane thing to do.

Just clip on your parachute and go, so the next man can go, and that's what John Low did.

He thought it would be like a dive off the high board. It wasn't. The bomber was barreling forward at 200 miles an hour, the propellers thumping a few feet away. The slipstream grabbed him violently, and he began to tumble.

He pulled his rip cord. It was too soon—he was at 10,000 feet—but the only thought when you're free-falling is whether your chute will open, and the anxiety left him only one option. The jerk was a surprise, like being dropped out the window at the end of a fifty-foot rope. There was no give, only the crushing jolt as the stiff harness wrenched against his stomach and sternum. The USAAF never practiced jumps. There were too many airmen. Besides, nobody ever got used to the violent collision of opposing forces, the feeling of your organs plummeting through your body toward your toes.

And then he was drifting, floating upward and backward, it seemed, as the ship hurtled forward, and even when the next man fell through the hatch seconds later, he was too far away for Low to see who he was.

It was gone: the clanging alarm bell, the pungent smell of cordite and fuel, the intensity of the jump. The formation was gone too. He saw seven other parachutes in the air, but there was no way to reach them or communicate. He was alone, floating slowly toward the flat Dutch countryside, with nothing to do but hope the Germans weren't waiting when he hit the ground or, worse, lining him up in their sights.

Low landed in a thicket of fir trees. By extraordinary good fortune, the crew had bailed out over the largest national forest in the Netherlands, Koninklijke Houtvesterij Het Loo, a 40-square-mile nature reserve crisscrossed by cycling and walking paths. Low's parachute snagged in the trees, suspending him from his canopy with no way of seeing the ground below. He unbuckled. The drop to the ground was mercifully short.

He breathed a sigh of relief. He was safe.

Safe? What was he thinking? He was alone in occupied territory. Low collected his pack and hurried into the forest, away from his parachute, which the Germans had no doubt spotted coming down. After ten minutes, he rested, changed his heavy flight boots for the pair of Oxfords that airmen kept tied to their bodies, and continued on.

He was on a forest path, walking quickly, when he heard a motor and dove for cover. Three Germans in an amphibious car, driving slowly and scanning the forest. The soldier in the back, leaning on a mounted machine gun, seemed to look right at him, but it was dusk, Low's flight suit was green and his bomber jacket brown, so they passed him by. Low thanked his luck, then wondered who else in the crew was on the run. He hadn't seen anyone since he'd hit the ground.

By early evening, he was skirting small farms. One had a haystack tucked up near the forest line. The farm was a bit run-down, and nothing was stirring except cows and a curl of smoke. No telephone lines. So he clambered up the haystack, burrowed into the top, and tried to sleep.

He was startled awake by a sudden sound. The sun was down, only a touch of light in the sky. He heard the sound again. Thrashing. Steady breathing. Looking over the edge of the haystack, he saw a young man pitching hay three feet below where he was hiding.

He needed food and civilian clothes. He needed directions. He was a long way from home.

*"Amerikaan,"* he whispered.

The young man stopped and looked around.

*"Amerikaan,"* Low said, louder this time.

The young man stepped back in shock. He raised his pitchfork. Low raised his hands to show he had no weapon. The young man looked around to see if anyone was watching, then moved into the shadow of the haystack. Low extended his hand. The young man took it and smiled.

Low reached for his language card, standard issue for airmen, and tried a few basic Dutch phrases. It was a comedy of mispronunciations and inadvertent insults, but soon the situation became clear: the young man was afraid.

*Wait*, he signaled to Low. He looked around, as if to make sure once again there was no one to see them. *Wait.*

He finished his chores, then retreated through the double back door to the farmhouse. In a flash of the interior, Low saw four large eyes staring out. Two cows, inside a barn that was part of the house. A half hour later, according to his watch, an older man stepped into the darkness, looked around, then looked toward Low and nodded. The young man walked past his father and approached the haystack. Hidden under his coat was a bottle of fresh, warm milk and a loaf of bread stuffed with butter and raw bacon. As Low extended his hand to thank him, the young man suddenly reached into his pocket, as if surprising himself with something unexpected, and handed him a hard-boiled egg.

"Good night," he muttered, perhaps the only English words he knew.

Low thought of his wife and parents back home in Laurel, Mississippi, as he lay in the cold, damp hay. Above him, clouds blocked the stars. Rainwater seeped through his flight suit. There are few things lonelier than a flyer in occupied territory with no direction home, and few things worse, he imagined, than receiving a War Department telegram saying your husband or son is missing in action. He wondered again who had made the jump. He wondered if anyone else was out in the night, on the run.

Suddenly, it all seemed very stupid: this haystack, his training, the bombing run, the war. The only thing he wanted was to be home in bed with his wife.

In the morning, the fog was so thick he couldn't see across the yard. But he heard the creaking of the barn doors and smelled chicory coffee. He was gone by first light.

By midday, he was miles from the crash site, and the forests had begun to thin. Desperate for civilian clothes, he approached a man hacking at a tangle of trees. The Dutchman spoke little English, but took him to a tiny hut in the woods. It was four feet high and buried half underground. A hunting blind.

A few hours later, another man arrived. "Hello, friend," he said in English. He had blankets and hot chocolate, a huge friendly smile.

"If you tell me your wife's name and address," the man said, "I will send word through the Red Cross that you are alive."

Low demurred, saying his unit would inform his wife, then lay awake. He didn't like the man's questions, and he didn't like his smile. Was he being paranoid? Was it worth it to find out?

Despite his exhaustion, he left before dawn, when the man was scheduled to return. By afternoon, he had walked another dozen miles to the edge of the forest. The land in front of him was open fields. The Germans were sure to find him there. But he had to keep going. What option did he have?

A fence ran along the tree line, with a path on the outside. Low had been walking the path for an hour, avoiding other pedestrians, when he realized he was being watched. A man on a bicycle was trailing him. It was too late to hide, so Low kept walking. The man passed slowly, looked him over, then pulled to a stop just ahead.

He didn't turn around. He just sat. Waiting.

"English?" the man whispered, as Low crept up beside him.

"American," Low replied. "Do you speak English?"

The man shook his head no, but stepped off his bike, then lifted it over the fence. He signaled for Low to follow. Once in the forest, the man set down his bike and reached to shake Low's hand. He wanted Low to wait while he ran an errand. Low nodded, then wedged himself into a comfortable position with a wide field of vision, in case he had misjudged his new friend, and tried not to drift to sleep. It was late afternoon. He had been on the ground for two days.

Eventually, the man returned with a boy in his teens. "Are you hungry?" the teenager asked in English.

"Yes."

The teenager opened his bag and handed him a sandwich. "Bacon and cheese," he said.

Low took it eagerly, hoping the bacon was cooked this time. It wasn't.

"Where did you learn to speak English?" he asked, as he chewed the small chunks of raw meat. A Dutch delicacy, or a condition of the war?

"Public school. Now I have questions for you."

The teenager asked about his hometown, his education, his favorite sport—baseball, of course, the American game—then translated the answers into Dutch for the older man. This was different than the night before. They weren't interrogating but testing. English-speaking Germans posed as Allied airmen. The Dutch Resistance had to be careful. And these men had to be Dutch Resistance, right?

Still, when the teenager and the older man started arguing in Dutch, Low worried. They were glancing at him and gesturing, clearly at odds. Had he said something wrong? Had he misjudged their intentions?

"One more question," the teenager said, turning away from the older man. "Do you know a Lieutenant Bill Moore?"

"Know him? He's my pilot!"

"We found him too," the teenager said. "He is here in these woods. We will take you to him now."

# CHAPTER 23

# FAITH

— ★ —

*Emilie Michiels van Kessenich*

Spring 1944

She lost the baby. Her fifth miscarriage. It clapped like thunder, froze her like a sudden rain. *The Lord is kind and merciful*, she reminded herself.

*Life is good.*

*My life is good.*

She had her children, the ten the Lord had allowed her to keep. She had her health, her home, her husband at her side. And no matter the darkness, no matter how bleak the morning, God provides.

# CHAPTER 24

# MOTHER

— ★ —

*Bill Moore and John Low*

April 1944

Shortly after the crash of Bill Moore's B-24, the local fire duty officer spotted a parachute in a tree near a watchtower. He and a colleague quickly pulled it down and hid it, knowing German soldiers and Dutch collaborators would be looking for survivors. They were searching the forest, in case the flyer was injured, when a vehicle pulled into the clearing. A man stepped out. Tall. Stern. The local gamekeeper. It didn't take him long to spot the American boots, survival vest, and leather helmet, or the two fire duty officers stepping out of the woods, trying to act as if nothing unusual was going on.

"I have him," the gamekeeper said.

The fire officers looked at their colleague, then sighed with relief. Four years of occupation, and they had never dared to ask his loyalty.

Bill Moore was luckier than Low. The gamekeeper fed him and gave him a place to sleep for two nights before turning him over to the teenage resistance fighter. He was in the forest less than a mile from Low, being questioned by the teenager—Joop "Joke" Bitter, seventeen years old, Jewish, and in hiding from the German forced labor program—when the cyclist told the boy he had found another American.

It was an emotional reunion. One American officer trapped behind enemy lines was a bad situation. But *two* American officers, hundreds of miles behind enemy lines, with thousands of enemy troops between them and freedom? That felt like fair odds.

They didn't know each other well. Low was not a regular member of Moore's crew. He was the group bombardier, responsible for training the bombardiers and briefing them before missions. Occasionally, to make sure there was no disconnect between planning and execution, the group bombardier would go up. Low was on his first flight with Moore's crew when the plane went down.

The two men talked over their situation. As the pilot, Moore was the last man to leave the plane. He knew the entire crew had bailed out, but Low was the first he had encountered on the ground. They agreed on a plan: they should try to get to Spain, where boats waited to carry downed airmen back to their bases in England. How they were going to do that, neither was sure. The kid hadn't even given them his name. For safety reasons, they hoped.

"Do you trust him?" Low asked.

"Yes," Moore said. "I do."

So Low fell to talking of home as they huddled in the forest, waiting for the boy to return. Low, an only child, was twenty-four years old. He'd been married for three years. He missed his wife, Josephine. She was a fiery redhead. Low laughed, remembering the fun they had shared.

"I hate to think of that Western Union man walking up the sidewalk of our home," he said. The standard telegram: *Your husband is missing in action. Regrets.*

Bill Moore didn't talk much. He was twenty-three. He was from Atlanta. He had attended the University of Georgia before dropping out and taking a job at an engineering firm. Even that information had to be drawn out. As to a girl back home? Bill Moore had nothing to say about that. He was either a quiet man, Low reasoned, or he was reticent because of his position. There was a distance between a pilot and his crew. To keep discipline, there had to be.

"Well, you've got someone who misses you," Low laughed. It had been a long few days, and he felt like chatting.

"I guess."

"You've got a mother and father, at least. Everybody does."

Bill Moore nodded, but didn't look at the officer. He was studying the forest. "Yes," he said. "I suppose they do."

They reached for their .45 caliber pistols when they heard the snap of a branch, but it was only the teenager. He handed them civilian suits and turned away as they dressed. As he walked them silently through the forest, they heard him sigh.

"I wish I was a soldier," he muttered.

"You are," Bill Moore insisted. "An underground man is as much a soldier as a man in uniform."

The kid walked on, his head down. "I wish I was a real soldier," he said finally.

A man and a woman, both in their early twenties, were waiting at the edge of the forest with three bicycles. "The two of us will ride together," the woman said. "You two follow thirty meters behind, so if we are stopped, you can turn around and wait for us here."

The flyers nodded.

"Now," she said, "we will not speak again until we reach our destination."

The kid waved good-bye, and the resistance members and the airmen rode off. It was six harrowing miles to the town of Apeldoorn. At one point, two German soldiers came walking toward them on the narrow path, talking with each other, and Low lost his nerve. He didn't know which way to go around them, left or right, changed his mind at the last second, and slammed into one of the soldiers. Knocked the man completely on his ass. As the soldier cursed him in German, Low stood up from his seat and pedaled furiously away. Bill Moore, coming behind, breezed right through without breaking a sweat.

They arrived at the safe house at 10:45 p.m., fifteen minutes before curfew. Aart van Kliest, the male resistance fighter, shared the house with his father, mother, wife, wife's sister, a brother, and a lodger. His mother greeted them at the door. She made a pot of ersatz coffee. But when it was ready, and they were sitting at the table, she went to pieces.

She didn't speak English. Moore and Low had no idea what she was saying. But eventually the female resistance fighter calmed her. "She didn't know you were coming," she told the Americans. "She is worried the Germans have seen you and everyone will be killed. But we told her it is safe, it is only for a day or two, so now she is okay."

Aart took them to the attic. It was triangular and unfinished, with two-foot walls on each side. Behind the walls was a crawl space wide enough for two thin mattresses. Low and Moore listened to the nightly BBC radio report with Aart and Jaap. It featured a report on the raid in which they were shot down, but already the flight felt like a distant memory, a million miles away. Where was the rest of the crew? Who else had survived? There was no way to know. So, heavily, sadly, they collapsed into the crawl space and slept for twelve straight hours. They had their first bath in four days the next evening, after the curfew, when the blackout curtains were drawn.

It was a fine arrangement. They were only waiting a day or two for their false papers and a transport to Belgium, so Moore and Low thought it . . . well, it was an adequate arrangement.

A week later, the man they were waiting for finally arrived. He was young, twenty-three years old, an English officer fluent in Dutch who had parachuted into the Netherlands three years earlier to help downed Allied airmen. There were two routes out of the country, Dick told them, but one had just closed. It would be eight days before they could leave. Hold tight.

Then, clearly homesick, he asked how things were going in England, but Low and Moore knew next to nothing; they had barely left their air base.

Five days later, Aart brought home another airman, a waist gunner named David Smith who had been shot down on the same mission as Low and Moore. He had been hiding for two weeks in a pigpen, fed by the farmer.

"Coffee?" Moore asked, because Mother—she was Aart's mother, but everyone called her Mother—always served a pot at five. "Or do you want a wash first?"

"Wash," Smith said, then danced around like a gorilla, making everyone laugh, he was so excited to be out of the pigpen.

When Dick finally returned, days later than promised, he brought bad news. He had been ordered not to move any flyers through France, and he strongly advised against them trying on their own.

"Why?" Bill Moore had the calm, confident demeanor of an officer. He spent his evenings studying Dutch with Jaap, while Dave Smith and John Low smoked cigarettes and played cards. A man named Henk de Vries came each week to share a small bottle of gin. He co-owned a candy factory, and he bartered chocolate for the alcohol, since both were valuable on the black market. Moore often told Low to go ahead and drink his share.

"For Jo," he smiled, meaning Low's wife, Josephine.

John Low was energetic, a talker and a gambler, and from his stories it was clear he'd met his match with Jo. She had a personality that gobbled up the air in the room, he bragged to the Underwater Boys, as the airmen had taken to calling themselves. A beautiful laugh, a mind for mischief. He was clearly proud of her, and clearly deeply in love. He was anxious to get out of Apeldoorn and back to Jo.

Moore was patient. This is war, he reminded the Underwater Boys, and these men and women are fellow soldiers. They know this battlefield, so they are giving the orders. And the Underwater Boys follow orders.

By the time Dick returned, though, it had been more than a month, and even Moore's patience was running thin.

"Why?" he insisted again, when Dick soft-pedaled another delay. "What is happening out there?"

"The invasion," Dick whispered, as if there might be spies. "It's coming."

# CHAPTER 25

# PAIN

— ★ —

*James and Edward Norton; Emilie*
*Michiels van Kessenich*

April–May 1944

O n May 23, a freight truck pulled into the Nortons' driveway in
Conway, South Carolina. It had been a year since their sons had been
declared missing. Six months since Dr. Jamie and Miss Ed had learned
James was dead. All that time, they had been trying to have the boys' foot-
lockers and barracks bags returned. Dr. Jamie understood the immense
burden on the Quartermaster Corps (QMC) supplying hundreds of thousands of soldiers going one way, while sending the last possessions of tens
of thousands of soldiers the other way. But these were the last items their
boys owned, among the last items they had touched, and the bureaucracy
frustrated him and compounded his grief.

He had written the Army Quartermaster Corps in June 1943,
then again in December. Then he wrote to his United States senator:
"I do not wish to bother you with this matter. . . . I have written the Effects
Quartermaster in K.C. Mo., and they knew nothing about it, that was some
six weeks ago. Colonel Von Kolnitz wrote that [the boys' possessions] were
being sent to the Quartermaster in London who would forward at once,
and that was last June."

He was not naive. He knew the odds of hearing good news about
Edward were long. "I just wished to thank you most sincerely for your
kind letter and sympathy," he wrote a business associate, "for we have
been terribly hard hit by this affliction. These boys were twins . . .

just twenty-two years old, and being our baby boys we were of course crazy about them. But they were flying in the same plane, Marauders, in the fateful raid of May 17 last, and while one has already been reported dead, we of course can have but scant hope for the life of the other."

Their possessions would not bring the boys back, and the QMC's mistake would never dilute the memories of their constant smiles, their joy, their love for each other. But those possessions were all Dr. Jamie and Miss Ed had left to grieve over, and they needed a point of contact. Something solid. Something to hold on to. Without that, they were lost.

By April 1944, Dr. Jamie's pain had turned to anger. How could it not, when his heart was breaking, and his wife seemed broken, unable to return to the life they had once led?

"I know that war is going on and that other things might take precedence at this time," he wrote the Quartermaster Corps office in Kansas City, "but it seems to me these things should have been delivered before this, for it has been nearly one year now that my boys have been missing. Why were we not told at the beginning, either from England or when I wrote you last December, that these things were required held in England for six months before sending over here? Had I known this, I could have at least been more patient, but no, I had to learn this little item of some needless army mandate the hard way."

Finally, on April 15, 1944, the QMC forwarded two U.S. Treasury checks, one for $47.96, payable to James, and the other for $607.86, payable to Edward. It was their pay, which the boys had intended to send home.

Five weeks later, the delivery truck finally arrived. Into the family room in Conway the movers carried a 60-pound footlocker and a 37-pound barracks bag that had belonged to James, and a 103-pound locker and a 35-pound bag that had belonged to Edward. Boots, socks, pants, shirts, underwear, neckties, handkerchiefs, bath towels, service caps, swim trunks, hairbrush, whisk broom, flashlight, sewing kit, pencils, and personal mail. They were the same things a million soldiers and flyers carried, but fate had converted them into priceless objects. To cry over hair in a brush, or a pair of socks, to hug them to your chest and feel the fabric tearing straight through to your soul, is to know that you loved, and loved well, and now you've lost.

— ★ —

In the middle of the night, Emilie awoke in pain. *All I need is rest*, she thought. *All I ever need is rest.* She tried not to wake Willem. She was reluctant to bother him with small things. But she couldn't sleep, and the pain did not go away. By the next day, it was unbearable, even for a mother who had given birth to ten children and recently lost another to miscarriage.

Two male orderlies were sent from Calvariënberg Hospital, a half mile away. She saw Jenneke at her bedroom door as they entered, panic on her face. *My child*, she thought. *Please don't worry. Have faith.*

They lifted her out of bed and put her on a stretcher. "Please don't cry," she pleaded as the children stood in two lines by the front door, watching their mother pass between them, too weak to reach out and touch their hands. "It's only a pain. Mathilda, Anna-Marie, Louis, don't cry. I'll be back."

She was diagnosed with twisted kidneys, the result of malnutrition. "Take care of them, Manka," she pleaded when the doctors ordered convalescence at the hospital. She worried. She was a mother, of course she worried. But Bonus Simplicitas had watched over her and her family before. And Manka was a loving father. And Agnes was there.

Four weeks of mental and physical rest in the care of Nurse Elise, Sister Humphride, and Mother Bernardine revived her body and spirits, even as the world slid dangerously. On April 24, a family friend, Willem van Sonsbeeck, the governor of Limburg Province until Max Marchant et d'Ansembourg replaced him in 1941, was arrested by the Germans. On May 10, several local priests were executed. Soon after, Chaplain Joosten, Chaplain Tilmaas, and the rector, three hospital leaders, disappeared.

That night, an American bomber was shot down, and chunks of flaming metal fell into the hospital yard. The concussion shattered windows. Collisions on the roof shook apart the light fixtures, knocked supplies from shelves, sent water and plaster showering from the ceiling. "Our house is dripping with oil," Emilie wrote from her sickbed, but nobody was badly hurt.

"The children are fine," Manka told her. "They are caring for each other."

"You are doing nothing, then?"

He smiled. "Nothing at all."

She relaxed, though it wasn't easy. *The Lord is my light and salvation*, she reminded herself. *My family is fine.* By the end of May, she had gained twenty-two pounds, and after another five weeks of strict bed rest at home, she was almost back to herself again.

# CHAPTER 26

# D-DAY

— ★ —

*Robert Cole*

June 1944

O n the evening of June 5, 1944, four-star General Dwight Eisenhower
made a surprise visit to the 101st Airborne Division, the Screaming
Eagles, at their base in Greenham Common, England. In December
1943, he had been promoted from commanding Allied units in the
Mediterranean to supreme commander of the Allied Expeditionary Force
in Europe following the success of operations he had overseen in North
Africa, Sicily, and mainland Italy.

"You are going to command Overlord," President Roosevelt told him,
when he bestowed the appointment. Operation Overlord, the invasion of
continental Europe from across the English Channel, was to be the pivotal
moment in the European Theater.

Overlord, designed by a joint Anglo-American military staff, was presented to Ike when he arrived in London on January 15. It was the largest
amphibious assault ever contemplated, involving more than 5,000 ships
and 40,000 men, but it had to be. The Allies had one shot. If they failed to
gain a foothold, it might be years before they could mount another attempt.
So Ike increased the invasion force from three assault divisions to five and
added three airborne divisions, bringing the totals to more than 6,900 ships
(including 4,000 landing craft) and 186,000 assault troops.

With the difficult, stressful months of planning over, and the hinge
of history reached . . . the weather turned foul. The operation had a three-
day window where a full moon phase created a low tide, but the first day

was lost to a storm. The next evening, June 5, the weather was miserable, but the forecast for the morning offered a glimmer of hope. And time was running out.

"Is there any reason we shouldn't go on Tuesday?" Ike asked General Montgomery, his subordinate commander.

"No," Montgomery replied immediately. "I say go."

Ike paced back and forth. "Okay," he finally declared. "We'll go."

With that, he put aside his maps and left his headquarters in Bushy Park, London, for Greenham Common. Tomorrow would be the D-Day, a general term for the day a military operation begins. Ike wanted to look into the faces of the men of the airborne: The first to land. The first to die. The young paratroopers and glider infantry, 17,000 Americans and 8,500 British, many of whom would never return to their wives, children, friends, and families.

He told his driver, Kay Summersby, to cover the stars on his license plate. His flag was not flying at the front of his car. It took the men a moment, as he walked silently through the airfield, to realize who he was. But then word went down the ranks, and the paratroopers began to roar.

He shook their hands. He looked them in the eye, as they whistled and cheered, wishing them success. "It's very hard to look a soldier in the eye," he later admitted to Summersby, "when you fear you are sending him to his death."

He was surprised when a familiar face stepped out of the ranks: Lieutenant Colonel Robert Cole, commander of the 3rd Battalion, 502nd Parachute Infantry, the promising young company commander from his days at Fort Lewis with the 15th Infantry. Paratroopers were among the toughest, most highly trained soldiers in the United States Army. They were men who had looked a near-suicidal new combat concept full in the face and said, *I volunteer*. But even among such men, Cole was a standout. After six months in the airborne, he was promoted to battalion adjutant of the 502nd Parachute Infantry on the day it mustered. In May 1943, he was promoted to commander of the 3rd Battalion, responsible for 700 paratroopers. When he kissed his wife Allie Mae good-bye on September 5, 1943, and shipped out for Europe, he was already a lieutenant colonel, a startling four promotions in less than four years.

Ike, in his crisp service uniform, reached out his hand to his former company commander. Robert Cole, in his baggy jump trousers and jacket, reached out to take it. His face was smeared with vegetable oil and charcoal. His pockets stuffed with survival gear. The paratroopers were mere hours from heaving themselves out of an airplane at 600 feet above 50,000 enemy troops, with no relief or escape if things went absolutely FUBAR, but Robert Cole was smiling.

Not a false smile. Not a for-the-camera smile. An easy smile, accompanied by a wink, as if to say, *Ah hell, General, don't worry. We got this.*

"They say you never get to the point that butterflies don't flit around your stomach," one paratrooper wrote home from training. "I doubt I'll ever jump as many times as I have already. I'll never make an unnecessary one. But when one is necessary, I know I'll never fail to go out."

He was talking about the experience of standing at the jump door, waiting for the signal. He could have been talking about the night before a combat jump. There wasn't a paratrooper that evening in Greenham Common not chewing butterflies. There wasn't a soldier who didn't feel fear. But every man in the 3rd Battalion was prepared to do his part.

And Robert Cole was smiling.

"Full victory," Eisenhower told the paratroopers, "and nothing else."

Cole and the paratroopers went to their staging area and checked their weapons: M1 Garand rifle, M1 carbine, Thompson submachine gun, cartridge belt, hand grenades, trench knife, M1911A1 semiautomatic pistol, two pounds of high explosives. They settled their gear: canteen, compass, medical kit, rope, flares, bouillon cubes, Nescafé, four pieces of gum, four chocolate bars, Tootsie Rolls, Charms candy, cigarettes, halazone tablets to purify water, and enough food to last several days, because there would be no resupply. The only things guaranteed were the things they carried.

As the propellers turned and the engines sputtered to life, they packed the last of their personal equipment, supplies, photos, mementos, and good-luck charms. They donned their gloves and distinctive steel-pot helmets, with their wide chin straps, then trundled past the control tower and the ground crews, who gave them the thumbs-up and V-for-victory signs. Many had to be helped into the planes. The average paratrooper carried seventy pounds in his pack. Radiomen, mortarmen, and machine gunners carried more.

Ike watched from the roof of the control tower as the C-47s embarked on the "Great Crusade," as he called it. They poured down the runway, then gently lifted into a night sky lit by a bright white moon. The planes circled overhead, waiting for their fellows to lift off so they could form up and fly in formation. Soon, there were hundreds in the air. As they began to tail off and swing toward Normandy, Ike turned and walked away. His head was down. His solitude complete. On the way to his car, he stopped and turned to his driver, and she saw that he had tears in his eyes.

"Well," he said, "it's on. No one can stop it now."

He went back to his cottage and jotted a quick note, known as the "In Case of Failure" speech: "Our landings in the Cherbourg-Havre area have failed to gain a satisfactory foothold and I have withdrawn the troops. My decision to attack at this time and place was based on the best information available. The troops, the air and Navy did all that bravery and devotion to duty could do. If any blame or fault attaches to the attempt it is mine alone."

By then, the planes were beyond the English coast. Like the others, Cole's C-47, *The Snooty*, held 28 paratroopers. If everything went right, the men, known as a stick, would jump less than a second apart and land in a line. And the other 700 paratroopers in his battalion, spread out in 25 planes, would be nearby.

Many of the men were resting, their heads back against the aluminum skin of the plane. It was a couple hours to the drop zone. There would be no rest below. Some talked quietly. Some contemplated their mission objectives, thinking through their actions on the ground, or said their prayers. Cole stood at the open door of the cargo bay, the wind whipping around him, watching the gray humps of the squadron flying beside him. Beyond those planes were more planes, and then more planes, and then more. Dark humps and pinpoint navigation lights were everywhere, spreading to the horizon: other squadrons, other transports, other sticks.

Cole chuckled as the plane hit its first turn and an NBC radio reporter lurched away from the astrolabe observation dome at the top of the fuselage, his comically oversized helmet rattling on his head. "It's cold back here with the wind whipping in," Cole said, as the reporter staggered toward him.

The night was calm and clear. The moonlight glinted off the channel. The dark hulls of the C-47s seemed to swim like enormous whales, undulating in the prop wash of their fellow planes, their engine drone so steady it put the world to sleep. And then, one by one, the transports switched off their navigation lights.

Thirty minutes later, *The Snooty* plunged into a bank of fog off the French coast. For two minutes, there was nothing but gray, and then the hedgerows were beneath them, so close it felt as if they could step out into the moonlit fields.

The antiaircraft fire began to crack and flash, ripping open the night sky.

Cole felt the intensity. The fear. He was scared, there was no other way to say it. All the men were scared. You'd be a fool not to be, and the paratroopers were no fools. But Cole didn't flinch. It was his duty as the commanding officer to remain confident and calm.

"Stand up! Hook up!" he yelled, as the sky became frantic with flak. The stick jostled quickly into position, each man attaching his static line to the anchor line that would pull his rip cord when he jumped. They hated being up here, now that planes were exploding and going down. They wanted to jump. They wanted a fighting chance.

"All set?" Cole asked Major John Stopka, his executive officer. Stopka nodded. "Then get this thing hooked for me." Cole was the first in line. It was the job of the man behind to check the anchor line of the man in front of him, since the man in front couldn't see to check his own.

"All set," Stopka said.

"Close up!" Cole shouted against the whipping wind. "And move to the door!"

And then, as the radio reporter watched, the signal light blinked and Robert Cole was gone into the flak-filled night, with Stopka and the rest of the stick tight on his heels.

The 3rd Battalion was supposed to parachute into Drop Zone A, west of the town of Saint-Martin-de-Varreville, but Cole's first sensation upon hitting the ground was tearing and pain. He had landed in a massive rose-bush. It took him fifteen minutes to hack himself free. When he finally found his bearings, he didn't recognize any landmarks, and his stick wasn't with him. The night was full of searchlights and bright white tracers, so many that the clouds looked red. He scuttled across a field to a tree line, bursts of machine-gun fire echoing around him, the night incredibly loud for thirty seconds, a minute, before the firing slowed and the din of the antiaircraft guns fell to a rattling instead of a roar.

The planes were gone. The paratroopers scattered. But he had an objective, and if he didn't reach it, the men on the landing craft would be outgunned, so he chose a direction and started running. As he crossed the open fields of the Cotentin Peninsula, the young wheat barely six inches high, several misdropped paratroopers joined him. The night echoed with small arms fire, but Cole's group was fortunate. They met no resistance. After twenty minutes, they still had no idea where they were.

Cole knocked on a farmhouse door. "Where are we?" he asked.

Sainte-Mère-Église.

They were too far west. They had been moving in the wrong direction.

It was some time after 2:00 a.m. when they ran into their first enemy, a group of German soldiers with horses and carts. Instead of the 700 men under his command, Cole had just seventy-five paratroopers from the 502nd's regimental headquarters; Company G, 506th (not his regiment); and the 82nd Airborne (not even his division). Some were fully armed; some with Cole, like Lieutenant Dick Winters of the 506th's Easy Company, had lost everything in the jump except their knives. Still, they were airborne. They ambushed the convoy, killed several Germans, took ten prisoners, and moved quickly toward the beach.

Around 4:00 a.m., Cole sent a reconnaissance group to check the

German battery emplacement near Saint-Martin-de-Varreville, his original objective. The German position had been hit by aerial bombardment and abandoned, so Cole moved forward with what was left of his force, now close to fifty. The Germans had flooded two miles of low-lying fields behind Utah Beach by opening a series of defensive locks originally devised by Napoleon, leaving only four paths out of the kill zone for the men coming ashore, which Army planners had designated Exits 1 through 4. Cole's battalion was responsible for securing Exits 3 and 4.

At 5:30 a.m., Allied warships began pounding German coastal batteries, blanketing the shoreline in smoke. Some support landing craft were fitted with heavy weapons. They opened fire at 6:00 a.m. The landing craft carrying the first wave of 4th Infantry Division troops hit Utah Beach at 6:30 a.m. By then, Cole and his paratroopers had cleared Exit 3. They set up in the low defiles along the narrow causeway, the only route of retreat for the German soldiers manning the beach defenses.

Around 9:30 a.m., the Germans appeared. Cole's men waited, then raked them with fire, killing fifty to seventy-five enemy soldiers and destroying their ability to reposition on that stretch of the beach. Then they waited again. Currents had pushed the landing craft 1,500 yards south, toward Exits 1 and 2, so the morning was strangely calm. It was several hours later, around 1:00 p.m., before the first American soldiers—the 1st Battalion, 8th Infantry, 4th Infantry Division, with Brigadier General Teddy Roosevelt Jr. shouting encouragement—appeared out of the smoke at Exit 3. Those who had come ashore from the water, and those who had come ashore from the sky, had linked at last. The Germans were far from beaten, but the lodgment at Utah was secure.

CHAPTER 27

# NEWS

— ★ —

*Frieda van Schaïk*
June 1944

In Maastricht, the local collaborationist newspaper—only collaboration-ist newspapers still existed—reported the Normandy landings on the morning of June 7. Without permission, apparently. By midmorning, the Nederlandse Landwacht, a Dutch paramilitary organization created by the Nazis in late 1943, were scouring Limburg, confiscating all copies.

"Where did you get this?" the two men at the door demanded of Dave van Schaïk, waving the paper in his face. They were young, bullheaded, and angry, wearing the black uniforms of the NSB.

"You gave it to me," he said.

The evening edition mentioned nothing of the invasion. But it was too late. The citizens of Limburg Province would never forget. They brought their radios out of hiding and tuned to the BBC and Radio Orange. After the 9:00 p.m. broadcast, Pappie brought a large map of Northern Europe down from his attic, and the family gathered eagerly around it, searching for Bayeux, Caen, and other unfamiliar names.

# CHAPTER 28

# PURPLE HEART LANE

— ★ —

*Robert Cole*
June 1944

Robert George Cole was born into a military family. His father, Lieutenant Colonel Clarence Cole, took a leave of absence from college in 1898 to join the 20th Kansas Volunteers in the Spanish-American War. Clarence became a doctor and was commissioned into the U.S. Army Medical School. He was assigned to Fort Sam Houston in San Antonio, Texas, where he eventually led the laboratory that serviced all Army hospitals in the southwest. Robert, his second son, was born in the base hospital in 1915.

Clarence Cole died when Robert was three. The Army said he "died en route to France in 1918," implying he was killed as a result of World War I. In truth, he never deployed to France. His death was a suicide. His wife, Clara, found him with a gunshot wound to the head. He had been relieved of his duties as head of the laboratory and treated at Walter Reed General Hospital in Washington, D.C., but the reasons he took his own life, like many suicides, were unknowable. He was buried with full military honors, having given his life to the military he loved.

Robert Cole and his two siblings never had a chance to get to know their father. It is unclear how much Robert knew about the circumstances of his father's death. But he grew up with his father's legacy, in a small house three miles from Fort Sam Houston, and he understood from a young age the many deprivations and hardships Clara had to endure as a result of her husband's death. His mother was stern. She worked her children hard and was stingy with praise. But Robert adored her. He did everything she asked of him. It wasn't easy to raise three children alone on a schoolteacher's pay.

Twenty-six years later, Robert Cole was a lieutenant colonel, just like his father. And he had his own son, Robert Bruce Cole. The boy was six months old when his father kissed him good-bye at Fort Bragg on September 5, 1943. Cole was a professional soldier. He could focus when duty demanded.

But as soon as the fighting was over, like all good soldiers, he let that hyper-human focus lapse. D-Day was Cole's first combat experience, a test no man is truly sure he'll pass. It wasn't simply a question of dying, though that was part of it. It was the deeper question of whether you would perform under pressure, or crack when death was near. Would Cole, with the added burden of leadership, command his men with grace in battle? Would he make the right decisions when men's lives were on the line? Only combat would tell, which is why every soldier, every one, is relieved to find himself alive and proud on the other side. It is a rush like little else on earth, followed by terror, exhaustion, reflection, relief, and joy.

Like many soldiers, after the rush had passed, Cole's thoughts turned to home. He was a prolific letter writer to his mother and Allie Mae, always in pen, on stationary, very clean. He couldn't write them from the lodgment. There was no post. But he must have thought of them, there on the edge. Composed lines in his head. Words of reassurance. Of confidence in the days ahead. What else would a man think of than the people he loves, when he has gone through the killing field and survived?

He wasn't idle. The 502nd put its 3rd Battalion in reserve in the early morning of June 7, 1944, rotating the other two battalions forward and giving Cole's men rest. He probably slept. Briefly. They were barely beyond the range of the German guns, and there was work to do. Regimental reserve was the time to assess actions, give and receive reports, organize, treat wounds and injuries, restock ammunition, and replace lost or damaged equipment. Patrols were sent on reconnaissance, forward areas swept, defensive positions manned against a German counterattack.

But in the quiet moments, he surely thought of his son, Bruce, toddling across the living room, his first toy in his fist. He surely thought of Allie Mae, at Fort Bragg with the other wives, listening to reports from the landings.

"Don't cry," he told her when he kissed her good-bye. "This is what I do."

He didn't need to say it. Allie Mae knew. She kept their home in order. She raised their son. She prayed for the safety of her husband and his men, but she never shed a tear over the life he had chosen. She was as dedicated to being a soldier's wife as Robert Cole was to being a soldier.

The 3rd Battalion came out of reserve on June 9, D+3. A precarious time. The Allies were barely off the beaches, and the success of Operation Overlord hung in the balance. Cole's battalion was tasked with taking the causeway to Carentan, a nearby town and one of Overlord's primary objectives. Since the Germans had flooded the low-lying areas, Carentan was the only viable link between Utah and Omaha Beach. Airborne units had attacked the mile-long causeway on D-Day, but they had been beaten back at the second of four bridges. If the Allies couldn't secure the causeway, the generals worried, the Germans would use it to drive the Allies back into the sea.

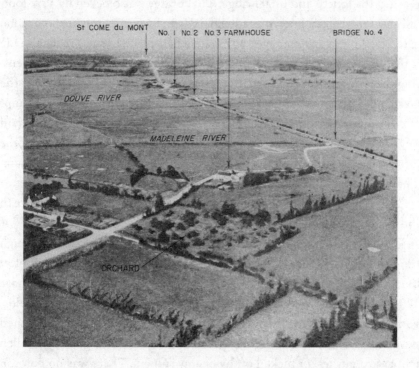

The operation began at 3:00 p.m. on June 10. By 3:30, Lieutenant Colonel Cole, leading from the front, had reached the second bridge. It was destroyed, but Cole's men discovered that, if they strung a rope for a handhold, they could walk across an intact beam that had been placed across the opening by an earlier patrol.

The afternoon was quiet as, one at a time, the paratroopers snuck along the low wooden beam. Cole urged them to spread out, not to bunch up and create targets, as for three hours the paratroopers crawled over the gap and along the exposed causeway. It wasn't until the head of the column reached the fourth and final bridge, and the bulk of the battalion was spread out over almost a half mile of open road, that the Germans opened fire from numerous positions on the right- and left-hand sides. Cole's men hit the ground, using marsh reeds and the embankment of the elevated causeway as cover. From then on, the advance was under a constant barrage of bullets, grenades, mortars, and artillery. Whenever a head popped above the road, it was a target for German snipers.

It was evening by the time Cole, crouching through devastating fire, reached the fourth and final bridge. That bridge was blocked by a six-foot-tall anti-tank barrier known as a Belgian Gate. By pushing against the metal gate, the Americans managed to create a fifteen-inch gap. Six men made it through, but the Germans opened fire from a nearby farmhouse, cutting them down. A second attempt, more losses. Cole tried to dislodge the Germans with mortar and artillery fire, but it was no use. A third attempt at crossing the bridge was repulsed with equal fury. The Germans had positioned a significant force behind the thick walls and windbreaks of the farmhouse, so embedded the men of the 3rd Battalion couldn't see them. There was no way to advance, but no thought of retreat.

And the paratroopers kept coming, crouching single file through fire to the uncrossable divide.

By dawn, Cole had managed to slip portions of two companies through the Belgian Gate, with another three exhausted companies at the foot of the bridge. The farmhouse was less than two football fields away, but those 170 yards were a no-man's-land of open ground and wet sucking fields, with the Germans covering every inch from their hidden and entrenched positions. The dawn's first light exposed dozens of bodies, good men fallen in forward pushes, or picked off by enemy snipers. There was no point in waiting, and still no thought of retreat.

"We're going," Cole told his executive officer, Major John Stopka. "Pass the word down the line."

Climbing onto the causeway with only his M1911A1 pistol in his hand, Cole stared toward the enemy position. Dawn was breaking. Bullets cracked past his head.

"What's wrong, fellas?" he asked, looking down at three of his soldiers crouched behind the embankment at his feet.

"We're pinned down, sir!"

"Aw, we ain't pinned down. Let's go get them sonofabitches."

"Reload rifles and fix bayonets," Cole ordered. And then, seeing the hesitancy of his men, he broke into an impromptu speech. "We will take the farmhouse. We will teach those goose-stepping Heinies how to fight a war. If you have a cigarette, smoke it now, because for some of you, it will be your last."

"When I blow my whistle," he yelled, "I want every one of you God-damned jayhawks right on my ass. If your best friend gets hit, you don't stop. You keep coming."

He called for a smoke screen and artillery barrage shortly before 6:15 and then, as the smoke blew cover across the fields, Lieutenant Colonel Robert Cole charged the entrenched enemy farmhouse, firing his pistol.

Two seconds, three seconds, and no one was coming. In the pounding din of the battle, only the men closest to Cole had heard the order and knew what the whistle meant. So Cole reached down to a dead soldier from an earlier charge, grabbed his bayoneted rifle, and yelled once again for his men to follow. The fog broke, exhausted men found their courage, and as Cole sprinted toward the farmhouse, the paratroopers of the 3rd Battalion, 502nd Parachute Infantry, came streaming across the field toward the farmhouse, charging through the smoke and the enemy machine guns, screaming and firing as they ran.

"We were scared to death," one soldier said. "They were mowing us down like corn." But they stormed across those sucking fields and hit the enemy like a tidal wave. It took a full day of vicious attacks and counter-attacks, close quarters combat and precision artillery. They fought for the farmhouse, and then the orchard behind it, and then the cabbage patch beyond that, until they had routed the Germans from their defensive stronghold and blew open the road to Carentan.

# CHAPTER 29

# HOMECOMING

— ★ —

*Frieda van Schaïk*
Summer 1944

In the heat of summer, as the Allied forces fought their way off the beaches and into the hedgerows of Normandy, Frieda's brother Wim and his friend Fernand decided to sneak through the caves of Sint Pietersberg into Belgium. They had been smuggling Jews and downed Allied aircrews through the caves since the autumn of 1942, but their primary contact on the Belgian side had gone missing, and they needed to meet with their network face-to-face. Moekie begged her only son not to go. She knew about Wim's work. Of course she did. She was his mother. She had endured the stress silently, bravely, as she endured all things. Now she asked him simply, "Please, Wim. For me. Don't go."

Since the D-Day landings, the Nederlandse Landwacht and Gestapo had become more aggressive. They felt the rising hope of Limburgers, and they were determined to crush it. Searches were volatile, sometimes violent. Arrests were rising. There were death sentences and executions. One morning, Frieda watched a woman trade her wedding ring for a cart of produce. The citizens of Maastricht were scouring the countryside for food, carrying away handfuls of nettles, terrible to eat but full of iron, and other greens of less obvious nutritional value. The woman had secured enough for several families. But a hundred yards down the road, a patrol of Nederlandse Landwacht confiscated the cart, laughing, leaving her crying beside the road.

It's too dangerous, Moekie insisted to Wim, to risk this kind of work now.

Wim thought of Tilly Cats, a young Jewish girl, the first person he had guided through Sint Pietersberg. He thought of how she had grasped his hand, in the feeble light of his lantern, and whispered in gratitude, "I'll never forget this."

The Americans and their allies were making slow progress. The combined armies took 10,000 casualties on D-Day, including 4,427 killed. In the next three weeks, they lost 40,000. By July 7, a month after the landings, they had progressed only to outside the town of Saint-Lô, barely twenty miles from the beaches. At that rate, it might take them a year to reach Maastricht. Or they might never arrive.

No, Moekie, Wim told his mother, I can't stop. This work is a matter of life and death.

The trip through the caves with Fernand was easy. They had done it dozens of times. They crossed the Albert Canal near the Belgian village of Lanaye, then boarded a bus to Liège. But just beyond the town of Visé, the bus was stopped by a roadblock. A German soldier with an automatic rifle climbed aboard. "Mensch, du!" the soldier ordered. "Papiere! Ausweis!"

Wim searched his pockets as the soldier stood in front of him, then searched them again. He was frantic, unsure how this could have happened. He held up his empty hands, confusion and worry on his face. It was all an act. He had intentionally left his papers at home. He was not authorized to be in Belgium.

"I've got one!" the soldier yelled, pushing him off the bus. The young soldier was so excited, he forgot to check the rest of the passengers. Fernand, sitting a few rows behind Wim, continued on.

The Resistance brought the family the news later that day. Frieda didn't miss the pain on Moekie's face as she absorbed the details of her son's arrest, the anguish in her eyes when she heard that Wim had been spotted entering an interrogation room in Lanaye. This was what she had feared since the moment she buried the first jar in the garden. This was the terror she had been living with for years.

The Germans didn't know Wim's real purpose. He and Fernand had a cover story: cigarette smuggling. It would work, the messenger assured them. Or maybe she was trying to assure herself. If Wim broke, after all, it could mean many people's lives, even hers.

Moekie didn't hear the reassurance. Or if she did, she didn't respond.

When the messenger left, she staggered to her bed. Frieda cooked a simple dinner, potatoes and a few greens from the garden, a little fat for the pan. It was all they had. She took a plate to her mother in bed, but Moekie turned away. She was sixty-three years old and weak from hunger and fatigue. They all were. Frieda feared Wim's death would kill her.

*Pull up your socks, Moekie*, she silently begged. That is all we can do.

The house was full of visitors: Frieda's sister Margaret, her husband and infant child, the local priest. Pappie brought the map of Northern Europe down each night, and they ran their fingers over it, searching for the landmarks mentioned in the nightly radio reports. But there was no joy in the Van Schaïk household. There could be no joy when Moekie, who had always accommodated everyone, barely left her bed when another worried guest arrived. There could be no joy without word of Wim.

He was in Maastricht, four miles away, locked in the Court of Justice, which had been converted into a political prison. His communal cell held eight men, with a table for meals, sleeping pallets, and a communal toilet. As the new man, Wim had the pallet next to the toilet. He walked the cell each day for exercise. Listened to the screaming late at night, when the Germans tortured. One screamer was a woman, he was sure of it. After a few days, two of his cellmates were taken away. "To the transports." It was death, and they knew it. Wim was haunted by the look on their faces.

"Don't cry," a priest said. He was a prisoner, too, and seemed to have been for quite some time. "We've all had the same experience. Felt the same feelings. They will make a man out of you here."

Wim heard the carillon of the bells of Sint Servaas, one of only two sets in Maastricht not melted down by the Germans. It was a sound from an almost-free world. A sound he had heard almost every Sunday but never like this. The bells of Sint Servaas had rung since 1515, through famine, epidemics, siege, and war. For 400 years, they had survived.

"As long as you can hear the bells," the old priest said, "you know you are alive."

It was three days, maybe four, before Moekie was able to get out of bed and get on with living. After a few more days, she began walking outside. She would shuffle a short way down the Bemelerweg toward Maastricht, then back. They needed food, she told Frieda. Women she had known for a decade might have something to spare for a neighbor who had helped them in years past. Frieda had abdominal pains. She was malnourished, and it was taking a toll on her body. But she knew Moekie wasn't wandering for food. She was wandering for Wim. They knew he had been transported to the Court of Justice, but there was no way of knowing if he was still there. He might have been transferred to the north. Or to the camps.

The waiting. The lack of information. It was a slow accumulation, a tightening vise of pain. Especially for Moekie, who looked weaker by the day.

And then one evening, as Moekie walked along the Bemelerweg, she saw a figure on the road. The sun was behind him, so he was a shadow to her, but something about the way he moved made her stop. He ambled toward her, surrounded by light, and it wasn't until he was a dozen paces away that she muttered, "Wimmy?"

"Mother."

"Are you alive? Is it really you?"

The NSB guards had come for him, laughing, "Van Schaïk! Transport!" Dutch boys, laughing, thinking he was condemned to death. They took him to Schneider, the Nazi who had been interrogating him day after day.

"You are going to a concentration camp," Schneider said, with a vile smile. Wim realized the man enjoyed this. "We will send you to a concentration camp . . . if you do this again."

Perhaps he had fooled them with the cigarette-smuggling story. Perhaps he had a friend somewhere, but if so, he had no idea who. He was so stunned to find himself outside the Court of Justice, free, that for a long moment he couldn't think. He couldn't move. But now, he rushed the last few steps to his mother and threw his arms around her. *She's worse off than me*, he thought, as he felt her thinness and the hunch of her shoulders.

"Yes, Moekie," he said. "I'm here. It's me. I'm alive."

"Never again," she whispered, shaking in his arms. "Please, son. Never again."

# CHAPTER 30

# TRUST

— ★ —

*Bill Moore and John Low*
August 1944

"We gotta go," John Low insisted. On August 17, after more than two months of fighting, the Allies had broken the back of Germany's Army Group B. General Patton's Third United States Army and General Courtney H. Hodges's First United States Army maneuvered from the south while British General Montgomery pressed from the north with his 21st Army Group, surrounding and trapping them near Falaise, France. Ten thousand Germans were killed and 50,000 captured. Now the Western Allied armies were racing across Northern France toward Belgium and the Netherlands, almost unopposed. Low wanted to run to them, to meet them on the road.

Moore didn't agree. "John," he said calmly, "where is your trust?"

The Resistance knew the Underwater Boys wanted to return to the fight. The Resistance was making arrangements. Moore and Low were in an unfamiliar, enemy-occupied country. They didn't speak the language, beyond Moore's rudimentary lessons with Jaap. It was better, Moore insisted, to wait.

On August 19, American and French troops reached the outskirts of Paris. Just 300 miles separated Apeldoorn from the City of Lights. The Underwater Boys could cover that distance in eleven days, Low argued, maybe twelve. And who knew how much closer the Allies might advance toward them in twelve days? They might be only eight, nine days away.

Aart van Kliest insisted that leaving was a bad idea. The Underwater Boys were safe. Plans were being made. This time Low wouldn't back down, so Aart sighed and left the house. A few hours later, visitors started arriving. At 8:00 p.m., the blackout curtains were drawn, and Low, Moore, and the three other Americans hiding in the attic were brought down to a room full of ordinary Dutch citizens: young and old, thin and worn, the shopkeepers and farmers of Apeldoorn. Good people, but stern.

No, not stern. Concerned.

Members of the underground, Low realized. Aart had gone for reinforcements.

"John, I understand you want to leave in the morning," a man said, after a pot of chicory coffee had been shared. His English was impeccable.

Low explained the plan: twenty miles a day, staying off main roads, hiding if anyone came along. He had a compass. A map. They would make it. He and Moore had been told they were staying eight days. That was five months ago. Now their comrades were on the march, and every man was needed to roll up the Germans once and for all.

"I agree," the man said carefully. "There is a decent chance you can make it. But if you are caught, you will be handed over to the Gestapo. I know you will not tell them anything while in your right senses, we trust you on that, but any man will crack under the torture they employ."

"They won't do that," Low protested. "We're soldiers."

"If you had just been shot down, yes, there would be no point in torture. But the Germans know the day you came down. They know you have been hidden. They will assume the Resistance helped you. They will turn you over to the Gestapo."

"They don't know how long I've been here."

"They know," Aart assured him, and it was only later Low thought of his parachute hanging in the trees. It had his name on it. Was that how?

"They don't want you," the first man said. "They want us. They will torture you until they have everyone in this room, and then everyone we know."

Mary, the twenty-five-year-old who had met them with bicycles, whose real name was Narda van Terwisga and who was the actual leader of the Apeldoorn Resistance cell, spoke softly but firmly. "We won't stop you," she said, "if this is what you want to do. But we won't help you. And if you go, we will have to disband this operation and move all the other men we have hidden in the area. You know too much. It will be too dangerous."

Low looked around the room: at his friend Bill Moore; his fellow Underwater Boys; these ordinary Dutch men and women who were risking everything; even Mother, their secret guardian, who hadn't left the house since their arrival, because someone had to be home in case of trouble.

"Trust them, John," Bill Moore said.

You are as much a soldier, Moore had assured young Joop Bitter in the forest, as a man in uniform.

Looking around the room now, Low realized Moore had been right. If members of the Dutch Resistance weren't soldiers, there wasn't any such thing.

He stayed.

# CHAPTER 31

# EXODUS

— ★ —

*Emilie Michiels van Kessenich; Frieda van Schaïk*

August–September 1944

On August 18, the day before American and French forces reached the outskirts of Paris, the Allies bombed Maastricht. There was no air raid siren, just a "hellish whistle" followed by "deafening explosions." The bombs were targeting the railroad bridge over the Maas, but they fell mostly on the area called Krejjedörrep, destroying several blocks.

"What havoc!" wrote a Dutch teenager, Hette de Jong, who ran to the wreckage to help. "Dozens of houses in ruins! . . . In the hall of the Butter Mine already three corpses. Horrible sight! Completely twisted and torn apart! Twisted, pale faces! Entirely covered in dirt!"

"I will never forget! Those dismembered bodies and faces will always remain in my mind."

Emilie's son Eduard was slightly wounded. If he had crossed the river thirty seconds later, he would have been killed, she fretted.

Ninety-two people were dead. More than 200 wounded. The next day, eighty coffins were displayed in the town's Vrijthof Square, where their German overlords made the city's officials kneel before them and place flowers. Thousands lined the streets on August 22, as a procession carried the coffins through the center of town to the cemetery.

"A fearful smell surrounded the procession," De Jong noted. "Moisture ran from the bottom of the coffins! Rest in peace poor inhabitants of Maastricht! You are remembered as a fallen front line soldier."

"So these are your friends?" the Germans taunted the Dutch crowd, snapping off Heil Hitlers as the coffins passed. They thought it was good propaganda, portraying the Allies as killers, but the Dutch didn't listen. There was sadness, bitter sadness, but this was the price of regaining their freedom, and they were willing to pay it.

A few days later, the leading edge of the German exodus reached Maastricht, though no one noticed at first. A few cars here, some high-ranking officials in a black Mercedes there, all traveling from France and Belgium. By September 1, the stream of traffic was becoming hard to miss. By September 3, it was obvious to everyone: the rats were abandoning the sinking ship. Collaborators, French and Belgian "Kraut girls" who had taken up with Nazis, German officials and sympathizers, were elbowing each other through the narrow streets that led to the bridges over the Maas.

They were fleeing with the leading edge of the retreating German army, which was being pushed northeast by the Allied advance. This was no orderly evacuation. This was a riot of columns in wild flight, so many uniforms mixed with so many civilians it was impossible to determine who the people were or how they had served the German cause.

The Germans were "confiscating" everything on their way out: baby carriages, tables, sewing machines, wine. The Michiels van Kessenich family's oldest boy, Willem, had his bike stolen by a German soldier, despite trying to fight him off. Cars were being "commandeered." Taxis and buses were hijacked and packed with household goods. In one car, two pigs were crammed into the back seat like human passengers. Cows were being herded through the center of town, wild-eyed, boxed in by Germans on foot almost as wild-eyed as the animals. Allied prisoners of war shuffled past, their clothes torn and tattered. Many were barefoot. Had they been marched that way from France? A Dutch woman stepped out of the crowd, offering water or bread to the prisoners, but the German guards knocked away the water and ripped the bread from her hands.

Workhorses, the kind from the fields, were being yanked by the bridle. Or kicked by impatient riders. They pulled farm carts packed with loot, or the hay the carts had been filled with when they were stolen a few miles or a few days down the road. In several carts, drunk soldiers rolled in the hay, wine bottles at their feet, roughly fondling French and Belgian women who had fallen in love with German soldiers and had no choice but to flee.

"Heimat" ("Homeland"), a few soldiers sang, a patriotic German song. "Keine Sorge, wir kommen wieder," they yelled to the Dutch. ("Don't worry, we'll be back.") But most were bleary-eyed and unshaven, eager to avoid notice in their haste to get away.

"Aachen!" two German Red Cross medics in helmets and uniforms yelled at passing motorists. "Are you going to Aachen?"

"Yes."

"Can we go with you?"

"No."

The column was crawling so slowly, one medic opened a car door and tried to get in, but the driver cursed and threw him out.

"Damn you!" the medics yelled, first at the German driver and then at the Dutch, who were laughing. Then they both climbed onto one stolen bicycle and wobbled slowly away, making the Dutch laugh even harder.

Else Hanöver, Willem Michiels van Kessenich's twenty-two-year-old secretary, lived above her family's music store on the Wycker Brugstraat, between the bridge and the train station. Her grandmother had escaped an Allied bombing in Aachen by fleeing into the basement as her house exploded and burned. Now she stood on the narrow balcony, watching the wild, degenerate exodus below. Else noticed she was crying.

"What is the matter, Oma?"

"I am ashamed to be German," the old woman replied.

By September 4, Maastricht's NSB officials were joining the exodus, along with local collaborators. The Dutch stood on the sidewalks and hurled curses at these traitors to the city. Overnight, someone had thrown nails into the road, so teenagers ran to find more. The Dutch cheered when the nails punctured tires, forcing the NSB officials to get out and make repairs. Some Germans had branches tied to the tops of their cars, since Allied aircraft were watching the roads. When cars drove by with brooms tied to the front of their wheels to sweep aside the nails, the Dutch jeered.

The next day, the bulk of four German divisions arrived in long, disorganized columns. They had been decimated in France and rebuilt with parts from whatever the Germans could scrounge. This was the end of the exodus. The soldiers had driven all the German officials and NSB traitors before them. Behind them, somewhere, were the Allied armies.

"Parachutes!" someone yelled the next afternoon, as white objects appeared in the sky, but they were only pamphlets, dropped by the Allies, urging the Germans to surrender.

By the evening of September 7, the city was quiet. A curfew had been imposed. Life suspended: no newspapers, no mail, no trains. The opening of the school year was postponed. The daily bread ration undelivered. Going out to survey the damage before the 8:00 p.m. curfew, the Dutch found hundreds of papers balled up in the street. They were pamphlets written by the commander of German forces in Western Europe, Field Marshal Walter Model, who was trying to rally the retreating soldiers at Arnhem, a hundred miles to the north. "Everyone must do his duty!" the pamphlets read. "Fight to the last man!"

That evening, the Germans blew up the railroad bridge, the one the Allies had failed to destroy in their deadly raid three weeks earlier. Camouflage transport trucks rolled through the streets, loaded to their canvas tops. Everything was taken: sugar, potatoes, bicycles, bedsheets. The banks were looted of currency. Dozens of trucks were spotted outside the warehouses where the city's rations were stored. At dawn, the transport trucks were gone, and so was the food. That night, the first artillery shells hit Maastricht, although it was unclear to the residents which side had fired them, and whether things were about to get better or worse.

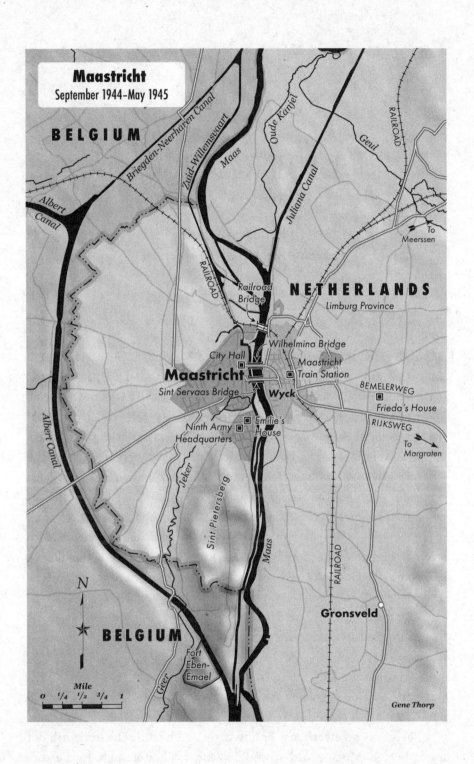

**Maastricht**
September 1944–May 1945

BELGIUM

Briegden-Neerharen Canal

Zuid-Willemsvaart

Maas

Oude Kanjel

Juliana Canal

Geul

RAILROAD

To
Meerssen

Albert
Canal

RAILROAD

Railroad
Bridge

NETHERLANDS
Limburg Province

Wilhelmina Bridge

City Hall

Maastricht
Train Station

BEMELERWEG

**Maastricht**

Sint Servaas Bridge

Wyck

Frieda's House

Albert Canal

Emilie's
House

RIJKSWEG

To
Margraten

Ninth Army
Headquarters

Jeker

Sint Pietersberg

Maas

RAILROAD

N

**Gronsveld**

BELGIUM

Geer

Fort
Eben-
Emael

Mile
0   1/4   1/2   3/4   1

*Gene Thorp*

# CHAPTER 32

# LIBERATION

— ★ —

*Frieda van Schaïk;*
*Emilie Michiels van Kessenich*
September 1944

For four days, an eerie quiet enveloped Maastricht. A jittery calm, a resounding silence, except for the distant sound of artillery and the occasional Allied warplane overhead. The Luftwaffe was beaten. The German refugees were across the border in Aachen, their stolen pigs making a mess of the rear seats of their cars. But the Sicherheitsdienst (the SD, German secret police) and hundreds of fanatical soldiers from the 176th Infantry Division had been left behind. They set up machine-gun positions and patrolled the streets, shooting at anyone foolish or desperate enough to appear. So the citizens of Maastricht sheltered in their basements. They lived on local apples and pears. They filled their bathtubs with water, in case the water supply was cut. Rumors passed from neighbor to neighbor: The Germans were setting booby traps and mining the bridges. The Americans had been seen at such and such a place.

"Get the flag," Dave van Schaïk said when he heard someone atop Sint Pietersberg had spotted the American vanguard, or something that looked like it, anyway.

Out came the Dutch flag from its hiding place of four years. "This won't do," Moekie said when she saw the deep creases and folds. "This will not do. It must be ironed."

There was no electricity. Frieda suggested heating the iron with hot water, but no, Moekie said, it would never stay hot enough. In the end, they folded the flag neatly and put the heaviest object they could find, Moekie's hand-sling Singer sewing machine, on top to press it.

At nightfall, a huge explosion in the east, a cloud of smoke. Was it the Americans? The Germans? If the Germans made a stand, Maastricht would descend into chaos, and who knew what would happen then.

Later, much later, Frieda woke to a strange sound: a pulsating pounding. She peeked out the attic window and saw soldiers on horseback in the distance. They were galloping down the Rijksweg toward Germany, the shoes of their horses sparking on the asphalt as they raced away with carts of loot. These weren't workhorses. They were show horses with fancy saddles and stirrups.

She thought of the morning four years before, when Hitler's tanks had rolled down that very road, and how the German infantryman had laughed at her defiance.

"So ein Witz. So ein Witz." What a terrible, terrible joke it had been.

The next day, a Belgian Resistance fighter snuck across the Albert Canal and through the German lines. He carried a letter from American Major General Leland S. Hobbs of the 30th Infantry Division to the mayor of Maastricht. It said, in French, that the Americans were at the gates of the city, and that all enemy personnel must leave by 7:00 a.m. the next morning or the city would be destroyed. In the early afternoon, the letter reached Willem Michiels van Kessenich, who was not the mayor. The NSB mayor had fled, but the SD and the 176th Infantry Division held the city, so there was nothing for him to do but prepare the bomb shelter in the basement, marshal his wife and ten children, and prepare for the war to fall on their heads.

A few hours later, out of a second-floor window, Willem took two photographs of the large white house down the block, which the German occupation authorities had commandeered in 1940 for their headquarters. The first showed the representative of the Reichskommissar in Limburg Province, Wilhelm Schmidt, scurrying into his black Mercedes. In the second, five German guards were fleeing on bicycles.

"Our view from our children's bedroom has never been so heart-warming," Emilie wrote in her Memory Book.

Dave van Schaïk snapped awake. The night was so deep in darkness, he thought it was a dream. Then he heard it again, a pounding on the door. When he stumbled out of the basement, he found six German soldiers, heavily armed but disheveled. They had lost their way. They hadn't eaten for days. They were so beaten down they wouldn't look him in the eye.

Dave wanted to throttle them where they stood. But he thought of the words in his Bible: if your enemy is in need, give him food and something to drink.

Without a word, he went to the kitchen and sliced the family's only loaf of bread. As the soldiers grabbed for it greedily, Frieda appeared at the top of the stairs, groggy with sleep. When Dave explained the situation, she turned away.

"I'll make the coffee," she said.

— ★ —

The morning of September 13 was filled with artillery fire. Explosions in the north, then the south. Shells whistling overhead, as they had for days, and Allied reconnaissance aircraft in the sky. The Dutch hunkered in their cellars. German soldiers ran from corner to corner, German artillery fired from the edges of the parks and the soccer fields. The Wilhelmina Bridge exploded—German charges—and collapsed into the Maas. Sint Servaas Bridge took a pounding just after 3:00 p.m., two rapid explosions, but the old bridge was tough. Only the newest section, the drawbridge, came down with a splash.

Then nothing. No running Germans. No trucks. No artillery. Only silence. It stretched for minutes, then hours, as the Dutch in their basements wondered what was happening overhead. Were the Americans coming? Were the Germans waiting? Was it safe to go out?

And then a shaking, a rumbling, as much a feeling as a sound. A rumor flashed through the apartment buildings of Wyck: The Yanks are at Gronsveld. They are coming down the Heerderweg. They have circled around and crossed the Maas south of the city. They are coming from the *east*, not the west. They are coming here, to Wyck.

Could it be true? Was that the rumbling sound of American tanks? The cheers were growing louder, surging down the Meerssenerweg, but were there no Germans left? Where was the counterattack?

The Dutch crept to their windows, peeked out their doors. At the end of the Wycker Brugstraat sat the ornate brick railroad station, hit by both German and Allied bombs but not destroyed. It stood impassively, almost completely intact, a symbol of the town's resolve. And then, from the right, a tank crept into view, its white star blazing in the sun. It stopped. It turned its gun down the Wycker Brugstraat toward the river and the bridge.

And the sky cracked open, and the cheers began to shake the buildings. From every door, and every window, the Dutch poured into the streets, shouting and cheering. They sprinted down the Wycker Brugstraat as a line of tanks pushed past the station and up the road. The Americans waved from their turrets. They threw their rations into the crowd, mostly cigarettes and chewing gum. Hette de Jong pushed to the front with his camera.

"We are free! The long-awaited hour has arrived!"

Down the block, an eight-year-old boy was swept up in the rush, swirling like a leaf in a stream until two hands reached down and lifted him up, up, up: an American soldier, riding on the front of a tank.

"Where are you headed?" he yelled over the noise.

The boy pointed up the street.

"Do you want a ride?"

The boy nodded as the American sat him down on the front of the tank, next to the gun. Soldiers were walking alongside. The crowd was screaming and banging on the tank with joy, but the boy was above them, riding down the Wycker Brugstraat toward his parents' store, there on the corner; he could see it now, his mother in the doorway, smiling and waving to him. This was the greatest moment of his life.

Dave van Schaïk sent Frieda down the road one way, then the other. The boom of artillery hung in the distance, but along the Bemelerweg all was quiet.

"Nothing, Pappie," Frieda said.

The Americans had swept through Heer on their way to Wyck, but they had bypassed the Bemelerweg, so the family hadn't seen them. Frieda wondered what was taking them so long to return. Had the Germans truly surrendered Wyck without a fight? If the townspeople were celebrating, it must be true, but where were the soldiers? Where was the confirmation, after four hard years, that they were free?

"Check again," Dave said, pacing the kitchen, and Frieda went out to look first toward Maastricht, and then toward the east.

"Nothing, Pappie," she said.

The Americans might be staying in Wyck, Moekie suggested. They might be waiting at the river, said Frieda's sister Margaret, her infant daughter in her arms. Perhaps they aren't coming this way at all, but using some other roads.

Dave refused to hear it. "Hang the flag," he said.

Proudly, Moekie brought it from its hiding place, crisp and pressed. With Frieda's help, she draped it from the ledge above the door.

And then they heard it, a growling from the direction of Maastricht, like a huge beast on the prowl. An M5 Stuart light tank appeared at the bottom of the road. As it turned and started toward them, another Stuart appeared, and then another.

"Look!" Frieda yelled. "The Yanks! It's the Yanks! They've come all the way across the ocean to save us."

Along the road, the Dutch stepped from their doors, waving and cheering as the great beasts barreled past. It was only a portion of the 2nd Armored Division, a tiny sliver of the American war machine, but it was more firepower than Frieda van Schaïk could comprehend.

Thousands of pounds of metal in motion, in a grinding line. How did the tanks get here? What factory could have made them? What ship could have brought them? How many miles must they have already pounded and chewed? They were impervious, rolling past like elephants, until one slowed and stopped next to her home.

Hatches opened, and heads popped out. Three men, older than Frieda but still young. *What would convince a country,* she wondered, *to send its young men so far?*

"Can we hold the baby?" one asked.

Frieda was holding her sister Margaret's infant daughter; the American clearly thought the girl was hers. She turned to her sister.

Yes, Margaret nodded. Of course, yes.

The men climbed down from the tank. They were wearing overalls and helmets. "We've been away for a long time," one said. "I haven't seen my daughter in years."

"I have a daughter I've never met," said the man beside him.

They passed the girl from soldier to soldier, father to father. "We've seen so much death," one man said, as the little girl squirmed. "It feels good to hold a child who's so alive."

They stayed for a minute. Maybe three. Then they handed the toddler back to Frieda, climbed into their tank, and passed on, down the road and out of sight.

Because this was not the end. No one had come across the ocean to free Limburg. Few American soldiers had heard of such a place. It was not even the U.S. Army's objective to free Maastricht; it just happened to be on their way to their real target: the German city of Aachen.

So the tanks rolled on, past the Van Schaïk home, up the Bemelerweg and, a day and a few miles later, straight into the German counterattack at Valkenburg.

The day after Frieda met the Americans, in the quiet hours before dawn, a boatload of U.S. soldiers slipped across the Maas River to assess the conditions in the old section of Maastricht. The commander, prepared for a dangerous landing, was surprised to find about a hundred Dutch citizens waiting to greet them. The SD and the 176th Infantry Division, fearing being encircled, had retreated. After four years, four months, and four days of occupation, the city was free.

At 10:00 a.m., the Michiels van Kessenich family raised the Dutch flag to the top of the pole in their yard. It was a dignified ceremony. A fitting celebration. Then an American truck came up the road, followed by soldiers on foot, and even Emilie couldn't resist the urge to run into the street and greet the liberators. The first American she met was Staff Sergeant Albert Girardi from Chicago, Illinois.

A crash from the white house on the corner startled her. The night before, an explosion there had almost knocked Emilie off her mattress. She had sprung up to comfort the children, thinking it was a bomb or artillery, but it was only the Germans destroying their telex machine before retreating. Now, a cheer went up as something heavy hit the ground. The Americans were pulling down the stone Nazi eagle that had been affixed above the door. Emilie grabbed the rug from her entryway and ran to join the crowd. The Americans threw the orange rug, the color of a free Netherlands, over the shattered eagle to more loud cheers.

Louis, all of six, came running. He had been out in the celebrating crowds. He grabbed Emilie's hand and tugged hard. "Mutti, Mutti, they are just swell. Can we talk to them?"

"Of course, darling."

He leaned in close to whisper in her ear. "Can we tell them the truth?"

It had been four years of lies: No, Papske isn't home. No, Mutti doesn't know where daddy is. No, we don't have a radio.

The lying was one more thing, Emilie realized, that was over now.

# CHAPTER 33

# HELL'S HIGHWAY

— ★ —

*Jacob Herman and Robert Cole*
September 1944

Jacob Herman Sr.—Jake—was born in 1891, the year after the massacre at Wounded Knee, in the South Dakota Badlands. He was a member of the Lakota Nation, the victims of the massacre, and he was born and raised on the Pine Ridge Reservation, home of the Oglala Lakota. As a young man freshly returned from Indian School in Pennsylvania, he had wanted to be a cowboy, but he couldn't make it work. He was fired from Jack King's Wild West Show and Rodeo Royal Circus for being, in the opinion of his employer, the worst "Indian imitator" he had ever seen. He finally found his calling as a rodeo clown, where his most famous act involved a mule, a dog, and a skunk. By the early 1940s, Jake Herman was ranching, farming, and raising his five children on the 420 acres of land he had inherited from his father.

Then, in late summer 1942, the Herman family, like 125 other Lakota families, was informed that their home of fifty years was now the property of the U.S. Army Air Forces. The United States government had used eminent domain to seize 341,726 acres of South Dakota Badlands, including the northern section of the Oglala Lakota Nation's Pine Ridge Reservation, for an aerial gunnery range. The Hermans were ordered to leave within thirty days. So they relocated their horses and cattle to other homesteads, loaded their carts, and walked eighty miles across the rough and treacherous Badlands to No Flesh Creek, near Kyle, South Dakota. Their crops, close to harvest after months of work, were left to rot.

A few weeks later, Jacob Jr., the eldest son, returned to the family home to retrieve his mother Alice's prized possession, her 400-pound cast-iron stove. It had been too heavy to move with their other possessions. Several tribal members helped him load it onto a horse-drawn cart, and Jacob walked with it for several days back to No Flesh Creek. There was no housing available in No Flesh Creek, so Jacob, his four siblings, and his parents were living in a government-issued canvas tent. Winters in South Dakota were brutally windy and cold, especially in makeshift quarters, but at least the Hermans had the stove to keep them grounded in their memories, and to keep them warm.

Jacob enlisted the next summer, shortly after graduating from Holy Rosary Mission, a Jesuit school. That was fine with Jake Sr., who thought "one rodeo screwball in the family" was enough.

His mother didn't want him to go. But Jacob had recently turned eighteen, and he was determined. He became part of a wave of recruits being trained to fill the ranks of the soldiers killed during major battles in Europe and the Pacific. Most of those boys were destined for the infantry. But Jacob Herman volunteered for the airborne. He completed jump school in May 1944 and was assigned to the 82nd Airborne, the All American Division, so named because its members had hailed from every state in the Union during World War I.

A few weeks later, he returned on furlough to visit his parents in No Flesh Creek. His people had been stripped of their property and rights not once, but three times: first when the U.S. government forced the Oglala Lakota onto the Pine Ridge Reservation in 1889; then when the U.S. Cavalry killed some 300 mostly unarmed men, women, and children at the Wounded Knee Massacre in 1890; and finally in 1942, when the U.S. Army Air Forces took their land to create a bombing range. Nonetheless, Jacob informed his parents that he would soon be jumping behind enemy lines in the service of his country.

"Don't do it," Alice begged. "Please, Sonny. For me." News accounts of D-Day were fresh in her mind. Not the glory of the landing, but the thousands of boys who were never coming home. "I'm your mother, Sonny. I love you. I need you. What has this country ever done for us?"

Jacob shook his head. He was a warrior. He knew the risk. And he knew that you didn't just volunteer for airborne. You were *chosen*. "You didn't raise a quitter," he told his mother. "I won't let my brothers down."

Three months later, he was in Europe, preparing to assault the Siegfried Line.

The Westwall, as the Siegfried Line was known in Germany, was a heavily manned and fortified series of 3,000 bunkers, foxholes, walls, and tank traps nearly twenty miles wide in places that stretched north to south for almost 400 miles along Germany's western border. As many as 100,000 German troops had slipped away from Allied forces in France, including most of the high-ranking officers. Many were filling holes and swelling the ranks of the soldiers on the wall, an enormous, dug-in army determined to protect their homes and families. The centerpiece of that line, the most heavily fortified city on the Westwall, was Aachen, twenty miles due east of Maastricht.

British Field Marshal Bernard Montgomery, seeing the meat grinder ahead, proposed an alternative to Eisenhower's "broad-front strategy" of building up forces before launching the final drive into Germany. Instead of waiting and attacking at multiple points along the length of the Siegfried Line, as Eisenhower favored, Montgomery wanted to bypass the Wall at two narrow points. His 21st Army Group would sweep around the northern end near the Dutch city of Arnhem. Lieutenant General Omar Bradley's Twelfth United States Army Group would sweep around the southern end through the Hürtgen Forest, on the Belgian-German border. If they could meet on the other side, across the imposing Rhine River, they could encircle the Germans behind their vaunted Westwall. From there, it was a straight shot to Berlin and a chance to end the war by Christmas.

The success of Montgomery's attempt to blitzkrieg across the Rhine hinged on capturing nine bridges near the Dutch cities of Eindhoven, Nijmegen, and Arnhem, where Frieda had hidden from the Arbeitseinsatz in spring 1943. If American, British, and Polish paratroopers could hit precise landing zones, seize the well-guarded bridges, and hold them long enough for Montgomery's infantry and armor to sprint across ninety miles of an open, elevated, single-lane road, they could blast open a quick strike path into Germany.

When Lieutenant Colonel Robert Cole, a combat veteran whose actions at Carentan were already the stuff of legend, saw his orders on September 15 or 16, he was stunned. He wrote an "eve of battle" letter to Allie Mae which, for security reasons, wasn't sent by the base post office until after the paratroopers made their jump. "At Normandy, we were all scared," he wrote. "Even I was scared. But this is beyond anything I have ever seen."

Operation Market Garden—"Market" for the air, "Garden" for the ground—would be the largest airborne operation in history: 34,000 paratroopers and glider infantry from multiple countries and divisions, 50 percent more than the D-Day landings. These paratroopers would be dropped much farther behind enemy lines—ninety miles!—than had ever been attempted by Allied forces. Risky. Very risky. But the reward, if it worked, would be a deathblow to organized German resistance on the Western Front.

And so, at 1:00 p.m. on September 17, three days after the liberation of Maastricht, Private Jacob Herman, Company D, 505th Parachute Infantry, 82nd Airborne Division, nineteen years old and barely a year out of Holy Rosary Mission in Pine Ridge, South Dakota, followed his stick out of a plane over Nijmegen, the Netherlands, to confront the enemy for the first time.

Thirty miles to the southwest, near the Wilhelmina Canal, Cole did the same with his 3rd Battalion, 502nd Parachute Infantry.

The jumps were similar, but the circumstances on the ground were not. Herman's stick landed safely and, within hours, secured their landing zone.

Cole's plane flew into ground fire so heavy that, just after his stick cleared the doorway, their plane burst into flames and crashed, killing the pilot and copilot. One of his units, Company H, was blown off target and became lost in a nearby forest. Cole barked over the radio for the men to head for their primary objective, a nearby bridge. Scattered landings were an airborne operation's lethal weakness. If the 3rd Battalion's three rifle companies couldn't form up, they risked being overrun.

After considerable scrambling, Company H found a road. But they had gone in the wrong direction, and the Germans were waiting. While Herman's company had dropped into relatively light resistance, Cole's paratroopers had unknowingly landed in the middle of Field Marshal Walter Model's reconstituted German Army Group B. Soon it was splintered trees, hastily dug foxholes, and a relentless barrage of automatic fire as Company H faced the Germans from opposing tree lines across an open field. One rifle platoon managed to claw its way up the road to within 100 yards of the bridge, but it was scattered by withering fire and forced to retreat. Out of 100 men, only fifteen soldiers and three officers survived.

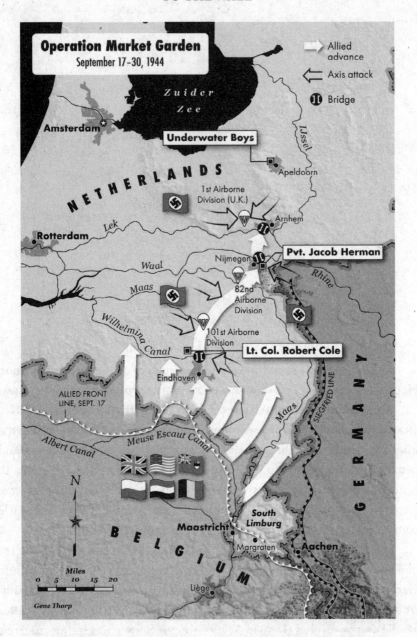

**Operation Market Garden**
September 17–30, 1944

Allied advance

Axis attack

Bridge

*Zuider Zee*

Amsterdam

Apeldoorn

Underwater Boys

N E T H E R L A N D S

1st Airborne
Division (U.K.)

Arnhem

*Lek*

Rotterdam

Nijmegen

Pvt. Jacob Herman

*Waal*

*Rhine*

*Maas*

82nd
Airborne
Division

101st Airborne
Division

*Wilhelmina Canal*

Lt. Col. Robert Cole

Eindhoven

G E R M A N Y

ALLIED FRONT
LINE, SEPT. 17

*Albert Canal*

*Meuse Escaut Canal*

*Maas*

SIEGFRIED LINE

N

B E L G I U M

South
Limburg

Maastricht

Aachen

Margraten

Miles

0   5   10   15   20

Liège

*Gene Thorp*

Around 6:00 p.m., Cole set out on a rescue mission, but stymied by rain, darkness, and enemy fire, even the hard-charging hero of Carentan was forced to dig in. Hours of pounding stalemate followed, as darkness swallowed the forest and running skirmishes echoed through the night. By the time Cole's men and Company H linked up, it was dawn of the following day. They tried a push for the bridge, but the German fire was too heavy, and by midmorning the battered 3rd Battalion had retreated back to the foxholes and the tree line.

As the men paused for rest, Cole pulled out a can of sliced grapefruit he had brought with him on the jump—a treasure in that time and place more valuable than diamonds—and shared it with two of his enlisted men, radioman Technician Fifth Grade Robert E. Doran and his loyal runner Private First Class John E. Fitzgerald. They shared a few words, a quiet communion over fruit. Then Cole turned to study the terrain: heavy trees, a small farmhouse, a flat field. The distance they needed to cover wasn't far, but the German fire was thick. He could hear the crack and sizzle as the bullets whizzed past.

*Naww*, he thought, *we ain't pinned down.*

He called for air support to knock the enemy back. Major Stopka, Cole's dependable XO, raced along the tree line, placing orange recognition panels and popping orange smoke grenades to mark their positions as a flight of P-47s came in low against the morning sun. The men dove for their shallow foxholes as the bullets snapped through the tree line. Despite the bright orange markers, the P-47s were strafing the wrong side.

"Commander wants you," someone barked at Stopka.

He sprinted to the command post, which was nothing more than a shallow trench. Cole was wiping blood and brains from his uniform. His radioman, Doran, had been trying to reach headquarters about the P-47 "roadhunt" when German machine gun fire took off half his skull.

"Take the radio," Cole snapped. "I'll take the panels."

Cole raced along the tree line through a heavy barrage, moving the orange panels to make them more visible along the P-47s' flight path. The planes came in low once again, but this time they strafed the enemy, knocking down their fire. Cole was near the edge of the forest, shielding his eyes against the sun as he watched a P-47 circle, perhaps contemplating its return angle and line of fire, when a single shot rang out from a small farmhouse on the other side of the clearing. His knees buckled, and Robert Cole went down.

His men were stunned. Cole was invincible. He was a pioneer of airborne infantry combat. He had jumped into Normandy. He had rallied seventy-five paratroopers behind enemy lines. He had led multiple near-suicidal charges against fortified enemy positions on the road to Carentan, and he had organized and emboldened his men. He had always come through. He had always *brought his men through*. And now, on the edge of a forest near the southernmost mile of what would become known as Hell's Highway, he was shot through the helmet and the temple, bloody, battered, and struggling for breath.

His men pulled him to cover. They yelled for the battalion surgeon, who was stunned to hear the colonel was down. He sprinted to the shallow trench and knelt beside his fallen commander. Cole's eyes were open, but the surgeon knew immediately it was no use. So he cradled the young father's head in his hands as Cole's loyal runner, Private Fitzgerald, pushed through the gathered soldiers and fell to his knees beside his leader, his commanding officer, a man he adored. It seemed only a moment ago that they were sharing a can of fruit.

"Why don't you do something for him?" Fitzgerald cried to the surgeon.

"I'm sorry, John," the surgeon said sadly as Cole blinked, looked skyward, then died. "There's nothing I can do for him now."

They wrapped Cole's body in a parachute. They placed him in a foxhole. In the frenzy of the battle, there was nothing but this hole, this shroud, the tools of his trade.

"It's the sniper!" someone yelled as a German ran from the farmhouse holding a rifle. A machine gun opened up, fired, kept firing long after the man was dead. Then a squad charged across the open field, in the berserker state that sometimes accompanies the death of a beloved comrade in arms, routing the Germans from the farmhouse without losing a man.

The next day, September 19, 1944, Private Jacob Herman and his 82nd Airborne company reached their main objective, a railroad bridge in the middle of Nijmegen. Halfway across, they came under relentless fire. Herman's young lieutenant dove for cover behind a boxcar. Turning, he noticed the replacement trooper, who had been advancing right behind him, crouching in the open. He yelled, "Get down, get down!" Then he noticed the neat round bullet hole through the center of Herman's forehead.

Jacob Herman's sacrifice, along with so many others, did not lead to the breakthrough Montgomery had hoped for. Market Garden pushed a sixty-five-mile bulge into the German front, but it came at the expense of an Allied attack on the port of Antwerp, which could have freed a million Dutch citizens while alleviating the Allies' supply problems. And the price, in terms of lost American and British paratroopers, was far too dear. While Montgomery's infantry and armor was able to reach the two American divisions, the British 1st Airborne Division was cut off and torn to pieces as they heroically attempted to hold the last remaining bridge in the face of a relentless German assault. Nearly half the men who dropped—15,000 British and American paratroopers—were killed, wounded, or captured in eight bloody days of fighting.

In the end, the operation was a plan too ambitious, a "bridge too far." Montgomery's army group didn't advance into Germany. The Allies didn't outflank the Siegfried Line and establish a bridgehead over the Rhine. The momentum rolled up since the breakout from Normandy was halted at Market Garden, at Aachen, and at numerous other points along the German frontier. By the end of September, Limburg was one of the few areas of the Netherlands firmly in Allied control. The retrenchment, to Eisenhower, was less a setback than a chance to build troop strength for a broad assault across the Siegfried Line and then the Rhine. He thought the buildup would take two months, but the U.S. Army would remain in Limburg for five months, through the bitterly cold winter of 1944–1945.

It was a coldness shared by Allie Mae Cole—a numbness—when she learned her husband was dead. She was notified on Friday, October 6. She kept her feelings in check, her heart together, for almost a week, until the following Thursday, when she met Cole's mother, Clara, for dinner at the officers' club—the Oak Room—at Fort Sam Houston. That's when Allie Mae, distraught, broke down in tears. Her beloved Robert had joined West Point's most sacred brotherhood, "the long gray line stretching for centuries told," of those who had given their lives for a better world.

Clara Cole, who had known her daughter-in-law nearly her whole life, looked at her sternly. "Losing a husband is devastating, Allie Mae," she said, "but it doesn't compare with the loss of a child."

That coldness—that emptiness and pain deep in the soul—was shared by Alice Herman when she learned her eldest son had died 4,000 miles from home, in a land she didn't know.

"He gave his life," she cried, "to the country that took our home."

Jacob "Sonny" Herman died a twentieth-century death, in a twentieth-century war, but his community honored him in the tradition of a Lakota warrior. They couldn't scatter his ashes from a high place or give a lock of his hair to the Keeper of the Soul, so they cut their own hair. Some of those who loved him cut their flesh. There was no spiritual center in which to hold a ceremony, because his community had been scattered by the U.S. Army Air Forces, but each evening before sunset, Mrs. Rough Feather, an elderly survivor of the Wounded Knee Massacre, traveled the high desert road from Kyle, South Dakota, to the Herman cabin in No Flesh Creek to weep with the family, and pray with the family, and sing the Akicita Honoring song:

> *Friend, I remember, Friend, I remember,*
> *Friend, I remember, Friend, they have gone.*
> *All over the world, soldiers went, I'm helping. . . .*
> *Friend, remember, Friend, they have gone.*

# PART III

# HOMEFRONT LIMBURG

— ★ —

## September 1944–January 1945

*The soldier is the Army. No army is better than its soldiers. The soldier is also a citizen. In fact, the highest obligation and privilege of citizenship is that of bearing arms for one's country.*

General George S. Patton
Commanding General, Third United States Army

# CHAPTER 34

# THE PROCESS

— ★ —

*Margraten*
October 1944

T he U.S. mobilization for World War II was an enormous undertaking. Frieda van Schaïk was right when she marveled at the American tanks rolling down the Bemelerweg: the time, energy, effort, money, and brainpower expended to assemble those tanks, build the boats to carry them across the Atlantic, train the men who crewed them, deliver them to the battlefield, and then use them to push an enemy as formidable as Nazi Germany back 400 miles toward their last redoubt was extraordinary for its muscle power and persistence as much as its strategy.

And that's before considering that, in September 1939, the United States had only 189,867 active-duty soldiers, making it the seventeenth largest army in the world, after Romania. It had 1,600 airplanes, mostly obsolete, and 380 ships of all classes, only 159 of which were warships. As for tanks: only 35 had been built between 1920 and 1935. The first new order, for 329 M2A4 light tanks, wasn't placed until October 1939.

Less than five years later, nearly 1,100 American vessels (including landing craft) and more than 8,000 American aircraft supported the D-Day landings. An extraordinary display of raw tonnage and power, and much of it built by women, who by October 1944 made up 22.3 percent of the workers in the American iron and steel industries.

And planes and boats were only the biggest, showiest items. Even a partial list of the other supplies the Allies transported across the Normandy beaches in the six months after D-Day is staggering:

- 137,000 jeeps, trucks, and half-tracks
- 4,217 tanks and tracked vehicles
- 3,500 artillery pieces
- 300,000 telegraph poles
- 16 million tons of fuel, food, and ammunition
- 240 million pounds of potatoes
- 54 million gallons of beer
- 1 million gallons fresh drinking water (in the first three days alone)
- 210 million maps
- 10 million vomit bags
- 2.4 million tent pegs
- 800,000 pints of blood plasma

And this doesn't include the 850,000 men who came across the beaches in June 1944—or the 260,000 wooden grave markers. The Americans would need 2,500 of those markers within the first 24 hours. By the end of operations in Normandy in August, they would use another 16,300.

The 260,000 grave markers attest to the number of soldiers war planners assumed would be killed defeating Hitler and his forces. They also attest to the respect the United States was intent on providing each of its fallen soldiers. The remains of every dead American, to the best of the Army's ability, would be recovered. The remains of every dead soldier would be identified, so that no family was left without word of their fallen loved one. Every man or woman would be buried in their own grave, under their own serial number and their own name, so that each would remain an individual, fallen in a global conflict but honored and valued for the life that they had led.

The U.S. Army reflected the beliefs of the society that produced it: that freedom and democracy, the ideals for which it was fighting, meant valuing every life. Sacrifice was necessary, but sacrifice was more than duty; it was a sacred gift to be revered each time it was given.

This emphasis on respectful burial may seem obvious. We might think it inhumane to do anything less. But past efforts had been sporadic. On April 3, 1862, in the midst of the American Civil War, the War Department issued a general order declaring it the duty of Union Army commanders to identify and bury their dead in individual graves with registered wooden markers. In practice, though, retreating forces usually left behind their dead, so burials fell to the victorious army. Mass graves were dug, one for those in Union blue and another for those in Confederate gray, and dead bodies dragged into the pit by a rope tied to their legs. Some bodies were never recovered, left to rot or for someone else, usually the farmer whose land had become the killing field, to bury. Some mass graves weren't marked. In the best cases, the bodies were covered with a blanket and a few feet of soil, but the dirt of many burial pits was measured in inches, not feet.

President Abraham Lincoln's Gettysburg Address, delivered on the grounds of one of the Civil War's greatest battles, paid respect to the dead by giving meaning to their sacrifice while issuing a challenge to the living:

> Fourscore and seven years ago our fathers brought forth, on this continent, a new nation, conceived in liberty, and dedicated to the proposition that all men are created equal.
>
> Now we are engaged in a great civil war, testing whether that nation, or any nation so conceived, and so dedicated, can long endure. We are met on a great battle-field of that war. We have come to dedicate a portion of that field, as a final resting-place for those who here gave their lives, that that nation might live. It is altogether fitting and proper that we should do this.
>
> But, in a larger sense, we cannot dedicate, we cannot consecrate—we cannot hallow—this ground. The brave men, living and dead, who struggled here, have consecrated it far above our poor power to add or detract. The world will little note, nor long remember what we say here, but it can never forget what they did here. It is for us the living, rather, to be dedicated here to the unfinished work which they who fought here have thus far so nobly advanced. It is rather for us to be here dedicated to the great task remaining before us—that from these honored dead we take increased devotion to that cause for which they here gave the last full measure of devotion—that we here highly resolve that these dead shall not have died in vain—that this nation, under God, shall have a new birth of freedom, and that government of the people, by the people, for the people, shall not perish from the earth.

Stirring words of appreciation and respect . . . and yet the stench of rotting bodies was so potent that Lincoln's audience could barely breathe. The battlefield was so full of ravaging animals that wild dogs were dragging corpses out of shallow graves, even as Lincoln invoked the "honored dead." This was four and a half months after the end of the battle.

In practice, it was usually only officers who were buried with honor and given their own marked graves, although some towns sent wagons hundreds of miles to pick up their dead and transport them home. It wasn't until after the Confederate surrender at Appomattox that the Union Army exhumed its dead and transferred them to national cemeteries. By 1870, four years after the end of the war, 299,696 of the approximately 360,000 Union soldiers killed in the war had been buried. Only 58 percent were identified. The Confederate dead were not permitted to be buried in national cemeteries. To the victor go the rules of commemoration.

During World War I, a concerted effort was made to rectify these nineteenth-century shortcomings. Soldiers who died in field hospitals were buried beneath grave markers, either in existing local cemeteries or, later, in battlefield burial grounds. But those who died on the battle-field were rarely recovered, in part because they were dying in such large numbers. It was left to their comrades in arms to bury them in small mass graves or individually where they fell, often with a simple wood or iron cross. Many photos of the trenches show them pockmarked with these crosses.

The nature of modern trench warfare, though, made even this level of honor and remembrance difficult. Bodies in no-man's-land between trenches were often left for weeks, until a short ceasefire could be arranged to recover the dead. Men disappeared in tunneling operations. Trenches collapsed, burying whole units. Artillery blew apart bodies. It was common in some battles, such as Ypres, for living soldiers to be pulled down into the sucking mud of shell craters, never to be seen again. The front moved back and forth over a limited area, trampling and upending graves. By the second half of the war, artillery, mortars, and bombs not only killed living soldiers but blew apart the bodies of dead and buried soldiers too.

Most countries developed special organizations, called graves registration units in the U.S. Army, to identify and mark graves near the front lines, establish cemeteries, keep records, and inform friends and family members of their loved ones' deaths. In many ways, they succeeded. The Faubourg d'Amiens Cemetery in Northern France, for instance, contains the graves of 2,650 British Commonwealth soldiers who died there. Only ten are unidentified. Respectable, until a visitor sees the stone memorial carved with the names of the 34,725 Commonwealth soldiers missing after the battle. The Germans had more than 80,000 missing soldiers at Flanders, assumed dead but never found. At Verdun, there is an ossuary: a building piled high with the bones of 130,000 dead men never identified.

In World War II, the U.S. Army intended to do things differently. No mass graves. No memorials to the missing carved, as at Faubourg d'Amiens, with the names of 92 percent of those lost. It was the duty of the living, as Lincoln preached, to honor the dead, and for all of 1942 and much of 1943, this burden fell on officers and soldiers at the tactical level, much as it had in the Civil War and World War I. Combat units handled extraction, identification, and burial, usually designating their quartermaster troops—those responsible for cleaning, cooking, and supplies—to handle the task. In the smaller-scale North African campaign, this proved effective. But it was ad hoc and unorganized. Units were handling deaths and burials in different ways, with few formal rules or guidelines.

With the planned invasion of Fortress Europe, American generals knew casualties would surge. The ad hoc system would have to be replaced. The first theater-wide graves registration effort was implemented during Operation Husky, the Allied assault on Sicily in July 1943. Specialized companies, under the direction of the Army's Quartermaster Corps, planned and conducted recovery of remains and burial throughout the battle space. Their dedication is evident in Chaplain Fowlkes's story of the graves registration soldier who searched three days for one missing pilot. No task was too hard, or too dangerous, when an American was missing.

On September 11, 1943—the same day friendly fire brought down twenty-three airborne transport planes—War Department Circular 206 officially created the American Graves Registration Service (GRS), a new organization under the command of the quartermaster general designed to standardize policies across all army groups and theaters. By D-Day, the GRS had refined procedures for quick retrieval, field identification, and burial. That's why Normandy's cemeteries are so complete and close to battlefields. Operation Overlord was, among many other things, a breakthrough in the practical handling of combat deaths.

The process began when a platoon of GRS soldiers (between twelve and twenty men) set up a collecting point just behind the front line. The objective, according to GRS handbooks, was to remove bodies quickly "but in a most considerate manner," so as to "sustain the morale of the troops."

Combat units often took their own dead to the collecting point. This was the most basic and heartfelt honor fallen soldiers received: the devotion of friends. Many of these men had been honored where they fell, like Lieutenant Colonel Robert Cole wrapped in a parachute, the tool of his trade, by his heartbroken men. The collecting point offered another opportunity for commemoration, especially if a graves registration officer was present for buddies to identify their friend's remains and provide the details of his death for GRS records. This testimony was a solemn ritual, even in the midst of battle. To say his name, and briefly recount his final moments, was a soldier's good-bye.

Once the pace of operations slowed, the GRS soldiers scoured the battlefield in teams of four, carrying out the dead on stretchers. Many bodies were difficult to find, since they were dressed in camouflage and hidden "behind banks, mounds, hedges, rocks, trees, fallen logs, arbors, in ruined buildings, or in any place offering the slightest degree of protection." As the GRS field manual stated, in almost poetic terms, "Self-preservation is the first law of nature, and these actions spring from no lack of bravery—rather they are the result of the calm courage of good judgment and training."

In the heat of summer, bodies might bloat to twice their original size. GRS troops learned to roll these corpses onto their stomachs, put a knee in their backs, and push. "One develops a strong stomach quickly," a GRS soldier recalled, "the gas escaping is the worst you will ever encounter."

In winter, a body might freeze to the ground. It might decompose, from the bottom, where the rot was hardest to see.

If a man had been hit by large-caliber weapons, as many pieces as possible were recovered. No part of a soldier was intentionally left behind. If several men had been killed by mortars or heavy artillery, the pieces were gathered on one stretcher and sorted later.

"As gruesome as it may sound," that same GRS soldier wrote, when a shell exploded inside a tank, "a mess kit cup and spoon were the tools of the trade."

At the collecting point, GRS soldiers covered the bodies (or body parts) with white cloth out of respect, especially if they were "mangled or in an unpresentable condition." Once their names and service details were recorded, the bodies were loaded onto trucks. The standard vehicle was a three-quarter-ton weapons carrier with a trailer, which held about fifteen bodies. When available, two-and-a-half-ton trucks, the famous Deuce-and-a-Halfs, could haul 150. The trucks delivered the bodies to the designated burial area, ideally within two days, where the details of their injuries and deaths were identified and recorded by medical technicians.

The GRS did this for every American soldier. Every one. It did this for every Allied soldier who fell in a joint operation. It did this for every human being recovered, even enemy soldiers. All remains were evacuated, evaluated, and cataloged. Every person was buried with respect, as an equal, side by side, without regard to rank, religion, sex, or color, even as the United States failed woefully to apply that basic fairness to its Black citizens and other minorities at home.

Initially, the Wehrmacht did this for the Allies. The respect they showed the body of James Norton when it washed ashore on the north coast of the Netherlands was the same they afforded thousands of Allied dead. Their care allowed the bodies to be identified and gave grieving parents like Dr. Jamie and Miss Ed Norton a degree of closure. The Germans were so diligent in the burial of Allied soldiers and airmen in Sicily that even Patton, a noted hard-ass and Nazi hater, forwarded his positive assessment up the chain of command.

Of course, it was impossible to identify every soldier, no matter how rigorous the GRS effort. Some bodies were too badly mangled. Some slipped through the safeguards of the system. In some operations, like Market Garden, the fighting was too intense and remote for timely extraction. Robert Cole, as a beloved commander, was buried by his men in a field grave as soon as the fight allowed. The British Army's 286th Battery, 97th Anti-Tank Regiment, 51st Highland Division, which was able to eventually reach and rescue Cole's ravaged 3rd Battalion, found the grave near the tree line, a hundred yards south of where he fell, marked with his dog tags. The GRS attached to the 101st Airborne had begun digging a graveyard, only to be thwarted by a shallow water table, so the Son U.S. Military Cemetery, near Eindhoven, was established on higher ground. Robert Cole was disinterred and buried there at 5:00 p.m. on September 19, 1944, the day after his death, still wrapped in his parachute, just as his men had honored him.

Cole was fortunate. Most of the paratroopers who lost their lives during Market Garden were not able to be buried by their men. Many fell beyond the reach of the infantry, and thus the GRS. When their bodies were finally recovered, they were too decomposed to be identified. Unidentified bodies were cataloged with an *X* and a number in place of a name. The 82nd and 101st Airborne Divisions in Market Garden had some of the highest percentages of unidentified remains in the European Theater.

Son was a common type of GRS cemetery, established near a battlefield at the division level. There were four American field armies in Europe, and three of them—the First, Third, and Seventh—buried their men at the corps or division level. This kept them close to the battlegrounds where they died, since corps commanded divisions that fought together. The cemeteries in Normandy were organized at the corps level.

Lieutenant General William Hood Simpson, commanding general of the Ninth Army, a man complimented by Eisenhower as "excellent in every respect," saw it differently. The Ninth Army assumed control of the southern Netherlands from the First Army, the army that had liberated Limburg, in early October 1944. On October 22, it set up its headquarters in Maastricht, in a Catholic school two blocks from the Michiels van Kessenich home. That same day, it assumed control of the XIX Corps and the famous 30th Infantry Division, known as Old Hickory, the liberators who had marched and rolled down the Wycker Brugstraat to the cheering of the citizens of Wyck.

General Simpson made a promise to his soldiers: no man under his command would be buried in Germany. To Simpson, that was leaving a man behind. More importantly, he said, *his soldiers* felt the same way, and he would never disrespect their wishes by leaving their bodies in enemy soil.

At the time, the Ninth Army GRS was sending its dead to Henri-Chapelle, First Army's cemetery twelve miles southeast of Maastricht, across the border in Belgium. That wasn't practical for an 80,000-man field army being positioned for the next major offensive. The Ninth Army needed its own cemetery. Given General Simpson's promise, the logical place to put that cemetery was in the liberated territory closest to Germany, where most American lives in the next offensive would be lost: the Dutch province of Limburg.

And so, in the first week of October 1944, Captain Joseph J. Shomon, a forester from Connecticut with a background in engineering, arrived in Maastricht. As the commanding officer of the 611th Quartermaster Graves Registration Company, Shomon was responsible for siting, plotting, and overseeing the Ninth Army's cemeteries.

Every GRS officer took this work seriously. They did not know if the cemeteries they were establishing would be permanent—the Army would evaluate that when the war was over and the body count known—but they treated each with the respect of a final field of honor. In Shomon's case, the details felt especially important, since the cemetery he established would be the only one for his army. Even before the Ninth Army officially took command of its area of operation, he was driving the roads of Limburg, conferring with local experts, searching for the ideal location. The fighting in the eastern reaches of Limburg and along the Siegfried Line was fierce; the Ninth Army was losing more than 100 men a week. The need for a cemetery was pressing.

Soon, Shomon found the perfect site: a rolling piece of land twelve miles northeast of Maastricht near the town of Sittard. The bulldozers arrived on October 17. Almost immediately, an artillery commander came running, screaming, "What the hell are you doing?"

But saltier. Far saltier.

An American artillery battery was hidden behind the ridgeline where Shomon's engineers were churning up the muddy ground to build the cemetery's entrance. The enemy was only a thousand yards away. The commander was enraged because the Germans had mistaken the bulldozers for tanks and began firing toward his position. Clearly, the area was too dangerous for a cemetery. The work was called off, and Shomon went looking for another site.

His search took him south to the Rijksweg, the primary road between Maastricht and Aachen. The Rijksweg was the road the Wehrmacht had rolled down in May 1940 as arrogant conquerors. It was the road they used to flee the Netherlands—and the oncoming U.S. Army—in September 1944. It was the road where, from her attic window, Frieda van Schaïk looked out across the orchards and heard horsemen galloping home in disarray. For Shomon, the Rijksweg meant access to supplies from Maastricht and a convenient way to bring back bodies from the front.

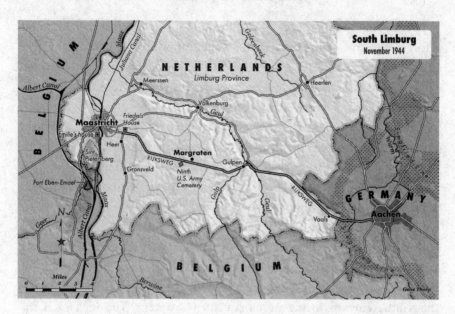

It was the village clerk of Margraten, Joseph van Laar, who alerted Shomon to the advantages of his small village of about 1,500 people. Margraten was a classic Limburg farming community—fruit orchards and wheat fields, horse-drawn carts, the outdoor ovens used to bake traditional breads and pies—but it had ideal access to the Rijksweg, which went right through the center of town. Van Laar spoke English, one of few in the village who did, so he personally showed the Americans around. Shomon was considering another site, but Van Laar suggested a piece of farmland a half mile west of the village center. It was on a high ground of gently rolling hills close to the Rijksweg, but screened from the road by a row of trees. This was important because, while a finished cemetery could inspire morale, a cemetery at work—with unburied bodies—could easily damage it.

When Van Laar, who became Shomon's primary translator, told the GRS captain it was not only a working farm, but the finest farmland in the area, Shomon was undeterred. "Listen, Joe," he replied, "even the best soil is not good enough for our boys."

By day's end, the Ninth Army had a site for its cemetery.

# CHAPTER 35

# LENDING A HAND

— ★ —

*Emilie Michiels van Kessenich*
October 1944

"I am not looking forward to their visit," Emilie Michiels van Kessenich wrote in her Memory Book about Major General Charles "Cowboy Pete" Corlett, the commander of the XIX Corps, and his staff, who were coming to their home for a meeting with Manka and other Maastricht officials.

It wasn't that she didn't enjoy entertaining official guests, or that she wasn't good at it. She was the wife of a mayor; she knew how to host a social event.

And it certainly wasn't that she disliked the Americans. Everyone in Maastricht loved the Americans—except the Nazi collaborators, of course, many of whom had been rounded up and marched through the streets to the cheers and jeers of crowds. The Americans were polite. They were optimistic. They smiled. They didn't bark orders, harass, or steal. The Germans wore hobnail boots. The sound of metal on cobblestones as they marched was the constant *click-clack, click-clack* of impending doom. The Americans wore rubber-soled boots. Even their silent strolling lifted the spirits.

Not that the Dutch were quiet in those first few days of liberation. They poured into the streets in jubilation, thankful, unburdened, relieved to finally be free. They rushed out of their houses to hug their liberators on the second, third, even fourth day after their arrival. They cheered when American tanks rolled past for the tenth or twentieth time. They stood in the streets, watching the soldiers. Rejoiced in old friends. Laughed with acquaintances. Brought out their last hidden bottle of liquor and shared it around.

When little Hubert Michiels van Kessenich, eight years old, received a piece of gum from a GI, he was so excited he started jumping up and down. He had never chewed gum; it was an American invention. He almost popped it into his mouth . . . but then, what about his brothers and sisters?

The children decided to share it. Hubert chewed first, since it was his gum, then passed it to Willem, the oldest. He chewed it and passed it to his twin, Eduard, who chewed and passed it to Jenneke, and on down the line by age until it got to Louis, the seventh child, who was six years old. Louis swallowed it.

"It didn't taste like anything!" he yelled, as if that was an explanation, but Mathilda, the next in line, was crying. Before Emilie could intervene, Willem and Eduard had Louis upside down by the legs, trying to shake the gum out. They were laughing, but Mathilda was genuinely disappointed when the gum didn't reappear.

"Did you know?" a teenage neighbor came running in a few days later, screaming for Emilie. "Did you know? Your husband is driving through town with Prince Bernhard!"

Willem had been reinstated as mayor by Queen Wilhelmina's government shortly after American forces arrived. He was busy, night and day, trying to help the city back onto its feet. But as the senior Dutch official in Maastricht, it was also his honor to welcome the prince, who was on a goodwill mission to thank the Americans and raise morale. For security reasons, the visit had been kept a secret. Even Emilie wasn't told.

"You are so thin," the prince said, when the two men met in the beet field where Bernhard, piloting the small plane himself, had landed.

"I would be ashamed to be anything else," Willem replied.

They rode in a U.S. Army jeep across a pontoon bridge built for tanks and transport trucks by an American engineer unit. Wild applause greeted the dashing husband of their beloved Queen Wilhelmina's eldest daughter, Juliana, as Prince Bernhard toured the first, and so far only, major Dutch city liberated by Allied forces.

*Wonderful,* Emilie thought.

Then she remembered the note Willem had left her that morning:

*You must be home and dressed at 3:30 p.m. because I am expecting an urgent conversation with some gentleman and may need your help.*

The gentleman was the prince, she realized! He was already in Maastricht. And there was precious little food in the house, especially food fit for a prince.

So sandwiches were thrown together quickly, quickly. The sitting room was converted to an entry suite. Agnes scrubbed the children with a wet cloth and threw them into their best clothes. And the prince appeared! Suddenly, right there, in Emilie's living room! But only for a quick hello, no sandwiches, before he and Willem had to sneak out the back door, past a basket of dirty diapers, and through the garden to avoid the crowds. They wouldn't have been able to make it to city hall for Bernhard's speech from the balcony otherwise.

The next day, Dutch flags were flying across the city. That night, September 19, the streetlights came on in Maastricht for the first time in years.

On September 20, a local paper admonished:

*It is very difficult to defend one's self against the amiability of the Americans. They are like magnets to people. They don't show it at all when one stands in their way. And yet: we are hindering them. We are standing on our toes against their vehicles. We clamber onto their vehicles out of enthusiasm, we gather in groups right in front of their columns of tanks, we want to give them souvenirs. . . . And the Americans are smiling!*

*And yet: we are hindering them. Do stay off the streets, because there is a war on, and it really is not a circus which is making its triumphant entry.*

The Allies had wrested air superiority from the Luftwaffe, but a few German fighters appeared almost daily over Maastricht, despite American reconnaissance planes and antiaircraft batteries. The front was so close, a chorus of artillery fire rang clear. V-2 rockets were often overhead. Their distinctive *whoosh* meant safety for those in Maastricht, since the rockets were hurtling toward France or England. If you saw but didn't hear one, though, you ran for cover, because the rocket had malfunctioned and was going to crash. When a German V-2 destroyed the butcher shop of a notorious NSB collaborator, it was both a delicious irony and a warning.

The day after liberation, Emilie had taken the mattresses out of the basement, where the family had been sleeping since the botched Allied air raid on the rail station a month before. Almost immediately, a bomb explosion rocked the city. It was enormous. It scared her almost to death. She moved the family back into the basement. The war was still too close.

The streetlights, so glamorously turned on, were turned off again to deny the German pilots easy targets.

So there were good reasons—practical reasons—why she wasn't excited to entertain the leaders of a U.S. Army corps. Reasons beyond her family being malnourished and her continuing recovery after a long convalescence at the hospital. Beyond the fact that she had children to raise, and a household to run, and lessons to teach in the afternoon. Beyond even the fact that she had nothing to serve to such distinguished guests. As the mother of ten in a barely liberated city, she was simply too fatigued for an evening of conversation, even with a general.

"I am not looking forward to their visit," Emilie had written, but she changed her mind after meeting them. "They are all so down-to-earth," she wrote, "showing such great interest, and warmth, that the evening passes by very quickly, one of the most interesting that I've ever had."

The next day, Emilie rode her bicycle to the XIX Corps headquarters to return a pack of cigarettes General Corlett had left behind. The city was a mess: branches down, bridge spans collapsed, mud in the streets. But it was a beautiful day. She could almost smell the excitement, the joy, in the late summer air. To be riding her bicycle, without fear of being stopped or harassed. To be out, on a quiet morning, making a social call.

She had just reached the gate in front of the American headquarters when the air raid siren blared. A German plane appeared in the sky. Emilie saw the small black objects floating behind it, heard the whistling as they fell, but nothing could mar this beautiful day, this crisp, new feeling of freedom. It wasn't until the MPs scattered for cover that Emilie realized what was happening and dove into a nearby bed of plants.

She stayed there, face-down in her finest dress, until she felt someone tugging gently at her elbow.

"You're alright," he said, pulling her up. It was General Corlett himself, smiling kindly. The bombs had fallen somewhere else. The general was calm and clean. Emilie was a bit shaken as she brushed herself off.

"I brought your cigarettes."

"I left them for you," Corlett said. A valuable gift, since American cigarettes were a prized form of currency in Maastricht. "But it is so nice you came."

"And it's as if I've landed in a fairy tale," Emilie wrote in her Memory Book that night. "I am taken inside, given real coffee, cookies, chocolate, and everyone is so warm and nice! I am taken home in a magnificent sedan, my bicycle in a truck behind it!"

More amazing: When Manka fell ill later that day, Corlett arranged for a U.S. Army doctor to come straight away. Manka received medicine that night. Medicine had been nearly unattainable under German occupation.

Two days later, Emilie and Manka were summoned to the white house next door, formerly the residence of the representative of the Reichskommissar, Wilhelm Schmidt. The Americans had taken it over when they arrived.

The liberation of Maastricht had not only released a great outpouring of joy, but a pent-up rage for revenge. Collaborators were mocked and beaten, both before and while being paraded through the streets to the police station. Some turned themselves in to the Americans, fearing for their safety. The heads of young women who had fraternized with German soldiers were brutally shaved while bystanders cheered, often resulting in cuts to their scalps. Then the Dutch poured tar on their bald heads. Neighbors, perhaps succumbing to the petty grievances that build up during a long and stressful occupation, denounced each other, often with little or no evidence. Hundreds of people were arrested. Soon, the jails were overflowing.

In that scrum of accusations, someone complained to the Americans about their mayor. Accusations were made about his conduct in office. They revolved around the morning of the German invasion, when the adjutant to the commander of the 4th Panzer Division demanded Willem provide the names of ten prominent citizens to be held as hostages in the event Dutch partisans wounded or killed German soldiers.

There was an oft-repeated story of the mayor of a Limburg village telling the Germans, when they made a similar demand for hostages, "My name will have to do. I'm sorry. I don't know anyone else in this town."

At that exact moment, the parish priest walked by. "What about him?" the German officer asked.

"Oh, you can put me on the list," the priest said, when he heard what was happening. "The mayor is right. It is only the two of us here."

Some Maastricht citizens believed *that* was how their mayor should have responded to the German demand. No one was accusing Willem of being a collaborator. He certainly was not. The NSB itself confirmed that, stating in a secret assessment from April 11, 1941, that Willem was "opposed to National Socialism . . . likewise the NSB," and any indication he had "pro-German leanings" was "mere pretense." But the fact that his name was not on the list of hostages condemned him, in the eyes of some, and rendered him unfit to be returned to office.

Emilie thought the accusation shameful. She believed in her husband's integrity. Of course she did. She loved him. She knew that he strived, always, to do what his Catholic faith and his duty as a public servant told him was right. She had no doubt he had done the best he could in difficult circumstances.

The Americans must have come to the same conclusion. Or perhaps they simply didn't want to undermine the government of a fragile, newly liberated city, or interfere with a decision rendered by Queen Wilhelmina. Willem continued as mayor.

About a week later, on October 15, he delivered a speech from the balcony of city hall, welcoming the Americans. General Corlett stood beside him on the balcony. Below them, members of the Old Hickory infantry division that had liberated Maastricht stood at attention. A thousand Dutch citizens, maybe more, crowded into the square.

"We understand so well how hard it must be for you to be here far from your homes, your wives, children, and friends," Willem said. "We know how you have left your work, your studies, your comfort; how you are risking your lives; and our most heartfelt thanks are going out to you."

His remarks included a farewell: General Simpson's Ninth Army was assuming control of the area of operations from the XIX Corps, and General Corlett was being transferred to Honolulu, where he was to take command of the XXXVI Corps in the Pacific Theater.

"I had an uneasy time standing at attention 'on the spot,' while the Burgomeister read his long speech," General Corlett admitted in a letter to Eisenhower. This probably had little to do with the length. Corlett was exhausted from the long push from Normandy. The weather was cold and rainy. And Willem gave his speech in both English and Dutch.

Afterward, there was a reception at city hall. Emilie, at ease, glided confidently among the American military officers and Dutch civil servants, some of whom she hadn't seen since before the occupation. There was champagne to toast the victors, but she didn't drink alcohol, and she didn't need it; she was giddy already. To be here with their liberators. To speak freely, once again. To mingle unafraid. To hear her husband's speech, with the Market Square full of free Dutch people. She looked across the room at Manka. He was chatting with an American officer, smiling, wearing his uniform of office. It hung loose off his shoulders. He was so thin.

*We can never thank them enough,* Emilie thought, as she approached General Corlett to say her good-byes.

"Is there anything I can do to help you?" she asked him.

It may have been a formality. She may not have expected an answer. But Corlett had one. "You can organize diversions, like pleasant dance meetings with Dutch girls and boys, for my frontline soldiers," he said.

The XIX Corps had entered Aachen on October 2. It was a "skeleton city," observed one American officer, destroyed by a relentless Allied air campaign. "You can read all kinds of descriptions of the destruction caused by air raids, and see any number of pictures, but the sensation of being in one of these dead cities just can't be imagined."

But Aachen wasn't dead. Amid the rubble and teetering facades, the Wehrmacht hounded the leading edges of Eisenhower's forces in fierce urban combat. By October 15, General Corlett's men were physically exhausted and psychologically worn down by the weeks of vicious, close-quarters fighting. A few nights of "pleasant dance meetings" was the kind of wholesome fun they needed to revive their fighting spirits.

"I will, sir," Emilie replied. "Yes, gladly, I will."

She would have done almost anything, really, for the army that had driven back their occupiers, for the boys who set them free.

# CHAPTER 36

# TROUBLE

— ★ —

*Bill Moore and John Low*
October 1944

The failure of Operation Market Garden was a costly setback for the Western Allies. For those still trapped in Nazi-occupied Netherlands, including the citizens of Apeldoorn, it was a disaster. Having advanced almost 450 miles from the beaches of Normandy, Allied forces had been turned back less than twelve miles from the house where the Underwater Boys were hiding. Expecting liberation, or perhaps because of simple bad luck, the Apeldoorn Resistance group had admitted a new member without vetting him carefully. The young man, only twenty-one and from Amsterdam, passed information to an SD (Sicherheitsdienst) officer. On September 30, four days after British Field Marshal Montgomery's audacious plan to cross the Rhine collapsed at Arnhem, the SD used this information to round up Mary's cell.

De Vries, the man who had shared his gin with the Americans, talked his way out of custody, rushed home, and guided the English pilot he was harboring safely out of town. Two other airmen, an American and an Englishman, were seen coming out of a safe house in the custody of the SD, the Englishman's face bloody and clothes torn. Within hours, eight Dutch Resistance fighters had been captured, including their leader, twenty-five-year-old Narda van Terwisga, a.k.a. Mary.

Aart escaped. He had been sick for a month, so he had no contact with the others while the SD informant was in their midst. As soon as he heard what was happening, he rushed out to find someone to take the five

Americans hidden in his attic. Someone who had never been associated with Narda van Terwisga's Resistance group and therefore couldn't be identified when—and it was almost certainly a when, not an if—one of the arrested members broke down under torture.

Around 3:00 p.m., a man John Low and Bill Moore had never seen arrived to take them to a new location. Even Aart didn't know where they were going, in case he was captured and interrogated. He, Jaap, and Jaap's wife were fleeing town. Mother was going to pretend to be bedridden and ignorant of anything that had gone on in her house. Her husband, Abe, said he was too old to leave his wife, and he was not afraid to die. It was a risk, but a man in his eighties must be allowed to make up his own mind.

The good-byes were hard. The Underwater Boys had come as refugees. They had been taken in against Mother's wishes and despite the fears. But they were leaving as family. Bill Moore, who kept his emotions close, was touched. He hugged Mother, said a few words to Jaap in Dutch.

It wasn't just Mother who cried. She just cried the loudest.

And then they were out in the street, following a man they had never met. Five months in hiding, never having set foot outside, and here they were, blinking against the sunlight. They were wearing civilian clothes, walking casually, but Low imagined every window held eyes, every passing person noticed the strangers. If they saw any German patrols. If they had to show identification. If anyone asked them anything in Dutch. There were so many things that could go wrong.

And then, suddenly, they were inside. The moment had stretched forever, but the house was barely around the corner. It had only been a three-minute walk.

Their new savior was an older woman. She was sorry, she said in English, she could only shelter them for a few days. Her boarders were out of town, but they would be back at the end of the week. She took the airmen to her attic, where a false wall in a closet concealed a hidden room. That was the strength of the Dutch Resistance: it was mostly small, independent groups. The woman had clearly sheltered people. She lived just three minutes from Aart. But even now, thanks to the intermediary, they had no knowledge of each other.

Once again, Bill Moore, John Low, and the Underwater Boys settled in. The failure of Operation Market Garden was a crushing setback. Listening to radio reports of the Allied progress, they had felt so close to freedom. Now, the chance was lost. And who knew how long it would be before it came again?

At least the old woman's secret closet was large enough to stand up, with just enough space for two small beds. The five men had to take turns, but Moore and Low slept on a real mattress that night for the first time since England, five months before.

"I'm praying for Mother," Bill Moore said, as he lay in the darkness. There was a light in the secret room, but they didn't dare turn it on.

"I'm praying for them all," Low replied. They could hear shouting outside. The roundup was still underway.

The woman left for the grocer at ten the next morning. Within half an hour, she was back. The Germans were displaying dead men in the streets, she said. They were hanging signs on their bodies labeling them terrorists, and saying anyone who removed the bodies in the next three days would be shot. Two of the dead were the American and English airmen captured by the SD the morning before. Six were resistance fighters, including a man Moore and Low knew as Photo Joe, because he made fake identities.

Low thought of his wedding anniversary, when De Vries had brought him a cake, and Mary brought flowers. Certainly a nicer celebration, Low had thought grimly, than Jo's lonely one in Laurel, Mississippi.

Now Mary was under arrest, and their hostess was near panic. The Underwater Boys decided to wait until nightfall, then slip away. It was a grim decision. Hundreds of German soldiers had been pushed back by Operation Market Garden into the Apeldoorn area. Killing five more American airmen meant nothing to them.

Soon after, the old woman left again, this time to see the mysterious man who had brought them to her. She returned in better spirits. The Germans were hunting spies and saboteurs, she said. It was unsafe for them to leave. They should stay in her house. She would spend the night with a friend and return the next morning. "Put a candle in the window," she told them, "if it is safe for me to come in." And don't worry. Her friend would come up with a plan. Then she prepared them a meager dinner, packed a bag, and left before the 8:00 p.m. curfew.

The other three Underwater Boys went upstairs to the secret room, but Moore and Low stayed downstairs. They made a small fire in the large fireplace, cherishing this small chance at comfort. Soon, they began talking. After five months together, they were more than pilot and bombardier. Although they never said it to each other, the men were brothers: the quiet one and the talker, the responsible one and the adventurer, a relationship forged in a harrowing experience only men in combat could understand.

A knock at the door, and immediately, they fell silent. It was dark. No streetlights. No uncovered windows. Nothing but the flickering of a small flame. Low peeked through the blackout curtain and saw two men at the front door, Gestapo agents, he was sure of it, with their guns drawn. Moore snuck to the rear window and saw another at the back.

*Up*, Moore signaled to Low, and Low nodded. They may have been brothers, but when it was time for action, they knew their ranks and roles.

Low started up the stairs, not an easy task since it was "as dark as the inside of a black cow's stomach," and the stairs creaked. He tiptoed as quietly and as quickly as he could, staring into the pitch blackness in front of him. At the second-floor landing, he looked behind him and realized Bill Moore wasn't there.

In the flickering light, he could see his pilot crouching beneath the back window. Moore must have seen him stop, because he raised his hand, as if to say, *Keep going*. He smiled, just as the Gestapo broke through the doors.

Without hesitation, Bill Moore threw open the window and leapt out. The Gestapo agents shouted, their attention drawn away, and Low took the opportunity to climb the rest of the way to the attic. He fumbled through the dark, searching for the hidden door, terrified of making a sound. He found it so quietly that he startled the other three Underwater Boys, who were crouched inside, listening intently. Low hissed to indicate he wasn't Gestapo, they hissed back, and the four of them hunkered down in the secret room as the Germans began searching the ground floor.

When the creaking told them the Germans were making their way to the second floor, they decided they couldn't wait for Moore any longer and pulled the trapdoor shut, sealing themselves inside. There were no windows. They didn't dare turn on the light. They could hear the Germans in the attic and then, suddenly, in the closet that hid the secret door.

Low held his breath. My God, the inhaling of the man beside him was deafening. They were captured, for sure. But after what seemed like forever, the Gestapo agents left.

"Where's Bill?" someone whispered.

"I don't know," Low admitted, "but I don't think they got him."

Should they run? Low dared his flashlight to check his watch. "Let's give it two hours," he whispered, as the other men nodded in the gloom.

Ten minutes later, the Gestapo agents were back with reinforcements. They began to pull apart the walls and flooring. The Underwater Boys could hear the violent tearing. A German, or maybe a Dutch collaborator, entered the closet. They could hear him tossing the clothes. He tore away the shelf that dropped down to cover the edge of the secret door. For a second, nothing. Then he yelled for his comrades.

A moment later, there were several men in the closet, beating at the wall. Low could taste their blows vibrating loose a cloud of dust. A crowbar was jammed into a crevice. Again, the terrible tearing, but this time at their door. The four men slunk back, but there was nowhere to go. Boards were ripping. Fingers were crawling through, prying for leverage. On one, Low saw a swastika ring. His mind said, *Give yourself up, end this thing*, but he was too afraid to move.

Then, just as suddenly as it had started, the tearing stopped. The men started arguing. One dropped the crowbar. It hit the floor with a clang. More arguing. A few last half-hearted taps, as if searching for a secret lever. Then they moved on. The old woman's secret room was a miracle; it had survived a direct assault.

Low clicked on his flashlight. "Two hours," he whispered, resetting the time until they would leave. The Underwater Boys nodded, their faces grim.

Several men came back one last time, an hour later, but only to loot. "Two hours," Low said again, setting the time forward once they had left.

Eventually, more than six hours after the Gestapo arrived, the Underwater Boys—all except their leader, Bill Moore—pushed open the secret door, exited the ransacked closet, snuck down to the back door, and ran.

They made it out of the city. After walking for three miles, they came to a farm. It was nearly dawn, so they hid in a haystack. The farmer was friendly. He helped them hollow out the top of the stack to form a room. Covered with a tarp, the hole was dry and sheltered from the blowing wind and pounding rain, so the Underwater Boys—now four, not five—settled in, exhausted, scared, depressed, and even more alone.

# CHAPTER 37

# TRANSITIONS

— ★ —

*Emilie Michiels van Kessenich; John Low*
October 1944

O n October 17, two days after the reception with General Corlett, thirteen-year-old Eduard Michiels van Kessenich received permission from the Americans to cross the border to Belgium and stay with one of Manka's colleagues from the paper mill. A doctor had diagnosed him with malnutrition, and the Belgians had more rations. They had sophisticated black markets, developed during World War I, and Eduard could be fed more easily there.

On October 18, a soldier with a "bright white star on his jeep" drove Emilie to Valkenburg and Heerlen. The family car had been confiscated by the Germans during the occupation, and even if she'd had a car, civilians weren't allowed to travel that far. She met with friends from her social circle and charity work to discuss logistics for Corlett's dances. She needed female leaders, meaning ladies looked up to by other women, since women did not hold official leadership positions in Limburg Province in 1944, to help her compile a list of appropriate girls. Her dances would be chaperoned. Transportation would be offered by the Americans to and from their homes. But the girls must, Emilie insisted, have sterling reputations. She wanted the kind of girls any mother 4,000 miles away would want her son to meet.

She worked through a steady rain. She worked around Eduard's illness. She worked, even though General Corlett had returned to America that morning. She worked not *despite* being a mother but *because* she was a mother of ten, and no one had ever asked her to do anything like this before.

"I'm entering a curious stage in my life," she noted in her Memory Book, on the night she returned from Valkenburg. "So far, I've not really done anything but look after the household and the children's education—and giving birth in between! But now, after General Corlett asked me to set up this organization, my days are filled."

He could say nothing of his rescue, John Low told the British journalist. He could tell him everything up to the Underwater Boys in the haystack, but the four months after that, nothing. The failure of Market Garden had scattered and stranded the remnants of the British 1st Airborne Division. The British, with the help of the Dutch Resistance, had organized a rescue mission, Operation Pegasus, to bring the paratroopers home. Several downed Allied airmen were swept up in the operation and its sequel, Pegasus II, including John Low and the three men hiding with him. At the time of the interview, not long after Low's arrival in England, Operation Pegasus was top secret, because the British were preparing more rescue missions. He was under orders not to speak of his journey from the haystack to his home base.

One detail, though, he did share. On the Allied side of the line, just before sailing for Britain, he ran into Dick, the undercover British operative who had met with them in the Van Kliests' attic. Dick had spoken with a Dutch Resistance fighter who had escaped a prisoner of war camp. The resistance fighter mentioned an American he had met there: a pilot named Bill Moore.

# CHAPTER 38

# THE STRIPPING LINE

— ★ —

*Margraten*
November 1944

The 117th Infantry, one of the 30th Infantry Division's three regiments, freed the Dutch border village of Cadier en Keer on September 13, meaning they passed within a mile of the Van Schaïks' home on the first day of their liberation. Like most combat troops, they didn't linger. By October 2, they were on the northern outskirts of Aachen, attacking the Siegfried Line. At the end of the month, after brutal fighting, Aachen was in American hands. U.S. forces were on the far side of the city, still in the meat grinder of the Siegfried Line. The 117th Infantry's job was to slug their way toward Düsseldorf, maintaining pressure on the Wehrmacht and preventing them from regrouping at the Rhine, where they would make a perilous Allied crossing more difficult.

On November 18, after two days of particularly intense fighting, they reached Warden, yet another heavily defended village barely ten miles past Aachen. The plan was to attack at 7:30 a.m., but the commander of the supporting tank company insisted the German anti-tank guns be knocked out by artillery or aircraft before exposing his men. The 117th Infantry charged in without the tanks and were driven back by machine-gun fire. They attacked again in the late morning, with the tanks firing from cover, not advancing with the exposed infantry. They were driven back a second time, with even heavier casualties.

Finally, the tank company commander was replaced, and eleven tanks, each with four infantrymen riding on the outside and hundreds charging on the ground, roared into Warden. The fighting was fierce, pillbox to pill-box and house to house, but by 7:30 p.m., the village had been cleared.

The 117th lost several hundred men in and around the village of Warden. In the second assault alone, Company B, usually comprising about 190 soldiers, lost more than seventy men. One platoon, about forty soldiers, lost all but six. The leader of that platoon was Second Lieutenant John Land, a student of the Medical College of South Carolina who had completed officer training before shipping for Europe in summer 1944. John Land died in that battle near Warden, twenty-three miles east of Maastricht. He was twenty-four years old.

Almost as soon as Land fell, the GRS stepped in. His body was transported to a temporary collecting point behind the line, perhaps by his men, perhaps by GRS soldiers with stretchers. His name was recorded, his body covered with a white mattress cover. After the battle, he was loaded onto a truck with dozens of other fallen heroes and driven back through Aachen and down the Rijksweg to the Ninth Army cemetery at Margraten.

On arrival, the bodies were unloaded at the stripping line. When it was Land's turn to be processed, his remains were stripped of weapons and ammunition. This was a dangerous job, since soldiers often clutched weapons primed to fire, wore ammunition damaged by the violence that killed them, or held grenades with the pin pulled, their stiff, locked fists the only thing keeping them from exploding. That was the reality of war: one instant you are in the thick of it with your buddies, fighting for your life; the next, you are frozen in time, forever clutching your last chance in your fist.

Once disarmed, Land's body was carried to a canvas tent, where his identity was confirmed using dental charts and the two dog tags worn by soldiers around their necks. Eyewitness accounts were considered definitive if the dog tags were missing—for instance, when a head was severed. If neither dog tags nor first-person accounts were available, the medical sergeants took fingerprints, although identification required all ten fingers. Odd anatomical features and tattoos were noted. All injuries were marked on a crude outline drawing of a human body. The cause of death determined.

Land's cause of death was succinct but devastating: "SKULL CRUSHED. REMAINS COMPLETE."

The medical technicians worked quickly, because the bodies were often bloody and fetid. John Land died in the cold. It was snowing by November, so his body was intact, except for his skull. In warmer weather, pieces softened and fell off. Wounds putrefied. Entrails slid out. GRS medical sergeants were issued rubber gloves, but they were cumbersome and easily torn, so many handled bodies with their bare hands. They suffered septicemia, a blood poisoning caused by bacteria in the corpses. It caused blue streaks up the arm and a knot in the armpit. If untreated, it could be fatal.

But the work never stopped, because trucks pulled into Margraten every day with viscera spilling out beneath the tailgate, with arms or legs sticking out of tarpaulins, with bodies piled to the roof. There was no end to the killing and dying, so there was no end to the work at Margraten.

This work was vital. Identifying John Land meant he could be buried beneath his name. His mother and father in South Carolina could be notified. Land had married his college love, Elizabeth, in the backyard of her mother's home, two days after he was commissioned a second lieutenant. The young couple were "prominently connected throughout South Carolina," a local newspaper noted. They were happy, hungry for life, barely back from their honeymoon when Land shipped off to Europe. Now Elizabeth, like thousands of other young brides, rich and poor, north and south, white and Black, was a war widow, heartbroken and bereft.

At Margraten, John Land's personal effects were cataloged: a billfold, four souvenir coins, his wedding band. A pair of eyeglasses, a wristwatch, a pipe, tobacco, and second lieutenant bars. They were boxed and shipped to a depot in Kansas City, where local businessmen and women stepped in to help the Army deal with the enormous amount of storage, sorting, and shipping, and then on to Elizabeth and his parents—after checking for appropriateness, of course. The GRS was in the business of accounting for the dead, not caring for families, but they tried as best they could to lessen the trauma. That didn't always happen. Dr. Jamie and Miss Ed Norton's year-long wait for their boys' effects was devastating. But for most, the process worked, even as the volume of personal objects reaching Kansas City exploded. Elizabeth Land must have been saddened and comforted, as much as any widow could be comforted, by the return of her husband's wedding ring. He had worn it for a year and a half.

And then, when everything was cataloged and bagged, examined and noted, the final step: two GRS soldiers lifted Land's body from the table and carried it out of the tent. When they reached the burial ground, they placed it in a line of bodies waiting to be buried. Not so bad, really—until the soldiers walked back to retrieve another body, revealing another stack of corpses, in a long line of stacks, disappearing into the freezing rain of Limburg.

# CHAPTER 39

# A NECESSARY TASK

— ★ —

*Jefferson Wiggins*
Fall 1944

Jefferson Wiggins, still only nineteen after more than two and a half years in the Army, stepped ashore on Omaha Beach at 10:30 a.m. on September 13, 1944, the day the Old Hickory division reached the Maastricht neighborhood of Wyck. More than three months had passed since D-Day, but Normandy was a beehive of activity, as soldiers and supplies came and went from temporary harbors. If ever there was a sight to make a man feel small, this was it.

Wiggins was assigned to the 960th Quartermaster Service Company, an all-Black unit led by white officers. When the 960th shipped to Glasgow, Scotland, in February 1944, Wiggins and his fellow Black soldiers rode crammed on the lowest deck of USAT *Frederick Lykes* with several hundred other Black soldiers, while the white soldiers rode on the decks above. No windows, since they were under the waterline. No private rooms. No air circulation, except for two large fans. With only brief daily walks on the outdoor deck for fresh air, the Black GIs made their own entertainment: dice, cards, Bible study. The saving grace, for Wiggins, was the gospel singing. The Black singers were so good that white soldiers descended into the holds to hear them.

It was a time, he noticed, when people who were nonreligious, who were nonbelievers, became believers, because no one was sure if they would survive what was coming.

Jeff liked the men in his unit. He liked his commanding officer, Captain William O. Solms, an upper-class Southerner whose father owned hotels in South Carolina and Georgia. Solms was fair, and he respected his soldiers. The men were so efficient moving supplies that, after the unit's first work assignments in England, they received a commendation.

Now here he was, finally, crossing the English Channel to the fight. A few days later, his company trucked through Saint-Lô, France, known as the Capital of Ruins because 90 percent of its buildings had been destroyed by aerial bombardments and a major battle in July, fought primarily by General Corlett's XIX Corps. A tearful French woman stood with a backpack, indifferent to the destruction around her. "You don't know what it is to lose your freedom, and then to regain it," she said as the 960th passed. "You cannot know how much this means."

*Madame*, Wiggins thought, *you have no idea.*

By November, the 960th was outside Sittard, ten miles northeast of Maastricht. One night, Captain Solms pulled Staff Sergeant Wiggins aside before lights out. "Get your platoon together, Sergeant," he said. "We're moving out in the morning."

"Where to, Captain?" Wiggins asked, although he assumed it would be more of the same: cleaning, warehousing, inventory, supplies.

"You'll see," Solms said. "Just make sure the men are ready."

They drove southwest to a school in the village of Gronsveld, the Netherlands, five miles southeast of Maastricht. "Don't let anyone sleep too hard," Solms told Wiggins, as the men were climbing into their sleeping bags. "We have to be out of here by 0430."

"Where to?" Wiggins asked again.

"You'll see."

The next morning, not long after sunrise, the lead vehicle in the convoy ground to a halt, half a tire deep in mud. Bulldozers were struggling up the ridge 100 yards ahead, moving logs. There was nothing else around but fields, a few trees, some rough olive-drab tents on the horizon line. Wiggins assumed the truck was stuck, until he saw Solms step down and begin to walk the convoy, telling his men to dismount. It was a few days before Thanksgiving, and it was dull and gray, the cloud cover thick and the precipitation pounding down, a mixture of ice and rain. It was so cold

Wiggins could feel the sharpness in his chest, so wet his uniform stuck to his skin the moment he stepped off the back of the truck. In the distance lay a vast field of mud, soggy and sucking, chewed to hell and riddled with sinkholes and mounds. Black soldiers were crawling across it, heavy tools in their hands.

"I know this is the most gruesome task that any of us has ever had to do," a white officer began, as the 960th formed up. It was Captain Shomon. "But it is a necessary task. I don't envy you, but at the same time I don't feel sorry for you because someone has to do it. The graves have to be exactly 6 feet deep, 6 feet in length and 2.5 feet in width. Every single grave. Sometimes a chaplain will be here, sometimes not, but you have to bury the soldiers respectfully. It will be hundreds a day, so remember that each young soldier you bury could have been you, your brother, or your cousin. He is a fellow American."

*Graves?*

Wiggins recoiled. He looked out at the muddy field with horror. The ground was foul and full of holes. The stench was overpowering. Wiggins had smelled that odor on his journey across France and Belgium, had tasted it on his tongue when it was at its worst, but it had never been this bad. It was the smell of death. The biological fact, not the idea. He wondered why he'd never placed it before.

*Graves?* he thought. *Hell no.*

If he had read the Quartermaster Field Manual, he would have known this was a possibility. Helping the Graves Registration Service was a listed duty. But that was not something the officers told the men of the 960th Quartermaster Service Company, and they had received no training in handling bodies or digging graves. Other men, probably Black men, must have been trained for it, Wiggins reasoned. A company of Black grave-diggers was already working. Surely the Army wouldn't force the 960th to join them. Regular quartermaster duties like supply and transport felt mundane, suggesting the Army didn't trust Black soldiers with complicated work. And yet that work was paradise compared to this freezing, hellish field. The Army couldn't do this to him. Could it?

"You'll be given a pick and shovel," Captain Solms said, and that was it, pep talk concluded.

As Wiggins walked to a tent to requisition his shovel, he watched the Black men of the other unit, the 3136th Quartermaster Service Company. Each was laboring at a hole, he could see now. Above them, white officers walked the rows, inspecting their work. He turned away in disgust . . . and saw the piles, fifteen or twenty, covered with tarpaulins and a rim of ice. The bodies, he realized, were underneath.

"Move along," a white officer said.

The weather had been brutal since the middle of October: rain almost every day. The road to the cemetery was supposed to take one engineering company three days to build, but no matter how much they bulldozed and packed the dirt, it was impassable by morning. So Shomon sent trucks to the destroyed city of Aachen to bring back rubble for a roadbed. No matter how many layers of rubble they put down, it disappeared into the mud. Finally, he sent men to the Dutch-German border to cut down trees. They laid the trunks across the road, tied side by side frontier style, then held in place with massive iron spikes. It was called a "corduroy road," and it worked. Finally. What was supposed to take thirty men three days had taken 400 men forty days.

And all that time, Ninth Army soldiers were dying and being sent to the First Army cemetery at Henri-Chapelle. Only in the last couple weeks had the bodies been trucked to Margraten. But already there were so many.

*And so many more*, Wiggins thought, *yet to come.*

He walked to the nearest stack of bodies. He lifted a corner of the tarp.

He saw what he expected, a young man like himself, but white. Almost all combat soldiers were white. Wiggins dropped the tarp and turned away. "Where are the coffins?" he asked the nearest white officer.

The officer laughed. "No coffins."

Jeff Wiggins couldn't believe it. Even his sister Othel was given a coffin, and she was a poor Black girl in Alabama.

"You'll get used to it," the officer said.

He was wrong. Most of the men of the 960th never got used to it. But they fell to their work like the soldiers they were. At 4:30 p.m. on that brutal first day, in Plot C, Row 4, Grave 99, they buried Second Lieutenant John Land.

# CHAPTER 40

# ENTERTAINMENT

— ★ —

*Emilie Michiels van Kessenich*
Fall 1944

Maastricht was full to bursting. The city was the headquarters for the Ninth Army, so for operational safety, the border with Belgium was closed to trade and civilian traffic. The curfew for citizens was 8:00 p.m. No one was allowed to travel more than ten miles from their home without a pass. Guards checked identification on the bridges, and antiaircraft guns and combat companies ringed the town.

Meanwhile, the Allied war machine kept rolling forward, thousands of officers and headquarters support personnel, many stationed in Maastricht, and tens of thousands of soldiers, many headed to the front. Tanks and trucks and artillery rumbled past the Michiels van Kessenich home and across the temporary bridge a thousand feet away. The Americans established a huge open-air ammunition dump in a field behind the railway station in Wyck. Once full, they piled their ammunition along the Rijksweg, which rumbled with military traffic all day and most of the night. They requisitioned public buildings for offices and barracks, and asked the citizens to billet American servicemen. Throughout the South Limburg region, people offered their homes. The Dutch appreciated their liberators. They wanted to help. Plus, billeting American soldiers paid in rations, and food was scarce.

And that was before the soldiers encountered the horde. They came stumbling out of a driving rain, hungry, terrified, dragging their children and elderly with them. They were human shields, evacuated from the

eastern Limburg city of Kerkrade and forced at gunpoint onto the road by the retreating Germans. They knew Allied army doctrine required the care of civilians before troops advanced. They figured this crowd would cost the Allies a week. But in every town the refugees entered, the Dutch provided them food and temporary shelter in barns, public buildings, and their homes. Then, Major Leo P. Senecal and his U.S. Army Civil Affairs Detachment C1E1 arrived. In less than a day, Senecal's soldiers assessed their condition and found them food, clothing, transportation, and more permanent shelter in twenty-three Limburg towns and villages. It would have been an impressive feat for a few hundred refugees. It was miraculous for 30,000.

Major Senecal, in civilian life the mayor of the small town of Chicopee, Massachusetts, was the head of the U.S. Army Civil Affairs office for the province of Limburg. He was said to have scrambled across the Maas River on the rubble of the Wilhelmina Bridge on the morning of the liberation of Maastricht, and whether that was true or not, the people of Limburg loved him for it. It symbolized his determination to do his job and help the Dutch. Since access to Maastricht was curtailed by the military authorities and almost all its rations and supplies were provided by the U.S. Army,

Senecal and his officers controlled the life of the city. Willem Michiels van Kessenich, while technically the mayor, answered to him.

Conditions were far from ideal. There was no fabric. No rubber or bedding. No bicycle tires. Before the occupation, there had been 800 delivery trucks in Limburg. Now there were only 350, most in a state of disrepair. In Maastricht, there were only seventy-three. There were almost no cars, so even if they had access to supplies, the citizens couldn't transport them. The Red Cross distributed clothes to children six to fourteen years old, but otherwise no clothing could be bought at any price, even undergarments. Seven thousand citizens never received a voucher for shoes.

Space was so tight that the Americans closed the city's schools. They needed the classrooms for offices and billets. While American soldiers were offered beds by thankful citizens, refugees who managed to escape from parts of the Netherlands still under Nazi control were often shunned or vilified, accused of eating into the city's limited supplies. Most found themselves at the mercy of Senecal and his ingenuity. So it wasn't just schools turned into housing and offices. Soon, it was stores and factories and public buildings too.

The most pressing need was food. The Germans had ransacked the rations depot before their retreat. The cattle had been slaughtered, and the fields trampled. There was canned meat, but only a little, and no butter. The only flour was for brown bread, and even that was limited.

"Our distribution is miserable," a Maastricht woman wrote on October 18, the day Emilie traveled to Valkenburg and Heerlen. "There has been only one allocation of meat in 5 weeks, and that is 125 grams [about a quarter pound], bone included, per person."

The daily ration had fallen to 990 calories, less than half the amount needed by a healthy adult. It was less food than the Germans had distributed, even in the worst months of the occupation.

And yet, Emilie Michiels van Kessenich was optimistic as the rainy October crept toward a cold and rainy November. She was fortunate, that's true. Willem's position gave her access to the highest reaches of the Ninth Army's leadership, and she was often invited to events: the ribbon cutting for the reopening of the Sint Servaas Bridge, a fund-raising piano concert for the Red Cross, the "world premiere" of the movie *Rhapsody in Blue* at the home of General Simpson. Because of her contacts, she had been able to get Eduard a pass to Belgium, where the effects of his malnutrition were waning. The family was hungry, like everyone, but she no longer feared her children starving.

Her optimism, though, was for the future. After years with the enemy, the citizens of Limburg were now among friends. They weren't really free, not with so little food and so many travel restrictions, but they no longer had to fear arrests, death sentences, or reprisals. They no longer had to worry about the next revolting Nazi law or action. These might be hard and hungry days, but they were great days too. *The Lord is my shepherd.* Thanks to Him, and the U.S. Army, her children would grow up free, and there was nothing more for her to want. In the meantime, she had faith that Major Senecal would solve the city's most pressing problems, because Willem believed in Major Senecal.

And Emilie believed in her work. In addition to being the Ninth Army's headquarters, Maastricht had been designated its recreation area. There were other recreation areas in Limburg, but Maastricht was the largest. Even in the midst of the struggles, the Americans were converting the historic city-center buildings once occupied by the Germans into theaters, Red Cross clubs, and kitchens for their soldiers' rest and recuperation.

"May the diverse entertainment to which the city of Maastricht welcomes you," read a letter from Mayor Willem Michiels van Kessenich accompanying a cartoon map of the city center, "be a slight compensation for the hardships you went through and the sacrifices you made in order to bring it its freedom."

This was no debauchery district. Senecal and the Americans were respectful partners. They worked with church leaders, especially the Catholic leaders who dominated the life of the province, to make sure the entertainment was in line with local morals. There were plays, concerts, and tours of area sights. Church services in English at the Catholic and Protestant churches on the Vrijthof Square. The Americans took over hotels, so the soldiers could have clean beds, hot showers, and hot meals, cherished luxuries for troops who had spent weeks in muddy foxholes in the rain.

Still, Emilie knew the primary activity in the city-center clubs was drinking. She knew the prostitutes were busy in the Stokstraatkwartier, a poor area of the city, where for a decade she had done charity work with a local priest.

That's why her dances were important. Emilie had lived through the terror of war: hiding in her basement during bombing raids, cowering from artillery and small arms fire. She knew the nearness of death the soldiers must be feeling, because she had lived with it too. And yet, she could barely imagine the horror of the front. She had only been near the shooting. These boys were being shot at. They were charging into enemy fire. They were watching their friends die. They were not much older than her fourteen-year-old twins.

Drinking wasn't healthy. It only blotted out the pain and fear. The prostitutes carried the possibility of disease. Her dances were *good*. They were simple affairs with chaperones, real American coffee and donuts, and no alcohol, where the soldiers could chat with nice girls—the ones who spoke English, at least, and she had managed to find quite a few—about nice things. Where they could touch a woman lightly on the arm and back during a nice American song. Where they were reminded of the free society they were fighting and dying to preserve, and the happiness that awaited them back home. They were the perfect wholesome distraction, Emilie thought, from the hardship of war.

So she was shocked on October 31, when an urgent appeal "To the Girls of Limburg" appeared in a local newspaper. The subtitle, in a box below the title: "How girls can help maintain and increase the glory of our nation." The text read, in part:

> The girls have already been urged from the pulpit in a number of parishes of the liberated parts of our fatherland to restrain themselves and behave with dignity. Sensible people who mean well … have made similar appeals in the newspapers. … [But] Priests and the government are almost powerless in this regard. THE GIRLS THEMSELVES can and must avert this looming danger. Exemplary behavior is needed. …
>
> We fully understand that everybody wishes to express their gratitude to the soldiers that have liberated us. … We fully understand … that any other, less charitable welcome should not have been expected. We understand therefore that fathers and mothers invite the soldiers to have a pleasant evening in their family home. … [But] What we offer to the soldiers should make them a better person and a better soldier. We should seek to avoid anything that could put the soldier at risk. … This most certainly includes the flirtations of many girls in the dark evening hours.
>
> We therefore also feel that we must point out the risk involved in the dancing evenings that some feel should be organized. We do not doubt that such suggestions are well-intended.
>
> M. Jenneskens, Head of Catholic Action, Meerssen

Emilie was a conservative Catholic, offering a nice evening to battle-weary men at their liberators' request. She and Willem had met at just such a chaperoned dance, way back in her youth, and she knew how invigorating a night of talking and laughing with a kindred soul could be. She found the accusation that she would turn a blind eye toward canoodling, much less that it might lead to fornication, deeply disappointing, if not outright insulting.

She clipped the article out of the paper and pasted it into her Memory Book. Underneath, handwritten: "The opposition is now becoming stronger and wider; not a single founded complaint is ever presented."

# CHAPTER 41

# NEW FACES

— ★ —

*Frieda van Schaïk*
Fall 1944

Like most Limburg girls, twenty-two-year-old Else Hanöver, Willem Michiels van Kessenich's secretary, didn't need dances to meet American soldiers in fall 1944. She had hustled downstairs to the Wycker Brugstraat on the second morning of liberation as soon as she saw a tall, lanky soldier leaning on his jeep outside her apartment building. A group of Americans were moving into the Victoria Inn on the corner, and she was worried. German soldiers had been quartered in that hotel, and she had seen them entering the building with a large box just before their retreat.

The soldier eased himself up from his lean and told her he'd look into it. "Don't worry," he told her an hour later. "My lieutenant and I searched the building." There were no bombs.

The next afternoon, a blast shattered the ground floor of the hotel and hurled a dozen American soldiers through the windows into the street. A soldier had sat down to play the dining room's piano. A key was struck, a booby trap tripped, and a bomb exploded. The piano-playing soldier, Private William Greentree, was killed. Many others were injured, mostly by flying glass.

Soon, there was a knock at Else's door. It was the soldier from the jeep, Staff Sergeant Wilson Clifford White, of the 247th Engineer Combat Battalion. He had his lieutenant at his side and his hat in his hand. "Excuse me, miss," he said. "Do you know of any other buildings occupied by Germans?"

"Oh, yes," Else said. They kept a list at city hall.

White took the list and rushed to examine the buildings. Several more booby traps were found. When White came to thank her for keeping more soldiers from being blown through more windows, Else invited him to her parents' home. The least she could offer one of their liberators was a home-cooked meal. The Hanövers didn't have much, but Sergeant White didn't mind. He hadn't had a home-cooked meal in almost a year.

The drive between the front lines and Maastricht was only a half hour, and Staff Sergeant White had access to a jeep, since his job was to inspect bridges and other installations. He often dropped by the Hanöver house for dinner. He always brought gifts. Else's favorite was a jiggly block of pink meat.

"It's called SPAM."

"It's wonderful."

White just shrugged his shoulders. He'd been eating it since his unit landed on the Normandy beaches on D+5.

Soon, he was bringing his GI friends. So Else invited a few of her own friends, and they did what "M. Jenneskens, Head of Catholic Action" and the other moral scolds feared: they danced to records in her bedroom until the 10:00 p.m. curfew. The GIs took to calling her Glamor Girl, a phrase Else didn't understand, since she wasn't familiar with the English word "glamor." Whenever she asked about it, they laughed and said, "Just like a glamor girl."

Not every interaction was so innocent, of course. The war was a massive cultural upheaval in a conservative Catholic area where, before the war, horse-drawn carts had been far more numerous than cars. The younger generation, deprived throughout the occupation, had been thrown into a more modern world, and many were eager to explore it.

Plus, the Americans were handsome, the girls thankful, and the proximity of death a powerful incentive to throw caution—and cultural norms—to the wind. "Pernicious" relations were inevitable. The 130 or so out-of-wedlock babies born in Limburg in 1945—and those were just the ones officially reported—were the proof.

But most Dutch girls were like Else Hanöver, or Frieda van Schaïk, who spent the first weeks after liberation talking with Americans GIs who stopped to rest in the nearby orchards. It was a beautiful time. The weather was ideal, the apples so ripe the soldiers ate them straight from the trees. Pappie chatted and shared cigarettes with the soldiers, and Frieda joined them when her chores were done.

There was nothing scandalous about these encounters. The soldiers were on their way to the front. The conversations were a diversion of a few minutes, or at most an hour, and besides, Frieda had made that wartime promise to Peter in Arnhem in spring 1943, that they would marry after the war. She didn't consider it serious, and Peter was trapped on the occupied side of the front line, unable to write. But Frieda was a woman of her word. She didn't flirt. But she always asked the soldiers if they wanted her to write to their mothers.

By October, the weather had turned rainy and nasty, and the Van Schaïk household returned to the way it was before the occupation: a constant buzz of activity. But the joy was missing. It was tempered for the same reason Frieda's sisters had raced home. Moekie had suffered another stroke.

It was probably the cumulative effect of the last four years of hunger and worry, and especially of those painful ten days near the end when Wim was a captive of the Gestapo. But it was a cruel irony to survive the German occupation, only to be stricken in the first few months of freedom.

She nearly died. When Frieda sent a message to her siblings, *Come quick, Moekie is ill,* she wasn't sure her mother would survive. All the children responded except Wim, who had been hiding with Resistance friends in Rotterdam (now inaccessible on the other side of the front line) since his imprisonment, and Jacoba, a Red Cross nurse in Belgium. The family wasn't sure how to reach her. Their only option was a Resistance radio broadcast that had been used throughout the occupation to communicate with people far away. The message was simple: "SOS, Jacoba van Schaïk, come home." Fortunately, a Dutch truck driver who had worked with the Resistance heard the plea. He knew Jacoba, and he regularly drove from Belgium to Limburg. (Smuggling, of course, as the border was closed.) He smuggled Jacoba home.

By the time she arrived, it was clear Moekie would recover. But she was frail, and thus the household burden fell on Frieda, her youngest and most accommodating daughter. So Frieda was home working, as usual, on the brisk, clear October morning when a Civil Affairs officer stopped Dave van Schaïk as he bicycled along the Wilhelminasingel.

"Excuse me. Can you tell me the way to the big church in Maastricht?"

"Catholic or Protestant?"

"Protestant, I'm afraid."

"You're in luck, friend. I'm going there myself." Dave stepped off of his bike. "Walk with me."

After the service at Sint Jans Church, Dave invited the officer to the house. It was a long walk from the center of the old town, but the men chatted the whole way. Limburg was a multilingual province, but Dave's conversational English was rare.

"We have a visitor," he declared, throwing open the front door. Frieda was in the kitchen, finishing the afternoon meal. She stepped out in her apron to find a handsome man in uniform, about forty, his hat in his hand. Her sisters and brother-in-law were already crowding around him, thanking him and shaking his hand.

The arrival of Captain John A. Hoadley was a blessing. He spent the afternoon with the Van Schaïks and, after that, seemed to spend every spare moment at their home. He would drop by unannounced, with rations or cigarettes for Dave. Despite Moekie's continuing weakness, there was an open invitation to the family table, and he tucked into potatoes and greens from their backyard garden many a night. Hoadley worked at a Red Cross substation a short distance down the Bemelerweg. He was a Civil Affairs officer, but lower ranked than those Willem and Emilie Michiels van Kessenich knew. Still, he was able to provide medicine for Moekie and real coffee for the family.

Hoadley had a habit of asking his fellow Civil Affairs officers if they had anything planned for the evening. If not, he'd say, "Well, I have some wonderful people for you to meet." And then two, three, or four middle-aged officers would appear at the Van Schaïk door.

It was like the evenings with the amateur scientists before the war. No matter when Hoadley's friends dropped in, they were welcomed. They chatted and smoked for hours with Dave, enthralled by his knowledge of the history, geology, and biology of his small corner of the Netherlands. His adventures in the caves, his stories of maps and skeletons and bats: the Pioneer of Sint Pietersberg had returned, in fine form.

Hoadley and his fellow officers were educated, accomplished professionals, and Frieda, nineteen, found herself eavesdropping on their conversations as she filled their drinks (non-alcoholic) and emptied their ashtrays. They were good company, unfailingly polite, and she enjoyed their kind eyes, their quick laughter. And, like everyone, she was eager for information about how the war was progressing. She often lost herself as she listened in on the conversation, standing with her serving pitcher thinking, *This is what I remember, this is how it should be,* until Moekie, who was getting stronger, touched her lightly on the shoulder and whispered, "Come away now, girl. It's almost midnight. Let the gentlemen have their fun."

# CHAPTER 42

# PAPA

— ★ —

*Emilie Michiels van Kessenich*
November 1944

Emilie Michiels van Kessenich met Major Leo Senecal, the Civil Affairs officer in charge of Maastricht, at a luncheon for war correspondents in early November. Afterward, he made a point to drop by their house for a visit every few days. She knew it wasn't just for her, though they loved each other's company, or even Willem, whom he worked with almost every day. It was for the children too. Senecal, a fifty-one-year-old bachelor who lived in a small house in his small hometown a few blocks from his mother, was smitten with the Michiels van Kessenich clan. There was something about seeing children going about their lives in the middle of a war that inspired the lifelong bachelor.

The children loved Senecal in return. Papa Senecal, as they called him, was a funny little man, not much over five feet tall, with jug ears. He always brought a gift, usually food. The ration situation was improving. By November, the citizens of Maastricht were receiving 1,200 calories a day. By December, they would be at almost healthy nutrition levels. Still, it was nice to get extra treats for the children.

One afternoon, he brought a tin of sardines, and the children all sat around the table with Papa Senecal at one end and Emilie at the other. Plates were passed, and each child received one sardine, in a little pool of oil. Emilie-Hélène, almost three and a half, gulped hers down right away, then grew restless.

"What's the matter, darling?"

The little girl came over and whispered in her mother's ear.

"Yes," Emilie whispered back, "but under the table."

"What is it?" Senecal asked, when he saw Emilie-Hélène grab her plate and ooze out of her chair. "What's she doing?"

Louis looked under the table and laughed. "She's licking the plate!"

Emilie looked at Senecal, who looked back at her and laughed. "Great idea," he said. "Please, lick your plates."

Soon all the other children were laughing and licking the sardine oil off of their plates.

Afterward, the adults went to the sitting room. The resistance of the Catholic clergy to Emilie's dances had spilled over into the general population. Young Dutchmen complained that they couldn't compete with the American soldiers, who could offer Dutch girls chocolate and nylon stockings.

"We do not wish that girls, *who now sell their honor for a pack of cigarettes, a piece of chocolate, etc,* will after this time be on a line [respected as highly] as other, honorable girls," read anonymous announcements in the papers. "The Dutch boys, who during the occupation put their lives on the line in underground actions, went into hiding or sabotages, are no longer sufficient because, yes . . . *they have no good gifts to offer.*"

The Americans responded by posting notices warning soldiers of venereal disease.

Ignore it, Senecal advised. He wouldn't have approved the dances if the soldiers, and their commanding officers, didn't want them. You have to understand, he said, that a soldier's two-day pass is not a weekend. They are not issued automatically. Some are for good behavior or a tough job well done. But many are for soldiers the commanders can tell are weary, scared, or in danger of breaking. The fighting at the front was brutal. Bloodier than some people of Maastricht comprehended. Some of the men had been fighting since D-Day. A night in a clean bed, with a hot meal, after a dance with pleasant girls, wasn't a luxury, Senecal explained, it was vital to the mental and physical health of the Ninth Army.

The voices against you are loud, Senecal said, but they are the minority. I assure you, the Americans and the Dutch are great friends, and the more they know each other, the greater those friendships will be.

On November 17, Emilie visited the U.S. Army's 91st Evacuation

Hospital, which had been set up in a Jesuit monastery a few miles outside Maastricht. She was there to visit a wounded friend, Lieutenant Colonel Thomas Crystal, but she was soon engulfed by the pandemonium of an American military field hospital: trucks slamming to off-load the wounded, nurses screaming orders, emergency surgeries in open operating theaters. The facility was top-notch. It had running water and electricity, when many field hospitals were little more than tents, but the screams echoed down the halls as Emilie pushed through with her required American escort.

It was one thing to know the American boys at her dances were returning to combat. It was another to see what happened to them in combat. Broken boys rushed past on trolleys, their bandages soaked with blood. Men slumped against walls, unable to stand. Classrooms full of bodies in beds. They were the lucky ones, having made it this far. A vast majority of the men in the 91st Evacuation Hospital survived. But to a civilian like Emilie, this was almost unbearable. On the day Emilie visited, 414 wounded soldiers arrived at the hospital. Four hundred and fourteen sons, brothers, fathers. It was the busiest day the 91st would face in the entire war, but not by much. In their first forty-eight days in Limburg, the unit treated more than 7,400 men.

"Wish I could show those front [line], ripped-apart soldiers for an hour to my opponents preaching moral and theological righteousness," she wrote that night in her Memory Book. "[They are suffering] without a cigar or a drink to comfort themselves or control their nerves."

Two days later, the Apostolate of the Front, volunteers whose mission was to entertain Allied troops, held its first meeting in the Ursuline Convent and Chapel in Maastricht. The official founders were a Catholic Army chaplain who had established a similar program in England and a local priest, along with a committee of twelve ladies. In truth, the priest and the other women had been recruited to the group by Emilie. The Apostolate was her organization. It was her answer to General Corlett's request and her response to those in Limburg who begrudged those "ripped apart" boys an evening of dancing and conversation. But she had no objection to being in the background, letting Catholic priests take the credit.

# CHAPTER 43

# COURAGE

— ★ —

December 1944

The thirteen men were marched to the waiting room of the administration building in the bitter cold of a December pre-dawn morning, then left to wait. The guards smoked cigarettes, laughed darkly, but gave no explanation. A few days before, Dutch Resistance fighters had snuck through the outer perimeter. Two had been shot dead, with detailed maps of the prison camp in their pockets. The prisoners didn't know that.

They shuffled nervously, their hands shoved into the pockets of their jackets, their breath visible in the cold. They were hard men, Dutch partisans, but they huddled together and whispered reassurances, reminders to stay strong. They had all been interrogated. They all had been tortured. None had cracked. They assured each other that, no matter the tactics, they would not crack this time either.

One man stood apart. He seemed calm. He might have been staring out the window at the darkness; he might have been thinking. He had been tortured, too, they knew, but he hadn't talked. He kept his own counsel, even with his fellow prisoners. He had spoken mostly with an American chaplain, a prisoner himself. But the chaplain had been transferred a month ago.

The men flinched as the door opened and Guard Commander SS-Oberscharführer Bender and the commandant of the barracks, Adolf Glück, a Luftwaffe officer, entered the room. A group of guards they didn't recognize followed. Heel-clicking and heiling, as usual. At a nod from Bender, the soldiers signaled for four of the prisoners to separate and follow. The men looked warily at each other but complied.

213

The air was cold in the little room. The men huddled in their coats, wondering what this was all about. Until they heard the gunshots. The guards weren't smoking or laughing now. Their eyes were hard, their hands on their guns.

The guards returned and signaled for the next four. Nobody moved, so the guards put the death end of their rifles to their backs. There was nothing else to do, and no place else to go.

A few minutes later, they were back for the last five. They marched the men across the yard, the ice crunching under their boots. Prisoners hung at their windows of the barracks despite the early hour. They shouted encouragement, promises to never forget. It was just after 6:00 a.m. in the dead of a Dutch winter. The sun was not yet up. But when they rounded the corner of the barracks, the prisoners could see the dark stains on the gray ice, and the quiet man stopped.

"I will not," he said.

Two guards grabbed him by the arms.

"I am an American officer."

He lurched backward, but the guards were ready.

"I am a soldier!" he screamed. His heels gouged parallel troughs in the ground as the guards struggled to pull him forward. "I am a prisoner of war. You cannot execute me. I am a prisoner of war."

One of the visiting Nazis, an SS officer named Wigger, stepped forward. "Schweinehund!" he yelled in German. "Wir werden Euch helfen mit Bomben zu schmeißen auf unsere Frauen und Kinder." ("We'll teach you to throw bombs on our women and children.")

If it was meant to reassure the guards that this man was no soldier, it didn't work. They seemed to falter.

"This is a crime!" the soldier yelled. "I am an Ameri . . ."

But the man's last "can" was swallowed by the explosion as Glück put a bullet through the thick of his back below his heart. Lieutenant Bill Moore, United States Army Air Forces, jerked forward, his left ribs shattered, then fell to his knees gasping for breath. As his head bent left, Glück stepped closer. The second shot was through Moore's skull, just behind his eye.

"Tell no one," Wigger said to his second-in-command, turning away.

# CHAPTER 44

# THE WORST JOB

— ★ —

*Jefferson Wiggins*
December 1944

The bugler blew reveille at 5:30 a.m. and within minutes, all 200 men of the 960th were dressed and lined up in the hallway of their damp and drafty barracks at the school in Gronsveld. It was Sergeant Jefferson Wiggins's job to count them off. Once Captain Solms cleared the count, they were given breakfast. In the past, there had always been chatting and joking at the breakfast tables, someone telling stories, mostly exaggerations and half-truths. But once they saw Margraten, the men became quiet, awed by the task ahead.

*Here we go again*, Sergeant Jefferson Wiggins thought, as he felt the truck jolt to a stop at the cemetery around 7:00 a.m. He pulled back the canvas flap and looked out at the freezing rain. They'd been working at Margraten for weeks, and it had rained, snowed, or sleeted every day. It was raining so hard he could barely see the olive-drab tents where the white officers and medical technicians of the 611th Graves Registration Company worked. The white wooden crosses, several hundred, were as thick as leaves, leaning in every direction as the ground shifted beneath them. The water ran in furrows, sticky with clay. The stacks of bodies stretched behind the tents, ominous as always, but smaller. Wiggins was sure the stacks were getting smaller.

He leapt off the truck and sank into the mud. Behind him, a few lucky men headed toward an idling Deuce-and-a-Half, pulling on their gloves.

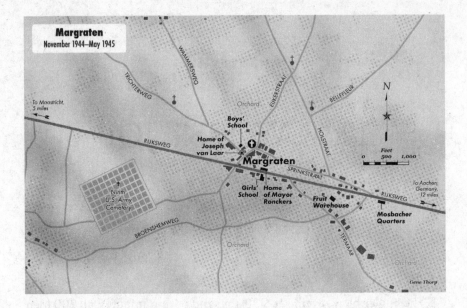

They had the easy assignment, unloading bodies. The front lines were less than an hour away, so the corpses were rarely stiff, unless the truck driver had stopped for breakfast at Sergeant Urban Brennan's kitchen; then, they might freeze up in the cold. Brennan was a butcher from Wisconsin. He ran the 611th's mess hall in Margraten. His food was so good, the drivers liked to stop for breakfast on the way in.

Not today, Wiggins noticed. Today the bodies weren't too stiff.

He grabbed his pick and shovel and headed into the field. As always, the mud grabbed his boots, dragging him down. Beside him, Black men plodded, jerking their feet from the earth with every step. They were used to it by now: the mix of ice and rain, the staggering cold, the extra pounds of mud, but it never got any more pleasant, or any easier.

At the end of his line of graves, Wiggins threw down his pick and began to dig. The first bite was wet, and it came away quickly, but before he could get his shovel back into the earth, the hole filled with water and the sides slid in. The first few feet were like this, a race to pull the soil out before the elements rushed back in. His muscles ached as he shifted shovelfuls of heavy mud, only to watch the hole refill. Even at age nineteen, digging holes in a driving rain was hard work. So, no wasted motion. No tossing or stopping. No talking. Only the steady rhythm of the shovel fighting the water, fighting the mud.

By midmorning, he had made it through the collapsing muck to the frozen loess beneath. He put down his shovel and grabbed his pick. Around him, several hundred Black men were spread out in rows, working their way into the ground. White officers strolled between them, bundled against the wind. The rain was sideways. The job of the 611th's officers was to make sure the graves were perfectly sized and aligned, but there wasn't much to measure. Originally, each man had been expected to dig three graves a day. In this weather, the goal was one, and it often wasn't reached.

He hefted his tools and turned back to his work. The cold wind was almost enough to make him wish he was back in the cotton fields under the boiling sun of Houston County, Alabama, with his parents in front and his siblings up the row, with the laughing conversations and the old women singing as they planted, slow and low. Almost.

"Come and get it, boys, but don't hog!"

It was Sergeant Brennan, with his Wisconsin accent and usual joy. Captain Shomon and his second, Lieutenant Edwin J. Donovan, lived with Joseph Ronckers, the mayor of Margraten, in his large brick house on the Rijksweg. It had an electric stove, coal heat, shower, tub, modern toilet, and enough space for Shomon and Donovan to have their own bedrooms. Joseph van Laar, the village clerk and translator, housed two officers in his more modest home. The transport sergeant lived in Van Laar's stables with the company's vehicles. The rest of the officers were billeted in Margraten's girls' school, across the street from Ronckers's home. The enlisted men of the 611th, including Brennan, lived in the boys' school two blocks away.

Wiggins and the other Black diggers rarely went into the village. The segregated 3136th, the other company of Black men digging graves, was housed in a large, drafty fruit warehouse on the far edge. Wiggins's 960th lived in the school in Gronsveld. They usually ate lunch under the tents at the cemetery, instead of at the dining hall in town. Brennan was a good egg. Generous and kind. He baked extra pastries and breads when the weather was particularly bad. There was nothing malicious about serving their meals at the cemetery. Most of the truck drivers were Black, and they were welcomed at Brennan's mess. It was just orders, Wiggins supposed.

"Cook's here," he said, putting down his shovel and pulling his boots out of the muck. Beside him, the man kept digging.

"Cook's here," Wiggins said again.

"Not today," the young man said, shaking his head. "If I stop today, I'll never start again."

It wasn't unusual for guys to skip lunch for that very reason: after drying out and stiffening up, it was murder on the body to get back to work. It was murder on the mind to sit for half an hour, thinking about what they were doing. It wasn't unusual for men to break down in tears when lowering a body into a hole. It might be your first hole, might be your fourteenth, there was no telling when the trauma would overwhelm you. I don't pity you, Shomon had insisted, because someone has to do it.

But why them? *How,* Jefferson Wiggins wondered, *did I end up here, in this country, outside this small village, doing this job?*

The sun was close to setting by the time Sergeant Wiggins finished his hole. Six feet long by two and a half feet wide, he could measure it with his shovel. Six feet deep, a few inches above his head. He clamored out of the earth, knocking mud to the bottom, and marched to the tents, where the bodies were stacked.

He leaned on his shovel, resting, watching the men from his company preparing bodies. New bodies, thank God. Sometimes, the bodies were old, and the handlers couldn't touch them until a GRS officer sprayed them with disinfectant. Sometimes, a special team had to help corral the parts. It was enough to lose your lunch and break your heart.

His man was whole, he could see, as the handlers lifted him from the pile. A white man. They were all white men. It was the parallel nature of their sacrifice: one chosen for glory at the risk of his life, one forced to stay behind and bury him.

They laid him on a mattress cover. They pulled it over his feet and up his legs. They put a dog tag in his mouth. They pulled the cover down, hiding his face. They tied it off at the waist by knotting the extra material, a makeshift body bag. It was easier when the dead man was like this, with a body and a head.

A Black soldier took a white cross and nailed the dead man's second dog tag to the center. He laid the cross on the body. Then they waited for the GRS officer. There were hundreds of Germans among the dead. They had their own burial area. The British, Dutch, and other Allies had their own small sections too. The officer checked the records, confirmed the identity and nationality of the soldier, noted the grave number and time of burial.

A chaplain stood at the top of the grave as Wiggins and the young man who had skipped his lunch lowered the mattress cover into the hole. The chaplain touched his shoulders and forehead, said a prayer into the storm. *So this dead man was Catholic*, Wiggins thought, but he would go no further down the rabbit hole of who he was, where he came from, who he loved, and who loved him. The Ninth Army had Jewish, Protestant, and Catholic chaplains. The dead man's religion: that's all Wiggins wanted to know. After the first few days, he hardly ever knew the dead man's name. It didn't matter. He was a man, and he was dead. You got used to it, or the sadness broke you down.

It was cold. The sun was down—it set around 4:30 p.m. The pile of dirt beside the grave had developed a white crust while they retrieved the body. In the icy rain, it usually did. Wiggins cracked the shell, then shoveled the dirt into the hole. The Catholic chaplain was two rows away, blessing another grave. The Protestant chaplain was a few rows behind him. The Dutch weren't allowed into the cemetery, except with special permission, but at the very edge black figures huddled under black umbrellas. Local girls. They often came to watch.

He picked up the white wooden cross. With his shovel, he pounded it into the mud at the head of the grave. Captain Shomon had asked Father Pierre Heynen, a priest from the area who was not assigned to a parish, to perform a memorial service at the cemetery's first burial. Now Father Heynen performed a memorial service in the big tent beside the graveyard every day. Villagers came to honor the dead. Wiggins had never gone. None of the diggers had gone. The service wasn't for them.

Seven shots rang out. A flock of blackbirds sprang from the mud. A bugler began to play taps. The American flag was lowered from the fifty-foot white spruce pole. The service was finished. The girls with the umbrellas turned for home.

The men of the 960th rode back to Gronsveld in silence. In Margraten, Burgemeester Ronckers served Shomon hot tea. Townspeople dropped by with gifts, like fresh apple pie. After dinner, Shomon and Donovan played bridge with Ronckers and Father Heynen in front of a roaring fire.

"We were most fortunate to be in such a grand place as Margraten," Shomon wrote. "The people were so friendly."

There were no bathing facilities in the converted school at Gronsveld. Once a week, a shower truck came from Maastricht. But most nights, the men heated water in their helmets, then scoured themselves with rags. The mud peeled off in thick layers, streaked brown stains across the floor, but they never got clean. No matter how hard they scrubbed, they never got rid of the odor. They only washed their uniforms once a week.

They ate dinner in silence, except for "pass the mustard" or "hand me the salt." They went to bed without a word. The bars and clubs in Maastricht were for white soldiers only, a rule of the U.S. Army. Dances were for white soldiers only. It didn't matter. The gravediggers weren't given rest and recuperation. Even if they had been, they were emotionally and physically exhausted. They fell straight to sleep, filthy with mud and reeking of the grave, and woke up at 5:30 a.m., when the thought of another day at the cemetery brought them to silence once again.

But Jeff Wiggins was optimistic. The number of dead appeared to be decreasing, and the stacks of bodies were almost gone. He was sure the 960th would soon be back to unloading supplies and organizing warehouses, work that seemed like paradise, though it had felt demeaning not so long ago.

Then, on December 17, the number of bodies noticeably increased. The next day, it increased again. That night, Jefferson Wiggins got his wish: his tour in hell was over. The 960th was called away from the cemetery in Margraten. But they weren't going to supply depots in France. They were being rushed to Belgium. Forty miles to the south, in the Ardennes. The Germans had broken through.

# CHAPTER 45

# CHRISTMAS

— ★ —

*Emilie Michiels van Kessenich; Margraten*
Christmas 1944

On December 20, four days into the Battle of the Bulge, the U.S. military newspaper, *Stars and Stripes*, ran an article, "Holland Girls Urged to Shun American GIs." Some of the reporting was accurate: The Catholic Church was divided. Dutch boys were jealous. An anonymous group that had posted the names of "Kraut girls" during occupation was threatening to do the same to girls seen in "compromising" situations with Americans. But the article was "untrue and destructive," Emilie thought, and the consequences unfortunate. An infantry unit refused to attend a dance. The American ambassador complained to the Dutch government-in-exile in London, which asked the Queen's Commissioner in Limburg Province to investigate. The U.S. Army threatened to cut the province's food rations, an idle threat. Lieutenant Colonel Senecal, who was recently promoted, would never have executed such an order.

An angry American private wrote to the editors of *Veritas*, a local newspaper, complaining, "It's almost as bad as if we were Krauts!"

A village priest declared from his pulpit that he preferred the German occupation to the current "pernicious films and dancing," shocking his congregation.

It was a tempest in a teapot, made ridiculous by the fact that the Germans were, once again, on the march. As the Wehrmacht advanced through Luxembourg and Belgium, "bulging" the front line to within a few dozen miles of Limburg, Maastricht fell into a panic.

Rumors started to swirl of black-clad parachute teams dropped near the city during the night, now hiding in the woods. The Germans were marching to Maastricht, people feared, to seize the Allied ammunition dumps. The Americans dropped nets on the upriver side of the Wilhelmina and Sint Servaas bridges to catch floating mines the Germans might have released upstream. They reinforced their antiaircraft positions and closed the bridges to civilians.

By December 20, when *Stars and Stripes* published its article, some in Maastricht were packing their bags and preparing to flee. They had nowhere to go. The Bulge was to the south, the German line of march was heading west, and the bulk of the Netherlands was in Nazi hands.

Jenneke Michiels van Kessenich, meanwhile, was sick from the lack of fat in her diet. Eduard had put on so much weight in Belgium (sixteen pounds) that he popped his garters on his return. Emilie managed, only barely, to send Jenneke to the same friends in Belgium on a pass from Colonel Senecal just before the German advance sealed the border. But then the younger girls came down with whooping cough. The food rations were scaled back, and hunger set in once again. The Luftwaffe was back in the sky above the city. Many Dutch returned to their basements, as they had when the Americans were advancing on Maastricht, and prayed the Germans wouldn't make it this far.

Christmas lifted Emilie's spirits. The fighting was ferocious in the Ardennes, so the threat of the city being overrun was on everyone's mind. But the whooping cough epidemic had worn itself out and Manka, who spoke often with Senecal and his men, was convinced the American lines would hold. It had been a long four years, four months, and four days of occupation. It had been a fall of intermittent hope and fear. Emilie was going to celebrate their first free holiday season.

On Christmas Eve, Emilie and Willem lit their family Christmas tree, with General Simpson and other American officers on hand to celebrate. A triumphant moment missed only by Jenneke, still in Belgium recovering from malnutrition.

That night, Emilie and Manka attended a concert given by the American 55th Anti-Aircraft Artillery Brigade. At midnight Mass, they prayed for the Dutch in the north, who were starving under a brutal Nazi occupation, and the brave Walloons—southern Belgians—trapped by the

German counterattack. The air raid siren had sounded on their way to church, a Luftwaffe attack. The antiaircraft batteries chugged outside as the congregation sang.

Six miles away in Margraten, the village children had spent the morning decorating the auditorium at the girls' school, where some of Shomon's officers lived, with flowers, evergreens, and colored crepe paper. A Christmas Eve Mass was held in the school. As candles were lit to start the celebration, the Luftwaffe attacked, the sounds of the battle a backdrop as Father Heynen read the Gospel and gave his homily. An accordionist accompanied a children's choir. There was only room for fifty, so the grave-diggers billeted in the drafty fruit warehouse weren't invited, but Captain Shomon praised "an atmosphere of indescribable spiritual uplift, an exalted feeling of great splendor, sensed by all of us who attended."

In Maastricht, the Brothers of the Immaculate Conception of the Blessed Virgin Mary were loaded into U.S. Army trucks, with military motorcycles as escorts. The streets were dark because of the blackout, and quiet, until the air raid siren blasted—the same raid heard in Margraten by Shomon and by the Michiels van Kessenichs and their fellow worshippers—and the sky exploded with machine-gun and cannon fire, the tracers a violent fireworks display. Twice, the convoy was stopped for inspection before it reached Schark, a former quarry dug into the side of Sint Pietersberg, now owned by the monastic order and used for recreation. Two Americans stood guard at the entrance to a tunnel, but they let the Brothers pass.

Inside, the Brothers lit lanterns to illuminate the passage into the mountain. The walls were covered with drawings, the work of current Brothers and others lifetimes before them, each work lit by a lantern left beside the wall. As always in the caves, it wasn't long before the outside world disappeared—the gunfire, the tracers—and the universe became these walls, these drawings, this chamber carved in the 1600s. At the far end sat an altar of marlstone. Behind it, glowing in the lantern light, was a wall painting of shepherds receiving the news of the birth of Jesus. On a side wall, at the Brothers' invitation, an American soldier, Salvatore Barravecchia, had drawn a large mural to honor the liberation of Europe.

By the time all the lanterns were burning, the American soldiers had begun to arrive. Many were friends of the Brothers. Antiaircraft companies were stationed around Maastricht, and some lived on the old quarry grounds. Others lived in a school where the Brothers had taken up residence after a wing of their monastery was destroyed by German bombs. Many had visited Schark before. Some had taken their meals in the large main cavern. They knew what to expect. Their Catholic chaplain and the magister of the monastery had planned this evening together.

Other soldiers entered with their jaws dropped, staring at the murals on the walls, the support pillars carved and painted like statuary. These young men walked with heavy steps, their uniform pockets stuffed with gear, their boots covered in mud, their rifles slung across their shoulders. They had come from antiaircraft positions farther from the city, and most would be going back to their positions as soon as midnight Mass was over.

They took their places on benches: several hundred American soldiers and thirty Dutch Brothers, silent in the soft light of the lanterns. The music began, a harpsichord the Brothers had brought from the monastery. A choir of young Brothers sang "Adeste Fideles" ("O Come, All Ye Faithful"). The magister and the chaplain spoke of the Christmas miracle, the birth of Christ, the manger and the hay. Outside, the sky was full of lead and steel, the temperature well below freezing, but the cavern was warm. So intense, one Brother remembered. So peaceful. Almost mystical.

At the end of Mass, an American soldier approached the harpsichord. He banged out "The Star-Spangled Banner," and the soldiers sang along, their hands on their hearts, facing the large American flag hung in the corner. He played several more patriotic songs, and the soldiers roared those too.

The Brothers had scraped a large section of wall, until it was white and flat. At the top, an inscription read in English:

*On Christmas 1944 at midnight a solemn Highmass has been celebrated by Reverend Father Dobrzynski in this cave for the American soldiers. We Dutch Brothers of the Immaculate Conception wish all of them a Merry Christmas. May the Holy Christ-child bless you and all your families far away in America. May the battle soon cease and peace rule over the world and you all return to your families safe and sound. We shall always thankfully remember that you liberated us from the terrible German occupation.*

The first soldier to sign his name on the wall was the brigade commander, Brigadier General Samuel L. McCroskey. Beneath him, the rest of the soldiers signed in charcoal too. Then, many piled into a convoy of trucks and headed back to the fight.

A few days later, at the American military cemetery in Margraten, a solitary man walked among the graves. It was a bleak and freezing day, much colder than earlier in the month, and the workers had gone back to their barracks, the corpse trucks back to their motor pools. But Joseph van Laar, the village clerk of Margraten, took pride in the cemetery, and his friendship with Shomon granted him access to the ground. He often walked there in the evening, straightening crosses and removing debris. It wasn't Van Laar's job to take care of the cemetery. The Americans oversaw their own burial ground. But he felt compelled to honor the fallen soldiers, and the men still fighting.

There were a few other men in the cemetery that evening. American soldiers, he would have known them even without their uniforms. A handful came every day, searching for the graves of buddies, or men who had fallen beside them. Men who, perhaps, had lost their lives saving them. Or men, perhaps, they tried but couldn't save.

On this evening, one of the soldiers approached Van Laar and asked the Dutchman if he spoke English.

Van Laar said he did.

The soldier introduced himself as Captain Lane. He couldn't stay, he told Van Laar, he was on his way to the front. But his cousin was buried here. They had grown up together. They had been friends all their lives. Would Van Laar, perhaps, look at his cousin's grave, from time to time?

Van Laar said he would.

*Thank you, sir.*

*What is his name?*

*Second Lieutenant John Land.*

# CHAPTER 46

# SPECIAL FRIENDS

— ★ —

*Frieda van Schaïk; Walter Huchthausen*
End of December 1944

O ne December, years before occupation, Moekie had heard a rustling sound outside. She went to the front window, where she saw a small girl trying to lift her baby brother, so he could see their Christmas tree. The tree was an oddity in the early 1930s. Strict Catholics considered it pagan and an affront to the spirit of the Lord's birth, and almost everyone in Heer was strictly Catholic.

"Come in, come in," Moekie said, opening the door and motioning to the girl. "Would you like a closer look?"

The girl seemed scared, then unsure. Finally: "May my brother come?"

"Of course. If you get your parents' permission."

The girl returned with a second little brother . . . and about twenty other children, the entire village, almost. Moekie, delighted, invited them inside. She played the piano while the children sang carols and drank hot chocolate, laughing with excitement. From that year forward, the visit of the local children was a Van Schaïk Christmas tradition, the date and time announced during Mass by the village priest. Every child drank hot chocolate, and every child left with a gift—the Van Schaïk children were each expected to sacrifice one of their own toys, while Moekie contributed her needlework dolls and Pappie his little wooden carvings of tops, boats, airplanes, and cars.

The tradition died during occupation. It was from another time. No one wanted that tradition to return more than the Van Schaïks, but for one more year, at least, it was not to be. The blackout. The Bulge. Moekie was still weak, recovering from her stroke. So, the family Christmas tree was lit behind blackout curtains, the food parceled carefully to the family—all except Jacoba, back in Belgium caring for the wounded, and Wim, still in hiding in Rotterdam. The family attended church on Christmas Eve, as always, then turned into bed with the sound of antiaircraft artillery overhead.

On December 26, Captain John Hoadley, the Civil Affairs officer who had asked Dave for directions to the church, arrived with several fellow officers, and the conversation was boisterous, lasting deep into the night. This was the house at its warmest and most cheerful, where liberators became friends.

The next day, Hoadley dropped by again. He had a new officer with him, Captain Walter Huchthausen. Hutch had been a casualty of D-Day . . . sort of. After the landings, the Germans had retaliated with a barrage of V-1 and V-2 rockets. Hutch, in London teaching Allied soldiers basic German, was badly wounded by a missile. He endured months of convalescence, during which he created a glossary of common German terms for English-speaking soldiers.

He was assigned to the Ninth Army on December 9, 1944, months after most of the other Civil Affairs officers had taken their posts, and arrived in Limburg three days later. By the time he met the Van Schaïks, he had spent two weeks conducting inspections across Limburg, in the northeast of Belgium, and across the Siegfried Line in the battered city of Aachen.

He had an instant connection, Frieda noticed, with Miel, her sister Margaret's husband. They turned toward each other in the midst of the larger conversation, delving into Maastricht's aesthetics. Miel was an artist. Huchthausen, an assistant professor of architecture at his alma mater, the University of Minnesota. There was much to be admired, he thought, in the rowhouses that crowded the city's center, the ancient bridges, the old fort atop Sint Pietersberg, the steeples. It was a city of many eras and cultures, filled with beautiful architecture and historic monuments, so different from the open spaces of mid-century Minnesota or even Harvard, where Hutch had received his master's degree. Miel, Frieda noticed, seemed to have an opinion on every angle and limestone slab.

The next night, Hutch and Hoadley returned, and again the architect sat with the artist. Pappie brought down his sketches of local plants, and Hutch's eyes lit up not at the anatomical accuracy, but the quality of the lines. He had just turned forty, but he had a youthful face, made younger by the happiness that seemed to so easily reside there. When he made eye contact with Frieda, who was refreshing their drinks, he smiled and said, "Let me help you."

She found him alone in the front room later that night. Miel had gone upstairs, where he lived with Margaret and their daughter. Pappie was enjoying a cigarette with Hoadley at the kitchen table, his tie loosened and his suit coat off, the most informal and relaxed her father ever was. Hutch was sketching by the Christmas tree in the glow of a Tilley lamp. From the doorway, Frieda could tell it was a building. She watched as he bent over the drawing, his hand gliding across the paper. There was no sound except the scraping of his pencil, the soft *whoosh* of the lamp's gas flame.

She started to turn, but he looked up. "How are you, Frieda?" he said with a smile.

She hadn't known he knew her name. "Is that Sint Servaas?" The basilica was the largest and most important church in Maastricht.

"No. It's Aachen Cathedral." He turned the notebook so she could see its rounded cupola, its thick tower. "One of the most important in Europe."

"Charlemagne built the chapel. The first Holy Roman Emperor. Twelve hundred years ago." She had never been to Aachen Cathedral, although it was only seventeen miles away, but she knew her history.

Hutch smiled again. He was a man, she thought, who always seemed to be smiling. "Twelve hundred years," he said. "Isn't that incredible?"

"Why are you drawing it?"

"It's my job." He laughed, seeing her confusion. "I'm a monuments and fine arts officer. My job is to save culturally important objects. Buildings. Art. Documents and archives. Aachen Cathedral is standing right in the middle of the rubble of a demolished city. Making sure it survives is my most important assignment."

"Why?"

He paused. "Because it's been there for a thousand years. Who would we be if we were the ones to allow its destruction?"

She studied his sketch. The thick and thin lines. The steady hand. It was quite good. Had he drawn it from memory, or was he only working out the details of what he had already drawn? The building in the sketch seemed remarkably intact. She wondered what it really looked like, considering the past two years of Allied bombing.

"Have you seen the art vault in the mountain? We saw the paintings go in, Wim and father and I . . ." she paused, counting back, "two years ago. Rembrandt's *The Night Watch* is in there. The most famous work of art in the Netherlands. And others too."

He shook his head no. "One of my colleagues has visited the cave. My job is to inspect historic structures before heading to Germany with the Ninth Army."

"Oh," she said. She had met many soldiers. Most were on their way to Germany.

"I do hope to visit the art vault before leaving, though. It's a once-in-a-lifetime chance. I hear the caves are beautiful too."

"Oh, yes," Frieda said, feeling herself on solid ground. "They are. They definitely are. You should see the bats."

# CHAPTER 47

# THE HONEYMOON ENDS

— ★ —

*Paschal Fowlkes*
January 1945

"Christmas Eve here is clear and cold and pretty," Chaplain Paschal Fowlkes wrote his mother from England on December 24, 1944. "I hope it is there too."

Five days later, to his wife Lib: "Love, the honeymoon is over for a while."

On D-Day, Fowlkes had watched from the British air base as the transport planes took off into the sky. Thousands of planes, tens of thousands of men doing their part, and he had been left behind. Two months later, he wrote to his mother (not his wife) that he was applying for a transfer to the airborne: "There are opportunities open and a real need, which someone, putting his trust in God, must fill. The training is rather vigorous, but I think I can stand it all right and will immensely enjoy it compared with this unsoldierly life I slouch through now. It is perhaps more dangerous than just riding the airplanes as I do now, but I believe its dangers are often exaggerated. I haven't decided to try it without full thought of Lib and my family. Instead I have prayed about this as I believe I have never prayed before and believe that it is God's will that I should go ahead."

"Love, you need not to worry about any heroics on my part," he wrote to Lib a few months later, after he had completed training and been assigned to the 507th Parachute Infantry, 17th Airborne Division. "I promise if I ever do go into it I'll be careful. Don't worry about that."

The 507th were called to action on Christmas Eve, mere hours after Fowlkes's letter to his mother. They were rushed to France that night. By December 29, they were marching through the Ardennes with Patton's Third Army. This was unspoiled forest: the hills thick with broadleaf and pine, their trunks so numerous a man could barely see his way through. The ground so heavy with snow and ice the paratroopers had to follow the treads of tanks down narrow tracks or risk the waist-high snow that blew up around the blueberry bushes and buried the ferns.

A curl of smoke. A village, pinpointed on their map. The paratroopers spread out, followed a path of crushed snow across a frozen field and down a slope to a simple settlement, centuries old, made of mostly wood and stone. But the smoke was not a hearth or cooking fire. It was the remains of a house, a modest dwelling laid to ruin. The village, when the paratroopers walked down its quiet streets, was smashed and littered with debris. Dead bodies slumped against walls, or face-down in the snow. Dead horses. Dead pigs. Bloody ice. In a barn, five cows were dead in their stalls, executed with a bullet to the head. In another village, 100 people had been tied together by their wrists to form a circle, then executed by machine gun. Their arms were touching but their bodies were wrenched in every direction, covered with frost.

Survivors crawled from their basements and hiding holes, traumatized, shaking against the shock and the cold. They looked at the bodies of their families and neighbors. They had been too slow, a survivor said, to offer information on the French Resistance.

But nobody in this village knew anything about the French Resistance.

The war was "one of the greatest struggles against the massed forces of darkness the world has ever known," Pat Fowlkes had declared from the innocence of his Virginia pulpit in May 1942, a few weeks before he volunteered. That darkness was the reason he had volunteered. It was the reason he became a paratrooper. But the darkness in the Ardennes shocked him. It shocked the hardened soldiers of the 507th. They had heard stories of German atrocities, but it was something different to see a hundred men and women tied wrist to wrist, murdered for no reason.

There was little Paschal Fowlkes could do to ease the suffering. For the survivors, starving and freezing: meager rations, a few bandages, a prayer. For the bodies: a white sheet, a simple blessing. For his fellow soldiers: a reminder that God sees all, justice will come, the dead will be taken care of. It was the paratroopers' role to march on, moving east over the ridges and across the frozen streams.

It was bitterly cold. So cold truck engines did not want to start, and the water in their canteens froze. The soldiers took their boots into their sleeping bags. Otherwise, the damp would freeze them stiff by morning. Many never took their boots off, even when they broke through the ice, or went down chest-deep in a snow hole. The men suffered every malady: frozen toes, frostbite, trench foot.

They took fire from Germans hidden in the tree lines or waiting in ambush behind dead falls. They withstood sudden armor attacks that over-ran strung-out positions. In temperatures of twenty degrees, the medics struggled. The wounded went into shock almost before they hit the snow. The blood plasma was too slushy for the IV lines. Pat and the other chaplains took to carrying plasma packets inside their clothing, pressed against their chests to keep them warm.

The medics set up triage centers in abandoned homes. They tacked blankets over the windows to black out the light and preserve the heat, lit fires in the hearths. But even inside, the cold was brutal. Pat Fowlkes had wanted this: To be on the ground, in service to the paratroopers he admired. To be one of them, although without a weapon. But he struggled to give them comfort when the enemy was as much the weather as the Germans. He put away the Communion chalices he had packed in his drop bag. They were wrong for the field. He read Scripture in the foxholes, led freezing men in benediction. He prayed in the small country huts, with their pitiful fires and makeshift operating tables, where his men were dying.

It was so bitterly cold, for so many weeks, that soldiers lost their way, especially the enlisted men. "Sometimes out here in the cold it's a little hard for the average doughboy to keep his perspective," Pat wrote Lib. "The average one, honestly, has no real idea what he's fighting to avoid or gain. And it's difficult to try to interpret [for] them through all their discomfort and fatigue."

"I often find myself thinking," Pat wrote Lib one quiet night, when the moon was shimmering off pine branches heavy with snow, "how strange it all is. I wonder what the civilians in, say, Luxembourg think—the Germans hurry out of town and make for their border, and into town rumble the tanks and march the weary foot soldiers of, not Luxembourg, not Belgium, not Holland, not France, but the men of a strange country four thousand miles away across land and sea.... I wonder what, if anything, goes on inside them when they see a load of our dead coming back."

On February 9, the 507th suffered casualties on the bank of the Our River. Only then did the arctic gear arrive, the large hooded jackets and woolen gloves that would keep them sane and safe against the cold.

The next day, they were recalled to France to rest and prepare for the assault on Germany. They had been in the Ardennes for seven weeks, on a plodding advance, pushing the Germans back to the Siegfried Line.

Five days later, on February 15, Paschal Fowlkes conducted a memorial service, where he delivered his "Eulogy for Fallen Comrades":

*Words always compare so feebly with the deeds they describe that it is difficult to say anything this morning that will not detract from the occasion. Wherever in this life we meet that which is perfected by the Creator himself we feel the futility of trying to do justice with any words to perfection. The perfection of one flower in the field is such that Solomon in all his glory could not equal it.... Perfection in a human life, which paradoxically is the willingness to lay down that life for one's friends, is something that we cannot add to with words. Our fallen comrades have written with their deeds what we can only poorly comment upon with our words. But these few thoughts I would leave with you.*

*In the first place, I do not conceive that we ought to feel sorry for them. They would not have wanted us to feel sorry for them. They took their wounds in the very forefront of the fight. No soldier worth his salt wants to die. Any soldier worth his salt, if he must die, wants to die as they died.*

*It is too much like the Nazism-Fascism that we are fighting to glory in the combat that can bring death to those so young and fine. We are a nation that has never looked on war this way. But there is a middle ground, and we may as well take warning. If that day ever comes when we shall not be eagerly willing, as they were, to fight for our freedom and if necessary to die for it, we shall be deader by far than they, though we may not be in our graves. We will no longer be living. We will be vegetating—which is a poor way for man, created in the image of God, to exist. And we shall not be free.*

*It is recorded that after Lee watched Pickett's charge across the wheat field at Gettysburg, after he'd seen the first great gaps appear in the gray line and be filled, after he'd seen the remainder march unhesitatingly into the very cannons' mouths—15,000 going in, 5,000 to return—a scene that was glorious even in its hopelessness—he turned to those who were near him and said, "It is well that war is so terrible; else we would grow to love it too much."*

*It is well. For the heroic example of those who have gone before us is a legacy for which we can be grateful even through our natural sadness....*

*With this much in mind, we can pray, not first that we would be safe, but that we would be kept loyal, and not first that we ourselves would be spared death but that we would be spared an unwillingness to face that which they faced and that which God and Country may require of us. Though they were dead, yet shall they live in our resolve, inspired by their example, to finish that which they had begun and for which they gave their last full measure.*

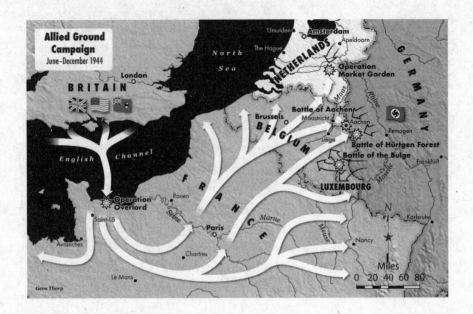

PART IV

# OVER THE RHINE

— ★ —

January 1945–June 1945

*Volumes have been, and more volumes will be, written on the col-*
*lapse of world co-operation and the true significance of the events*
*that accompanied the tragedy. For us, all their words will amplify*
*one simple truth. Freedom from fear and injustice and oppression*
*will be ours only in the measure that men who value such freedom*
*are ready to sustain its possession—to defend it against every thrust*
*from within or without.*

General Dwight D. Eisenhower,
Supreme Commander, Allied Expeditionary Force

## CHAPTER 48

# CURLEY

— ★ —

*Bill Hughes*
January 1945

M4 Sherman medium tanks like those used by the 784th Tank Battalion had five-man crews: commander, driver, gunner (for the main gun), machine gunner, and a loader for the main gun. Each position had a limited range of vision, and everyone had a specific role. The commander, seated above and behind the driver, had the widest view of the outside world and barked clipped orders—"Driver, move out," "Driver, stop," "Gunner, traverse left"—into the tank radio, but it was the responsibility of the four other men, who often could not see much of what they were doing or why, to perform each task. A tank was like a hand: five working as one.

Hard enough in ideal conditions, but then add a cramped compartment so small the men had to move together to make space to fire and reload the main gun. The airflow was limited, so the interior was stifling and prone to smoke. Even a small engagement was deafening, as every shell, including their own, seemed to reverberate the metal sides of the hull. Adjustments were constant in a firefight. When the radio broke down, the commander used his feet to direct the driver: a stomp on the right or left shoulder to turn, a tap on the head to stop, a push to the back of the head to advance. When a crew member was hit, the other men worked quickly to leverage him out of the hatch and get help. If a tank was disabled, the five men had mere seconds to execute a coordinated escape. A disabled tank meant an enemy gun had them bracketed, and it would almost always keep firing until the tank was on fire.

There was no freelancing in a tank. The gunner and drivers followed the commander's orders. The commander followed the orders given before the engagement. The tanks in the 784th Tank Battalion were split into four seventeen-tank companies, Company A, B, C, and D (in M5 Stuart light tanks). Each company worked together: each tank was given an objective, like a bridge or an intersection, and it was their job to lead the advance, secure that position, and hold it until the infantry arrived. You had to trust the infantry, because without them the tank was stranded beyond the advance. But the tankers in the 784th usually wouldn't know the infantry they were fighting with. As a separate tank battalion, they were assigned temporarily to infantry units, constantly moving to wherever they were most needed. Their real trust was in their fellow tankers: that they would reach their objectives and be in their positions, forming a cohesive front. You had to trust, in all things, the men in your company. Tank warfare was, even more than other types of warfare, built on teamwork.

The 784th spent a year at Camp Hood, Texas, forging that coordination and trust. They had classrooms and manuals, but spent most of their time in the field working on night marches, assaulting fortifications, close combat, street fighting, and other basic operations. The instructors gave them "problems" to solve, then assessed their performance and offered advice. They practiced combined operations with infantry and artillery, since the tanks would never fight on their own, but in task-organized units with infantry. They even, on occasion, fought against each other.

By summer 1944, the men of the 784th were a brotherhood. They had refined the ballet within an individual tank, and they knew how to work together in the field. They knew each other's lives and stories. They knew each other's personalities. They trusted every man to do his job, and to be where he was supposed to be no matter how thick the fire or how violent the battle. And yet, in late September 1944, almost four months after the landings at Normandy, the 784th Tank Battalion found itself stuck at Camp Hood, Texas, awaiting orders.

The other two Black tank battalions had deployed: the 758th to Italy and the 761st, featuring a twenty-four-year-old star athlete named Jackie Robinson (who did not deploy, because he was under investigation for refusing to sit in the back of one of the Army's segregated buses), to Northwestern Europe in support of the 26th Infantry Division.

Some in the 784th were disheartened, worried they would not be called. Bill Hughes's mother in Indianapolis felt the opposite: she was happy her son was stuck in Texas. The success of the D-Day landings and advance through the French hedgerows had inspired the nation but terrified its mothers. In a month and a half, nearly 16,300 American boys were killed in the Normandy Campaign, about 2,700 per week. By comparison, 116,000 Americans were killed in the nineteen months of U.S. fighting in World War I—about 1,400 a week. Not since the Civil War had the nation been forced to contend with combat deaths coming this quickly, and of this magnitude. And the numbers were certain to increase. Those 16,300 American boys had liberated just twenty miles of enemy-controlled territory. Berlin was still 680 miles away.

Bill Hughes never wavered. He wanted to fight. He had been trained to fight. He had faith his time would come.

But when the 784th finally left Camp Hood on October 3, 1944, it was in secrecy. Nobody told the men their destination, for fear of leaks. Their troop train traveled with the windows covered, so the men couldn't see which direction they were headed. Their tanks weren't on board; their weapons and equipment had been left behind. Bill Hughes was relieved when word came whispering down the cars that the train was headed east. Europe then, not the Pacific.

Europe, where the Allies had stormed their way onto the beaches in Italy and France. Liberated Rome, Paris, and Maastricht, although Bill Hughes didn't know that last name, and if someone had told him, it wouldn't have meant anything. He'd never heard of the place. He probably didn't know about the failure of Market Garden as their train crossed the eastern United States. All he knew was that the Allies had a long and bloody road in front of them to reach Berlin.

Chaplain Paschal Fowlkes wrote of Germany's Siegfried Line in one of his typically lyrical letters to his beloved wife, Lib:

> You picture it as a fifty-yard wide strip of concrete dragons' teeth. It would be
> a pushover if that were all it was. But it runs through hills, over mountains,
> through the densest forests, for hundreds of miles, and is miles in depth. It
> is sown full of camouflaged pillboxes that they've been building since Hitler
> came to power. Underneath are dugouts and tunnels that make the occupants

*safe from practically anything but direct hits from the heaviest bombs. Some are fifteen feet thick in concrete. With fortifications like that they can hold a whole line with an amazingly small number of men. The weapons emplaced here are zeroed in to the finest degree and practically no visual firing is needed to hold whole stretches. All they need are forward observers with telephones to call back for certain fire patterns listed on charts and then there's not much more to it than the pressing of buttons to lay down a curtain through which nothing living can move and survive.*

Would he be ready, Bill Hughes wondered as the train slipped toward New York, when the 784th hit the line? Training was one thing. Combat was something else. He was ready to fight. But was he ready, Bill Hughes wondered, to give his life?

The 784th left New York Harbor the day before Halloween on board the British transport *Moreton Bay*. Many troop transports were converted passenger liners, but the *Moreton Bay* was a tub, old and rusty, its interior a big hollow space strung with hammocks instead of bunks. Unlike Jefferson Wiggins's 960th, the tankers had access to a deck, but there were few amenities and little to do but play cards and dice. The weather was awful, the waves rough. They rarely saw their white officers, who had their own sleeping quarters, mess, and recreation area. Twice a day, the junior officers came down to conduct lifeboat drills. There weren't even close to enough lifeboats.

"What am I supposed to do?" Bill asked First Sergeant Daniels, the senior enlisted member of Company D. "You know I can't swim." Bill had jumped into the pool for his swimming test and sank. Daniels pulled him out and stamped his papers "PASSED."

"Look, Hughes, even if you could swim, how far do you think you could go in the middle of the ocean?"

Bill looked out at the cold waves, the harsh gray sea. There had not been any land in sight for days.

"Don't worry, Hughes," Daniels said. "We're all in this together."

They landed in Liverpool, England, processed through, and boarded another train. In Cardiff, Wales, new M4 Sherman and M5 Stuart tanks were waiting for them. They spent days tightening the bolts and cleaning the guns. Some of the men had worried their race had caught up to them, and they were being diverted into the Quartermaster Corps. Now, even the most skeptical believed: they were going over not as clerks but as a tank battalion.

They crossed the Channel to Le Havre, France, 100 miles east of the Normandy beaches, in the bitter cold of Christmas Day, 1944. Bill Hughes couldn't help but admire the logistics, as there were boats in the Channel as far as he could see. As a radioman and bow gunner/assistant driver in an M5 Stuart tank, he understood the complexity of coordination among men. And that was just for one tank! Imagine the coordination needed to move hundreds of thousands of men and millions of pounds of equipment. Could the 784th retain their discipline, he wondered, if the battlefields were anything close to this size? Would they stick to their objectives in the face of a ferocious enemy onslaught? Could they hold together, and fight as a team, once everything went FUBAR and the dying began?

The next afternoon, the battalion rendezvoused with an ammunition train, since tanks made the Channel crossing unarmed. The Luftwaffe attacked, or maybe a bomb accidently went off—no one was sure exactly how, but a train car full of ammunition exploded. Fiery concussions rippled from one car to the next. A tank commander drove forward and hooked his Sherman to the last car and began to drag it down the tracks. Another tank hooked and dragged away a second car, as men raced with chains to the third and the fourth. There was no panic, only determination, a grim relay of tanks and chains. The 784th saved more than 100 train carloads of ammunition. That night, they were given a sit-down meal and French wine.

They passed through Maastricht soon after, in the closing days of 1944, driving their tanks across the Maas River, down the Rijksweg, through Margraten and on toward Aachen. The Battle of the Bulge raged to the south, mostly in the Ardennes Forest. The Luftwaffe was above them. On New Year's Eve, the Germans unleashed a vicious bombardment on Maastricht, killing seventeen Dutch civilians. That evening, the 784th linked up with the 104th Infantry Division, known as the Timberwolves, at Eschweiler, Germany, on the west bank of the Roer River, ten miles east of Aachen.

This was the front. On the other side of the river were ten German divisions, about 200,000 troops. Bill Hughes couldn't see them, since they were hidden in pillboxes and dugouts, concrete fortifications and dense clumps of forests, but he knew what he was facing: heavy artillery, Panzerfaust (shoulder-fired anti-tank weapons), and the dreaded German Tiger tanks, whose 88mm guns could pierce the armor of any American tank. When a GRS soldier said recovering remains in a tank hit by direct artillery fire was best done with "a mess kit cup and spoon," he was talking about the kind of damage an 88mm shell inflicted. No American tank could fight the behemoth German Tigers head-to-head and hope to survive.

"We'll get through it," Paschal Fowlkes assured his wife, after describing the kill zones of western Germany.

> Because with flame-throwers, dive-bombing, etc., we can, slowly, do it. But I can scarcely tell you in strong enough words how different it is doing it from thinking about it. It's because this is so that I've never for a moment regretted being out here with the boys who'll do this thing and others like it. There have to be thousands and thousands of jobs in the army, few of them at the front. Every man ought to serve where he is best fitted to serve. And no one ought to judge a man who is doing that, regardless of where he is serving. But honestly, until you have been up there and seen the boys who really do the work, you just plain cannot begin to know what we all owe to them.

Bill Hughes was one of those boys who would "really do the work," and he couldn't help but wonder, as he stared across the Roer River, how well he'd hold the line.

Men in his company were going to die, some in gruesome ways. Bill knew it was no use thinking like that, but as the 784th bedded down in an old coal briquette factory, one of the few buildings big enough to shelter their tanks and trucks, he couldn't help but ponder it. Men he had trained with—buddies, brothers—burned to cinders, torn apart by ricocheting bullets, vaporized by explosions. Who would it be? The man beside him in their makeshift barracks, writing a letter home? The man across from him, eating his tin of beans? Himself?

Was he ready to face that fate? To give not just his life, but every ounce of flesh? He feared death. Every honest soldier did. But what if his body was decimated and destroyed, leaving nothing to mourn?

He thought of his mother in Indianapolis. He prayed the Lord would keep his family safe. He prayed that every man in the 784th would make it out alive. How terrible would it be, he wondered, to see his best friends die?

How terrible would it be to take a life?

He was confident he could do it. But would it be right? How could he pray to God to keep his friends safe, then kill someone who prayed for his own safe return? Whose mother sat at home in Germany, just as his mother did in Indianapolis, waiting for her child?

He knew one thing for sure: he could depend on every man in the 784th Tank Battalion. And that was a combat soldier's most comforting thought.

On January 10, he watched from the yard of the factory as waves of Allied bombers flew overhead, heading toward the German city of Cologne. They were so close to the front, the ground shook when the bombs hit the battered city. The sorties were so regular Hughes could time them, twenty minutes between waves. The journeys back were more staggered, with bombers missing or limping toward home.

It was four hours into the bombardment, about 2:30 p.m., when someone yelled, "Take cover! Close your hatches! They're bombing us!"

It didn't seem possible. The sky was clear, visibility perfect. Orange ID panels surrounded their position. But Bill Hughes saw the black dots in the sky, and he knew the man was right. He ran. The first bomb hit 300 yards away, rocking the ground. Hughes reached a tank, scrambled aboard, and slammed the hatch closed as a second bomb exploded. It must have been close, because the shrapnel raked the tank, deafening the men inside.

First combat, friendly fire . . . and he panicked. He thought, *My God, I have to get out, the next one might be a direct hit.* He forgot that bombs from a single plane fell in a skipping pattern, a few hundred yards apart.

He threw open the hatch and sprinted across the yard. The pressure wave of the next blast knocked him to the ground. He got up and ran toward the exit as the driver of the company commander's jeep, Private Curley J. Ausmer, ran past him the other way. The jeep had a mounted .30 caliber machine gun. In the confusion, Curley was preparing to shoot back. But just as Hughes reached a door, the concussion of the last bomb rocked the factory, and the machine gun began to fire on its own. In half a minute, it burned through its ammunition belt. Private Curley Ausmer was raked across the stomach and almost cut in half.

Hughes cried as they carried away the lifeless body. He didn't just feel bad, or sad. He cried bitter tears. Curley Ausmer was the first soldier killed from the 784th. The first man down, at the hands of an American aircrew. It wasn't supposed to happen. Not like this. Death wasn't anything like what he thought that it would be.

The company clerk was told not to type the death report. No incident report was filed. No one from the battalion was allowed to visit the body in the basement of the factory. Hours later, a truck came and took the body away, but the battalion commander provided no comforting remarks, no prayers of mourning. Bill Hughes was stunned, angry. It felt as if the Army didn't want to acknowledge the screwup that had cut Private Curley Ausmer down.

No, death was not like Bill Hughes had imagined it. Not at all.

# CHAPTER 49

# RITCHIE BOY

— ★ —

*Stephen Mosbacher*
February 1945

Emil Mosbacher was the most prominent—or perhaps the second most prominent, depending on who you asked—Jewish gynecologist in Nuremberg, Germany. He was the head of maternity at a local hospital, with a thriving private practice he ran out of the front room of the family's large apartment. He delivered his first child, Sigmund, in that front room on October 14, 1923. A little over two years later, in January 1926, his wife died there, during a difficult childbirth. The baby, a girl, was stillborn. It was a too-common tragedy, even for prominent gynecologists.

Sigmund was a happy, outgoing child, despite the loss of his mother. He was close to his father, a political idealist who supported the Weimar Republic and universal state-sponsored medical insurance. Even at a young age, Sigmund argued with his schoolmates in support of his father's progressive politics. He loved reading and excelled in class. Too young to remember his mother, his life's first great shock came in 1935, when the Nuremberg Laws stripped Jews of citizenship. Like all Jewish children, eleven-year-old Sigmund was kicked out of school. In 1938, the state forced the closure of medical practices run by Jewish doctors. Emil's second wife, Rose, had been urging him to emigrate since Hitler's consolidation of power in 1933, but Emil was an optimist. He believed in the goodness of his countrymen. He had proved his loyalty in World War I, when he earned an Iron Cross, second class. And his reputation sheltered him. High-ranking Nazis secretly brought their pregnant wives to see him, tipping him off to raids and other abuses.

Still, by 1938, Emil often slept at the hospital to avoid confrontations. He and Rose used a secret code to determine when it was unsafe for him to come home.

In October 1938, days before Sigmund's fifteenth birthday, and one month before Kristallnacht, when the Nazi Party unleashed its hatred on Jews, the family fled. A distant relative in Chicago they had never met sponsored their visas; Jews could not immigrate to America unless they were sponsored. They settled in Queens, New York, where Sigmund Americanized his name to Stephen. Emil's savings and insurance had been seized by the Nazis, and the once-prominent doctor struggled to find work. The family moved from apartment to apartment as they slid into poverty. Stephen finished high school two years early, at sixteen, and took a job in a market.

Finally, at the suggestion of the Chicago relatives, Emil turned to the Midwest and landed an opportunity to resume his practice in Toledo, Ohio. The family moved there in June 1940, one month after Hitler's Wehrmacht invaded the Netherlands, Belgium, and France. The Chicago relatives helped with the down payment for a house. Stephen, who had been attending college on scholarship in North Dakota, transferred to the University of Toledo.

He enlisted in the Army Reserve on June 12, 1943. Jake Herman, the South Dakota teenager, and John Land, the South Carolina medical student, enlisted and commissioned the same year. Those two, along with tens of thousands of other young men, became replacement troops, filling the ranks of units that had taken combat losses in summer 1944.

Stephen Mosbacher took a longer route to Europe. He was transferred to Camp Ritchie, Maryland, because of his fluency in German, French, and Russian. Twenty thousand Americans of German or Austrian descent (known today as the Ritchie Boys) were being trained at the camp in espionage, intelligence gathering, translation, analysis, and interrogation. They were taught to identify and remove booby traps, conduct raids, organize searches, and defend against enemy attacks. Many of the Ritchie Boys would be working as translators and cultural liaisons for combat units.

It was a distrustful time. Americans of Japanese descent were rounded up and sent to prison camps. Germans were accused of dual loyalties. But the Americans at Camp Ritchie were intensely loyal to their new country, and grateful. After all, 2,000 of them, including Stephen Mosbacher, were Jews.

One had been Stephen's schoolmate in Fürth, a neighboring town to Nuremberg where many Jewish Germans lived. Opinionated boys, they often argued about politics and current events. That boy was also kicked out of school and forced into the same Jewish school as Stephen in 1935. His family also left Germany for America in 1938. Like the Mosbachers, they settled in Queens. They both joined the United States Army in 1943. Were trained at Ritchie. Became interrogators. The boy's German name was Heinz, but he would become well known by the Americanized version: Henry Kissinger.

Stephen had hoped to become an officer. He deployed instead as a sergeant and was assigned to Patton's Third Army as an interrogator. He returned to Europe in late November 1944. Soon after, the Third Army raced north to help stop the German advance in the Battle of the Bulge. Mosbacher was stationed at their headquarters in Thionville, France, south of the Luxembourg border. He translated captured maps, supply lists, and letters to girlfriends back in Baden-Baden or Stuttgart. It was tedious work, and he was restless. He spent his evenings chatting with the French family that was billeting him, or with the local priest. The priest was astonished that Stephen seemed to know every family in Thionville.

Eventually, the Third Army ordered him forward to Luxembourg City, twelve miles from the front, where he interviewed a group of recently freed Russian children who had been kidnapped by the Nazis and used as forced labor. A Russian girl told him, "Before, with the Nazis, we cried all the time; now, we sing all day long."

One day, he overheard a prisoner tell his buddy, Second Lieutenant Nephi Georgi, a German Mormon whose family had emigrated to Salt Lake City in 1928, that he was from Nuremberg. "Can I talk to him?" Stephen asked, after Georgi's interrogation was complete.

The two men had a long conversation about home, which neither had seen for far too long. Stephen's hometown of Fürth had been heavily bombed, the man told him, and all the Jews sent away, although the man did not know where. He assumed they were relocated to another city. When Stephen told him German Jews had been sent to prison camps, the man "almost fainted," as Stephen wrote his father, Emil.

"Then he asked me a peculiar question: Did we ever think of coming back to live there? He thinks things will change greatly, but he quite understands that one cannot live there again, maybe, after all one has experienced there."

On January 14, with the Americans routing the German advance in the Ardennes Forest, he was transferred from Third Army headquarters to Combat Command B, 8th Armored Division. In France, he had done office work in the comfort of headquarters; now he'd live a soldier's life close to the front as one of six soldiers in Interrogation Prisoner of War Team 149. "I think the work here will be more direct," Moose Mosbacher—so called because of soldiers' notorious fondness for shortening names and his permanent place at the head of the chow line—wrote his family, "and one can therefore easier see the results. I think we'll be on the move quite a bit, I'd rather stay in one place, you know, but I have to get used to that."

Limburg was pristine, Moose thought, compared to Luxembourg. The farm animals had been slaughtered or stolen, but the fields lay ready for a spring planting under their blanket of snow. The roads were muddy but not cratered. The Americans had placed a Bailey bridge over the ruined spans of the Sint Servaas Bridge, allowing people to pass over the Maas between Wyck and the city center, and the buildings pressed with Dutch precision along its banks. Signs hung in several windows, and Stephen used his fluent German to pick out a few words of the Dutch.

"They were friendly with the Germans," the host of their billet that night, a schoolteacher, told him. "But the jails are full. The signs shame them and declare them undesirable."

The schoolteacher had hidden Dutch Jews and brought them food. Others in her neighborhood had too. "There were more of us," the schoolteacher said, "than there were of them."

"Thus a great number of Jews were able to save themselves," Stephen wrote his father, "and I only hope that somehow some of our dear folks will be among them, when the whole of the country is liberated."

The next day, the six-man interrogation team split to cover more ground and Stephen's half reached Margraten, where 2,500 soldiers from Combat Command B would billet while awaiting their call to the front. Stephen's team was assigned to a farmhouse on the edge of the village. Their hosts, the Vroonens, were a family of nine: a husband and wife, a grandmother, and six children. They crowded around the three interrogators, speaking rapidly in German, their shared language. Chicory coffee was offered, and a plum cake, fresh from the oven. A bowl of apples sat on the table, "Bedienen Sie sich, jederzeit." ("Help yourselves, any time.") The back room had been set aside for the Americans. It had electricity, running water, two large beds, and a stove, so the three soldiers could heat a pot of water for a wash. Stephen spoke rudimentary Dutch to the children, but they shouted back at him, excited, and he struggled to keep up.

Oma, the grandmother, sat by the fire, laughing. "It was the same with me," she said in German. She had moved from Germany thirty-eight years before, and she rarely spoke Dutch. Stubborn. She reminded Stephen of his own German grandmother, who he hadn't seen in years.

There wasn't much to do. The military traffic on the Rijksweg was constant, but the front was stuck in its winter defensive positions. The weather was miserable, freezing and rainy. The interrogation team had access to a jeep, which they occasionally took into Maastricht. They saw a movie, *Sergeant York*, and drank Belgian beer, excellent and inexpensive. But Stephen spent much of his time reading. At Camp Ritchie, he had read *The Germans: Double History of a Nation*. Now he read *Babbitt*, *A Tree Grows in Brooklyn*, a book of Hemingway short stories, and Sholem Asch's *The Apostle*.

The Vroonens were eager to please. The soldiers' room was spotless. Their laundry always washed. Mrs. Vroonen must have thought they liked waffles, because she prepared them most mornings, even though there was a mess hall nearby, and the family's rations barely covered milk and flour. One Sunday, the family let them sleep late, until 10:30 a.m. On another, the team was scheduled to leave early, at 4:30 a.m. The family was already up when Stephen awoke. Mrs. Vroonen had prepared them chocolate milk and eggs.

*It's too much*, Stephen thought. *How can I repay such kindness?* He bought cigarettes (for the adults) and candy (for the children) from the post exchange. He talked the mess hall into giving the family some of its leftover food and its garbage slops for their pigs. But to Stephen, it still felt like an unpaid debt.

The Vroonens' great pride was their radio. Stephen often sat in front of it with the family in the evening, listening to the news. We did this before, Mr. Vroonen told him. Everywhere Stephen went, every Dutch person he spoke to, it was always *before*. Before the Germans, before the occupation. As if speaking not just of a different time, but a different place. One evening, Mr. Vroonen brought out his old drum-major uniform. Gold epaulets, golden V8s, cords, and big gold buttons. The jacket was dirty, dark blue with stains, but it had twelve medals on the breast. It was a symbol of *before*, and Mr. Vroonen took pride in it. Stephen opened a bottle of liquor he had bought at the post exchange, and everyone had a drink. Even Oma, who didn't have even three teeth, and had to cut her apples into very small bites, enjoyed a glass.

The family cried when the interrogators left. First Oma, whom Stephen called his Dutch grandmother, then the children. Then Mr. and Mrs. Vroonen. "Let me at least wash your overshoes," Mrs. Vroonen begged. "It may be the last thing I can do for you."

It was ridiculous, they were only going on an errand. They would be back in the evening.

But Stephen understood. The house was on the opposite side of Margraten from the burial ground, a mile and a half away, but death hung over the village. The citizens took pride in the cemetery. It was their offering to the Americans, a thank-you for their freedom, and it permeated their lives. The smell of death, always in the air. The Black gravediggers, mud-caked and exhausted, trudging to their billet in the uninsulated fruit warehouse 400 yards from the Vroonens' home. Nobody could miss the body trucks, churning down the Rijksweg every day. The guardhouse where the trucks stopped for inspections and paperwork was in front of the fruit warehouse, and Stephen saw them idling there: canvases pulled tight over a lumpy heap, viscera dripping over the edges, a loose arm or loose leg, a death-blind stare.

"IN GERMANY," Stephen wrote in caps, at the top of a letter dated February 9–10.

*Exactly six years, 4 months, and 5 days after we left this country I came across the border again. You can imagine the feeling that goes with it. It is something that can hardly be described. . . . We left our place accompanied by the tears of the [Vroonen] family, and then kept right on driving. The roads were bad and muddy, but. . . . All of a sudden, I see the customs control of the other country, and then we crossed a little bridge, and there was the Zollhaus, without any sentry. We had entered Germany. It was exactly 3:42 p.m.*

By February 14, Stephen was back in Margraten with the Vroonen family. That day, Valentine's Day, he visited a shop in Maastricht, still abuzz from General Eisenhower's visit with his commanders earlier in the week. The name of the pre-war proprietor, scraped away by the Nazis, had been repainted above the door. A similar thing had been done in Luxembourg, in honor of Jewish owners who had not returned. He asked the current shopkeeper for directions to the Jewish Committee, an organization set up by survivors for displaced Jews.

At the committee office, he was greeted by a Mr. Wijngaard. He had fled Limburg in 1942, Wijngaard told Stephen, and hidden in Belgium with his daughter. His wife and sister, though, had been captured and deported. He had not heard from them. Stephen told him about his family members in Germany, "our dear ones," as he wrote his father. Emil was one of the few of his family to get out, and the news from the Nuremberg prisoner in Luxembourg had been ominous. Mr. Wijngaard wrote down the names and addresses of Stephen's dear ones. In Eindhoven, a committee kept the names of all the liberated Jews. It was well organized, but of course not complete, with so much of the Netherlands under Nazi control. He promised to write if any of Stephen's names were on the list.

"I am with you in my thoughts all the time, my good ones," Stephen assured his family. "When I am driving through these areas, I always think of how grateful I can be to know you [are] safely over there. It is a wonderful feeling, and everyone confirms this. Seeing this all around destruction over here, which no one was able to escape, one thinks that it is really a miracle that America has been so untouched by this turmoil."

"Oh, how I wish that I could sit with you for a few minutes and talk to you. But otherwise I am glad that I am here, doing what I am, and I couldn't think of a place that is more right for me at the present than this."

The Vroonen house was comfortable, and their friendship a comfort. But Stephen knew, as every soldier knew, that the hard work lay ahead.

# CHAPTER 50

# THE CATHEDRAL

— ★ —

*Walter Huchthausen*
February 1945

Limburg's roads were packed with jeeps and transports, tens of thousands of soldiers on the move, though the Ninth Army headquarters was not. The countryside near Maastricht was saturated with ammo dumps and storage depots, the city stuffed with bars luring soldiers with allusions to home, like Oklahoma, a club with neither cowboy hats nor cattle. Not that Walter Huchthausen had ever been to the Oklahoma club. The bars were for enlisted men. There were clubs for officers, but he rarely went there either.

As a Monuments Man, Hutch spent most of his days on the road conducting inspections. The one place, though, that never left his mind was Aachen. The city center had been flattened by aerial bombardments, but the ancient Aachen Cathedral still stood amid the destruction. The stained-glass windows, the tallest in a Gothic structure in Europe, had been blown out and the altar severely mangled by a direct hit from an unexploded bomb, but First Army's Monuments Man, Captain Walker Hancock, had shored up the worst of the damage in October. Still, the buttresses of the enormous window walls needed reinforcement with cement and brick. The Hungarian Chapel had needed a temporary roof before the elements destroyed its eighteenth century Baroque interior. Hutch was overseeing a team of elderly German laborers, all the younger men having been either drafted into the German military or arrested by the Allies, who were rushing to complete that work.

It might seem strange, he knew, to be saving monuments on German soil while twenty miles away his fellow soldiers were in a life-and-death struggle against that enemy. But Aachen Cathedral, with its unique blend of Carolingian and Gothic architecture and priceless ecclesiastic treasures, belonged to the world. He was proud of the U.S. Army for preserving it.

But his work at lesser sites, repairing roofs and propping up walls, transporting little known works of art and minor cultural objects to safe locations, also mattered. To Hutch, every assignment was worthy. All artistic creations were stories, and all those stories mattered.

On February 13, he visited the art vault in Sint Pietersberg, as he had told Frieda van Schaïk he hoped he would. He was the third Monuments Man to inspect it, after Hancock and Lieutenant George Stout, their leader. The air-conditioning and moisture systems worked perfectly, just as Dave van Schaïk had designed them. The densely packed paintings were protected, still hanging on their metal racks. *The Night Watch* was safe in its custom niche. Masterworks all, but fragile objects, made by fragile men.

"[C]onditions of pictures and storage found to be excellent" was the extent of his report.

# CHAPTER 51

# "IT WILL BE DONE"

— ★ —

*Bill Hughes*
March 1945

The 784th Tank Battalion went into division reserve on February 9. The weather had been icy and cold throughout the month of January, and the Allied advance across the Roer River was postponed. The tankers spent their downtime with the Dutch. It was a rural area. Most of the farmers and villagers had never seen a Black man, but they were eager to help their liberators. Throughout Limburg Province—in Venlo, Heer, Margraten, Maastricht, and other towns—the Dutch welcomed American soldiers into their homes. They had little food to offer, but the Americans brought their own, and the Dutch prepared it.

Lasting bonds form quickly when death is near: those in Limburg Province having just been freed from it, the tankers facing it in the days ahead. One tank commander from the 784th, Sergeant Charles Jefferson, became so attached to his host family that he wrote about his "Dutch mother" in his letters home. The family had a newborn baby. When snow and ice prevented the godmother from traveling to the christening, Sergeant Jefferson volunteered. After the ceremony, they stood for a picture: a Dutch family and their Black American friend, a huge smile on his face, holding his goddaughter in his arms.

The 784th returned to the front on February 26, the third day of a long-planned Allied advance, Operation Grenade. After months of delay, the Allies were finally resuming operations where they left off in fall 1944, when they paused to wait out the weather and build up combat power for the crossing of the Rhine. Before they could do that, though, they had to cross the Roer. The river was a natural barrier, and the Germans had fortified it with troops and artillery on the eastern bank.

The Allies had exploded across the Roer on the first day of the operation, but the bridgeheads were narrow, and they had yet to take the operationally important village of Hilfarth, Germany, a few miles north. Company A, 784th Tank Battalion, in support of the 134th Infantry, 35th Infantry Division, rolled into the town under heavy fire. Mines and booby traps were everywhere. Automatic weapons fire echoed down the streets. But German forces in Hilfarth lacked tank-killing weapons. By 2:00 p.m., the Americans had taken the village without a single casualty.

A few hours later, as the tankers rested, a shell exploded near their position. They dove for cover, but a piece of shrapnel caught Sergeant Jefferson in the back of the head. As his horrified crew rushed to his aid, Jefferson fell, blood gushing from the wound. Soon, he was convulsing and in shock. He was evacuated to a field hospital, where he remained overnight, then was rushed to the U.S. Army's 105th Evacuation Hospital in Sittard, in Limburg, for emergency surgery. He died two days later, at 8:10 a.m. on March 1, 1945. He was the only soldier from the 784th mortally wounded in the month of February.

By then, though, February was gone, and the 784th was barreling north with elements of the 35th Infantry Division. They took thirteen villages and small towns in two days as they advanced toward their objective, the river town of Venlo. They raced so quickly to the bridge into the city that a German soldier on a motorcycle threw up his hands and surrendered without sounding the alarm. As they drove past the town's outlying buildings, Bill Hughes heard music and laughter. The Germans were eating dinner, completely unaware. Most of them surrendered too.

It was mop-up duty after that. The tanks drove forward, infantrymen riding on top. They dropped the men at crucial intersections, then raced ahead to block the Germans' escape. Infantry went door to door, rounding up stragglers. It was Bill Hughes's first taste of combat, and it had gone as well as an enemy encounter could. He rode in his M5 tank, yelling from the hatch to the infantrymen doing the "house calls." All the soldiers, white infantry and Black tankers, had a good laugh about that.

Then the civilians appeared. The first to approach a tank took a rifle butt to the face. Infantrymen raised their weapons. Then they realized what had happened. They had crossed back over the border: the citizens of Venlo were Dutch, not German. And they were starving.

The Dutch had risen against their occupiers as the Allies approached in September 1944, striking and closing the railroads, among other actions. The Germans retaliated by blockading Dutch ports. They cut off the cities of the north from the farming regions to the south. They lifted the blockade in November, once the front line had hardened, leaving most of the Netherlands under German control. It was too late for the Dutch. A brutal winter had set in, blanketing the country in bitter cold. The meager rations dwindled. By the closing days of 1944, they were all but gone. The Germans were unmoved. In Amsterdam and other major cities, people ate the leaves from the trees and drank the slush from the gutters. By March 1945, 20,000 Dutch citizens had died of starvation, many of them older men who sacrificed themselves so others could eat. Millions suffered severe malnutrition. Already, the tragedy had a name: the Hunger Winter.

In Venlo, the conditions were especially harsh, since the British had reached the west bank of the river in September, but were unable to cross. With the two sides targeting each other across the river, the town was blockaded. Almost nothing in or out for months. The only large cache of food was potatoes. The citizens ate them slowly through the winter. When the potatoes ran out, they ate the spring grass that had begun to sprout from the snow. One young man on the run from the Germans had hidden in an eighteen-inch crawl space for two years, daring to venture out only at night. He looked half the weight he should have been.

"And we thought we had it bad," one infantryman remarked.

That night, the people of Venlo ate American field rations. The 784th slept in comfortable Dutch beds. Bill Hughes had a warm bath, his first in many days. The Germans shelled the city, but even that couldn't dampen their spirits.

"What a day this has been," Captain Orval Faubus, an intelligence officer in the 320th Infantry, wrote in his journal.

*Tonight there are about 24 miles of the Siegfried Line Defenses which are no more.... The attack was led by Col Alexander's 3rd Bn, which was spearheaded by Capt Kurtz's K Co and two companies of Negro tankers.*

259

*The CO of light tanks led most of the way, and those black boys proved to be*
*good fighters. Today's action was more or less in the nature of an adventure*
*after some of the hellish battles we've been through. So we don't know how*
*the colored boys would be if there was only unrelenting hell as we have seen it*
*several times, but they did all right today.*

The 784th showed its mettle two days later. They were advancing
down a road five miles from the German border, near the town of Geldern,
when the bridge in front of them blew up. A Panzerfaust smashed into their
lead tank, disabling it and stopping the column. The infantrymen who had
been riding on top of the tanks leapt for cover, but buried mines kept the
tanks trapped in the open. They couldn't turn, go forward, or retreat, so
they unleashed a massive fusillade, blasting their big guns over the heads of
their infantrymen.

"Hey, white boy!" someone yelled down from a hatch. "Pick 'em out for
us, and we'll shoot 'em."

The tanks pounded the countryside for two hours, until they were reinforced by the British 8th Armoured Brigade.

That night, the task force started toward the village of Sevelen. They
drove in radio silence with only blackout lights, metal slats over the head-
lights to make it difficult for enemy aircraft to spot them. It took two
hours to reach the edge of town, though it was only a few miles. A halt
was called, and First Lieutenant Waters, commander of Company D, was
ordered to lead the charge in his M3 half-track personnel carrier, a truck
with tank tracks on the back instead of rubber tires. A corporal manned the
.50 caliber machine gun. Six infantrymen rode on the running boards. Bill
Hughes was reassigned from his tank to the half-track so he could man the
commander's radio.

The night was quiet as they crossed a railroad bridge and crept through
the darkened streets. No cats in doorways. No lights in windows. Hughes
could barely breathe, for fear of upsetting the delicate balance. He knew the
enemy was here, somewhere.

The half-track made the crossroads at the center of town. The lead
tank pulled up beside them, the infantrymen fanned out to check the
shadows. Twelve minutes ticked away as the rest of the battalion crossed
the bridge and trundled through the town. Bill Hughes gripped his radio,

watching the night, but there was nothing to report, and radio silence had been called.

Then the railroad bridge exploded. The lead tank, hit by a Panzerfaust, burst into flames. An anti-tank gun was hidden in a barn. The American tanks opened up and blew the barn to bits, but mortar fire and artillery were raining down. The Germans had preregistered the coordinates of the crossroads, then waited for the Americans to enter the kill zone.

An orange flare was fired: radios on. Hughes relayed his coordinates, heard the order to pull back. The half-track and remaining tanks backed carefully out of the crossroads, firing as they went. With the blown bridge at their back, the infantrymen laid down a withering barrage. A tank with a bulldozer blade scraped out defilades to give the soldiers cover. Bill Hughes called headquarters as the defensive lines formed.

*We're surrounded. Bridge blown. No means of escape.*

The call came back: *Hold your position. Reinforcements preparing to move. Call with further developments.*

Bill needed to get the message to the infantry commander, but the radios in his half-track and the tanks could not communicate with the radios the infantry carried. He had to deliver the message himself. He crouched behind the half-track, plotting his path, as the night lit up with muzzle blasts and mortar fire. No time for fear. He sprinted toward a fighting position. Enemy bullets whipped past him, while the 784th sent 37mm rounds the other way. No luck in the first foxhole, or the next. He finally found a lieutenant with a radio, who contacted the commander. The commander didn't want the message read over the radio—the Germans could be listening. He wanted Hughes to come another 200 yards and tell him to his face. So Bill sprinted through the bullets and the shrapnel.

The infantry commander requested they move the half-track closer so he could stay in better communication with the 784th.

Too dangerous, Hughes told him. In the dark, infantrymen hugging the dirt for cover would get run over.

"Fine," the commander said. "Stay awake. I'll be sending runners to you." Hughes braved the fire again to give Lieutenant Waters, commanding the company from the cover of a tank, the intel from the infantry.

"Keep me informed," Waters barked. "I need you."

Bill Hughes stayed on the radio, the crucial link between the task force commander and his company. He sent runners between his half-track and the infantry commander, and crossed the firefight six times with updates on the infantry-armor coordination. He saw Sergeant Walter "Pop" Hall, a forty-seven-year-old veteran of World War I, using a bulldozer blade attached to a tank to fill in craters on the road. He spotted men crawling out of the bottom hatch of their tanks for extra ammo, rations, and fuel. Bill watched medics running in the light of the muzzle flashes, leaping into defilades where wounded men were bleeding out, where soldiers blazed away at an enemy hidden somewhere in the night.

By morning, the firing slowed, as both sides succumbed to exhaustion. But the Americans were still taking a pounding, and reinforcements had not arrived. A decision was made: the only way out was through. The infantry and tanks would divide into three columns, on three parallel streets, and fight their way into the enemy.

The men counted their rifle rounds and said their prayers. They settled into their tanks, crouched in their fighting positions, studied the terrain and any strongpoints along their advance. Then, they burst out of the trap and barreled over the lip of the defilades toward Sevelen, the tanks riding high and the infantrymen sprinting behind them. The gunfire was so thick it felt seamless. The tanks shot so fast, they barely aimed. There were no targets anyway, the enemy was on top of them. The corporal firing the .50 caliber in Bill Hughes's half-track ate through the ammunition belts so fast the barrel became red-hot.

And then, somehow, it was done. They had reached the crossroads, where 100 Germans surrendered. Fifty more lay dead. Back home, the story was picked up on the wire and spread throughout the country. "A Negro tank battalion task force staged a miniature Bastogne in Sevelen today," the *Los Angeles Times* trumpeted, "mauling Nazi parachute units in savage street fighting while cut off for 18 hours."

The "tank-riding doughboys and the Negro tank crews" did a wonderful job, Orval Faubus wrote, putting white and Black soldiers together in victory. Whatever reservations he had about "the colored boys" after Venlo, he knew their fighting spirit now.

Bill Hughes was overjoyed. The high of the battle. The adrenaline of the fight. In that moment, he didn't think of the dead men in his company. In the future, they would come back to him, especially the faces of his friends. But his primary thought, in the afterglow of combat, was how proud he was to be in this battalion, with these men, the fighting 784th. They had been pinned down in an ambush, under constant fire. They had fought against being overrun for eighteen hours, without reinforcements. They had come through. Turned the battle. Routed the enemy.

"It Will Be Done." That was their battalion motto, and at that moment, to Bill Hughes, those words meant everything. Whatever had to be done, whatever the odds, Bill Hughes knew the 784th would get it done.

They rested on the other side of Sevelen: sleep for the men and maintenance for their machines. After a few hours, they were on the march. Morale was so high, Hughes didn't mind. He believed in these men. He wanted to fight. *Whatever it is. Wherever we go. It will be done.*

They saw action the following day in Kamperbruch. The day after that, a vicious firefight in Millingen. In four bloody days of fighting, in four small German villages and towns, the 784th lost multiple tanks and dozens of men. The white officer corps of Company C was wiped out, leaving the Black enlisted men to lead at Millingen. In one tank, only a lower leg of the commanding officer remained. The men buried it beside his destroyed machine.

They progressed, in those four bloody days, barely ten miles. When the 784th went into rest on March 7, they were still two miles from the Rhine.

# CHAPTER 52

# THE CIVILIAN COMMITTEE

— ★ —

*Margraten*
March 1945

"I will take care of your cousin's grave as if it were my own family. Indeed, I will adopt his grave." Those were the words Joseph van Laar, the Margraten village clerk, had spoken to Captain Lane in December. That was the promise made, and he intended to keep it.

It did not take long to realize he had unleashed a deluge. Many American soldiers were wandering through the cemetery, searching for fallen comrades. When they saw Van Laar at John Land's grave and asked what he was doing, they requested, even pleaded, that he do the same for their friend too. Van Laar always said yes. What else could he say? These boys had died for his freedom. But he didn't have the time, he soon realized, to honor all those promises on his own.

And yet, they kept coming: the soldiers, the requests. There was an intense desire to know a comrade-in-arms was being cared for and remembered, especially from soldiers who knew that, but by the grace of God, they might end up here too. They asked of Van Laar what they hoped their buddies would ask if their roles were reversed.

On January 24, 1945, Van Laar met at town hall with five other prominent citizens of Margraten. They had all risked their lives for freedom, in some way, during the occupation. Van Laar was a Resistance contact at the Margraten post office who passed messages and supplied Dutch Jews with false identification papers. Joseph Ronckers, the burgemeester of Margraten, had hidden from the Nazis for much of 1944 in a stable. He returned on September 13, after the NSB-installed mayor failed to hail a ride to Aachen during the German exodus and literally ran out of town, carrying his suitcase. The six men—they were, of course, all men—decided to form a committee.

"We as Dutch citizens feel an obligation towards the American soldiers who died not just for their country, but also for our freedom, and we want to do something for them in return," they informed Captain Shomon, the American officer in charge of the cemetery. Their idea was to collect money for a Holy Mass for the fallen, to be celebrated on the third Sunday of every month. Shomon cautioned the cemetery was temporary; the men were undeterred.

In early February, the Civilian Committee Margraten, as they called themselves, met at the house of Burgemeester Ronckers. Shomon attended the meeting. Mrs. Ronckers served a formal dinner using meat, flour, sugar, and coffee provided by Sergeant Brennan from the 611th's supplies. Shomon contributed a bottle of scotch. Plans were discussed, and priorities set: to beautify the cemetery and organize civilian access to the grounds.

But the conditions weren't right. The weather was brutal: even more ice than the terrible January. This was no weather for planting flowers or worrying about Dutch visitors. And the American GRS soldiers and Black gravediggers, after the struggles of the fall, had the burial operation firmly under control, the process from death to ground respectful and efficient. Within hours of Sergeant Charles Jefferson of the 784th Tank Battalion taking his final breath at 8:10 a.m. on March 1, his body was collected and taken to Margraten. He was processed through the stripping line and autopsy tent like all the others and buried in a mattress cover, with a white cross at his head and a chaplain at his feet, at 5:00 p.m., less than nine hours after his death. Two hours later, Father Heynen celebrated the funeral liturgy and the Rite of Committal for the men buried at Margraten that day, and for the thousands buried there in the last four months.

A few weeks earlier, Joseph van Laar had approached Burgemeester Ronckers. He had a letter: words of gratitude from Dr. and Mrs. Land in South Carolina for the unusually kind gesture of adopting the grave of their son. He mentioned the other soldiers—many other soldiers—to whom he had made the same promise.

Ronckers saw the solution immediately, and when he and Van Laar brought it to the Civilian Committee Margraten at the March meeting, they saw it too. Van Laar couldn't handle all these grave adoptions on his own, but surely the village could handle such a task.

"Why not have the committee," they said, "ask people to step forward and accept such a responsibility?"

# CHAPTER 53

# A RAGGED BUNCH

— ★ —

*Stephen Mosbacher*
March 1945

Combat Command B, 8th Armored Division, crossed the Roer River on February 23, the first day of Operation Grenade. In the early morning hours of February 28, they stopped at Hilfarth, Germany, and received orders to take a village to the north. This was only hours after Sergeant Charles Jefferson suffered his fatal wound in the same village. They joined the 35th Infantry Division in Sevelen, three days after Bill Hughes and the 784th managed their dramatic breakout from the ambush in the village. For the next two weeks, they traveled roughly parallel to the 784th, staying between three and ten miles to their south.

On March 5, they entered the town of Rheinberg. Once again, German forces let the American tanks roll into the town, then sprung their trap. Men in foxholes with tank-killing weapons fired point-blank into vulnerable flanks. Within minutes, eighteen tanks were crippled or on fire. The tankers scrambled from their burning machines, throwing themselves behind cover and fighting like infantrymen. A third company barreled into the firefight, blasting at anything that moved. Four tanks made it to the city center, but without infantry support, they couldn't hold and had to pull back. It wasn't until the 35th Infantry Division arrived in the afternoon— the same division that fought alongside the 784th—that the Americans were able to take and hold the city. The 8th Armored Division lost forty-one tanks in the brutal fighting, and took 199 casualties.

"We had quite an exciting trip," interpreter Stephen Mosbacher wrote his father the next day from Ossenberg, Germany, a few miles farther down the road. Even those miles weren't easy: the artillery fire was so thick, the GIs called the roadway 88 Lane after the caliber of the enemy shells. The infantry had to clear every house as the column advanced. "It wasn't easy going at all, but we are here nonetheless."

Typical military understatement. Most soldiers didn't want to alarm their loved ones, no matter how horrible the combat, and Moose was no exception.

The interrogation team set up shop in the offices of a mining operation on the edge of Ossenberg. The Rhine was so close, the Germans on the other side were lobbing artillery into the American ranks. The mine was ideal for cover, and also warm. The rain and snow were breaking, but it was still ice-cold in western Germany. The 8th Armored Division had taken 512 prisoners. It was going to be a long few days. Might as well be comfortable.

"First customer," Stephen joked with his friend Lieutenant Georgi, to settle the mood. No matter what he told his family, the carnage had unnerved him.

It didn't take long for Stephen to realize these weren't the German soldiers he had expected. Some were young, green recruits. Others were stragglers from other units, or men Stephen suspected of desertion. Many were sick or wounded, left behind when the stronger soldiers retreated. One company was entirely composed of men suffering stomach ailments, another of men deafened by artillery fire. They had been pulled out of German military hospitals and forced to fight with their backs against the Rhine. Others were much older than typical combat age, part of Nazi Germany's national militia, known as the Volkssturm. Almost to a man, they were polite. They answered questions, but knew little of value. They were relieved, it was clear, to be prisoners, instead of out there in Ossenberg with the 350 German dead. There was no other way, it seemed, off the German line.

A ragged bunch, Stephen thought.

And yet: They had fought like trapped animals. They had knocked out forty-one tanks and killed or wounded almost 200 men.

*If this is the rear guard*, Stephen thought, *what lies across the Rhine?*

The next morning, the miners arrived. They wanted to get back to work. The other two interrogators hated the idea. No one knew who these men with picks and shovels really were. Stephen saw the truth in their eyes: They were struggling to survive. Their families were hungry. The only thing that made them different from good-hearted, hardworking people like his Dutch family, the Vroonens, was a border. This war had hurt these ordinary Germans too.

He contacted a colonel. The colonel contacted a general. The general gave his permission for the miners to return to work.

The other interrogators laughed at Stephen for going up the chain of command. A sergeant didn't make requests to a colonel. He definitely didn't have his request forwarded to a general. Who do you think you are, Moose? You think the general has time to listen to you feeling sorry for the Krauts?

But as they walked out of the mine offices, laughing and joking about Moose's big request, Lieutenant Georgi put his arm around him. "You did the right thing," he said.

The villagers of Ossenberg were out searching the rubble, trying to piece together their broken lives. Moose saw a woman gesturing at two bored soldiers. He was often asked to interpret such encounters, so he saved the soldiers the trouble and walked over.

The woman was complaining about her piano, damaged in the attack. She was in tears. She couldn't believe this had happened to her. "We have never done anything against the Jews," she pleaded to Stephen. "We didn't break into their houses or stores. And, anyway, my boys would have been too small at that time."

Moose turned to the soldiers and told them what she said. One of them spit on the ground. "Tell her we heard different," he said.

# CHAPTER 54

# THE DANCE

— ★ —

*Frieda van Schaïk; Walter Huchthausen*
March 1945

Frieda van Schaïk checked herself in the mirror, her face bright against the darkness of her room. She was not used to seeing herself this way. She noticed Moekie standing behind her, her face in shadow. Her mother was looking at her closely, quietly. When she saw Frieda watching her, she smiled.

"Ik ben trots op je." ("I am proud of you.")

She lifted the brush and began to smooth the wave of hair at her daughter's forehead. Frieda shifted her gaze back to her own face. Her wide eyes. Her small nose, with a few freckles across the cheeks. Her firm, stiff jaw. She smiled, but the tension remained. She breathed deep, tried again, and it dropped away.

Her hair was up, showing her neck. She didn't wear it this way. She didn't usually wear it any way at all. But Moekie had rolled and shaped it into something like the style she saw on the fashionable girls in church. Moekie had chosen her dress and spent an hour ironing it. Straightened the lace. A few stitches at the seam. American soap, a gift from Captain Hoadley, for a stain. She gave Frieda a necklace she had worn as a girl in Arnhem, a piece of jewelry Frieda had never seen before. She had never seen her mother wear any jewelry at all.

"Ik ben trots op je. Heb ik je dat al eerder verteld?" ("I am proud of you. Have I told you that before?")

Frieda knew about the dances. She had read about the controversies in the papers. But she had never been invited to a dance. She had never, she supposed, been invited to anything. That was fine. Frieda had never wanted what she didn't expect to receive. But now she had been invited to a social event—not her father, not her older sisters, but her—and not by the Dutch, but by her family's American friends.

After five months in Maastricht, the Ninth Army was leaving. The Americans had crossed the Roer, and the headquarters staff was moving forward. The displacement included Captain Hoadley and many of their friends from the Red Cross office down the road. Chaplain Barsh, who stood in line to get her hot soup and bread when she rode her bicycle to visit him at the 91st Evacuation Hospital. Captain Lang, who had a jeep named Sally, and who once returned from Germany looking like a pregnant woman, his jacket so stuffed with contraband.

"Liberated material," he said with a smile. It turned out to be food, "liberated" for Frieda and her family.

The Red Cross sent a car. The driver helped her across the muddy Bemelerweg into the back seat where her chaperone was waiting. She didn't need the help. She had ridden her bicycle down blacked-out roads past German sentries, witnessed the crash of Allied planes, buried false identities, explored Sint Pietersberg with her father, and hooked hibernating bats by their claws to the front of her shirt while reaching out with her gathering pole for more.

She crossed the Bemelerweg a few times a week to talk with soldiers resting in the apple orchard on their way to the front. They were different now than in the fall, when the weather was perfect and their advance seemed unstoppable. They were weary after the failure of Market Garden, the brutality of the combat in Aachen, the German counterattack in the Ardennes. They had lost buddies, seen horrific things. They were young, mostly her age, but no longer innocent. They knew what lay ahead, and they were afraid, in a way they had not been before.

"You're not a coward," she told them, when they confessed their fears. She had a certain manner. They confided in her, like a sister. "All soldiers feel this way. Just remember what Christ has told us for centuries: 'All who are heavy ladened, come to me, and I'll refresh you.' Just say, 'Lord, I can't cope. Tell me what to do.' And He will be there. He will refresh you."

She thought of their faces as they started up the road, then stopped and turned. The peace in their eyes. What they were going down that road to do was hard. It was deadly. But for a moment, at least, the doubt had passed.

She thought of her friend Walter Huchthausen, who had visited her family several times. With the other men, she listened while Pappie talked, but with Hutch, she had conversations. He was often away, inspecting buildings or relocating art, but he always returned with a story. He, too, would be moving forward with the rest of the Ninth Army. Would he, she wondered, ever find it in his interest to return to Limburg?

The dance was in an attic above a store. The size of the space was a shock, after so many years confined to Moekie's kitchen. The light was soft. The ladies' committee had brought in lanterns. A military band played in the corner. Streamers looped along the roofline. Near a table of donuts, officers in uniforms talked in groups. At round tables, young women chatted in their own small groups. The dance floor was already full of couples, and older women were passing between them, watching, making sure everyone had what they needed and nothing more.

Frieda felt a moment of doubt: Did she belong? Even the older women, the committee members, were elegant. The younger women were stylish, comfortable, as if they'd been to many dances before. Or perhaps it was just nerves.

It was Moekie's necklace she touched for comfort, although she didn't realize it. *You belong*, she told herself, as she stepped into the room.

She recognized a woman who worked at the Red Cross office. They hugged and took a table. At the first lull in conversation, Frieda's eyes began to wander, and then they stopped, because there he was, across the room. She had never seen Walter in his dress uniform. He was tall, elegant, and handsome. Sophisticated. He was speaking with the Dutch couple who were billeting him, and she could see the ease in his posture, the way he leaned slightly forward, always interested in what others had to say. He was kind to everyone, of course. There was nothing special in that. There was nothing special, she realized, in his kindness to her. But when he turned and saw her, his boyish face broke into a smile, and the memory of their evenings together, talking at her mother's home, collapsed into a shocking, exhilarating thought: *I was hoping for this.*

And maybe, just maybe, he was hoping for this too.

He shook hands with the couple, then headed across the floor.

Her instinct was to look away, but she kept her eyes up, unafraid. Her smile, she suspected, was too wide. She couldn't help it. The smile was how she felt.

He didn't come to her. He went to her chaperone and asked permission to dance with her. The chaperone said yes.

"Would you like to, Frieda?" he asked, holding out his hand.

She could not have named the song. She could not have said how long they danced, or identified the steps. She didn't remember what he said, if he said anything at all. He was a good dancer. She knew that because he made it easy, he led her lightly, and while their time together seemed to run through countless perambulations, it was over in an instant.

The next morning, she grabbed her bicycle and headed into town. She told herself she was on an errand, but she ended up outside the Ninth Army headquarters. She circled once, then stopped. She looked past the gate. The building was silent.

No, it was foolish. What was she thinking?

She circled again. She watched the headquarters building. No one was around, but the duty officer was watching her closely. She put down her bicycle and approached the building.

"Is Captain Huchthausen here?"

"No, ma'am."

She felt her heart collapse. He didn't even bother to pretend to check. But as she turned to go, she saw him, that brilliant smile on his face as he came bounding down the steps.

"Frieda," he said.

"Walter. I mean, Captain . . ."

He hugged her. "Frieda, it's so nice of you to come."

"I thought you'd gone." Her heart was flipping over. The greatest joy, the greatest sadness, all in that friendly hug.

"Soon. Within a day. We're finally on the move." He was beaming. She could see how excited he was to finally get past Aachen to the great cities of the Rhine. "But I'll be back, Frieda, don't worry. I'm coming back at the first opportunity. I will see you and your family very soon."

# CHAPTER 55

# PROMISE KEPT

— ★ —

*Emilie Michiels van Kessenich*
March 1945

Emilie Michiels van Kessenich worked through her contacts in Heerlen, Valkenburg, and several other towns in Limburg, making sure the lists of girls were up-to-date. The Americans were moving east. The Apostolate of the Front had been holding dances across Limburg, wherever they were convenient for the troops, and the Allied advance meant she needed to move the dances eastward too. Some might even be held in conquered German territory, but that would take extra planning, since she didn't have contacts in western Germany, and it was too early to consider at this time. The Allies were barely twenty miles across the border.

She was pregnant again, and she was tired. The controversy had never really died, and the work to organize so many events was more than anybody besides Willem seemed to realize. The list of appropriate girls alone held 2,500 names. But this was a crucial time. The Americans were attacking at last, and she could not forget what her friend Colonel Senecal had told her: rest and recuperation was not just a reward, but a way to preserve the strength and sanity of the boys at the front. For this latest push, the boys would need all of the strength that they could muster.

She had not asked for this job. She had merely extended a hand of gratitude to General Corlett, as so many did to the Americans after liberation. The general had given her this assignment. He would not have done it, she believed, if the Lord did not agree that it was right. She refused to let them down.

# CHAPTER 56

# RESPITE

— ★ —

*Stephen Mosbacher*
March 1945

It was always the same: "We never did any harm to the Jews." "We never were for Hitler." "We never belonged to the party." One fellow swore he was from Poland. When a soldier asked him in Polish which city he was from, the man decided he was Dutch. The 8th Armored Division had taken 1,300 prisoners, and somehow none had done anything wrong.

It's like being a Fuller Brush salesman, Stephen thought: going door to door, being lied to again and again.

The third man on his interrogation team, Singer, was an anti-Zionist. He argued the European Jews brought it on themselves, being so insular. They needed to assimilate. When Stephen billeted for a day with a Dutch family in Venlo, the city liberated by Bill Hughes's 784th Tank Battalion, the daughters told him it was the Jews' fault for not fighting back. They took everything, the most brutal insults, without protest. They let themselves be deported like cattle. Their rabbis made lists. It didn't matter that they were threatened, said the girls, who had never been personally threatened. The Nazis should not have found one man willing to go along. "I'm sorry," they insisted the rabbis should have said, "I am the only Jew in this town."

It ground on him: the destruction, the lying, the racism. The American dead, the Germans in the rubble. He would not, he decided, let it change him. He kept his smile, his easy nature. He laughed at all the jokes about his spot in the front of the line for chow. He volunteered for the billeting team, whose job it was to enter towns and secure sleeping quarters, a kitchen, and other basic necessities for an army on the move. This meant cajoling information from hostile locals, Stephen's specialty, while advancing with the forward troops, ahead of the main body of Combat Command B. By the time those soldiers, cooks, and officers arrived, the arrangements for their comfort—if the bare minimum can be called comfort—had already been made.

For this cheerful attitude and service, Stephen was granted a special leave: three nights at the Hôtel de Paris, in the heart of the City of Lights.

He left the front on March 19. On a previous trip to retrieve his belongings from his old billet in Thionville, France, Moose's transport had turned south through an area of Luxembourg devastated by the Battle of the Bulge. Staring across the hood of a jeep, he had seen captured Germans repairing bomb-shattered roads, with Black American soldiers standing guard, sunglasses on and rifles resting on their shoulders.

He wrote to his family:

*It is very restful to see that landscape, even though it is dotted by rusty, ghost-like monster tanks, which, when they lie on the road with their tracks blown off and their wheels up in the air, look like giant, dead old beetles. And then you see the stores of discarded ammunition, shot-down bombers and gliders. It is an interesting picture. But when you come through the ravaged cities, where whole sections are turned into dust, and where only a few ragged pillars, the former cornerstones of former houses reach into the air as reminders of the past, then you really get a complete picture of the horrors and the devastation of war. And then you see old men and women standing amidst the rubble, and looking for the things that were once their own. It is pitiful to see them fishing in the dust for their furniture and minor belongings, and then, after some digging, they come out with the broken leg of a chair, or a broken doll.*

This time, Moose and the men passed through Aachen, then Maastricht. In Belgium, young children stood by the side of the road with their pockets full of beer bottles and cigarettes in their mouths. Whenever Allied jeeps came by, they held out a beer and pointed to the cigarettes. Moose figured most were six, maybe seven years old. Everything was for sale, he thought sadly.

In Liège, they passed a column of Black soldiers heading east. A little girl leaned out her window: "A bas les Negres!" she yelled. ("Down with the Negros!") The Black soldiers thought it was something kind and waved back. Moose turned away in disgust.

They reached the Hôtel de Paris on the evening of March 20. It was a grand old hotel, set aside for soldiers. The men slept two to a room, but the rooms were massive, with two soft beds, a balcony, and a private bath. Stephen stepped into the hot shower and never wanted to leave. In Margraten, he had washed with a hot towel from a steaming pot of water. The front was worse. Now he ate French food in a dining room, while a French band played for his entertainment. Baguettes. Lettuce. Roasted meats in sauce. The waiters brought whatever he wanted, in part because he was one of the few American soldiers who spoke French, and in part because the hotel was a French "merci" to the soldiers who had liberated them. It had a Coca-Cola bar in the lobby, and a donut and coffee counter in the basement. Every night, a free movie. The cost of a room for three nights was $1.20. The delicious French dinner cost 20 cents. That was less than the cost of one kilometer in a Parisian cab.

He walked the city, rode the bus, and drank real coffee in sidewalk cafes. He was stunned by the elegance: women in high hats and fashionable shoes, men in suits with their hair gelled flat. He tracked down people he knew: family friends escaped from the old country, Jewish acquaintances from New York, soldiers from Camp Ritchie. At one point, he was yelled at by a sentry, only to realize the soldier was a long-lost friend—well, close enough to a friend, anyway. They had a good laugh about that.

He took the subway to see a girl he knew from school in Germany. He brought a present, and bought her flowers in the station. Lore was the girl of his dreams. He thought of her sometimes, while standing in the rubble after another long day of interrogations. Truth be told, he had come to Paris primarily to see her.

She wasn't home. He left the gifts with her landlady and walked back to the Hôtel de Paris. Along the way, he visited Napoleon's tomb, but found himself more taken by a large square surrounded by walls, the Cour d'Honneur. He wasn't sure why, until he realized it was where the French had stripped the Jewish officer Captain Alfred Dreyfus of his honors in 1894, falsely accusing him of spying for the Germans.

At the hotel, he found a message from Lore, saying she had missed him and would return that evening. He ran outside, bought a bunch of daisies, then ran back to the hotel and found her sitting in the lobby. They hugged, kissed on the cheek, and went to a cafe to talk. She took the next day off from work, and they met on the hotel terrace to plan their afternoon. He bought her rations at a U.S. Army post exchange and lunch at a restaurant. But the reunion was not what he had hoped. He found Lore pleasant, but not ravissante—or ravishing—as he had before. They had changed. Of course they had. They had spent the last few years on different continents. They were living through war. Stephen was barely fifteen when his family fled from Fürth.

The disappointment didn't get him down. Quite the opposite. When he got back to headquarters, Stephen thanked his commanding officer, Major John R. Elting, so profusely for the special pass that the man was forced to laugh.

"Whoa, slow down, Moose," he said. "You'll shake my arm off."

His return to the Vroonen home in Margraten was accompanied by happy tears: the children, of course, he brought them gifts, but also Oma, his Dutch grandmother. They hadn't seen him in weeks, they wanted to hear all about the front and his trip to Paris, but Stephen was tired, and he told them he'd feel better in the morning.

But when the morning came, he didn't feel much better. He watched Mrs. Vroonen scurry around the kitchen, making waffles, and felt saddened by her effort. He thought of the klompen he had bought a few weeks back for his much younger half sister, Marianne. When the Vroonens saw him packing the wooden shoes, they insisted on adding to the gift. Stephen had given the Vroonen children an imitation pearl necklace. Mrs. Vroonen used the extra pearls to make a bracelet for Marianne. She made her a ring with a pearl setting, using her twelve-year-old daughter's finger to approximate the size. Mr. Vroonen gave him some Dutch coins and four local apples, wrapped in silk paper. He took the photo of himself in his drum-major uniform out of his shirt pocket—his token of *before* that he always carried with him—and stamped it on the back with the Vroonen family mark, then stuffed it in the box. Finally, he stood on a chair and reached atop the refrigerator. He brought out a bar of Kwatta milk chocolate. The family had hidden it there five years before.

"Real Dutch chocolate," he said proudly, holding it out like an offering, insisting Stephen send it to his family.

Stephen refused. It was too much, he insisted. He couldn't take everything. And now, looking back, it seemed so foolish. So pointless.

"Stephen, was ist nicht in Ordnung?" Mrs. Vroonen asked. ("What is wrong?")

She came to him across the kitchen. She put her hand on his shoulder. "Was ist los, mein Junge?" ("What is wrong, my boy?")

"Mutti, ich komme niemals mehr nach Hause," he said, collapsing into her and throwing his arms around her waist. ("Mom, I'm never getting back home.")

It was March 25, 1945. The previous day, March 24, Operation Plunder, the Allied assault across the Rhine, had finally begun.

# CHAPTER 57

# FIRST JUMP

— ★ —

*Paschal Fowlkes*
March 24, 1945

"What Easter signifies is the ultimate victory of good over evil, of right over wrong," Chaplain Fowlkes wrote to Lib on March 20, twelve days before that year's celebration of Christ's rebirth, "so if we pray hard enough that we may be good enough and right enough, I think we're entitled to see in it the day of Hope that it is. May we never never be apart from one another! Hug and kiss my babies. God bless you and keep you all. Your very own, Pat."

He knew that he was jumping in Operation Varsity, an airborne assault to support the long-awaited Operation Plunder, the Allied crossing of the Rhine River. The Allies had known the Germans would destroy the bridges across the Rhine, making the crossing of the wide, fast-moving river the largest obstacle between the Siegfried Line and Berlin. Field Marshal Bernard Montgomery had been tasked with planning the crossing; he considered it a war-defining event on the level of D-Day. But while he spent six months worrying about every detail, American General Omar Bradley's forces discovered a shortcut: an intact bridge at Remagen, near Bonn. Bradley managed to slip five divisions across the Rhine after March 7, establishing a bridgehead on the other side.

Still, Montgomery waited, and tinkered, and waited through most of the month of March. Bradley's crossing was important, but it was dwarfed by Montgomery's plan, which involved 1.25 million soldiers and three Allied field armies: the Ninth Army, the First Canadian Army, and the

British Second Army. Montgomery had thirty divisions. The Ninth Army alone had eleven. There were only ten Allied divisions in total at Normandy on June 6.

The plan called for infantry and armor to cross the river on pontoon bridges and advance rapidly to the Ruhr Valley, the heart of German coal mining, steel production, and manufacturing. The British and Canadian armies would circle the northern edge of the Ruhr, the Americans the southern edge. If they could meet on the far side, it would trap Germany's Army Group B and isolate the industrial area, starving Germany of the troops and materiel it needed to keep waging the war.

The crossing would be treacherous, the long pontoon bridges susceptible to damage and demolition, the soldiers trapped on the narrow expanses and exposed to German artillery fire. So Montgomery planned two actions to help them cross. The first was the largest aerial and artillery bombardment in history. The second was Operation Varsity. More than 16,000 paratroopers would drop across the Rhine a few hours after the river crossing began to attack and disable German positions. D-Day only had 13,000.

Chaplain Paschal Fowlkes's 3rd Battalion, 507th Airborne, 17th Airborne Division, marshaled at Prosnes Airfield A-79, twelve miles southeast of Reims, France, on March 23, 1945, the day before Operation Varsity. The aerial bombardment had already begun, targeting rail lines, bridges, fuel depots, and storage sites. That evening, as the last of the 11,000 bombers passed over the Rhine and the time for the river assault drew near, Chaplain Fowlkes addressed the men whose souls were in his care.

*You do not need me to tell you that we stand on the eve of a great mission.... The battle for the preservation of decency and of freedom and of justice is a battle that never begins and never ends; it just always is. This makes of life, your life and my life, a kind of warfare in which we are ever constantly engaged.... Life is warfare, requiring a strategy. Peace, therefore, is never mere absence of war. True peace is that knowledge that comes to us that in the midst of the warfare we are doing our duty.... We, therefore, who are in this Group preparing ourselves for an ever larger measure of service to God and our country, ought not to think of ourselves as men unfortunate in being so intimately drawn into a violent phase of the struggle between good and evil.*

*Rather we ought to be thankful that ours is the opportunity of a handsome contribution to a cause for which our best is none too good. Mr. Churchill, when he promised the British people only "blood, sweat, and tears," did no more than to paraphrase the New Testament which makes it forever clear to us that to struggle manfully against evil one must undergo risks and make sacrifices.*

Fowlkes ended with a prayer. The paratroopers filed out, each with his own thoughts. Whether they saw their mission in grand terms, like Pat Fowlkes, or focused on the smaller details of their individual objectives, all knew the morning drop might be the last great turning of the war, and the culmination of everything they had trained for.

They prepared their weapons: M1 Garand rifle, M1 carbine, Thompson submachine gun, M1911A1 pistol, hand grenades, two pounds of high explosives. They secured their personal keepsakes, lucky charms, photographs, and supply kits.

Alongside them, Chaplain Fowlkes packed his essentials too: hymn leaflets, copies of the New Testament, and his compact Communion set since, with the weather softening, he could once again use his cup for the Holy Eucharist rite. He packed blood plasma and bandages, since the paratrooper medical officers could never carry enough. He wrapped his cross in cloth. He kept the same gear as the boys, with its tools and food and emergency supplies. He wore the same distinct four-pocket jacket, baggy trousers, and metal helmet. But he carried no weapons. And once packed and arranged, he added a final piece: a large cloth brassard around his upper arm featuring the Red Cross, to mark him as a noncombatant.

Paschal Fowlkes did not consider his life to be his alone. He knew himself to be part of a larger plan, and he believed his life in greater hands. But God expected us, he knew, to take responsibility and be prepared.

The next morning, March 24, General Eisenhower watched from a hill overlooking the Rhine as the first planes passed overhead: C-47s, flying fifteen abreast, in perfectly straight lines.

Chaplain Fowlkes was in the rightmost plane of the third line, preparing himself to jump. The morning was clear, and the smoke screen meant to aid the attack blew off the Rhine, as if the river were on fire. Below him, he could see the boats of the infantry assault. In front were the fifteen C-47s carrying the men he had trained with, eaten with, ministered to, and loved. Behind him were the rest of the 1,572 transport and 1,326 glider aircraft protected by 3,042 fighters, a force so vast it stretched for 200 miles. Each transport plane carried 18 paratroopers. As the chaplain, Pat was the eighteenth and last in his stick, and his stick was the last in the battalion. But the battalion was the leading edge of the invasion force. He would land only two minutes after the first American paratrooper touched German soil.

"Stand up!" the jumpmaster called. The wind was whipping through the fuselage. "Hook up!" The cold pierced their jumpsuits and bit at their skin. They shuffled to the door. A moment for preparation, for prayers, and then the jump light flashed green. "Go, go, go!" They disappeared one after another, out into the sky.

Pat felt the familiar tug of the static line, the plummet and the unforgiving rope. He felt the turbulence of the prop wash, the moment of weightlessness, and then he was heading downward somewhere between a hurtle and a float. Below him, he could see the sticks from other airplanes, men of the 507th falling like a rain of arrows angling toward the enemy. He could see the first jumpers begin to land, their white chutes closing like evening flowers, their shrunken shapes left scattered on the ground. He could hear the chug of gunfire, the boom of artillery, but there was no time to worry, the ground was approaching fast, so he put out his feet, bent his knees on impact, and completed a perfect parachute landing fall. He popped up. He was in a field, a line of houses to the east. He started to run for cover.

But the stick had jumped a fraction too late, causing the men to travel a fraction too far. A German machine gun hidden at the edge of the field cut down the last five men to land, including Paschal Fowlkes, before they could reach safe ground.

# CHAPTER 58

# FRANTIC DAYS

— ★ —

*Jefferson Wiggins*
March 24, 1945

The last and heaviest bombardment had begun at 1:00 a.m., nine hours before the first paratroopers jumped. Every minute, for an hour, 2,070 artillery pieces fired more than 1,000 rounds over the river at the German positions, more than 65,000 artillery rounds in all. When it was over, Eisenhower walked toward the Rhine, where Old Hickory, the infantry division that had liberated Maastricht, prepared to cross in boats. In addition to the artillery, the Allies had laid a massive smoke screen fifty miles long to protect them.

"How are you feeling, son?" Ike asked a soldier headed to the embarkation point.

"General, I'm awful nervous," he said. "I was wounded two months ago and just got back from the hospital yesterday. I don't feel so good!"

"Well, you and I are a good pair then," Ike replied, "because I'm nervous too. . . . Maybe if we just walk along together to the river we'll be good for each other."

To which the soldier replied: "I meant I was nervous. I'm not any more."

The boats set out at 2:00 a.m., the moment the bombardment ended. By 3:00 a.m., two divisions were across. The artillery barrage had worked. The Germans were knocked down. Thirty-one men died in the crossing.

The airborne passed over the Rhine at 10:00 a.m. The last 240 planes were B-24s, which dropped 582 tons of supplies. The men from Sergeant Jefferson Wiggins's 960th quartermaster unit watched the aerial assault from the ground at the Ninth Army's forward operating base, three miles from the Rhine. The fleet took two hours and thirty-two minutes to pass. It was an awe-inspiring sight.

The 960th had reached the Battle of the Bulge on December 18. It was brutally cold, and they had been assigned to supply, not combat. And yet, with the front so close and moving so fast, there was always that thought: *If the company is overrun, the officers dead or missing, I'd rise to the occasion; there's a Dorie Miller inside of me, waiting for his chance.* The reality turned out to be a harrowing middle ground: The 960th distributed ammunition at an arms depot so close to the front they could hear heavy arms fire nearby, but so socked in by fog they couldn't see more than a few dozen feet. They had met the enemy, and he was . . . invisible.

They returned to Margraten in early February to bury German soldiers. On the first day, a fellow digger grabbed a body by his hobnail boots. "You were a good soldier," he said, with a gallows humor Wiggins never understood. "You were just on the wrong side."

Now they were at the front again, waiting to cross the Rhine. This time, they were driving trucks. The 960th was muscle to move and organize supplies on the other side of the river. This work was all the danger, with none of the agency. Most of them weren't even carrying guns.

Around 2:00 p.m., a pontoon bridge was operational. Within the hour, the 960th set out to cross it. They were driving twelve DUKW amphibious trucks loaded with gasoline in a convoy 2,000 vehicles long. They were, essentially, sitting on bombs. If the trucks were hit, there would be nothing left. Not of the trucks, and not of them.

By 3:30 p.m., the convoy was across the Rhine and headed to the airborne's supply dump at Bönninghardt. The 960th delivered their fuel, then stayed to help with unloading, organizing, logistics, and resupply. Another obvious target, another chance to be caught in a massive explosion that would leave their mothers with nothing to mourn, not even their bones.

The explosion never came, because the Americans were able to repel the German counterattacks. The only thing that arrived were Allied soldiers, thousands of them, and endless supplies.

A temporary airborne cemetery had been planned across the Rhine. Shomon had sent GRS officers forward from Margraten to collect, identify, and bury the bodies. They had already chosen a site and begun to lay out the graves when it was decided to scrap the burials. The casualties in the initial fighting were lighter than expected, nowhere near the scale at Normandy, so the airborne dead would be transported to existing cemeteries. First Army's cemetery at Henri-Chapelle in Belgium was full, leaving one logical option. So on March 27, three days after the initial crossing, the 960th packed their now-empty trucks with bodies and drove them seventy miles back across the Rhine to Margraten. Among those bodies, almost surely, was Chaplain Paschal Fowlkes.

They found the cemetery in chaos: an anthill kicked over, activity everywhere. White men were digging graves alongside the Black soldiers of the 3136th Quartermaster Service Company. White men were unloading bodies from a long line of trucks. They were carrying bodies to the stripping line and stacking them outside the morgue like firewood.

Two days into Operations Plunder and Varsity, as the bodies began to arrive, Shomon had asked the Ninth Army for more men. They turned him down. They were busy at that moment. They needed their quartermaster troops at the front to sustain the advance into Germany.

So Shomon went to Ronckers, the burgemeester of Margraten. "We need men. We need shovels. Can you issue a call to all the able-bodied men to report to the cemetery at once? We have a thousand bodies to bury."

"Just leave it to me, Captain," Ronckers said. "Just leave it to me."

It is impossible to say who dug the grave of Chaplain Paschal Fowlkes, but his body was buried at Margraten on March 29, during those frantic days, when the Black gravediggers worked like machines from row to row, and the citizens of Margraten answered the call, doing all they could to pay back his sacrifice with their own.

Seven months later, on a quiet October afternoon, as the leaves turned russet on Pat's well-loved Virginia hills, Lib opened a box of the items from the Army Effects Bureau in Kansas City. It contained the things her husband had been carrying when he died: his Bible, his prayer book, his captain's bars and chaplain's cross, a billfold, photos . . . and her August 1943 letter sharing the news of the birth of Betsy, the daughter he would never meet. He had carried it for nineteen months in his left breast pocket, above his heart. He had taken it with him everywhere, even into death.

*My Darling . . . remember and cherish. Betsy arrived at 2 a.m. . . . . [A] fair complexion and dark blue eyes. . . . [T]wo letters and today a V-mail. . . . [Y]our beautiful red roses. . . . I love you and thank you a million times for being so good to me. All three of us send love.*

# CHAPTER 59

# RIVER CROSSING

— ★ —

*Bill Hughes*
April 1, 1945

B ill Hughes crossed the Rhine on the night of March 26–27, day three of Operation Plunder. The pontoon bridge was narrow, the river wide, its black waters deep and moving fast. The only way was forward, but the rear of a tank was staring back at him and another five or six hundred vehicles were in front of that, the whole damn U.S. Army, it seemed. He could hear the whistle of artillery, the boom of explosions, but he worried less about enemy fire than the bridge. It seemed woefully inadequate, sure to collapse under the weight of so many tanks.

"If we go in the water, don't fight it," someone said. "Just go with the current."

Go with the current? There was no way. They would be trapped in the tank. And besides, he couldn't swim.

Bill Hughes had never been so happy to touch dry land. Even crossing the Atlantic was nothing to him compared to the bridge over the Rhine. Even the enemy fire was nothing, with the tanks of the 784th "It Will Be Done" battalion around him, and their old friends the 35th Infantry Division fighting alongside. This was not an accidental pairing. Infantry officer Orval Faubus might have been skeptical of the Black tankers after the ride into Venlo. He might have seen them as equals after the breakout from the trap at Sevelen. But the 35th Infantry Division considered the Black tankers among the finest tank battalions in the Army. One of their regimental commanders had commended them to the division commander

288

for their "high morale, aggressiveness, and willingness to fight." The 35th had requested the 784th.

At first, the going was easy, but it didn't take long to encounter tank traps, explosives, and German troops. They lost their first tank of the operation on March 27, the day after crossing the Rhine. They took their first combat fatality on March 28. At one point, the Germans lowered the elevation of their flak guns to fire on a flat trajectory at tank level, instead of at aircraft, and tore apart one of the 784th's companies.

Soon after, they turned inward, toward the heart of the Ruhr Valley. Eighteen divisions had been assigned to "reduce the pocket," in military parlance. To engage and kill enemy soldiers while the bulk of Allied forces completed their flanking maneuver. The Ruhr Valley was an industry-blackened landscape, miles of heavy factories, smokestacks, pipes, and coal scuttles. Historic buildings were smashed within shopping districts, near semi-detached homes and claustrophobic housing blocks. The rubble of buildings shattered by Allied bombs belched smoke and ash. The trees were shorn of leaves, the grass dirty with soot. The 784th advanced slowly, like animals on the prowl. The enemy was out there, Bill Hughes could feel them. But he was ready. Whatever the 784th Tank Battalion had to do, he knew, It Will Be Done.

# CHAPTER 60

# LOST

— ★ —

*Walter Huchthausen*
April 2, 1945

Shortly before 2:00 p.m. on April 2, 1945, Captain Walter Huchthausen and his driver, recently arrived Monuments Man Technician Fifth Grade Sheldon W. Keck, crossed the Rhine. About 3:00 p.m., they entered the northern edge of the Ruhr Valley. They were heading to an area controlled by the XIX Corps to investigate a report of a looted altarpiece. But near Recklinghausen, the roads were impassable, blocked by rubble and war debris.

Hutch suggested they try the autobahn. The men swung east and were soon making good time. In fact, the road was remarkably free of traffic; the lack of markers the Army used as guideposts meant combat in the area had recently ended. Keck didn't like it, but Hutch wanted to press on. The maps at the Ninth Army forward headquarters showed all territory this side of the Rhein-Herne-Kanal under Allied control. As long as they stayed more than rifle shot from the canal, which they could see off to their right, they should be safe.

They passed beneath three bridges, all in good condition. A fourth appeared destroyed. They slowed as they approached the rubble. At a few hundred feet, they could tell the road was impassable. At the same time, Keck looked over and noticed a helmeted head peering down at them from the edge of the road's embankment. An American soldier. He leaned over to ask where they were just as a machine gun burst slammed into the jeep from the direction of the ruined bridge.

"They're firing at us!" he screamed, as he flung himself out of the jeep and ran toward the embankment.

He saw Hutch lurch sideways, as if preparing to jump, and then jerk back. The machine gun raked the jeep, sparking an oil fire.

"Captain!" Keck screamed. "For God's sake, Captain, jump!"

Two soldiers pulled him into their foxhole as the Americans returned fire. A soldier crawled toward Keck's position. He had been in a foxhole farther east, with a view of the far side of the jeep.

"Your captain's hit, corporal!" he shouted over the German buzzsaw. "Head wound. He's white as snow."

"We need a medic."

The man shook his head no.

"An extraction team."

"We'll send word back, but that's an exposed position. I don't think they can get him there."

Keck crouched beside the road for forty-five minutes, as the Germans hidden across the ruined bridge maintained their steady fire. From his angle, all he could see was the knobby tires, the dusty jeep, Hutch's left shoulder, and the black smoke pouring out of the engine block. Finally, a lull in the firing allowed him to withdraw to the company command post. The commanding officer told him Hutch had been evacuated by medics from another company, and he should report to the battalion command post farther back. But when Keck reached battalion command, they had a different message: a captain had been killed on the autobahn, but because of heavy fire his body was still out there, where he had died, in the front seat of his jeep.

# CHAPTER 61

# MAN BEHIND

— ★ —

*Stephen Mosbacher*
April 2, 1945

O n March 26, two days after crossing the Rhine, the billeting officer for the 8th Armored Division was killed by a land mine. Major Elting, who had granted Stephen Mosbacher his leave for Paris, assumed command of the billeting detachment. His handful of soldiers, including Moose Mosbacher, were advancing along the edge of the Ruhr pocket in the early morning of April 2, when the 116th Panzer Division attempted a breakout. The German tanks were to the south, but the brutal fighting necessitated a change of orders. They were to enter the heart of the Ruhr Valley to find a place for the division headquarters to set up in the town of Lippstadt. An armored cavalry squadron and a platoon of military police would meet them at a crossroads and escort them in.

The Ruhr pocket where the detachment entered was a sooty, bomb-blasted mess. Whole blocks of buildings had collapsed. Roads were cratered and blocked by debris. Thousands of German soldiers and civilians were rushing to surrender, while mere blocks away well-trained infantry and tank companies fought on. The mechanized cavalry squadron got stuck in a firefight; the military police were delayed by crowds of civilians—what the U.S. Army called "displaced persons," or DPs—on the road. When daylight dawned on April 2, the billeting detachment found itself alone at the crossroads.

Major Elting decided to move forward. There was no front line in the Ruhr Valley; they were as likely to meet the enemy in Lippstadt as they were going back the way they had come. So they formed up and began to roll toward the town, their eyes searching for enemy soldiers, their guns squeezed tight against their shoulders.

The road wasn't empty. DPs were straggling along the dusty verges—slave laborers, Stephen learned, when he got out of a jeep to question them. In the town of Delbrück, they captured a small German outpost. Stephen interrogated the commander, but the men knew nothing. He was relieved to be in custody. At Sande, the same thing: a small outpost, thankful prisoners. At Schloss Neuhaus, they ran into a garrison of eighty men. The billeting detachment opened fire as the bullets struck the road around them, but the soldiers didn't have any fight. One German laid down his gun, and then others, and soon the entire garrison was standing with their hands raised and their guns at their feet. Stephen was moving among them, asking questions, when a company of black-coated SS fanatics topped a hill and descended on the town.

The Americans scattered for cover. They were outgunned, but they laid down a field of fire the SS couldn't cross. Until German tanks rolled over the rise and down into the fight. The detachment had no heavy weapons capable of taking out a tank. So Major Elting called a retreat, then stayed behind to cover the withdrawal. Beside him was his driver, Private Smith, and his translator, Sergeant Stephen Mosbacher. When he saw the enemy closing in, and his fellow soldiers in danger, Moose chose to stay behind.

"Get us out of here!" Elting yelled to Smith, as soon as the last man was clear. The private threw the jeep into gear and stomped the gas. Elting was beside him, Moose in the back, hammering away at the enemy with his Thompson submachine gun. They were almost out of firing range when Elting looked back and noticed a man running frantically, the jackbooted SS chasing him, firing as they ran. An American soldier. They had left a man behind.

"Stop the jeep!" Elting yelled, jumping out.

He was laying down fire with his M1 Garand, trying to drive back the SS troops, when to his surprise his jeep went barreling past toward the enemy. Smith was behind the wheel, and Stephen Mosbacher was manning his submachine gun, smiling as he fired. Not just smiling, Elting noticed. Stephen was laughing wildly as the two soldiers charged straight into the SS and its tanks. His smile was small, though, beside the happiness on the face of the fleeing soldier as Stephen reached out his hand and pulled him into the jeep, while Smith hit the brakes and skidded into a 180-degree turn.

They barely slowed down for Elting, who threw himself onto the hood as they sped away from Schloss Neuhaus and the sound of shooting began to fade. They had made it. Unbelievably, they had made it.

Ahead, just off the road, was a destroyed truck. Beside it, a wounded American soldier was lying in a ditch. Smith slowed and Elting slid off the hood, while Stephen reached out to grab the wounded man just as a tank round exploded with a deafening roar, and the entire world went white.

# CHAPTER 62

# O-910847

— ★ —

*Frieda van Schaïk*
April 4, 1945

It was Captain Sully, who drove the jeep named Sally and stashed so much food under his uniform jacket that he looked pregnant, who brought the news. Frieda was upstairs in bed. She had been struck by acute appendicitis and was recovering from emergency surgery. But she knew what was happening as soon as she heard his heavy tread on the stairs, along with the lighter steps of her mother.

"Walter!" she screamed, as soon as she saw their faces.

Maybe, she thought later that night, as she lay crying in bed, she had already known. When she woke from her surgery, the nurse told her that, in the depths of her unconsciousness, she had called out for someone by name.

Who?

Walter.

That was probably, Frieda calculated, about the time he died.

As soon as she had recovered enough, Frieda rode her bicycle to the U.S. Military Cemetery in Margraten, five miles away. She walked boldly to one of the tents, where a clerk was working on files. She wanted information, she said, on an American soldier. The clerk rifled through his files for information. He was kind. He walked her to the grave, then left her to her grief.

She fell to her knees. The dirt was trampled flat by footprints. A simple, white-painted wooden cross threw a shadow against the ground. A dog tag was nailed to its center, so small she had to lean forward to read it:

# OVER THE RHINE

*Walter J. Huchthausen*
*O-910847*

How could this be all? How could everything that was be here, under this small piece of ground? How could everything she knew about this man, everything he was—a person's entire life—be crammed into a few square feet, pressed up against his fellow fallen men in column after column, and row after row? She looked to her left: nothing but trampled ground and crosses. To her right, to the front: the same sad sight. Walter was dead, and this section was full, and the gravediggers were across the grounds in another area entirely, digging holes. All these graves, all these crosses, all these soldiers dead and buried.

She took her bouquet of flowers and placed them on Walter's grave. In all that desolation, they were the only spot of color.

*Please Lord,* she prayed, *let Walter be made aware that he is not, and never will be, forgotten.*

# CHAPTER 63

# THE LETTER

— ★ —

*Stephen Mosbacher*
April 5, 1945

*My dear good one, we haven't heard from you today either, again nothing after eight days. But we are still living off your interesting and packed report from March 17, like pondering, always thinking, where you might be right now. And I am looking for you in the radio reports and on the map, I always mean in Münster or Paderborn. Wherever you are, the main thing is that you are healthy, and that you do not suffer mentally from the changes in character that war and the atmosphere of war cause in everyone.*

*Today is the last day of Pessach [Passover]. I was in the synagogue for a short time and thought of you intimately and very much, my dear.*

*... Stay healthy, my dear. God bless you. We are with you with all our love, hugging you deeply.*

*Your Father*

This letter was returned unopened, with one handwritten word across the envelope: Deceased.

# CHAPTER 64

# SLAUGHTER

— ★ —

*Bill Hughes*
April 18, 1945

The Ruhr Valley was filled with slave laborers, mostly Slavs from Eastern Europe, but any ethnicity the Nazis despised, they had rounded up at gunpoint and put to use. Men and women, children and the elderly, Russians from the east and Dutch from the west: nobody was exempt from the German drive to produce enough coal, steel, iron, and ammunition to conquer the world, or at least Europe, the part of the world that mattered to Hitler. These laborers poured out of their hiding places when the 784th rolled through, abandoned, malnourished, and perilously thin. They pointed out where German soldiers were hiding, or in what direction they had fled. It was not the 784th's job to deal with the laborers. They took no prisoners and helped no refugees. That was for the soldiers coming behind. The 784th's place was in the vanguard, driving the Allied armies forward. Still, this was a wretchedness Bill Hughes had never seen before. This wasn't Indianapolis, or even Alexandria, Louisiana. This was worse.

The fighting was intermittent, but dangerous. March was the deadliest month for the 784th, with 180 casualties. April was almost as intense. One afternoon, Hughes felt a sharp pain and thought he had hit his elbow on his hatch. Then he saw the blood. He'd been shot in the arm by a sniper. At another point, his company was pinned down for several days on the lip of a canal with the 137th Infantry. But by April 10, the 784th was through the Ruhr Valley. The Allies would take 323,000 German soldiers prisoner in the pocket.

On April 12, the tankers arrived in Hanover, 120 miles northeast of the Ruhr. They were greeted by sheets, pillowcases, shirts, and even underwear waving from windows and railings. Anything white, to signal surrender.

The 784th bedded down for the night. Like cavalry units of old, the tankers cared for their horses first: added oil to the engines, lubricated the bogie wheels, refueled with gasoline from dozens of jerry cans. Then they took care of themselves: K-rations and instant coffee. They awoke before sunlight. By 6:00 a.m., they were pushing toward Berlin, 175 miles away.

It was Company B, not Bill Hughes's Company D, that spotted the smoke. The dawn was clear and bright, the spring grass fresh with dew. The tanks were speeding along at twenty-five miles an hour, the men riding with their heads out of the turrets, since the hull was cramped and airless, when the call went down the line: "Smoke at your ten o'clock. Prepare for contact."

Company B peeled off and sped toward the battlefield. As the tanks came around a sweeping turn, guns forward and ready to fire, their commanders spotted a wire fence. It was hung with laundry. No, not laundry—human skeletons. No, not skeletons—human beings, alive, clinging to the wire, too weak to move.

"Slow down!" came an urgent cry on the radio. "Slow down, dammit! Don't run over the bodies!"

The tankers threw on their brakes, slowing to five miles per hour as they came level with the wire. That's when the men saw the bodies strewn across the road. They were thrown down in all positions, contorted by the violence of their deaths.

As the Allies advanced over the Rhine, the SS and German paratroopers had evacuated prisoners from the Mittelbau-Dora and Neuengamme concentration camps. Near the town of Gardelegen, the railway tracks had been destroyed by Allied bombing, so the SS unloaded the train and began to march columns of prisoners in several different directions with the help of German soldiers and Volkssturm troops. The prisoners had not been fed. They were starving, begging for help. Anyone who fell, the Germans shot.

Soon, the SS herding the prisoners north grew tired and hungry. Or maybe the Germans despaired. Their country was beaten. Their dreams lay in ruins, and the consequences of their actions lay before them. They didn't want to deal with prisoners. They wanted to destroy the "evidence" and flee. So, they doused the hay in a barn near the Remonte Cavalry School with gasoline, herded the inconvenient "undesirables" inside, and barred the door. The fire went up in a flash, burning hundreds of men, women, and children alive. Some of the prisoners managed to break open the barn door, but as they rushed from the inferno, the Germans were waiting with rifles and machine guns. Not just SS, paratroopers, and soldiers. There were also Hitler Youth: boys in their teens, firing point-blank into unarmed prisoners. In mere minutes, more than 1,000 people were massacred. The fire was so hot that all but a handful of those inside the barn were incinerated. Company B, stopping their tanks in horror, stared out on several hundred bodies trampled and gunned down in the small yard between the burnt barn and the wire fence.

"Keep moving!" the voice screamed on the radio, as the tankers fought back tears. "Keep moving, dammit! There are soldiers behind you to help. The SS did this, and they are ahead. Keep moving! Keep moving! We have to catch those bastards!"

Bill Hughes's Company D, meanwhile, were almost to the Elbe River, the last natural barrier before Berlin. Before them was a tangle of forest. Hughes could have sworn the woods were empty, until a burst of fire sent the men scuttering into the bellies of their tanks. "On the right, on the right!"

Thirty seconds later, they were being hit from the other side. "Tell us where to shoot!" the tankers called out to the infantry, but the Germans were too well hidden for anyone to see.

Lieutenant Waters called for an assault. Forget hide-and-seek. The entire force would smash forward, overwhelming the small arms fire. It worked. Through the periscope in his tank, Bill could see the Germans fleeing as the mass of Company D, 784th Tank Battalion, bore down on them. He felt the relief, the elation when a battle turns and a dangerous advance becomes a rout, but then an infantry commander screamed into his radio: "Look out! Here they come! Two o'clock! Two o'clock!"

Bill saw the shadows moving, the shapes through the trees, as the task force laid down a blistering barrage. Small arms, machine guns, tank main guns, artillery. He could hear the thudding of bullets entering flesh, could see bodies being torn apart. He thought of death. First theirs, and then his. If this was it, he thought, then he was going out in the full majesty of the American military.

Eventually, the firing slackened, until Hughes could hear the ping of individual rounds. A few dark shapes bounded away, disappearing into the forest.

Deer.

My God, they were deer. The mighty American military had slaughtered a herd of deer.

They found the Germans huddled half a mile away. They were sitting on fallen logs, squatting on their haunches, standing in small groups sharing cigarette butts, their weapons in a pile. They were waiting to be captured.

*War is insane*, Bill thought. *Half an hour ago, these men were trying to kill me. Now they are calling out "Genosse, Genosse"* ("Comrade, Comrade") *and asking for water.*

Some of the Germans were stretched out on the ground, exhausted. Most were malnourished. Several Americans offered them cigarettes, gave them food from their rations.

*Would the Germans have done the same?* Bill wondered, then answered himself: *Hell no. Certainly not for a man who looked like me.*

He hadn't seen the blackened skeletons and machine-gunned corpses of the massacre at Gardelegen. He didn't yet know about the Final Solution or the concentration camps. But Bill Hughes had seen the starving laborers in the Ruhr Valley. The human beings made slaves because of their ethnicity, their country of origin, their religion, or their political affiliation. He knew what the enemy was capable of.

After the prisoners had been turned over and the battalion bivouacked, the talk turned to Berlin. They had cleared the resistance on this side of the Elbe. Once they crossed the river, Berlin was only fifty miles away. They could reach the city in two days. They might, someone suggested, be the first tank battalion to enter the capital of Hitler's Reich.

How would Hitler like that? Bill Hughes laughed. A bunch of battle-hardened, butt-kicking Black men leading the charge.

It was not to be. Eisenhower had made the decision to turn south, where the holdouts of the Nazi regime were rumored to be planning a last stand in the mountains. Let the Soviets have the glory of taking Berlin, Ike thought, anticipating the fighting there would bring a brutal and costly climax to the war in Europe.

The 784th would never cross the Elbe. They waited in their bivouac until elements of the Soviet Red Army met them there, on the west bank of the Elbe.

And then they had a celebration, since East and West had finally met: bonfires, singing and dancing, the homemade vodka carried by Soviet troops. Bill took a cup of vodka, raised it in salute: *To the fall of Berlin. To the end of the war. To our friends from the East.* He knocked it back in one long gulp.

He started coughing. His throat burned. The Wehrmacht couldn't stop the advance: not at Venlo, not at Sevelen, not at the Rhine or in the Ruhr Valley. The Wehrmacht, at every point, had proved no match for the 68 tanks and 750 men of the "It Will Be Done" 784th Tank Battalion.

But homemade Russian vodka? That poison knocked Bill Hughes to his knees.

CHAPTER 65

# THE END

— ★ —

*Lib Fowlkes; Jefferson Wiggins;*
*Emilie Michiels van Kessenich*
April 26–May 8, 1945

Lib Fowlkes stood at the front window of her mother's brick home in Richmond, Virginia, as a Western Union delivery man walked up the drive. This was before the box containing Pat's possessions, before the long and lonely summer that began right here, at this moment, with this slow walk. Lib was not from a military family, like the Nortons in South Carolina, but every civilian knew what a telegram meant:

THE SECRETARY OF WAR DESIRES ME TO EXPRESS HIS DEEP REGRET THAT YOUR HUSBAND CAPT FOWLKES PASCHAL D WAS KILLED IN ACTION IN GERMANY 24 MARCH -44 CONFIRMING LETTER FOLLOWS.

Her world collapsed.

Three weeks later, after receiving the "confirming letter" with more information, Lib sat down to compose a letter to the quartermaster general. She was a widow with two young children. She was overwhelmed by grief, alone and lonely, even in the midst of the new life laughing and playing around her. "My husband is buried at Margraten, Holland," she wrote, "but I can't find Margraten on a map. I would appreciate deeply your telling me just where it is or what it is near and all other details possible regarding it."

That was April 26, 1945, one day after long-distance telephone communication resumed in Maastricht. The city, long closed to the world, was suddenly open, and all the talk was about an end to the war, a Nazi surrender, a return to ordinary life. But before that could happen, there was work to do. More than 380,000 Dutch citizens had been in Germany, either by force or by choice, and after the Western Allied assault across the Roer, they had begun returning to the Netherlands. By May, there were more than 30,000 refugees in Maastricht, swelling the city of 70,000 to about 100,000. Many citizens wouldn't take them in. The refugees might be traitors, and the ones who definitely weren't traitors came from prison camps filthy with lice and disease. That's how the police ended up knocking on the Michiels van Kessenich family's door on the evening of April 27, asking if they had room. The family already had twenty-two people living in the house, including refugees from Venlo. Without hesitation, Emilie and Willem took in more.

The news from Germany was coming in dribs and drabs, and it was often devastating. Emilie and Willem's friend Maes van Lanschot was found starving and badly abused in a concentration camp. He would die before the year was out. Their friend Jos van Hövell had been worked to death in a labor camp. Erro van Manen came home in an ambulance arranged by Papa Senecal. He recovered, barely. But April 28 was a good day, because it saw the return of Max de Marchant et d'Ansembourg, the NSB governor whose vitriol and edicts had led Willem to resign. D'Ansembourg had been found hiding in Germany, in a castle near the Roer. Dutch partisans took him back to Limburg and marched him, thin and disheveled, through the streets he had once terrorized, as jubilant citizens waved orange banners and Dutch flags in his face.

The citizens of Maastricht and Margraten learned of Hitler's death on May 2, two days after he committed suicide. The next day, the newspapers trumpeted: "Berlin Fallen. Enemy Gives Up 900,000 Troops."

On May 4, the German army in the Netherlands surrendered. The next morning, May 5, Queen Wilhelmina declared her country free. On May 6, there was a celebration in Maastricht, presided over by Mayor Willem Michiels van Kessenich. Emilie stayed home in bed. She was eight months pregnant with a victory baby, conceived in late September or early October 1944, in the weeks after Maastricht's liberation.

A few hours later, at 2:00 a.m. on the morning of May 7, in a small schoolhouse in Reims, France, General Dwight D. Eisenhower accepted Germany's unconditional surrender from General Alfred Jodl. A newsreel and a radio message were recorded, but his staff struggled to come up with soaring words to match the moment. In the end, it was Eisenhower who dictated the official message: "The mission of this Allied Force was fulfilled at 0241, local time, May 7, 1945." No words could have been more understated, or simpler.

Eisenhower knew that after three and a half years of war, "he should feel elated, triumphant, joyful," historian Stephen Ambrose wrote of the moment, "but all he really felt was dead beat."

It was a "dead beat" tiredness shared by Jefferson Wiggins, who was in Senne, Germany, with the 960th Quartermaster Service Company; by Bill Hughes with the 784th Tank Battalion in Hanover; by hundreds of thousands of soldiers on both sides—and tens of millions of civilians. War is grueling. The first thing most soldiers felt when it ended wasn't joy. That would come later. It was relief.

It was a tiredness felt, no doubt, by Lib Fowlkes, mourning her husband in Virginia, and the Mosbachers in Ohio, the Huchthausens in Connecticut, the Coles in Texas, the Hermans in South Dakota, the Moores in Georgia, and the Nortons in South Carolina. For them, and hundreds of thousands other families across the United States and millions more around the world, the fighting may have been over in Europe, but the grueling personal war with grief was just beginning.

# CHAPTER 66

# THE PHOTOS

— ★ —

*Frieda van Schaïk*
May 1945

Frieda van Schaïk snapped awake. She had ridden her bicycle almost every morning to Margraten to visit Walter's grave. Sometimes, she took a flower from her garden or the countryside near her home. Sometimes, she talked to Walter about the war. Usually, she simply knelt and let the sadness overwhelm her. The American cemetery was a depressing place: sticky dirt and bare crosses, the grind of the processing tents, the smell of death. It crushed her to visit Walter this way, to think of his coy smile when he'd showed her his drawing of Aachen Cathedral, his confident stride as he'd crossed the dance floor to ask the chaperone for her approval. But it would have pained her even more to leave him here, alone, so she tried to never miss a morning.

Until this morning, when she sat up suddenly and thought: *The photo!*

In one of their last conversations, Walter had mentioned having his photo taken in his new uniform. It was a common practice. Many soldiers had their photos taken before heading to the front. The photo hadn't been ready when the Ninth Army moved out. Walter planned to pick it up on his next visit to Maastricht. He never came back.

So the photo had never been picked up.

Frieda hopped on her bicycle. She would visit every photo studio in Maastricht until she found Walter's photograph. She would buy it. She would give it to his mother, or his sister, or someone who also loved him. She would not let the last image of her Walter languish in a box, never to be seen.

She discovered two problems almost immediately: there were several photo studios in Maastricht, and because of a fear of spies, the names of the soldiers were never written down. Instead, the soldier was given a numbered receipt. They had to exchange the receipt for the photograph. Walter probably had his receipt with him when he died. Frieda had no way of knowing where it was. No matter: she would look through every photo.

The first photographer was skeptical. He knew many of his customers had died, but there was a procedure, and this wasn't it. So Frieda told him about Walter, his kindness and warmth. She told him how much her mother and father had admired him, how the whole family had loved him, how he had eaten dinner with them many times. There is a passion that can't be faked, a trauma that can't be denied. Perhaps, in other circumstances, the photographer would have followed procedure and turned her away. But how can you begrudge a man who gave his life to free your country, or a girl who wants a final memory of a person she loved and lost?

She did not find Walter's photo in that studio, so she went to the next one and repeated her sad, determined plea. Perhaps that photographer was moved by her passion too. Perhaps he had lost a child or a friend in the war. Or perhaps he was just kind. He let her look through his inventory: hundreds, perhaps thousands, of photographs of smiling young men and women in their uniforms. Walter wasn't there.

It was late afternoon when she finally found him, in a box in the back room of Photo Studio Werner Mantz, a small shop on the Vrijthof Square. It stopped her cold, in surprise, when his face was suddenly there, amid so many others. It was a sad, joyous moment to find her Walter smiling, staring out at an angle toward the right of the frame, his lips curled upward in his ever-present smile. His hair was a little longer, slicked carefully back and to the side. His face clean-shaven and freshly scrubbed. Those eyes that saw something in her no one else had seen were bright, but looking off into a distance that seemed filled with nothing now. She had only seen his face a dozen times, but every line came back to her, and every expression, every moment: the kitchen table, the front room, the dance . . .

"Is that him?"

She couldn't look away. She didn't want to leave those memories. It was all ending now. The war was over. Walter was dead. The Americans would soon be going home.

"How much do I owe you?"

"Take them," Werner Mantz said. He was Jewish. No doubt, he had been through many heartbreaks. Perhaps that was a reason for his empathy.

"I couldn't. I'll pay you what is fair."

"They're already paid for," Mantz replied, and later Frieda didn't know if that meant Walter had paid in advance, or paid with his sacrifice.

She took the photos home. She kept them in her room.

*I will never forget you. You will never be a number. Not to me.*

CHAPTER 67

# MEMORIAL DAY

— ★ —

*Margraten*
May 30, 1945

In 1868, three years after the Confederate surrender at Appomattox, a day was set aside at the end of May to commemorate Union Army soldiers killed in the Civil War. It was known as Decoration Day, a time to decorate graves. Five thousand people attended the first Decoration Day at Arlington National Cemetery in Washington, D.C., honoring the 20,000 Union soldiers buried there. By World War I, the practice had spread across the United States, and May 30 had been designated Memorial Day, a time a time to honor the American soldiers killed in every war. Memorial Day 1945 fell a little more than three weeks after Germany's surrender. The Ninth Army's work in Europe was done. Thousands of soldiers were returning home. But before they departed, the Ninth Army wanted to memorialize its dead, on their designated day, in the place where more than 10,000 American soldiers lay buried.

Captain Shomon's 611th Graves Registration Company started preparations at Margraten on May 9, two days after Germany's surrender. Bringing beauty to a vast field of trampled ground and endless rows of crosses was a daunting task. There wasn't even any grass! The only color was the red and blue of the American flag atop the fifty-foot spruce mast. And the dead were still arriving from the last engagements of the war. The body trucks idling. Registrars documenting new arrivals. The stripping line was busy, and so were the gravediggers.

So the citizens of Margraten stepped in, just as they had in March, when the bodies from Operations Plunder and Varsity overwhelmed the burial process. Those brutal weeks had changed the town's relationship with the cemetery. It's one thing to feel compassion in your heart; it's another to become part of the process, to have the calluses on your hands to prove your respect and affection. The American officials who billeted in Margraten had long been considered family. After the horror of March, the villagers had begun to embrace the dead as family too. But their help was not enough, so Shomon hired workers from the nearby town of Vaals.

They mounded dirt on every grave, then came with boards to shape the mounds into perfectly straight, perfectly uniform rectangles the exact size of the graves below.

They straightened and, in some cases, redug and reinserted crosses.

They planted cedar, juniper, and hemlock trees sourced from a nursery in Münster, Germany, to complete the windbreak along the Rijksweg.

The graveyard needed paths, so Shomon requisitioned 200 truckloads of gravel from a stockpile near the Maas. The gravel beat back the mud, but looked too ragged at the edges, so Shomon sent men to Aachen to find thousands of square stones in the rubble. He used the stones to line the paths and square the corners.

The Civilian Committee Margraten's task was flowers, finally in bloom across Limburg, as if they, too, were celebrating the end of the war. While Van Laar and Ronckers had been instrumental in the group's founding, a young priest, Father Johannes Heuschen, now took the lead. The thirty-two-year-old Heuschen had been assigned to Sint Margarita Church in Margraten as chaplain shortly after liberation, but he had already developed a reputation as a terrific footballer and energetic advocate of the Civilian Committee Margraten's efforts. While his fellow priest, Father Heynen, performed a nightly funeral Mass at the cemetery, Father Heuschen encouraged villagers to embrace the cemetery. He had seen an American mother in uniform, stationed in Europe, collapse at her son's grave. Knowing that villagers were taking care of him, she told Heuschen, was a comfort. That's what Van Laar and the others on the Civilian Committee Margraten were encouraging people to do. By May, Heuschen had identified several hundred Dutch volunteers willing to help the committee by adopting and caring for the grave of a soldier.

When Shomon mentioned the need for flowers, Heuschen leapt into action. Ten thousand graves meant ten thousand bushels of flowers—not individual flowers, but bright bushels—plus bouquets and wreaths. Heuschen contacted priests across Limburg, while Ronckers worked with other mayors. Committee members contacted friends and relatives. Dave van Schaïk, known for his knowledge of the local flora, led walks to take wild cuttings, at the request of Ronckers himself.

On the evening of May 29, Shomon sent twenty trucks to sixty villages to pick up the flowers arranged through Father Heuschen. The same trucks that once carried bodies now carried 100,000 flowers, maybe more. Two hundred men and women worked through the night to place them on graves. Six people made bouquets. Others laid the final stones, tied bows on wreaths, or smoothed the gravel paths. No one knew what to expect, or if the work could be done in time. But when first light broke on Memorial Day 1945, the exhausted workers, American and Dutch, beheld a glorious sight: 10,000 identical mounds of dirt, 10,000 perfectly straight and upright white crosses, and 10,000 armfuls of fresh-cut flowers, of every color and variety, resting atop every American grave.

The gravel, every piece in its place, framed the cemetery. A crisp, new American flag, hoisted that morning, flew proudly. Below it, the rubble of Aachen had been used to spell out in large white letters against dark brown soil: U.S. Military Cemetery, Margraten, Holland.

The attendees began arriving with the sun. They came on foot, on bicycles, and in farm carts pulled by drays. A few came in cars, but most walked, because they lived in the nearby towns and villages, and many of the Dutch had their cars and carts stolen by the Germans during the occupation. Soon, the crowd on the Rijksweg reached to the horizon. By 8:00 a.m., it stretched all the way to Maastricht, more than five miles away, and the crowds on the cemetery's gravel verge were ten or fifteen mourners deep. Still, they came: families with children and young men and women from the Resistance, farmers and storekeepers, those who were better off and those who were struggling, older couples who had lost a son, and young couples who had taken soldiers into their hearts and homes. The Dutch knew Americans. If they didn't know these Americans, they knew boys like them. There was no animosity, no squabbles over dances or rations. More than 30,000 Limburgers came to the first Memorial Day ceremony at Margraten because they loved the Americans. They held in reverence their sacrifice. They wanted to honor their friends.

At 9:00 a.m., volunteers began handing out small bunches of flowers to the children of Limburg. Dutch dignitaries, including Willem Michiels van Kessenich, were feted by their American counterparts, and then the Dutch honored the Americans in return. Thousands of soldiers representing every division of the Ninth Army lined the gravel perimeter, between the graves and the crowd. Many had been reluctant to come.

Some of their duty stations were 400 miles away in France, and they dreaded the idea of turning the death of their friends into a spectacle. Death wasn't neat and tidy, like this cemetery. It was messy and violent, heartbreaking and horrible. They knew its wrath. They had seen it up close, many times. Most just wanted to go home. What could a formal ceremony possibly add?

A hush fell on the crowd as a large black car rolled up the drive. Slowly, Lieutenant General William Hood Simpson, commanding general of the Ninth Army, emerged. He shook one hand as he passed through the crowd, that of Willem Michiels van Kessenich. As he ascended the wooden dais Dutch laborers had built for the ceremony, 1,000 Ninth Army soldiers saluted. General Simpson was flanked by his sixteen corps and division commanders. He saluted them, one by one. Shomon's 611th Graves Registration Company was in formation to the left of the platform. Beside them were the soldiers of the 3136th Quartermaster Service Company. Simpson saluted, acknowledging their work.

His speech was short—clear and crisp, but not loud. His voice didn't have the bravado of battle, but the gentleness, the awe, of a man confronting the magnitude of his army's sacrifice. He paused often to take in the crosses, the flowers, the 30,000 Dutch mourners standing at his soldier' backs.

"In happier days, they were our neighbors—our friends," he concluded of the fallen men. "Let us carry on. They would have it so."

He stepped down from the dais and lifted a large wreath from a nearby stack, delivered by Shomon's trucks the night before. With crisp ceremony, he placed it on the grave of an unidentified soldier. Saluted him. Turned. His sixteen lieutenants followed one at a time, each placing a wreath on the grave of a soldier fallen under his command. The chaplains spoke. Many soldiers, many Dutch men and women, bowed their heads and wept.

A twenty-one-gun salute. A lone bugler playing taps, the bugle call that signifies the end of a military funeral, while a Black soldier from the 3136th lowered the crisp, new American flag to half-staff. In the silence, the last note of taps rang over the hills, as 30,000 people stood quietly, contemplating the cost of their freedom.

The soldiers were the first to break, stepping out among the graves, searching for their lost friends. They had not wanted to come, one soldier wrote, but they were glad they did. "Because the ceremony was simple, honest and sincere. It was devoid of bunk, it had no fancy speeches. It was a neighbor's goodbye and a thank you."

Airplanes roared overhead, and the thirty war correspondents in attendance rushed to post their stories to London and New York. The Allied officers walked to their cars, grasping each other's shoulders in grim resolve. Eventually, the soldiers began to board their trucks, as orderly as they had come.

The Dutch didn't want to leave. They stood on the wide gravel verges, waiting for more. So Father Heynen, who had celebrated many funeral Masses at the cemetery, celebrated another one. The Dutch sang together, celebrating Christ's triumph over death. It was hours before the bulk of the crowd began to trickle away, back to Maastricht or their villages, their farms or stores. Twenty thousand left with a prayer card created by the Civilian Committee Margraten. The paper was donated by Léon Lhoest, Willem Michiels van Kessenich's friend who owned the paper mill, the printing costs covered by the employees of the Orange-Nassau coal mines in Heerlen. But the poem, written in English, was the committee's own:

*You, who enter this cemetery look*
*How the crosses above the graves are silent and white,*

# MEMORIAL DAY

*Remember the price that your freedom took,*
*The lives of lots of soldiers who died.*

*They came from their country far away,*
*Where they left their well and woe*
*And their hope of a return had to stay*
*Like their bodies in Limburg too....*

*As to buddies and brothers our country does honors*
*To those who fell, fighting our foes,*
*They are of our freedom the representatives and donors,*
*We consider them as our proper heroes.*

*You, who enter here, look at the thousands of men,*
*Don't forget the price of their lives anymore.*
*Remember, pray God for them*
*And that He preserves us from another war.*

CHAPTER 68

# A SIGN

— ★ —

*Emilie Michiels van Kessenich*
Summer 1945

Emilie's eleventh child, a girl, was born on June 4. Her parents wanted to name her Mary, after Jesus's mother, and Victoria, in celebration of the victory over Nazi Germany. But when their good friend Colonel Leo Senecal heard the name, he seemed disappointed.

"Would you consider giving her my mother's name?" the bachelor Senecal said.

Emilie and Willem talked it over. Senecal was more than a friend. He was the person who had, more than anyone, helped Maastricht recover from the occupation. He had provided food and clothing, resolved the housing situation, settled the refugees. He was Papa Senecal to their children. A confidante. A pillar of support in troubled times. A symbol of the bonds between the Dutch and their American friends.

"Willem and I have discussed it," Emilie told him, "and we'd like nothing more than to honor your mother. What is her name?"

Senecal smiled with pure delight. It was the largest smile Emilie had ever seen on his face. "Mary Victoria," he said, laughing at her shock.

The baby's godfather was the mayor of a nearby town, a good family friend. He could not attend the baptism because the roads were abysmal, the train service spotty at best. So Leo Senecal stepped in as godfather. Jenneke, thirteen years old and a second mother to her younger sisters, was the godmother. The two of them stood together, smiling, Senecal holding a huge bundle of fabric and lace that completely obscured the baby.

After the baptism, Emilie returned to her bed, to nurse her child and preserve her strength. Senecal and his Civil Affairs detachment were staying through the fall, but Emilie had chosen to wind down the Apostolate of the Front. After the Allied victory, the alcohol had begun to flow, and the Americans' behavior had, quite honestly, deteriorated. They were boys. They had survived. She didn't blame them. But the time for wholesome dances had passed.

"Please take time to rest," Willem begged her. Emilie had been sick during the pregnancy, from stress and the numerous illnesses swirling through Limburg. She was bedridden for parts of February and March. She was almost quarantined for typhus, after greeting the first bus of survivors from Dachau, some of whom were discovered to be infected with the disease. And she was still weak from the twisted kidneys, the result of malnutrition, which had hospitalized her the summer before.

"Rest, my love," Willem said gently. "You have worked yourself to the bone, and there is nothing more you need to do. Unless of course, God gives you a sign."

This was not a casual mention. The Michiels van Kessenichs discerned, like many Catholics, God's will through signs.

So when the letter arrived soon after, Emilie didn't think it was a sign from God. She *knew* it was a sign from God. It was addressed to the Mayor of Maastricht, and it was from the widow of a man who served God as an Army chaplain—Lib Fowlkes.

PART V

# LOVE AND REMEMBRANCE

— ★ —

June 1945–July 1946

*With all my heart I believe that no one who left a son over-seas should doubt the fittingness of his final resting place. That he should have, for time unending, a part of the ground he so dearly bought is supremely right and fitting.*

General George C. Marshall,
Chief of Staff of the United States Army

CHAPTER 69

# GOING HOME

— ★ —

*Margraten*
Summer 1945

Almost as soon as Hitler committed suicide, the trucks, jeeps, and armor started back down the Rijksweg, the Bemelerweg, and hundreds of other roads out of Germany. Some American soldiers had been away from their families for three years or more, between training and deployment. Many had seen years of combat in major operations and campaigns. Even the wave of soldiers who began training in summer and fall 1943, "new boys" like Stephen Mosbacher, John Land, and Jacob Herman, had been away from their wives and children, fathers and mothers, for nearly two years. By May 7, the day of Germany's surrender, Army planners were already discussing how to stand down units. Soon, they were trucking soldiers to nine huge tent cities in France and one in Belgium known as "cigarette camps," since they were named after cigarette brands. Lucky Strike, near the French port of Le Havre, was the largest, capable of holding 58,000 troops. These camps were the final stop in the complicated process of shipping three million American boys and girls home to their families.

Not every American was leaving. Between December 1944 and March 1945, the Ninth Army had issued from its stock in Maastricht—only one depot, for one field army—29 million rations, 24.6 million gallons of gasoline, and 42,000 *tons* of ammunition. It had taken 250 Deuce-and-a-Halfs and 150 tractor-trailers months to move the ammunition alone. Most of those resources had been expended in the fighting. Much of the rest was being driven back by the units who used it. But that left many tons of material to transport, organize, and pack, a job that fell primarily to quartermasters. Jefferson Wiggins and the other soldiers in the 960th would not leave Europe until January 1946.

Bill Hughes, who had skipped basic training and had joined his battalion after the other Black tankers, hadn't accumulated enough service time to qualify for discharge. Unlike most of the men in the 784th Tank Battalion, he remained in Germany as part of the American occupation force. He would not return to America for several years. But for the most part, in Western European areas like Limburg, the American presence was disappearing almost as quickly as it had arrived.

There was, however, a large segment of soldiers being left in Britain, France, Belgium, Luxembourg, Switzerland, and the Netherlands. Some 140,000 men (and a few hundred women) lay buried in thirty-six U.S. military cemeteries in the European Theater of Operations; 11,000 were missing in action; and 25,000 were scattered across the continent in isolated graves. Some GIs spent their last nights before the cigarette camps in watering holes like the Oklahoma bar in Maastricht. Others spent their final afternoons (and nights) with the Dutch they had come to know (and perhaps love). But no matter where they were, the thoughts of their fallen comrades sat heavy, despite their happiness, their relief, at heading home.

They were, they understood, the keepers of the memories of their comrades who didn't make it back, and especially of their final days and deaths. The U.S. Army, dealing with numbers on an enormous scale, relayed to families only two facts about their fallen loved ones: date and country of death. It was up to the commanding officers and the soldiers or airmen they served with to pass on the details, to individuate these men and their actions from the thousands who fell around them. Peace gave the survivors the space to confront their grief and to comfort, as best they could, the loved ones their friends left behind.

So it was in May, two months after Pat's death in March, that Lib Fowlkes received a letter from a chaplain who had served under her husband, assuring her Pat had not suffered. "I saw him lying on the drop zone," the chaplain wrote, "shot through the arm and hip. Others were there too. He was lying among his men, whom he respected and loved. It was hard to tell that he was dead. More like a man asleep, his peaceful countenance bore no sign of pain."

"I envied him. I knew of his devotion to you and his children. It was hard to face the grim reality."

Pat's assistant in the 314th Troop Carrier Group wrote to say that Pat had done true good in the airborne, and that he had always considered his life in God's hands.

A medic from the 507th, a participant in Pat's final jump, gave Lib the details of her husband's last day and death, assuring her once again that her husband didn't die in pain. "Pat was one of the finest men I have ever had the good fortune to know," he wrote. "I have never felt anyone's death as deeply as I did his."

The Army chaplain who had been imprisoned with Bill Moore, Captain Tildon S. McGee, knew only that his friend and fellow POW was from Atlanta, Georgia. In August, he traveled there and, after striking out calling every Moore in the phone book, asked the *Atlanta Journal* to help him locate Bill's mother. Helen Moore responded to the article immediately, and they met that evening. Chaplain McGee did not know Bill had been executed. When McGee was transferred by the Germans, Bill was alive. But he wanted Helen to know—he wanted the world to know—how valiantly Bill had stood up to torture, never betraying his fellow soldiers or the Dutch Resistance members who risked their lives to save them.

It was also in June that Stephen Mosbacher's parents received a long letter from their son's commanding officer, Major John Elting. The officer told them, in several detailed pages, about Stephen's last assignment with the billeting team, how he stayed behind to guard the unit's retreat, and of his brave attempt to save two fellow soldiers:

*Having your jeep hit by a high-velocity shell is something you can't describe. It was a glare of white light, a screaming crash. Then we were in the ditch. Smith and I were wounded, Stephen and the rescued soldier were dead. Stephen was still smiling and still had a firm grip on his submachine gun. . . .*

*Your son was a brave and honorable soldier. He was greatly missed, both because he was our best interpreter and interrogator and because of his constant good humor and comradeship. I have heard the same soldiers, who once "kidded" him about always being the first man in the mess line, speak of him with deep regret.*

*We served together, several times in dangerous and exciting missions. He was always willing, always cheerful, always reliable, always brave. There are not too many other men of whom the same can be said. This expression of regret and sympathy is delayed, but is deeply sincere.*

*I shall always remember this of him—that he spurned safety to fight beside me in the most desperate moment of life—that he was not afraid—that he died trying to save others—and that he died laughing in death's very face.*

*Few men, who lived out a full, smug lifetime in comfort and safety, did as much:*

*"As He died to make men holy, let us die to make men free."*

This extraordinary letter arrived not in June 1945, but in *June 1946*. The pain of loss was not a temporary thing, forgotten in a summer. Until Elting's letter, Emil and Rose Mosbacher had little more than the standard three-line telegram informing them of the date and place of Stephen's death. For fourteen months, they must have thought a thousand times of a thousand ways their son might have died. To finally learn that their Sigmund had suffered a sudden, painless death, in a heroic attempt to save his fellow soldiers, was the most comforting news they could receive.

Elting apologized for the long delay. He had been wounded and captured in the attack. The Germans took Elting to a hospital, which they surrendered *to him* the next day. That's how close Stephen's death had been to the end—the area where he died was surrendered without a fight less than twenty-four hours later. The main reason for the long delay in writing, though, was that Elting could not find the Mosbachers' address.

He apologized, as well, that Stephen's commendation had been downgraded from the Distinguished Service Cross he had recommended to a Silver Star. He was in the hospital at the time for jaundice. "Would have created a fuss otherwise."

He then offered one more comfort to the parents of a soldier he clearly admired and mourned, even fourteen months after his death:

*I understand that he is buried in the US military cemetery at Margraten, Holland. A Dutch family, with whom I stayed while we were there before our first battle, writes me every now and then. They had offered to take care of the graves of any of my friends who were buried there, so have asked them to take care of Stephen's. Their last letter stated that they had made application for that purpose with the cemetery authorities. The Dutch have been consistently grateful for our help and have gotten along splendidly with our troops, so there is not the slightest doubt but that this family will tend your son's grave with care and devotion.*

Elting's Dutch friends were far from the only visitors to the cemetery at Margraten. In September 1945, a few of Pat Fowlkes's friends visited his grave, a few of the hundreds, perhaps thousands, of American soldiers who made a final stop on their way out of Europe to pay their respects. They sent Lib photographs of Pat's grave and a diagram of the cemetery, which Emilie Michiels van Kessenich, when she wrote to Lib and then to Pat's sister Elizabeth that summer, had not thought to send. "As yet there is no grass," they wrote, "but the cemetery is in the process of being beautified and in time will be a beautiful place."

Most of the visitors, though, were Dutch. For the first five months of its existence, the Margraten U.S. Military Cemetery had been closed to nonmilitary personnel except by special exception, like Father Heynen's nightly memorial services. That began to change in March 1945, when the citizens of Margraten stepped in to help dig graves. After that, Shomon unofficially opened the cemetery to local visitors. A good thing, since many of the boys who died in March and April 1945 had lived their last months in Limburg, and their Dutch friends and host families wanted to honor and mourn them, like Frieda with Walter, or the Vroonen family with Stephen Mosbacher, buried less than two miles from their home.

By the first Memorial Day celebration, the Civilian Committee Margraten had several hundred adopters for American graves. At the ceremony, they handed out cards encouraging others to register: *If you are already caring for a soldier, let us know. Let us help you. If you need a connection, let us provide you a name, a young man or woman to think of as your own.* The committee gave tours to Dutch groups, more than fifty in that first single summer, including Boy Scout troops and the burgemeester's committees. They oversaw a ceremony on July 4, where the Dutch prime minister placed a wreath on a grave. But their primary focus, under the direction of the young priest Father Heuschen, was grave adoptions.

The Dutch did not need encouragement. On their own, throughout the summer, they came to the cemetery to mourn. They came—men, women, and children—out of a genuine love for the men who had freed them.

*Anne-Marie Peters*
*Hubert-George Hedy {Sjef.*

Shomon's company had a small tent, marked Inlichtingen—information office—where an officer could flip through file drawers of index cards to find the gravesite of specific soldiers. Heuschen tried to keep a volunteer or two nearby, to register these mourners as adopters. Many of the Dutch came to honor a special soldier—or soldiers—and were officially recorded as the adopter of that grave. But others, like twenty-year-old Mary Broun, came to honor the Americans in general. That morning, when she arrived at the tent with two friends, Paschal Fowlkes's three friends happened to be there, too, so the committee assigned Mary Broun to be Pat's adopter. His friends sent Lib a photo of Mary kneeling at Pat's grave, along with her address in Heerlen. The adoption program was what Major Elting was referring to when he said his Dutch friends had "made application . . . with the cemetery authorities" to care for Stephen's grave.

Captain Shomon and his 611th Graves Registration Company welcomed these developments. He understood the Dutch commitment to the cemetery, especially the villagers of Margraten, because he had lived among them for months. He knew that, in the three weeks between the German surrender and the first Memorial Day ceremony, the Margraten U.S. Military Cemetery had transitioned from a working burial ground—though men were still being buried, even after Memorial Day—to a place of remembrance. A sacred place for returning soldiers to mourn, and for the Dutch to give thanks.

Captain Shomon was determined to make it the most beautiful memorial grounds in Europe, despite the fact that everyone assumed the cemetery was temporary and eventually the boys would be brought home for burial on American soil. He had funds to purchase trees for a natural screen along the Rijksweg and a gracious approach to the burial grounds. He created beds for flowers and bushes, with a plan to plant 50,000 tulips, a symbol of the Netherlands, to honor the friendship between the two nations.

Much of this landscaping and maintenance was done by men from Margraten, under Shomon's supervision. The cemetery had expanded wildly since October 1944. What had once been confined primarily to a single orchard now covered more than thirty fields that had once grazed cattle and produced potatoes, sugar beets, and rye. Those farmers and farmhands, like many in the area, were out of work, and the Dutch economy was in shambles. Supplies were so scarce, many in Margraten wore clothes sewn out of the mattress covers the Americans used for burials. Shomon gave out the covers, unofficially, because he saw the suffering. Now his cemetery was one of the few places offering steady work.

The relationship, though, was about far more than jobs. The people of Margraten felt a strong attachment to the cemetery that had grown to dominate their lives. To soldiers like Stephen Mosbacher, who had stayed in the village. To the gravediggers, who had lived at the village edge. And especially to Shomon's 611th Graves Registration Company, whose members had eaten with them, worshipped with them, and slept in their homes. These relationships of convenience had turned into friendships, and those friendships had changed Margraten. The U.S. Military Cemetery was more than a burial ground for soldiers. It was more, even, than a source of local pride. It was a physical manifestation of the bond between the villagers of Margraten and the American army that built it. The cemetery, from the initial planning to the nightly memorial services, from digging graves during Operation Varsity to the flower-decked Memorial Day ceremony, was a collaboration. The villagers were as determined as their GRS friends to make it worthy of the tens of thousands of souls (and counting) who had given all and found eternal rest within their midst.

But not long after Memorial Day, Shomon received orders to prepare to redeploy. The 611th was being transferred to the Pacific Theater, where the war with Japan raged on. They were scheduled for training in GRS procedure.

*Training!* Shomon scoffed. His men had been working in the field for fifteen months. They had developed many of the methods they would no doubt be "trained" to use.

The citizens of Margraten were crushed to see them go. They streamed out of their houses on the day of their friends' departure. They jammed the narrow Rijksweg so full the American jeeps couldn't move. Another graves registration company was taking over the cemetery, but the citizens of Margraten knew they could never recreate the comradery of those frozen, fearful months. So they offered parting gifts: fresh-baked bread, homemade jams, a kiss on the cheek. A band struck up a jaunty tune. Dutch and American flags were waved. Burgemeester Ronckers gave a speech.

Then Shomon stood in the back of his jeep and said his own farewell, thanking the people of Margraten for making their village a worthy resting place for Americans. "We are proud of your friendship, your love," he said. "We are leaving, but we cannot forget you. . . . The friendship between Holland and the United States is closer because of Margraten. This is how we feel this morning; we shall always feel this way. May God bless you and your good work. May He always look after you, in times of joy and sorrow.

May He look after the dead which we leave in your care this bright but sorrowful June morning. Goodbye—and God be with you always."

On the way out, Shomon stopped one last time at the cemetery. The 50,000 tulips were never to be planted, but thousands of orange and yellow poppies had bloomed among the headstones, a spontaneous outpouring of beauty and hope. Life, they seemed to say, would go on. The summer would rise, the seasons roll. But this land, which he had loved for all his time in Margraten, was changed forever, and it was beautiful.

Two months later, it was Lieutenant Colonel Leo Senecal's turn to go home. In July, at Queen Wilhelmina's palace, Prince Bernhard made Senecal an officer of the Order of Orange-Nassau for his service to Limburg. On August 19, Burgemeester Willem Michiels van Kessenich made him an honorary citizen of the city of Maastricht, the first time such an honor had ever been bestowed. City hall was decked with green and orange gladioluses for the celebration. American and Dutch flags hung side by side throughout the city.

"I'll come back!" Senecal declared.

Before leaving, Colonel Senecal, like General Corlett before him, asked a favor of Emilie, which she recorded in her Memory Book: "I am now taking over the task of visiting and caring for graves in Margraten at the request of Colonel Senecal."

Nazi Germany and Fascist Italy were defeated. The Allied military presence was unwinding. But the war was far from over. As Lieutenant Commander Ernest A. de Bordenave, a friend of Pat's from Virginia Theological Seminary and a Navy chaplain, put it in a radio address: "Although I have ministered to wounded overseas for many months, and although I had buried American boys in the soil of many foreign lands, yet now that I am home I know that it is not the boys, but the parents and friends, the sweethearts, wives and children, who bear the deepest tragedy."

# CHAPTER 70

# MAIL

— ★ —

*Emilie Michiels van Kessenich*
September 1945

In the final days of August, as the U.S. Army prepared to pull out of his city, Willem Michiels van Kessenich wrote a letter of gratitude to the American people. Identifying himself as the "burgomaster of Maastricht, one of the first liberated towns in Holland," he thanked them for their sacrifices and their efforts (led by Lieutenant Colonel Leo P. Senecal, he noted) to clothe, feed, and care for Maastricht's citizens. The letter was printed in the August 27, 1945, issue of *Life* magazine. At the time, *Life* was one of the most popular and influential magazines in the United States; its issues reached 20 percent of the American population. In that same issue, it published—and thereby introduced to the world—the famous photograph of a sailor kissing a nurse in New York City's Times Square following the Japanese surrender and the end of World War II.

Two weeks later, on September 12, a letter arrived at Maastricht City Hall. It was postmarked August 25, meaning it must have been written as soon as that issue of *Life* arrived, since subscriptions went out only a few days before the newsstand publication date.

> *Dear Sir:*
>
> *... For some time, I have hoped that in some way I could learn the name of the Burgomaster of Maastricht. Fortune has been kind to me, for by reading my "Life" Magazine I have learned your name and I am now able to write you.*
>
> *My husband, Private Warren F. Feil ... was killed in Germany on his*

*birthday, April 18, 1945, and is buried in the U.S. Military Cemetery at*
*Margraten, Holland, near your town of Maastricht.*

*Since you live so near it I will be grateful to you all of the days of my life if*
*you can get me a snapshot of his grave. It is located in Plot HH, Row S, Grave*
*111. I have all this information and know the exact location of his grave but*
*have no picture of it and no hope of obtaining one, except through someone like*
*you. I cannot begin to tell you how very much it would mean to me to have such a*
*picture. My husband and I were so young and he was my whole life to me. I know*
*that he rests in peace and I have heard how beautifully the graves are kept and*
*how the kind people of Holland go to the cemeteries and place flowers upon the*
*graves. If only I could see for myself. The snapshot would help so much. . . .*

> *Sincerely,*
> *Mabel Rose Feil*
> *(Mrs. Warren F. Feil)*
> *Demopolis, Alabama*

Willem's secretary, Else Hanöver, read the letter, then gave it to Willem, who passed it along to his wife, saying that it seemed like something for her.

Lib Fowlkes's letter and Senecal's request had inspired Emilie to turn her attention toward the American dead. She was not alone in this. As Mabel's letter noted, stories of the generosity of the Dutch toward America's fallen soldiers had already reached all the way to Alabama. The idea of honoring graves had sprouted a hundred or more times, organically, across Limburg, especially in the homes of those, including Frieda, who befriended soldiers. Emilie was uniquely positioned to use her contacts with influential women from the Apostolate of the Front to encourage that effort. But she was nursing her baby girl. She had never fully recovered from her malnutrition and hospitalization the previous summer. And, as Willem often reminded her, she had "worked herself to the bone" to provide wholesome entertainment for American soldiers, and her children needed their mother healthy and strong.

So around the time of Senecal's request, Emilie reached out to the Civilian Committee Margraten. International mail delivery had resumed on June 1, and like Willem in Maastricht, Burgemeester Ronckers had begun receiving letters from America. In August, a particularly touching letter was passed on by a friend in The Hague. An American father, too ill to visit, offered to pay any expense if someone could send him photos of his son's grave in Margraten. Just as Mabel's letter, with its vulnerability and pain, pierced Emilie's heart as a wife and a mother, this letter touched Ronckers deeply. It was clear to both of them, and to Father Heuschen, whom Ronckers shared the letter with, that an adoption program should not only focus on soldiers, but the next of kin as well.

On September 9, five days before the first anniversary of the liberation of Maastricht, a short call to action appeared in three Limburg newspapers, the *Gazet van Limburg*, the *Advertentieblad*, and the *Limburgs Dagblad*. Emilie read it in her sitting room, after washing three-month-old Mary Victoria in the little zinc tub in the sink. There was still no better way to start the day than with a giggling infant and a warm bath. The anonymous writer urged readers not to forget, in the joy of liberation, the thousands of white crosses at Margraten. "They too speak to us during the general rejoicing in their quiet language; not on their own behalf; they found peace in their heroic death; but for their loved ones that are left behind."

Emilie smiled when she saw the paragraph about the moving letter, recently received by the author, that cried out in desolation, "He was my whole life to me!" and contained a specific request from the heartbroken widow: to visit her husband's grave and send a photograph.

Every family in Limburg that can, the article said, should adopt a grave and care for it "as if it belonged to one of their family members who have now been spared." The anonymous writer—and here Emilie couldn't help smiling even more, because this appeal, of course, had been written by her—envisioned an "army of understanding and affectionate hearts" to show grieving American women that their dear ones were dead but not lost, overseas but not alone. If you wish to be part of this effort, the article said, send your information to the "Burger Committee 'Margraten.'"

She was shocked by the response. Emilie understood the appreciation for the American soldiers. She believed in the kindness of Limburgers. She never expected that within ten days of the article, the Civilian Committee Margraten would receive 3,000 requests to become adopters. Mabel Feil's letter was, as Willem described it, no doubt with the shocking news of Hiroshima and Nagasaki fresh in his mind, "an atomic bomb of providence."

It wasn't her moving words, Emilie knew. It wasn't her personal influence, since the article didn't include her name. It was the timing. What better occasion than the anniversary of the liberation of Maastricht to remind Limburgers of the American sacrifice?

But mostly, it was Mabel Feil. Her simple emotion—*He was my whole life to me!*—and the straightforward nature of her request: visit, flowers, photograph. It meant so much to her, and yet it was so easy. Hundreds of Limburgers were visiting the cemetery already. Why not help an American widow or family member suffering overseas?

After the article, Emilie met with Father Heuschen. She had discussed the article with him in advance of publication, although the section from Mabel's letter—the soul of the piece—had been a last-minute addition, an "atomic bomb" of emotion dropped at exactly the right moment. Apparently, the flood of letters surprised Heuschen as well, because at that meeting or one soon after, the young priest went into his room at the rectory in Margraten and pulled a trunk out from under his bed. It was filled with unopened letters from Dutch citizens answering Emilie's call to action.

"I don't know what to do with all these," he admitted.

The flood of letters wasn't the only problem. While Shomon and his men had supported the grave adoption efforts, the unit that replaced them, the 603rd Quartermaster Graves Registration Company, had no connection with the Dutch or the local community. They saw the cemetery the way the GRS was instructed to see it: as American property to be safeguarded, not shared, and they *discouraged* the Dutch from thinking of it as an open memorial ground.

This made some sense, as Margraten was still an active cemetery. On June 8, General Eisenhower had declared it a priority of the U.S. military to find all American personnel missing in action or buried in an isolated grave and to inter them in a U.S. military cemetery. It was an *immediate* priority, Eisenhower wrote, to bring back those lost or buried in Germany. So even as combat and support troops were being trucked to the Atlantic ports for their journey home, GRS disinterment teams were pouring into Germany. Hiking through forests. Dredging rivers. Interviewing priests and undertakers. Interrogating enemy prisoners. Placing ads asking for assistance and studying old newspaper articles, tracking down every rumor and report. Every town was visited, and every mayor required to sign papers declaring they knew of no Americans killed or buried nearby.

When remains were found, the location was recorded and the area searched, since many of the lost were airmen, and other crew members might be nearby. The remains were carefully recovered or disinterred, then moved to a temporary collecting point. Within hours, they were on the way to the nearest U.S. military cemetery. That often meant Margraten.

This reburial effort started while Shomon was still in theater, but the vast majority of the bodies reached Margraten after the takeover by the 603rd Graves Registration Company. The numbers weren't as high as in spring 1945, but they were substantial: almost a thousand bodies from two cemeteries near the Ruhr Valley, hundreds from other cemeteries in western Germany, dozens of lone bodies found through the diligent efforts of the disinterment teams. The Black gravediggers of the 3136th Quartermaster Service Company had left, so German POWs dug graves. But the 603rd handled the bodies, many of which had decomposed. The work of sorting, autopsying, and identifying was difficult and often unsettling, but the GRS technicians took their duties seriously, treating every body—and every body part—with the respect and care they deserved. The U.S. Army demanded no less.

The needs of the Dutch, even the needs of the widows and mothers in America, were not their concern. Their duty was to the soldiers: to honor each with a dignified burial, and to keep their field of honor beautiful and clean. The 603rd had registry books containing the names and grave locations of soldiers buried at Margraten. They shared this information with the Dutch who visited, looking for specific soldiers. But no amount of coaxing from Father Heuschen or Burgemeester Ronckers could open the minds and hearts of the Americans to the idea of giving a copy of the roster to the Civilian Committee Margraten. And nothing could get them to entertain the idea of providing the Dutch with what Emilie, Ronckers, and Heuschen now realized they needed for their work to have the greatest impact: contact information for the mothers and fathers, siblings and spouses, back home who craved a photograph or word of comfort from someone near the final resting place of their fallen son, brother, husband, or friend.

To Emilie, that was absurd, and out of character for the Americans, who had always been friendly and open. So on September 27—barely two weeks after her article in the *Gazet van Limburg* and the other two papers had been published—she composed a letter to the one person she thought could cut through the bureaucracy and give Father Heuschen's committee access to the registers of next of kin: President Harry S. Truman.

*Dear Mr. President:*

*For months I have been thinking, if there could not be done something for the relatives of those brave Americans, who gave their lives for our liberation....*
*[A] very real comradeship has been established between your big country and our small one. And now that most of the Army has gone back to the States, and only your fallen heroes remain in our soil, we want to establish a lasting tie between their relatives and our people.*

*Captain Shomon, once at Margraten, where your vast Cemetery is situated, took the initiative for the adoption of their graves by our Dutch families. The "Civil Committee 'Margraten'" has been elaborating this scheme, and I have been propagating their splendid work among all the towns in South Limburg, calling upon the former hostesses, who had the occasion of meeting ten thousands of your boys....*

*There is one difficulty to surmount. The Cemetery at Margraten is under the supervision of American Authorities, who are frequently changed. They ... are not authorized as yet to give up the registration of the men buried there....*

*So my urgent request to you, dear Mr. President, is this: If you think it advisable for us to undertake this responsible task, that may bring a little comfort to 18,000 American homes, and give a chance of showing their gratitude and friendship to 18,000 Dutch ones, would you show me the way to contact the Commanding Officer, who has the authority to hand over a complete registration or have it copied by our volunteers.*

The widows and mothers knew the graves were well-kept, Emilie told the president, but "they want a warm-hearted, personal touch and thought." To reassure him, she suggested he appoint an overseer on the American side, perhaps Colonel Leo Senecal, who had recently gone home to Chicopee, Massachusetts, but was well-known and highly regarded in Limburg.

Then, after apologizing for her "dreadful impudence" in writing to him personally, Emilie laid out the reason for her passion so clearly that it was almost a mission statement: "I am a mother of 11 children ranging from 14 years to 3 months, and if it should happen that my boys were buried in American soil, I should be so grateful if an American mother would send me a photograph and should go there sometimes in my place . . ."

*I am a mother,* she thought. *I feel a mother's hope, and I know a mother's fear. I understand a mother's pain.*

We, the Dutch, understand. We are here, with your boys. We want to help.

# CHAPTER 71

# TOUR GUIDE

— ★ —

*Frieda van Schaïk*

September 1945

Frieda was frustrated as she walked home from the distribution center with her family's rations. In addition to the thousands of Allied
soldiers passing through Limburg, Dutch citizens who had been trapped
on the German side of the line for months or even years were returning.
One of those was Wim, her brother, whom she hadn't seen since he fled
for Rotterdam after his release from the Gestapo prison in summer 1944.
Another was Peter, her friend from her time in Arnhem.

Peter had asked to see her. She had been nervous about that. She
barely recognized the girl she'd been in summer 1943, before liberation.
And Moekie's two strokes. And Walter. She had no interest in the wartime
promises Peter had asked for and that young girl had made. It had been a
strange time. No one was sure if they would survive, much less ever be free.
Surely, she thought, Peter wouldn't hold her to the promises of a child.

He didn't. But what he did say when they met that morning was worse:
he accused her of betraying him by consorting with American soldiers. She
knew he was looking for a way out. He had been a child then too. Maybe he
saw in Limburg's anger at some of its young women a convenient excuse.
In that case, he was a coward. Or maybe he believed what he said, in which
case he had never really known her at all.

Either way, the accusation stung. He could have been honest with her.
They could have had a conversation.

"Frieda."

337

And the insinuation of that *consorting with*! And not just with a soldier. With soldiers! It was just . . . it was . . . How dare he! After all they had been through—all the Dutch, every man and woman, every single one of them.

"Frieda!"

She looked up. It was her older sister, Helen. Last September, in the excitement after the liberation, their sister Thea had met a young man. In October, when it was clear Moekie would recover from her stroke, they had taken a train to visit his parents in his hometown of Leiden. Market Garden failed, the front hardened, and for seven months, Thea and her Dutchman were trapped in the occupied part of the country. It was awful: starvation, fear, German patrols, while Maastricht was relatively safe in Allied hands. After their liberation, Thea had decided to stay in Leiden with her new husband. It was Helen who came home from Nijmegen, as if taking her place.

"Pappie needs you," she said, holding out a Tilley lamp and a pair of boots.

"It's not my day. It's your day."

"I'm not feeling well," Helen said. She looked fine to Frieda, except for the annoyed expression. What did Helen have to be annoyed about? She had a fiancé now, and he loved her.

"Hurry," Helen said, signaling for Frieda to take the lamp and hand over the rations. "You're late."

After liberation, Dave van Schaïk had been blackballed by the State Supervision of Mines on suspicion of collaboration. Ironic, since Pappie had refused to sign the oath of loyalty to the Nazis while most of the others signed, but such were the times. Accusations were rampant, especially toward those who had interactions with Nazi officials. The fact that Dave had conducted tours of the caves for Nazi officers—in particular General Christiansen, the highest-ranking German officer in the Netherlands—made him guilty in some people's eyes, even though he'd intentionally given Christiansen a terrible tour, helping to save Sint Pietersberg. He was forced to testify in front of the purification committee, a stressful experience, although he was ultimately cleared.

Fortunately, the Americans saw things differently. They helped him publish a fifty-page pamphlet on the caves, in English. His cave tours based on those writings became popular with soldiers. It was typical of her father,

Frieda thought, to finally strike on a successful idea at the very moment all his clients were leaving.

Each tour was a two-person job: Pappie the lead guide, Helen or Frieda at the back to make sure nobody wandered off. Frieda loved the work. The caves were her family's passion. She was excited to return to them. And the soldiers were polite. But it was four miles from the ration distribution center in Heer to the Market Square in Maastricht, where the tours began, and she practically had to run the whole way. By the time she arrived, the soldiers were scouring the area, looking for a young woman with a Tilley lamp, and her father was angry. Just what she needed. She boarded the troop truck in a foul mood, barely noticing the young airmen sitting beside her.

*Royal Air Force*, she noted. It was September. The British were about the only troops left.

The caves, as always, calmed her. The narrowness of the passageways. The depth of the darkness. The way the world fell away after the first turn. The Brits were rowdy at first, cracking jokes, but their voices died in the marlstone, and soon the stillness lulled them into a silent awe. The only sound was their soft footsteps, her father's voice in the darkness, her own voice repeating a quarter of what he said, since Pappie never could curb his enthusiasm.

"It's incredible," an airman said. His face hit the light as he leaned toward her, smiling, and Frieda wondered what he could see of her on the other side of her Tilley lamp. "Do you come here often?"

After the tour, the group had lunch at the restaurant atop Sint Pietersberg. A patio with a view of Maastricht's steeples in the distance, the rare meal she and Moekie didn't have to fashion from ration scraps. Frieda could not have recognized the young man who spoke to her in the cave. In their berets and uniforms, they looked so much alike. But when one of the airmen asked her if she wanted to go to the art show, Frieda knew that it was him.

"I'm an artist," he said. "This is such a rare chance; I'd hate to miss it."

The artworks from the vault in the mountain were being sent back to their respective museums. But first, some were being displayed in Maastricht, in an exhibition called *Zuid ziet Noord* (South Sees North). It was, as Gordon Gumn, the young RAF airman, said, a rare opportunity. Large art exhibitions rarely traveled to Limburg, and such an important collection of Dutch masterpieces was unprecedented. How could Frieda say no?

Gordon proved an excellent guide. He knew many of the artists. He recognized some of the paintings. He could talk about them. Like Walter. Or like Pappie and his caves. Frieda's only experience with the paintings was in passing, as they disappeared into the mountain.

"What do you think?" Gordon asked. *The Night Watch* had returned to the Rijksmuseum in Amsterdam in June, but these old Dutch burgers looking down at her from their huge, ruffed collars were impressive enough.

"It's nice to see them again," Frieda said.

"Give me your address," Gordon said, as they stood in the Market Square, near the truck that would take him back to his base. "I'll send you and, um, your father, some of the photographs I've taken."

She fell for it.

"How did it go?" his mates asked, as Gordon sat in the back of the idling truck, watching the girl of his dreams walk away across the square. He had told them the moment she walked up with her Tilley lamp and frustrated frown, *That's the girl I'm going to marry.* It was no accident he was in her truck to the caves, at the back of the tour, at her table in the restaurant.

"Not disappointed," he said.

"Not yet!" someone cracked. And then they were off, back to their base and, before he had a chance to see her again, all the way back to England.

# CHAPTER 72

# FAMILY AFFAIR

— ★ —

*Emilie Michiels van Kessenich*
November 1945

I t had been a surprisingly difficult six months for Willem Michiels van Kessenich since liberation, considering his family and city were finally safe and the Nazi threat defeated. In May, he had been nominated to become minister of the interior. But on June 22, two weeks after his daughter Mary Victoria's birth and the day before his selection was to be presented to Queen Wilhelmina, some resistance fighters once again voiced anger over the hostage affair. The controversy was too much for a newly formed government tasked with knitting back together a suspicious, hungry nation. Willem's nomination was withdrawn.

By the fall, his actions were being investigated by the Advisory Commission for the Purification of the Mayors of Limburg, one of many commissions established to probe the conduct of government officials during the occupation. In Willem's case, the charges were two: providing the German commander with the list of ten citizens to be used as hostages, and a two-day trip to München-Gladbach, Germany, he took with five Limburg mayors in 1941, which NSB leader D'Ansembourg had organized.

The commission cleared him of the charges regarding his travel to Germany. The trip was not an invitation but an order. The five mayors had no choice but to go.

It cleared him of harboring German or Nazi sympathies—"He had not failed to have the correct attitude in connection with the occupation," in the committee's wording—which would have caused his immediate dismissal from office.

He was reprimanded, though not publicly, for succumbing to German pressure to name hostages and for naming ten others instead of himself. The reprimand was placed in his official files, effectively ending his chances at higher office.

Still, there were those in Maastricht who insisted their burgemeester had performed poorly during the occupation. That in trying to protect the city from German aggression, Willem had acquiesced too readily to the occupier's demands.

"De beste stuurlui staan aan wal," thought Emilie. ("The best steermen were always ashore.")

If the accusations hurt Willem, he kept those feelings to himself. He went to city hall every day, worked the same long hours, showed no emotion over the public condemnation. That probably hurt him with the public, because it made it seem as if he didn't care. But that was the man: he was determined to be a solid rock in a raging sea, for his city and his family. It was how he thought a good public servant had to act.

Only Emilie, his heart's companion and confidante, knew how much it stung a man so careful of his morality to see his ethics questioned. "I have never admired him more," she wrote in her Memory Book, after Willem accepted the loss of his chance to become minister of the interior. It meant his career advancement was over. But that didn't much bother Emilie. Her dream was always to be the wife of a kippenburgemeester, and she loved their life in Maastricht.

Plus, she had her own project, the mission given to her by Senecal, Mabel, and Lib Fowlkes, and it was at a critical juncture. On November 6, she had finally received a reply to her letter to the president asking for access to the next-of-kin rolls. It was not from Truman's office but the Office of the Quartermaster General, and it was only a few lines: "We regret that we are not in a position to supply the information you desire."

Meanwhile, the Margraten grave rolls had been moved from the cemetery to the Army's Headquarters in Liège, Belgium. Cross-border travel was severely restricted. Even when a Dutch person was allowed to cross into Belgium, they could carry no more than the equivalent of $10, because the Dutch government was in the process of reminting and reprinting the Dutch guilders the Germans had confiscated and then outlawed in 1942, and they didn't want them spent outside the country. It seemed the Americans were doing everything they could to thwart the work of the Civilian Committee Margraten.

It would have been easy to give in to frustration, to think the program was a gift nobody wanted . . . except that each time a letter from an American mother or war widow arrived in the Maastricht burgemeester's office, Emilie saw once again how necessary this work was. American officials might be leery of the committee's efforts, but Americans whose sons and husbands had been killed were dying for the comfort a Dutch adopter could provide. Emilie read each letter carefully, translated it, and sent it on to the Civilian Committee Margraten. She wrote back if a letter touched her deeply, answering questions and offering her sympathies, so she had a growing list of correspondents. Of friends, really, who needed and appreciated, as Emilie had written President Truman, "a warm-hearted, personal touch and thought."

As the weather began to turn toward winter, she took her daughters Mathilda, five, and Emilie-Hélène, four, to Margraten to visit Mabel's husband's grave. The 603rd Graves Registration Company was hard at work. The recovery and reburial efforts were at their height, and there was a steady stream of bodies to process and bury. They were stenciling the name and serial number of each fallen American on each white cross and Star of David, now numbering almost 18,000. But the burial ground was enormous, and near Plot HH, Row 5, Grave 111, where Private Warren Feil's body rested, the cemetery was calm.

It was a chilly day, so Emilie had dressed the girls in identical short coats, with white knee socks and buckle shoes. Mathilda stood by the grave with her hands in prayer, while little Emilie-Hélène squatted to straighten the white chrysanthemums her Mutti had placed on the grave. The ground was bare dirt. The cross was plain white, with Warren's dog tag nailed to the center. The GRS would nail it to the back of the cross when they stenciled his name on the crossbar, but they had not gotten to his grave yet. Behind it, there were thousands of identical crosses, marching into the distance. Emilie thought of all the mothers, fathers, spouses, and siblings in America, mourning the brave men under all those crosses.

"Can you pray for Private Feil, please, girls?"

"We are, Mutti. Can't you see my hands?"

In the coming year, she would do this many times. Emilie was so moved by the Civilian Committee Margraten's efforts, and by the poignant letters she received from grieving Americans, that the Michiels van Kessenich family adopted fourteen graves, one for each family member. The children were so young, though, that Willem and Emilie were listed on eight of the forms as the official adopters. (Agnes and the other household girls each adopted a grave, as well.) She wrote to grieving loved ones for whom she wasn't an official adopter, including one of Paschal Fowlkes's sisters, Elizabeth, known as Hit, with whom she grew quite close. She sent Lib Fowlkes a photograph of two of her young daughters placing flowers at Pat's grave, his name clearly visible, stenciled on the cross.

But in Mabel Feil she found a kindred spirit. Her words—*He was my whole life to me, send a photograph*—were the inspiration that powered her, her simple request the template for Emilie and so many other adopters to follow.

In November, Manka fell ill. After a day, his condition grew critical, and he was hospitalized for three weeks before coming home and gradually getting better. Even a rock will succumb to scarlet fever.

On January 1, 1946, Emilie's father suffered a stroke. She sped to his bedside, but he awoke only briefly before dying on January 3, at the age of sixty-nine.

On January 10, she traveled to Utrecht, in the north, with Father Heuschen. They had been appointed to the Netherlands War Graves Committee, which oversaw the care of Allied graves on Dutch soil. While there, she met with the United States ambassador, Stanley K. Hornbeck. He was formal and intimidating. Unfriendly. As she stood to go, she paused, wondering if she should say anything more, and then turned back.

"Your Excellency should not take me so seriously," she said. "I am only just a kid!"

And suddenly, he smiled, and a light flashed in his eyes behind his smart round glasses. It was a light she would see many times, because that moment was the start of an unlikely friendship between this mother from the south and the highest-ranking American official in the Netherlands.

"After a 16-year marriage with 11 children, four times a foster child, many illnesses and worries," Emilie wrote in her Memory Book after the trip, "I am suddenly turned loose from the nursery and from the stocking basket."

Who, she wondered, could have ever foreseen all this?

CHAPTER 73

# HAARLEM

— ★ —

*Frieda van Schaïk*
February 1946

It wasn't quite the Christmas of her youth, with the big tree in the front window, Moekie at her piano, and the village children gathered for singing and gifts. But it was better than any Christmas during occupation, and much better than Christmas in Haarlem in 1944, when the citizens had been suffering through the Hunger Winter and deprivation was more common than a hot bun, even on Christmas morning.

Frieda had arrived in Haarlem in early December as a volunteer. The shock of the Hunger Winter and the devastation of the war had broken many Dutch mothers mentally and physically. Men, too, no doubt, but Frieda had come north to help children whose mothers hadn't recovered from the horrors. She had two families under her care. She spent most of her time helping with the cooking and cleaning. She had evenings off, and as the holidays approached, she liked to walk back to her narrow room through the Christmas crowds, admiring the well-dressed women with their shopping bags, the store windows lit up with displays of candied fruits, tinned meats. Even with most windows half-empty, it was still more merchandise than Frieda had ever seen. The gifts of her youth were Pappie's wooden carvings, Moekie's sewing, the togetherness of family.

She didn't notice him at first. She was lost in the holiday lights, and thoughts of home, and she didn't expect him. She saw the uniform, but there were hundreds of men in uniform in the Netherlands; she passed them all the time. It wasn't until he stopped suddenly, surprised, that he

346

caught her eye. Then she stopped, too, and looked, and there he was, up the sidewalk and across the street. Smiling. She hadn't seen that smile since *South Sees North*.

Frieda didn't have a shopping bag. If so, she would have dropped it. She sprinted into the road, dodging cars and bicycles, weaving through the Saturday crowd. She had the impression people were watching her, disapproving. *Another Dutch girl after a foreign soldier*. They were hoping, she felt, that he'd push her away. Instead, Gordon wrapped his arms around her and kissed her on the mouth, then the cheek, and finally on her woolen hat.

By the time Frieda pulled away, the pedestrians were walking and talking, as if they had never even noticed she was there. She imagined them disappointed. *Oh, she knew him. She's one of* those *girls*. But their resentment, real or imagined, didn't matter. Gordon was here.

"Where did you come from?"

He laughed. "England, of course."

"How?"

"On a boat."

"But how did you find me?"

"Frieda, I could find you anywhere."

She laughed. "But really, Gordon, how did you find me?"

"It was luck," he admitted. "But I knew you were in Haarlem, and you make your own luck, right?"

They had been writing feverishly since October, when he sent her a long letter with photographs, as promised. She had no one else, really, to talk to. Pappie was still running at the first hint of feelings, and she was too shy of her heart to bring it up with Moekie. She spoke to Walter at the cemetery. She had finally gotten his mother's home address by writing to Harvard University, where Walter had completed graduate school. She had written to let her know that her son was fondly remembered and deeply missed. The Huchthausens reached out to Major Hoadley, who confirmed the friendship between Walter and the Van Schaïks.

"The knowledge that someone lives so near his grave and gives it constant care is a real comfort, and I know my mother appreciates it immeasurably," Walter's brother Paul wrote to Hoadley. "As a family, we shall all keep in touch with this fine family throughout the future."

Days later, Walter's sister Martha wrote to Frieda. Walter was the only unmarried child in the family of six, Martha said, and he had taken care of their mother. Stunned by his death, Mrs. Huchthausen was too distraught to write, but after all the wonderful things Major Hoadley had said about the Van Schaïks, Martha wanted to thank them.

Frieda immediately wrote back; Martha wrote to her again; and already, a genuine friendship was forming. Still, Frieda kept her initial letters, and her feelings, vague. There was so much she wanted to tell them. So much. But this correspondence was for Walter's family, to help them through their grief. She could not make the letters about herself.

It was to Gordon she poured out her feelings, her experiences, herself. She wrote, in almost every letter, about the cemetery. How sunlight suddenly pierced the clouds and gave every poplar tree a yellow crown. How the citizens of Limburg descended with white flowers on All Saints' Day—white flowers, white crosses, the white mist of morning, a sight never to be forgotten. How November sun threw shadows that connected every grave.

"I was so impressed, Frieda," Gordon wrote, "by your description of your last visit to Margraten. You have such a delightful imagination. What Symbolism! crosses woven together in relationship. I saw photos of the Cemetery shown to me by your Dad. I do so look forward to you taking me there."

She hadn't taken him to Margraten. She hadn't seen him since the cave. Not until right now, on this busy Haarlem street, a complete surprise.

"Why didn't you write?"

"I only just got my leave. You know how the mail is, it takes five days at least. I knew I could get to you faster than that."

She was practically skipping. "Come on, Gordon. Come on. Let's . . . I don't know. Let's go somewhere."

They hurried down the street, holding hands, laughing and looking into the shops. They went to a cafe, where Gordon had real coffee, not the chicory of the occupation, and Frieda a slice of apple pie, warm like home. Frieda lived in a room in a big house with other volunteers, but she had friends in the city. They offered Gordon a spot on their couch. Every night after work, Frieda spent hours with him, walking, talking, laughing. The Christmas lights made everything bright. The holiday music made everything warm. The street-corner puppet shows, gift shacks, fires. The year before there had been no electricity, and burning furniture and branches had been the only way to keep warm. Now the fires were festive, made to be gathered around. Made for a young couple in love, and Frieda had no doubt that's what they were.

After five days, Gordon returned to England. His leave was up, and he had to report to his officer training course at Grantham. Frieda stayed in Haarlem, helping shell-shocked families. But in the evenings, she thought of Gordon. She knew by then that she was going to marry him. She told Walter as much, while walking alone along the icy river.

*He's a good man, Walter. You'd like him. He's like you, a soldier and an artist. I've told him that, I've told him all about you, and he understands. He knows me, Walter. He knows my heart. And he likes it.*

She thought Gordon might return. She waited for him through January and February, but he never came. Supplies were short, the continent bomb-blasted. The more confined people stayed, the civil servants thought, the better. No refugees. No leisure travel. Limited cross-border commerce. If he wasn't on a military pass, Gordon couldn't leave England, and military passes were difficult to acquire. No matter. Frieda had his love to keep her warm.

But then came an announcement on the special radio program, just as news had been relayed during the occupation. "Frieda van Schaïk, come home immediately. Your mother is very ill."

Frieda raced to her room. She threw her bags together. She tried to get a train to Maastricht. No use. It was too late. The best option was the last train to Amsterdam, then a night in the station so she could catch the first train to Maastricht in the morning. Several friends went with her to Amsterdam. They sat with her in the waiting room all night, so she wouldn't be alone as she cried for her mother. As she imagined what she would do, how she would live, if Moekie died.

Moekie survived, but Frieda never returned to Haarlem. The whole family had gone home to Limburg, and even though her four older sisters and her brother Wim, Moekie's favorite, helped out, Frieda slipped back into her role as caretaker. When guests visited, she took the role of hostess, food provider, and drink runner that Moekie had always filled. It was the same service she had been providing for the families in Haarlem. It was the job she had been doing since her return from Arnhem in 1943.

But this time, it was different. The house was the same: Pappie ensconced in his attic, Wim coddled, her now two nieces squirming underfoot, Moekie exhausted from sickness and worry, but Frieda was different. She had a future now. She knew where she was going, or at least where she wanted to be. She knew herself. And she liked the woman she had become.

She chose a sunny day to return to Walter's grave. She bought red tulips and, after cleaning up the family lunch, bicycled with her sister Helen to Margraten. The fields were a patchwork, green and brown, and the tips of the trees were beginning to bud. She could feel the life awakening, the spring pressing up from the soil. But it was still winter, the wind bone-chilling, so no one was at the cemetery, save a few American officers manning the tents, a few gravediggers, a few Dutch in the distance paying their respects. On Walter's grave, the first green threads of grass pushed through the mud, ready to unfurl, but the world was silent, waiting. She bent at his cross. She laid the tulips down. It was so cold, she had to pull her jacket tighter, even though she was wearing an extra sweater.

"Don't worry, Walter," she whispered, as she arranged the bright red flowers. "I am always here. Even when I am away, I am here with you."

She cried the whole way home. It was the cold, she told Gordon, when she described the visit in a letter. The bitter winter wind, whipping past her bicycle, had stung the teardrops from her eyes.

# CHAPTER 74

# REINFORCEMENTS

— ★ —

*Emilie Michiels van Kessenich*

February 1946

The letter section of the February 11, 1946, issue of *Life* magazine featured a photo of two little girls, one standing and one kneeling by a grave covered with white flowers. The girls were Mathilda and Emilie-Hélène Michiels van Kessenich, and the submitter Mabel Feil, who had formed a friendship, she wrote in the letter, with the Michiels van Kessenich family. They had adopted her husband's grave. "I assure you it is a great comfort to know that someone who cares is there to do for me what I cannot do."

"Dearest Mabel," Emilie wrote after receiving the clip, "I have no words to thank you for the sweet letter and the papercutting you sent me. I really did not believe my eyes, seeing those two naughty kids in a real American newspaper."

After *Life*, several family members of American servicemen reached out to Emilie. They wanted what she had given Mabel: the comfort of knowing someone cares. Some of their sons weren't buried at Margraten. They were at other American military cemeteries in Europe, but these mothers and fathers didn't know where else to turn. Might someone go there, too, place flowers, send a photograph?

There was such a movement in the Netherlands. That winter, the Civilian Committee Margraten had formalized its structure, adding "U.S. Military Cemetery" to the end of its name, giving Emilie the title of

"Patroness" (the governor of Limburg was designated "Patron") and Father Heuschen the title of "Secretary," meaning head of operations. Both were appointed to the Netherlands War Graves Committee, which oversaw the care of Allied graves on Dutch soil and had taken an interest in the Civilian Committee's work at Margraten.

Even the Americans, Emilie wrote Mabel, had noticed. Two men from the U.S. War Department had traveled to Margraten, then to Maastricht to talk with her about the adoption program. Impressed, they asked for help spreading the idea to other cemeteries. The committee, Emilie told Mabel, was working on that project.

She could not, however, contain her frustration over the American graves registration rolls being moved from Margraten to Liège, Belgium, where they were much more difficult for the Dutch to access. "I am convinced it is being done on purpose," Emilie wrote, "because the [Graves] Registration Officers belonging to Margraten are still here. I wish they would honestly tell me to stop the work if they have any objections, because this is extremely exasperating."

Mabel responded with a second letter to *Life*, published in March, urging those with loved ones at Margraten to reach out to the Dutch directly. It included Emilie's address. Emilie received more than 400 letters—more of the valuable next-of-kin contact information the committee had not been able to get from American officials.

Mabel's mother, Mabel Rose Levy (Mrs. Ernest Levy, as she identified herself, but those closest to her called her Ma), went further, writing a blistering letter to her congressman from Alabama, Frank W. Boykin.

"It would seem," she wrote, "that the Netherlands Government is more interested in our boys and their families than our own government. . . . [M]y daughter has received letters from all over the country and if you could read these pathetic missives from heartbroken mothers and wives, many of whom have never received any information about where their loved ones are buried it would break your heart. . . . It does seem strange, doesn't it that the records should be moved away from the cemetery and taken to another country?"

Boykin passed the letter on to the military brass and received a somewhat prickly response from the quartermaster general himself, Major General Thomas B. Larkin, stating that the U.S. Army took its responsibility for its fallen very seriously, and didn't need help from the Dutch. He then added, "I must tell you, too, that there have been instances which have pointed to commercialism and the solicitation of funds, even the actual victimizing of the next of kin."

Whoops. The statement was true. Fraud was a problem after the war, and some desperate Europeans were not above begging from the comparatively wealthy Americans. But Mrs. Mabel Rose Levy was a hard-bitten matriarch from South Alabama, and she had no truck with such rudeness. When Boykin shared Larkin's comments, she targeted her wrath on the quartermaster general:

> *Mrs. Michiels van Kessenich is a woman and a mother.... She can realize the awfulness of that telegram from the War Department, and the frustration in trying to get any information at all, the desire that some one who cares will place a flower there and send some information to the family. These things mean so much to a woman. My daughter, widow of Private Warren F. Feil, has received so many letters, and the majority of them have had no word about the location of the graves. Can't you see what it means to have some contact in the country where these boys are buried? These are not just* <u>*bodies*</u>*, but our boys, our sons, our husbands, who have made such a futile sacrifice. Mrs. Michiels van Kessenich is above any commercialism. She will not even allow me to send candy to her eleven children....*

She then loaded up for her final word:

> *I am writing you as a woman whose ancestors' blood is on every battlefield in America, whose family had many generals in it, and whose names are enrolled in the pages of the history of our country since 1653. My daughter and I must render an account to the many many bereaved families who have written us. Must we say to them that our government is more interested in bringing British brides to America than in bringing some balm to their aching hearts? If you have ever lost a dearly loved one you realize that those first months are the hardest to bear under the best circumstances. The women are not asking for any expenditure of money, only that the records be available when it is necessary to search for a grave location. Even though it is temporary, it will be of comfort when most needed.*

Emilie was wrong about a few things. The records had been moved to Belgium not to thwart the Dutch but because the American Graves Registration Command had centralized cemetery operations for the Netherlands, Belgium, and Luxembourg. In fact, after months of appeals, Father Heuschen had befriended an American Graves Registration official at the headquarters in Liège and talked him into opening the files. Father Heuschen's priesthood convinced the official the effort was honest, and God's work. Since November, Heuschen's volunteers had been crossing back and forth to Belgium to copy the information from the files. This was a vital step. With this information, it would be far easier for the committee to match adopters with soldiers.

Emilie was right, however, in her basic concern: the Americans were withholding vital information. The register in Liège was a list of soldiers and grave plots. It did not include the names and addresses of next of kin. Soldiers who enlisted before June 1943 had next-of-kin information listed on their dog tags. It was possible to get that information by copying it from dog tags nailed to crosses and Stars of David, and Father Heuschen's volunteers were doing just that. But for soldiers who enlisted or commissioned after July 1943, the committee had only one way of getting the information they needed: recording it off of the letters from America.

In this, Else Hanöver, Willem's secretary at city hall, was invaluable. Emilie had asked for her help, with Willem's encouragement, because the committee needed volunteers who could read and translate English. Else was happy to help, in part because she adored her boss and his family, but as always, Willem was a stickler for the rules. She could not miss any of her regular work hours for the effort, he told her; she would have to volunteer in the evening or on weekends. The people of Maastricht would not be short-changed a penny or a minute on Willem Michiels van Kessenich's watch.

Else began taking the bus to the village one or two evenings a week, but soon she was volunteering three evenings a week and on Saturdays. She convinced two friends to help her, and on some weekends the three of them became so enthralled with the work that they slept at Sint Margarita's rectory in Margraten, then woke up early the next morning to continue working.

Else adopted the grave of Ralph Van Kirk Jones of Ault, Colorado, who was a day older than her. A boy her age, almost to the day, had died, leaving his mother no chance to say good-bye, no way to visit his grave. How could she not be moved? From correspondence with his mother, who Else called Mother Ruth, she learned that Ralph had polio, and his right arm was withered, but the Army took him anyway. He was married six months before shipping overseas. He was killed two months later.

"If I ever have a baby," Else promised Mother Ruth, "I will name him Ralph."

The girls were young, barely twenty-four, and the long hours crimped their social life, but to Else and her friends, the sacrifice was worth it to help women like Mrs. Jones.

But what, Emilie wondered, about the other wives and mothers whose boys were buried at Margraten? There were thousands who had not thought to write to the leaders of Maastricht and Margraten, or were too heartbroken to compose a letter, or were, like Miss Ed Norton, struggling to rise from bed each morning without their child. What about the wives who assumed there was no one here, across the sea, who cared? The thousands suffering in silence, who assumed they were alone in their grief? Surely those women deserved kindness and comfort too.

The truth was, every time Emilie thought of a young American dead and buried, she saw the face of one of her boys. How could she leave these boys, so like her boys, to lie alone in a foreign land? How could she leave their mothers to suffer, when there was something she could do to ease their pain?

It had taken half a year for Father Heuschen to access the complete roster of names and grave locations. It had taken Major John Elting, Stephen Mosbacher's commanding officer, half a year to locate the parents of one of his own soldiers. Chaplain Tildon McGee had to resort to getting an article published in the *Atlanta Journal* to find Bill Moore's mother. With that kind of bureaucracy, what hope did Emilie have of navigating her way through the system to nearly 18,000 American addresses?

She wasn't giving up. She needed another plan.

# CHAPTER 75

# RELOCATIONS AND BEAUTIFICATION

— ★ —

*Margraten; Frieda van Schaïk*

April 1946

By April 1946, the remains of an additional 6,000 Americans had been located and reburied at Margraten since Memorial Day 1945: infantrymen, artillerymen, tankers, engineers, flyers, paratroopers, nurses, quartermaster troops, and civil affairs officers, a true cross-section of the volunteers, professionals, and draftees who had sacrificed their lives to win the war. That brought the total buried at Margraten to nearly 18,000 Americans, and 21,000 in all when accounting for other Allied and enemy dead. It was a monumental effort. Eighteen months before, this area had been farmland, barely liberated from German hands. The Americans had built roads and buildings, staked and graded the grounds, and laid out burial plots. They had driven thousands of miles, sometimes through hostile conditions; autopsied and identified; moved 1.6 million cubic feet of dirt, six feet by six feet by two and a half feet at a time, shoveled aside with nothing more than muscle. Nearly enough dirt to fill the reflecting pool on the National Mall in Washington, D.C.—twice. They used most of that dirt to refill those holes, with respect, one at a time.

They were far from the end of the mission. Lieutenant James Norton and other American pilots had been reinterred at Margraten from the graveyard at Huisduinen, but the graveyard at Son, where paratroopers who fell at Market Garden—including Lieutenant Colonel Robert Cole—were buried, was still spread across a rise near the city of Nijmegen.

In Germany, the GRS had searched 12,589 square miles, finding 7,651 isolated graves and unburied bodies. Of those, 971 were identified as Americans. By April, 477 had been interred in U.S. military cemeteries— less than 5 percent of the 11,000 missing Americans. Some of the remaining lost would prove relatively easy to locate, like Lieutenant Bill Moore, whose body had been recovered by Dutch Resistance fighters and buried in a church yard in Ugchelen, a village on the outskirts of Apeldoorn. Others would never be found. But the effort would continue for years, well into the 1950s, until every option and possibility had been exhausted. To call it monumental is an understatement. It was the most thorough effort to find and bury the remains of soldiers missing in action and those who had been killed and buried in some isolated grave in the history of modern warfare.

And all of it, at least at Margraten, was temporary. General Eisenhower wanted the thirty-six U.S. military cemeteries in Northern Europe consolidated. He envisioned two permanent burial grounds: Henri-Chapelle in Belgium, and one of the graveyards in Normandy. The bodies at Margraten, as at the thirty-three other temporary burial grounds, would be moved, the cemetery dismantled, and the farmland returned to the Dutch. Since the graves were temporary, officially like General Larkin reasoned, sentimental ties would only make the work of repatriation harder.

The Army's Quartermaster General's plan, submitted to the War Department in June 1945, questioned the need for any European cemeteries. It suggested giving the next of kin a choice for permanent burial: any U.S. National Cemetery, any local or private cemetery of their choosing, or a permanent military cemetery overseas near their current interment, *if enough loved ones chose that option to make the maintenance feasible*. The U.S. government would pay repatriation and reburial costs, estimated at $700 per soldier. If almost all of the 280,000 overseas dead (including the Mediterranean and Pacific Theaters) were repatriated, as the quartermaster assumed they would be, the total cost would be around $210 million.

"In the opinion of this office," the report stated, "comparative costs . . . are not in any event the primary consideration in a matter so involved with sentiment. Final disposition of our soldiers' remains, in accordance with the wishes of the loved ones, is an inherent obligation of the Government as the final gesture of a grateful country to those who paid the supreme sacrifice."

Everybody in the chain of command, from President Truman to Ike to Graves Registration troops on the ground at Margraten, were in agreement on that point: when it came to doing right by fallen service personnel, no expense in money or manpower would be spared. The officers of the 603rd Graves Registration Company gave their souls to the work at Margraten. They knew the quartermaster's plans might take a few months, or they might take years. Conscience, good grace, and duty required them to provide a beautiful, well-planned, and well-maintained site until then. Margraten was more than a burial ground. It was a monument to valor, freedom, and sacrifice. With the reburials slowing by spring 1946, the 603rd turned to completing Shomon's work of transforming it, at least for a little while, into a place of honor and remembrance.

They seeded grass over the graves. They planted flower beds, hedge-rows, and trees. They moved their offices and the morgue to the back of the site. The German POWs had built a white clapboard chapel there, much like the little chapels that dotted American towns. It came from a kit provided by the U.S. Army, but the Germans found a bell and added a steeple. A symbolic reversal of the Nazis melting down most of the bells in Limburg, though the POWs had no way of knowing that. Locating the work and worship spaces at the back allowed the 603rd to add a formal entryway to the cemetery from the Rijksweg, with the gravity and grace it deserved.

As a well-known amateur botanist and local flora enthusiast, Dave van Schaïk was consulted by Margraten's first superintendent, Johannes Straarup of Seattle, Washington. Or perhaps Pappie went to the cemetery to offer Straarup his expertise. Frieda never knew for sure how it happened; she only knew that Straarup had, like Walter and so many other American officers, been beguiled by her father's esoteric knowledge and enthusiasm. By April, she was frequently setting a place for him at their dinner table.

Afterward, Pappie retreated to his study. He was making landscape drawings. Pappie feared the Americans would make the cemetery into a park, Frieda wrote to Gordon, adorned with North American plants and trees. He wanted the site beautified with local trees, bushes, and flowers, so that it fit into the rolling hills of Limburg. He was only an unofficial consultant, though. Much of the advice Straarup sought, as far as Frieda could tell, concerned caring for the plants already chosen.

On April 8, she visited the cemetery. She had come often over the winter, not just to Walter's grave but to those of other men and boys her family had known. The first time she honored a death anniversary at a grave, it was for a family friend. Her sister Thea had promised the boy's mother someone would visit, and Frieda had been happy to oblige. But she found the experience grim, she wrote Gordon. A thick fog, cold and wet, socked the world with gray. She felt her kindness was nothing more than a small, weak candle against the cold, indifferent fog.

On the anniversary of Walter's burial, the day was cloudy but warm. Frieda and Thea woke early and walked to the florist, who cut fresh flowers from his garden. Superintendent Straarup gave them a ride to Margraten in his jeep. It was spring, and the air felt lighter. As they approached Margraten, the sun broke through the clouds, and the fresh white blossoms in the orchards exploded into brilliance.

"How I wish you could have been with me," she wrote Gordon. "We would have stopped the jeep and continued walking, to enjoy the beauty of the countryside."

At the cemetery, the daffodils were yellow beneath the enormous American flag. A troop of Boy Scouts were planting flags on graves. Perhaps they knew these men. Perhaps they had adopted the graves of strangers. A friend, visiting a grave, had seen a plane slowly circle the cemetery, then drop low over a particular section of graves and dip a wing before flying away into the distance.

*Never forgotten, Walter,* Frieda whispered, laying the flowers on his grave. *Never alone.*

She expected her usual afternoon routine: housework, cooking, writing to Gordon before bed. She wrote him every day, and he wrote back just as quickly. Many times, she sent her next letter before receiving his reply, confident his kind words, his professions of love, would cross hers in the mail, like ships on the English Channel.

That evening, though, her Pappie needed her. He and Helen had been working for three days, creating enormous landscape drawings of the cemetery—graves, trees, bushes, and buildings, even the flagpole. Pappie wanted her to transcribe his notes in English onto the maps. Carefully.

Very carefully! He insisted she measure each letter, make sure the inscriptions were straight and precise. Frieda had no idea what the maps were for. But she noticed a few additions, a few of her father's ideas, and she realized they did not reflect what was but what her father hoped the cemetery would be. Had the Americans asked for such plans? Were they paying him? It was exactly like Pappie to embark on a project with no guarantee his plans would blossom, or even be looked at by an interested party.

But what did it matter, in the end? Frieda stayed up until 2:00 a.m. penciling inscriptions on the beautiful maps. Helen and Pappie stayed up past three. And neither sister could have been prouder when Pappie brought those maps out the following day and discussed them in detail with Superintendent Straarup over Frieda's simple, delicious Dutch country dinner.

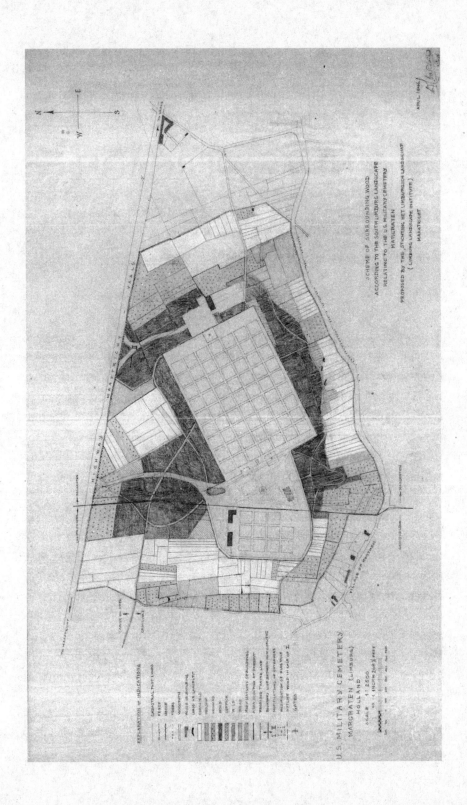

EXPLANATION OF INDICATIONS:

CENTRAL PLOT LINES
FENCE
HEDGE
TREES
GROWTH
MUD FOR BUILDING
LAND IN SUPPLY
CORNFIELD
WHEATFIELD
CLOVER
BEET
GRASS
ROAD
PATH
HIGH LEVELED GROWING
HIGH SUITING ATTENTION
TRAILING TRACING LINE
SURFACE NOT WITHIN NEW SURFACE
HIGH LEVEL OF GROWING
OUTFIELD OF PLANTING
OUTFIELD WOOD IN USE OF II
GUTTER

U.S. MILITARY CEMETERY
MARGRATEN (LIMBURG)
HOLLAND

SCALE 1:2500

SCHEME OF SURROUNDING WOOD
ACCORDING TO THE SOUTH LIMBURG LANDSCAPE
RELATING TO THE U.S. MILITARY CEMETERY
MARGRATEN
PROPOSED BY THE STICHTING HET LIMBURGS LANDSCHAP
(LIMBURG LANDSCAPE INSTITUTE)
MAASTRICHT

APRIL 1946

# CHAPTER 76

# A NEW APPROACH

— ★ —

*Emilie Michiels van Kessenich*
April 1946

It was hard for Emilie Michiels van Kessenich to say which came first, the publicity or the idea. It all seemed to arise organically, like the way Limburgers had rallied to the adoption program. For eight months or so, the effort had been a local affair, rarely known or remarked on outside of Limburg and North Brabant, the neighboring province. But at some point in the spring, as the world's attention turned to the first anniversary for victory in Europe, the interview requests began increasing. Writers and radio crews were beginning to travel to Margraten from the cities of the northern Netherlands, and from other European countries.

In Emilie, they discovered an ideal interview. She spoke Dutch, English, and French, very helpful in polyglot Europe. She was the wife of the mayor of Maastricht, adding a sheen of glamor she discounted, or didn't fully realize. Most importantly, she was a woman, a wife, and a mother eleven times over. The dedication of the Dutch to the soldiers buried in their soil was the story. It cut to the heart of the way most liberated people across Europe felt about those who had come across the ocean to their aid. But it was the idea of comforting grieving survivors like Mabel Feil, told by a wife and a mother who understood deep down their devastation and need, that struck the clearest emotional chord.

It was a virtuous cycle: the right spokesperson for the right cause at the right time. And Emilie enjoyed it. It was a nice respite, especially for a woman long devoted to childbearing and rearing. But she also believed, with her whole heart, in the service she was providing. A voice to speak for the voiceless. A mother to speak for the forgotten mothers. A wife to speak for the suffering wives. Much as when General Corlett asked her to provide recreation for his boys, it was a role she had never known she wanted, a role she dared not dream she might find once again.

She was good at it. She believed that, for this moment in her life at least, it was what God had called on her to do.

And the more she spoke, the more she felt the committee's efforts reaching across the miles to wounded hearts and anguished minds, the more it crystallized an idea that had been knocking around her head for weeks or maybe months: Someone from Limburg should go to America. They should talk one-on-one with General Larkin and convince him how much the adoption program meant to the loved ones of his soldiers. They should reach out to the lonely, grieving family members through American radios and newspapers. They should comfort as many family members as they could meet. They should try everything to get every address, so that every hurting soul could be reached.

The Netherlands War Graves Committee gave the plan their tacit approval. The American ambassador to the Netherlands, Emilie's unexpected friend, Stanley Hornbeck, declared it an excellent idea. A month-long goodwill trip, he called it. An opportunity to highlight the friendship between their "great big country and our little one," as Emilie had written in her letter to Truman, and show Americans their sacrifices were not only meaningful but appreciated. If Emilie could plan and finance a month-long overseas journey, through letters, to a place she had never been—had never considered going, until the Americans gave so much to her and the people of Limburg—she had their support.

She offered the opportunity to Father Heuschen. The adoption program was his. She was only its patroness, "propagating their splendid work," as she explained to President Truman. Father Heuschen declined. He was extremely busy finding and organizing adopters, because he had set the ambitious goal of having every Allied grave—every one—adopted by Memorial Day 1946. He was setting up a network of translators in villages across Limburg for those without "sufficient knowledge of English to consult with American families." And a tour of the United States was impractical for him for a simple, obvious reason: Father Heuschen's English was not strong enough for such an onerous undertaking.

Emilie herself was unsure. She had every reason not to go. She had eleven children, including little Mary Victoria, ten months old. She needed to help them navigate a period when food and necessities were still difficult to come by, when the hardships of the occupation were not so very far behind them. Life in Limburg was a grind of rations and clothing allowances, of uncertainty and confusion, of systems not yet back to where they once had been. There were thousands of refugees, many hungry. The priest in the Stokstraatkwartier had a list of suffering longer than both his arms, and she was his primary patroness too.

It wasn't until KLM Royal Dutch Airlines, which had been helping her travel to and from publicity events in the north, offered free round-trip tickets to New York City that she realized she might actually go. KLM's generosity was another sign, as Emilie saw it, not only of Dutch gratitude and giving, but of divine intervention. If Providence wanted her for this little part of the larger mission . . . if Mabel Feil kept writing for her advice and comfort . . . if all the letters from America the Dutch had been receiving represented even 10 percent of the need . . . she had no choice. She had to see it through.

# CHAPTER 77

# PLANNING

— ★ —

*Emilie Michiels van Kessenich;*
*Frieda van Schaïk; Margraten*

May 1946

It had rained for much of April, a blessing for Margraten. The newly planted bushes and trees were flourishing, the flowers bursting with blooms. Helen and Frieda, arriving at 7:30 a.m., helped the florist cut two large armfuls of flowers fresh from his garden. The dew was on the spiderwebs like diamonds. The air was fresh, with a pleasant chill, as it often was on the back side of a rain. At the last moment, Thea decided to join them, so they all piled into Superintendent Straarup's jeep for the six-mile trip to Margraten. At the cemetery, Straarup raised the large American flag. Beneath it was a golden cloth of daffodils, above a crisp blue sky.

A friend of Frieda's from Haarlem had sent her a list of seventeen Americans killed in Germany. Soldiers that people there had known and lost track of. She wanted Frieda to find out if they were buried at Margraten. The Van Schaïk girls searched a registry at the visitor's tent, under the guidance of the 603rd, but found only five. Whether the others were at Margraten or another cemetery, or still alive and back in America, they could not be sure. But they came back with their arms full of flowers to honor those five Americans. Unfortunately, the grass was newly planted, and several of the graves were in areas roped off to protect it.

So the Van Schaïk girls took their flowers and placed them on other graves. "I'm sure the families of the boys would have done the same and that they will appreciate it," Frieda wrote to Gordon.

A few weeks before Memorial Day, the U.S. military office in Frankfurt, Germany, issued an order: it was hereby forbidden to place flowers on the graves at Margraten. The stated reason was to protect the integrity and security of the Memorial Day celebration.

The Dutch took it as an affront. Which it was, since the Americans knew Dutch citizens came daily to place flowers on American graves. At best, the order was rude and unthankful. At worst, an attempt to rupture the Dutch bond with the cemetery. The order was so insulting, the florists in the North refused to fill American orders for ceremonial wreaths, saying there were plenty of flowers in Limburg.

Father Heuschen complained immediately to the cemetery authorities. In less than a year, the Civilian Committee Margraten had, against all odds, found a Dutch adopter for every grave. Every grave! All each adopter had to do was place one bouquet of flowers—from their gardens, from the wild, from anywhere flowers grew or were sold—on the grave of their adoptee. It wasn't difficult, now that that part of the organizing was done. Then the Memorial Day ceremony would be complete.

The president of the Gold Star Wives of America, Mrs. Marie Jordan, who was planning to attend the ceremony since her husband, Private Edward Jordan, was buried at Margraten, was livid. The Gold Star Wives bombarded General Eisenhower, and even President Truman, with emotional telegrams. The widows wanted flowers!

The order was rescinded, and the Civilian Committee Margraten's adopters went back to the "impossible" task of sourcing and placing a bundle of fresh-cut Limburg flowers on each of the nearly 18,000 graves.

On May 28, KLM flew Emilie to The Hague for a radio broadcast. Her speech was recorded to be played on air that evening. But due to a travel mix-up, she missed her flight home. KLM provided her a car ride back to Maastricht. On the way, they picked up a Dutch couple in their fifties who were hitchhiking, a common occurrence since cars were scarce, and gasoline even more so. The couple invited Emilie to relax in their home before heading on, which Emilie, ever eager to make a new friend, gratefully accepted.

When she saw it was 7:15 p.m., she casually mentioned, "If you turned on the radio now, you'd hear me talking about the care of Allied war graves."

The Dutch couple was stunned. They had lost both their sons in the war.

A minute later, they were all listening, rapt, in tears, to the radio broadcast, while the two young men, lost forever, stared down at them from photographs on the mantel.

"Only then," Emilie wrote in her Memory Book, "did I realize how much comfort we could bring through our devoted care."

That week, the last of May, Superintendent Straarup was dour over lunch. The grass had come in beautifully, but with so few lawn mowers, he didn't know how he could possibly cut it in time for the Memorial Day celebration. As usual, Frieda didn't say anything. She cleared and washed the dishes, then went out along the Bemelerweg, through Heer and the next village, Bemelen, to ask her neighbors to lend her their lawn mowers. Wim and Frieda spent the day gathering the lawn mowers and tagging each one with the owner's name. When Straarup arrived for dinner that evening at Dave's special invitation, since it was not normally a two-meal-a-day relationship, Frieda suggested he take a look inside their garage. Staarup was stunned to see fifteen lawn mowers, available for his use.

"Helen and Dad have gone out there this afternoon," Frieda wrote Gordon, giddy from her triumph, "and it really is going to look beautiful."

Again, the crowds began to arrive at dawn, by foot, by carriage, by horse-drawn cart. They came by bicycle, by motorbike, and occasionally by car, although the Rijksweg was so crowded between Maastricht and Vaals that the foot traffic was moving just as fast and the bicycles much faster. It was, after all, a two-lane road. By midmorning, the cemetery was full. By noon, the crowd was fifteen deep.

The burial ground, with its manicured lawn, was a sacred space. Grass covered the graves, softening the harsh mud mounds of the previous year. The paths were white gravel, the flowers blankets of color. A line of Norway spruces blocked the cemetery from the snarl on the Rijksweg, a series of cedars and hemlocks lined the approach. A low bandstand had been built for the speeches, with a row of giant wreaths propped on stands before it. The generals wore dress uniforms, the dignitaries, including Willem and Ambassador Hornbeck, top hats and tails.

Emilie's two eldest boys, Willem and Eduard, fifteen-year-old twins, stood beside the largest wreath. Willem wore his Dutch Boy Scout uniform, Eduard an American scout uniform given by a friend. The wreath was to be placed on a grave by Prince Bernhard, who was representing the Dutch royal family. The boys had been given the honor of guarding it. Emilie could see them standing proudly as she slipped into the grounds. How old they looked. How much they had grown.

She showed the business card of her friend Ambassador Hornbeck to the military guard. The ropes parted, and she entered the restricted area near the front. The crowds were thick. Her sons proud. The graves gorgeous: white crosses, green grass, flowers of all types and colors, thanks to Heuschen and his volunteers.

The crowd was larger than the year before. By some estimates, 40,000

Limburgers, the common men and women from the farms, the villages, the simple houses where the American boys had lived.

The Dutch had not forgotten. In fact, in the year since Germany's surrender, they had grown more thankful. Such a mass turnout on Memorial Day, the *New York Times* reported, "was believed to be without parallel in a foreign country."

A few months later, the Margraten U.S. Military Cemetery headquarters office released the official tally of the Dutch commitment to their friends, as organized and led by Father Heuschen: "Number of adoptions in American plots: all 17,738 graves; number of adoptions of Allied plots: all 1,026 graves; number of adoptions in German plots: none."

Frieda was in her bedroom when she overheard a conversation going on downstairs. It was June 1, two days after the Memorial Day celebration. She thought she knew the voice, but when she peeked over the railing, she didn't recognize the woman in the kitchen. She had a calm manner, despite her energetic enthusiasm, and no qualms about talking with her father as an equal. They were discussing a few enormous maps of the cemetery, which he had spread out on the table. Frieda couldn't tell if they were the maps she had worked on.

It didn't take much eavesdropping to catch on. The woman was the wife of the burgemeester of Maastricht. She was leaving soon on a goodwill trip to the United States. She had commissioned several large maps of the Margraten cemetery from Pappie, and she had come to retrieve them.

She was taking other things: lantern slides and color photographs. She was meeting so and so, and doing such and such; Frieda wasn't paying close attention, until she heard Mrs. Burgemeester mention the crosses. She was taking four, the woman told Pappie. Well, three crosses and a Star of David. They were wooden, with a slot to fill with soil. They were the idea of a Lieutenant Corman, a volunteer with the Civilian Committee Margraten. She planned to give the crosses to four special families. The soil in each would be from their loved one's grave.

"I know someone!" Frieda shouted. She was down the stairs before she considered what she was doing. "I know someone. A friend of our family. He was killed in Germany. I know his mother. I write to his sister. He is very special to me."

The woman was smiling. She was motherly, simple but elegant.

"May I write to them, if you have an extra cross? Or can you write to them? I want his mother to know that I . . . that we . . . that all of us are thinking of him."

Suddenly, the woman closed the distance between them. The hug was unexpected, especially in this kitchen, where emotions were so rarely shown.

"Of course, my dear," Emilie Michiels van Kessenich said. "I would be happy to. I happen to have another cross. What is the soldier's name? And who is his mother?"

CHAPTER 78

# APPROVALS

— ★ —

*Frieda van Schaïk*
June 1946

Frieda couldn't take her eyes off the horrible ginger caterpillar riding the lip of the little man reading through the letters Gordon had sent her, reading his private thoughts and feelings, his declarations of love. After all she had been through, she couldn't believe her happiness came down to this mustached little man. But it was the only way.

"Maybe we should get married," Frieda had written to Gordon. This was early in the spring, after Haarlem but before she'd gone through the process of trying to get a travel visa and discovered that, in practical terms, there were only two ways to do so: marriage or business. Marriage seemed easier. And it was something she had wanted since Christmas.

"Let's do it!" Gordon wrote back.

So Gordon went to his commanding officer and, after a series of interviews, the Royal Air Force gave him permission to marry an alien. That struck Frieda as appalling, that the British Armed Forces had the right to approve or deny Gordon's marriage since she wasn't British. But such were the times.

Now she needed Dutch approval. Thus, the bureaucrat ransacking Gordon's love letters, licking his grubby fingers as he turned the pages. Was he judging her for being that kind of girl? Or worse, did he not believe she was that kind of girl at all?

*Approved.* Finally, thank God, approved! Frieda felt the stamp hit the paper, as if imprinting on her heart. What a humiliation.

But now she was free: to visit England, to see Gordon, to live her life. Gordon's officer training program was holding a graduation parade on June 13. The visa approval had come just in time. Two days later, she was on a train, then a boat across the Channel. It was June 7, one day after the two-year anniversary of D-Day. So much had happened in those two years. Frieda stood at the railing, contemplating her bright new world. A world with Gordon in it.

She stayed five days with Gordon's family before she saw him, marching in his uniform with the other graduates, his eyes ahead, his head high. Her heart skipped. Every time she saw him, he was more than she remembered.

That was a Tuesday. On Friday they were married under a special license at the city hall. Afterward, they took a double-decker bus to the beach town of Weymouth. Gordon had seven days of leave. That was their honeymoon, but they didn't even get the seven days. Gordon had to report to Yorkshire, in Northern England, for his battle course. It was a two-day journey, so he had to leave after five.

Frieda wasn't ready to let him go. She insisted on going with him. "I'll find an inn when we get there," she said. "I can make my own way back."

Gordon laughed. Kissed her. "Why not?"

The journey, to her surprise, was by troop train. Frieda was the only woman on board. The other officers laughed at Gordon's temerity, but it was good-natured, all in fun. The trouble started when they arrived at their destination, because there was no inn. No town. Not a single building. The "station" was a platform in the middle of nowhere. It wasn't even on any maps.

The officers in charge were not amused when they saw a woman step off the train. A woman—a Dutch woman!—in an off-limits, military-only area. A newly minted officer who thought it acceptable to bring his wife— *his Dutch wife!*—to his training course. The officers were flabbergasted, flustered, and infuriated. There was talk of a court-martial.

A sergeant stepped in. He was living in a bungalow near the training grounds. If Frieda agreed to leave on the first train Monday morning, he would let her stay with him for the night.

She and Gordon couldn't thank him enough. "I'm recently married myself," he said. "I have an infant son. I know how you feel."

They spent the night together, husband and wife. They had breakfast together, in the quiet of an early, early Monday morning. Then Frieda kissed Gordon good-bye, he saluted with a smile, and she was driven from the camp and deposited on the railroad siding.

It was dark. A fog hung over the landscape. A bird called as the sun began to threaten the horizon, but for the most part she was alone. She stood on the wooden platform in her best dress, sewn for her by Moekie, holding her hard-sided carrying case. She was young, she was pretty, she was completely out of place in that desolate green landscape.

She smiled. She was Mrs. Gordon Gumn. She was Frieda van Schaïk Gumn. She was a young wife in love with her young husband, and the world—the whole world—was before her.

Eventually, she heard the distant rumble of the train. The steam of its engine appeared above the trees, thick against the thin, bright fog. There was no signal man. No flag. No whistle. As the train came into view, she saw the engineer thrust his head out the window, trying to figure out what was happening along the tracks.

Frieda waved.

He threw the brakes, a long shrill screeching. The train leaned back against its weight as it came sliding past. She had to walk a few steps to catch the last car, which wasn't a caboose, only another carrier. There was no conductor. No porter to take her carrying bag. Frieda waved to the engineer, who waved back in shocked surprise, and stepped onto the train.

# CHAPTER 79

# THE TRIP

— ★ —

*Emilie Michiels van Kessenich*
June–July 1946

O n the morning of June 8, 1946, Willem and Emilie left for Beek, the small town outside Maastricht where Willem had held his first position as mayor. The airport, built in spring 1945 as a U.S. military support airfield, was recently converted for civilian use. The first and only airport in South Limburg. *Another gift from the Americans*, Emilie thought.

It had been an emotional parting from the children. Mathilda, six now, had cried and thrown herself at her mother's legs, so of course Emilie-Hélène and Octavie had cried and thrown themselves at her ankles too. The older children were stoic, hugging Emilie as if she were going off to war, but little Mary Victoria was ill. Four nights before, they had celebrated her first birthday, with the poor baby sick in bed, feverish and dyspeptic. Emilie thought she might have to cancel the trip. But then the child's condition improved, and the doctors assured her the infant was out of danger. Now Emilie was leaving for five long weeks. It was a painful burden for any mother to bear.

But she trusted her intuition: that she was doing the right thing, for the right reasons. And Manka had managed during her hospital stay. And God, she knew, was always at their side.

"The flight is lovely," she wrote in her travel journal. "The sun is positioned so high in the sky that our own shadow flies along underneath us, a fantastic sight."

In Amsterdam, Emilie was greeted by reporters and members of the

Netherlands War Graves Committee. Airline officials presented her with a bouquet of flowers, which she cradled above her donated KLM travel bag as a photographer snapped publicity stills. A few family friends caught her in the tumult, offering encouragement. Ambassador Hornbeck handed her a card with a handwritten note: "Come back to Holland rested." Then she boarded a bulbous, shining silver Douglas DC-4 known as *The Flying Dutchman*. The land fell away, and Emilie Michiels van Kessenich was out beyond the Netherlands, out beyond the edges of her life.

She took notes in her diary: the curtained windows, the smoking passengers, turning down the "introductory martini" in favor of orange juice. By coincidence, she was seated next to Mrs. Marie Jordan, president of the Gold Star Wives. Mrs. Jordan, who had harangued the Army so effectively over its plan to prohibit flowers on graves, had missed the Memorial Day ceremony at Margraten because of travel delays. She had spent a week touring military cemeteries, but the tour wore her down. She was sick and exhausted. A flight across the Atlantic in 1946 took a full day, with fueling stops in Scotland and Newfoundland. Mrs. Jordan slept the entire way.

Emilie thought of her itinerary. She had only the first ten days planned out of a five-week journey. She thought of what she would say when she met the mothers, the wives, the grieving families. She was nervous. This was no vacation. It was a mission.

Emilie considered it a mission of mercy.

LaGuardia Field seemed a marvel, clean and modern, only seven years old, as Emilie stepped down the stairs of *The Flying Dutchman*. She crossed the tarmac and spotted a small crowd waiting for her in the viewing gallery on the roof of the Art Deco terminal: publicists, reporters, representatives of KLM Royal Dutch Airlines and the Netherlands Information Bureau. Two giants towered above the others, Eugene and Bill Feil, Warren's brothers. Nearby, barely five feet tall, a familiar face: Leo Senecal, her dear friend, who had come from Chicopee, Massachusetts, to greet her.

"Wanted to run to them; not allowed," she wrote in her journal. "Wanted to talk to them; also not allowed!" First, she had to pass through U.S. Customs.

The Customs inspector frowned at the sight of her luggage and carrying cases, so many they spilled over the edges of her porter's push trolley. He read her list of declared items: Dave van Schaïk's hand-drawn map, more than a meter long; oversized color photographs; lantern slides; printed materials.

"What are these maps and photos of?" the inspector asked.

"The U.S. Military Cemetery at Margraten, Holland," Emilie said.

"And what are they for?"

"The family members of fallen soldiers, so they can see where their boys are buried, and understand how much we Dutch care for them."

The inspector shook his head. "I'm sorry," he said. "You'll have to pay import duties."

"How much?"

He told her. It was too high. Her family, the whole Netherlands, was staggering under the cost of the war. She was not traveling with money to spare.

"Give me a moment," the inspector said. He walked off to have a conversation with the other inspectors, which eventually included several Black luggage porters in their starched white coats.

"We passed the hat," the inspector said, "and paid your import duties. Welcome to America, ma'am."

Emilie was stunned. Bonus Simplicitas, her guardian angel, was looking out for her. "I have reporters waiting for me. Can I tell them about this?"

"For God's sake, no," the inspector laughed. "We'll all get fired. Say you found the New York customs personnel agreeable and helpful. No one will believe that!"

That afternoon, she was the guest of honor at a reception of the Gold Star Wives, which her accidental travel companion, Mrs. Jordan, had thrown together at the last minute. A complete failure. Only four women attended. Gene Feil ferried her back to her hotel, exhausted, after only an hour or so.

The next few days were full of wonders: the offices of *Life* magazine, Rockefeller Center, Times Square, the docks of Lower Manhattan, crowded with boats. She went up the Hudson, accompanied by U.S. Army officials, to the U.S. Military Academy at West Point, where she was the honored guest for the night. She saw the Statue of Liberty, standing proudly in the harbor. It was dizzying to experience a city so full of life, to see people so well dressed and fed. Her country was shattered. The Dutch were scraping by on ration cards. New York City was energetic, laughing, almost untouched by war. The warm stone skyscrapers seemed unbreakable. The lights of Times Square brighter than a thousand German klieg lights scanning the sky for planes.

She met with reporters, including those from the *New York Times*. She was interviewed on the radio. Papa Senecal spent several days with her, their friendship as warm as it had been when they licked sardine oil from their plates. The Feil brothers accompanied her everywhere, like bodyguards. Paschal Fowlkes's twin sisters, Hit and Hyde, and Hyde's husband, Harvey Hallum, came from Washington, D.C., for an afternoon. Mrs. Berkhofer and Mrs. O'Neill, mothers of fallen boys whom she had never corresponded with, showed her around the city and let her into their lives. There was sadness, of course; their sons had died. But also friendship. A thankfulness that someone, anyone, had seen their need.

On Thursday, June 13, she boarded a train to Washington, D.C., a guest of the Dutch ambassador. The next day, she met with Quartermaster General Larkin. He was polite, but Emilie feared their meeting was a courtesy. That he didn't see a need for what she and the Civilian Committee Margraten were trying to do. The U.S. Army took care of its own, and it took care of them damn well. And for General Larkin, that was the end of the matter.

At 3:00 p.m., a large press conference, attended by thirteen media outlets.

At 5:00 p.m., a reception with members of Congress. It went so well that a young congressman from Texas invited her to Capitol Hill the next day. He wanted his colleagues to hear about the remarkable Dutch and their adoption program. The luncheon was followed by a tour of Washington and the National Mall, culminating at Arlington National Cemetery, with its rows of gleaming headstones. So many lost, not only in Margraten, but also here. Emilie thought of Lib Fowlkes, whose letter in summer 1945 was a clear sign of divine Providence. Lib lived three hours away in Richmond, Virginia, but with two young children to care for, or perhaps because of where she was in her cycle of grief, she and Emilie had not been in frequent touch. Instead, Emilie spent the night with Pat's sister, Hyde, and her husband, Harvey.

On Sunday, Emilie attended Mass. She was a week into her trip, and she already felt exhausted—and with very little to show for it. Her meeting with General Larkin had not succeeded in prying loose the precious next-of-kin information. She had planned to fly to Arkansas to meet with General Simpson, but he had to cancel. He was recovering from emergency surgery. So she had four weeks ahead of her, with no firm plans.

Marie Jordan wanted her to tour California with the Gold Star Wives, but Emilie suspected their primary interest was fund-raising. Each soldier designated a beneficiary before heading overseas, and many had chosen their mothers, not their wives. Helping them was a worthy cause, but she did not want money to be a motivation.

Another option was Texas. The young congressman who invited her to the Capitol was Lyndon B. Johnson. He insisted there were thousands in his home state who would love to—no, needed to—meet her and hear her story. Unbeknown to her, he had been making arrangements since the evening they met. His arguments were compelling; he wasn't known as the Great Persuader for nothing. But Emilie was unsure. She didn't know anything about Texas.

So she asked for intercession at Mass, and prayed for grace. She asked God to guide her once again.

After a visit to Mount Vernon, the home of George Washington, she took the evening train back to New York. A large stack of letters and telegrams from grieving family members awaited her, the result of the publicity surrounding her first week in America. One telegram was from Mrs. Charlotte Cymbalski, who had traveled twenty-one hours by bus from Detroit, Michigan, to meet with her. Emilie invited Mrs. Cymbalski to the Netherlands Information Bureau, where they looked at her photographs together. Until that moment, Mrs. Cymbalski had no idea what the Margraten U.S. Military Cemetery looked like: the rolling hills, the lines of trees, the white wooden crosses, so temporary after the stone memorials of Arlington and yet, somehow, in their imperfection, just as grand. Like most Americans, Mrs. Cymbalski had only vague impressions of the Netherlands, much less the province of Limburg. The silence when Emilie unrolled Dave van Schaïk's map was heavy and deep. In such a moment, what can any mother, any wife, say to another? Finally, Mrs. Cymbalski stretched a hand to the paper, touching the section where her son was buried.

What would General Larkin say, Emilie wondered, if he could see them now? Two women, not soldiers. Two mothers, crying over a map of his cemetery.

That evening, she was on an ABC radio program which went out live, coast-to-coast, to three million listeners.

The next day, more grieving families came to see her, widows and mothers, husbands and wives. So many the hotel manager sniffed at her to cease inviting in the rabble—the overlooked, the grieving, the working class who had traveled to her in need of kindness—they were a "decent" hotel.

"You would do well to listen to the radio," Emilie snapped back, in a rare moment of pique. She was on it, she told him, talking about her mission of mercy, almost every day.

That evening, at the Feil home in Plainfield, New Jersey, she presented Bill Feil and his wife with a miniature wooden cross containing soil from his brother Warren's grave. They gave her a pair of white leather shoes for Mary Victoria. It was the quietest, most private, most heartfelt moment of her trip so far.

She boarded a plane for Texas on June 20. The extent of her plans, as arranged by Lyndon Johnson, were passed on to her by the Netherlands Information Bureau, but only after she boarded her plane: "Mrs. Emily van

Kessenich, go to Dallas, get out at 4 a.m., go to the Adolphus Hotel and wait for Mr. Connolly."

Those names meant nothing to her, but she had faith.

When she arrived at Love Field in Dallas, to her surprise, two families were there to meet her. Five members of the Connolly family had driven overnight from their home in Lockhart, Texas. The Nances, whose son Otto lay buried at Margraten, lived nearby, in East Dallas. By agreement, Emilie went to the Nance home first to share her photographs and maps. It was a beautiful, bittersweet conversation. Emilie was not the official adopter of the Nances' son, but like many others buried at Margraten, she corresponded with his family and visited his grave.

A few hours later, she met the Connollys at the Baker Hotel in downtown Dallas, where they had a cup of coffee. Seeing her weariness, the Connollys suggested a second cup, and maybe some rest.

"No, thank you," Emilie said. It was an eight-hour drive to Lockhart, Texas. "Let's just go."

In Lockhart, she was greeted by a local reporter and a crowd of family members who had lost their boys. She gave a presentation, using Dave's map and her lantern slides for the first time, and answered questions deep into the night. She didn't get back to the Connolly home until after 1:00 a.m. That's when she learned that, fifteen minutes after they left Dallas, the Baker Hotel had exploded. A gas leak. Ten dead, thirty-eight wounded.

If she had accepted that second cup of coffee . . . if she had decided on a nap . . .

*Thank you, Bonus Simplicitas*, she prayed. The generous U.S. Customs inspectors and porters, Mrs. Cymbalski, Lyndon Johnson's suggestion to go to Texas—God had blessed her trip already, she was sure of it. Bonus Simplicitas was watching over her.

The next day, the Connollys drove her to an American Legion convention in Mineral Wells, Texas, where people had traveled across the state to hear her speak. Not all had a loved one at Margraten. More than 400,000 American men and women had died in the war; Margraten only held 18,000. This was, Emilie realized, about more than grave adoptions. It was communal grieving. An opportunity for a group of Americans whose losses kept them from the joy and optimism of that famous Times Square kiss to feel that they were not alone, not forgotten, that someone—a Dutch woman, from a region they had never heard of, representing people they did not know—cared about them, and was acting on their behalf.

The next day, Emilie spoke again to an overflowing crowd, telling them about her little corner of the Netherlands, the salvation their boys had brought to its struggling citizens, and the grave adoption program that was their small way of expressing a thank-you beyond expression. Once again, at the end, she was astonished to find a long line of friends and family members, mostly women, waiting to speak with her. General Larkin had refused to give the Civilian Committee Margraten their names, but these mothers, and it was mostly mothers, wanted Emilie Michiels van Kessenich to know their names. They needed to share their stories. They craved connection.

They had no means of visiting Margraten. The trip was long, and it was expensive. For some families, the trip to Mineral Wells, Texas, was the farthest they had ever traveled. So they reached out their fingers to Dave van Schaïk's map and, with tears in their eyes, came as close as they ever would to touching their son's grave. They hugged a Dutch woman, a complete stranger, a sudden friend, and came as close as they ever would to being with their child.

"Your son will never be alone," Emilie told them. "He will never be forgotten. Leave him with us, and we will watch over him, forever, as if he was our own."

"Everyone is equally lovely and pleasant," she noted in her diary that night, "as if I have known these people for years."

Because, in a way, she had. As a mother of eleven children, as a woman who had lived through war, she knew about hardship and deprivation. She knew about loss, between the mother she never knew and the miscarriages she had suffered. Yes, she knew these women, and cared about them, heart to heart.

In the days that followed, she traveled from Mineral Springs to Fort Worth, Birmingham, and Tuscaloosa, where she finally met Mabel Feil. "She is sweet and pretty," Emilie wrote in her journal. Emilie had developed a motherly relationship with the twenty-seven-year-old through months of openhearted, often emotional correspondence. Mabel was planning to remarry, which angered Warren's family. That's why Emilie gave the miniature cross to Warren's brother Bill, instead of Mabel. But she had encouraged Mabel, in a series of letters, to follow her heart.

*Don't be afraid to move on,* she told the grieving young woman. *You are young. You have a long life ahead of you. Warren would want you to live it.*

It was her message to all the grieving men and women she met in her travels: *Let go of your guilt at the thought of moving on with your life. Let go of your fear. Leave your child, your husband, your father, with us. You are not abandoning him in a foreign land. You are placing him in the care of those who love him.*

Mabel's spitfire mother, Ma Levy, told Emilie she hadn't had a moment's rest in months. She had written hundreds of letters to congressmen and journalists. She had been so overwhelmed with letters and phone calls from distraught mothers, she'd been leaving the food on the table uneaten, the water in the bathtub unused. But she smiled when she said it, clearly pleased.

*She has done more to promote our program and ease suffering than an entire office staff,* Emilie noted. And Emilie, of all people, would have known.

The mayor of Demopolis, Alabama, had arranged a police car to drive them to the town. Emilie was so tired, she could do little more than lean her head against the window and marvel at the similarity between Limburg and Alabama: the rolling hills, the green fields. At Ma Levy's house, a crowd was waiting, and Emilie rallied. If these grieving women were willing to travel hundreds of miles to meet her, she would give them everything she had, every last ounce of her energy.

Days before, in Birmingham, Emilie had awoken to her hostess dragging a wet rag across her face. "It's true," the woman muttered, shaking her head. She could not believe Emilie wasn't wearing make-up. But Emilie had never worn make-up, and even if she had, luxuries like make-up weren't available in Limburg in 1946.

In Demopolis, she found a box of gum on her pillow. The previous evening, she had told the story of the liberation of Maastricht, when her ten children passed around one piece of gum, and the youngest girls cried bitter tears when Louis swallowed it. The twins were so angry, they shook him upside down.

The box of gum on her pillow was accompanied by a note: "FOR THE CHILDREN. Hope this will go around and you won't have to turn the baby upside down. A Friend."

JUNE 9 - JULY 10, 1946

For the thousandth time, Emilie thought of her children, wished for them to be with her. For Manka to be at her side. Like any mother, she was homesick. But she was determined. The hugs from mothers and young wives assured her she was doing good.

By the grace of General Simpson's emergency ulcer surgery and LBJ's maneuvering, she had escaped the frustrating bureaucracy. She had left the power centers for the countryside, for the ordinary people of this beautiful land, and she had felt—in her bones, in her heart, in the hands she held as family members cried—what she had sensed from thousands of miles away: That America's postwar joy was cut through with sadness. That the pain of 400,000 families was more than a Gold Star in a window; it was a tightness in a mother's chest each time she woke, and an empty hole whenever she lay down to rest. That healing was not a logistics problem, as the Army seemed to think, but a feeling that needed kindness for catharsis, and reassurance for peace. Families who knew only a date and location needed more. They needed every comfort they could get. LaGuardia's Black porters, underpaid and suffering their own disappointments, understood this so well that they had given their hard-earned money to a stranger, because of her promise to address that pain.

She traveled from Demopolis to Atlanta, where she gave a miniature cross to the grandfather and aunt of a B-17 pilot from the Bloody Hundredth, the 100th Bomb Group, First Lieutenant Frank W. Harte, another young man whose grave Emilie's family had adopted. The next night, a woman from Tucker, Georgia, stood up from the middle of an overflow crowd at the Optimist Club. By now, Emilie was used to mothers telling her, "I didn't believe in you before. I wanted to bring my child home. But now I'm at peace, and I'm leaving my boy at peace with you."

The mother from Tucker wept as she said the opposite: That her son's death had destroyed her family. That her husband had suffered a stroke when he heard the news, and she feared he would soon die. She appreciated the Dutch, and what they were doing for the boys, but she already had a ticket on a ship to the Netherlands, and she was determined to find her son, bring him home, and bury him in the Georgia clay.

There was not a dry eye in the room.

From there, it was back to New York City for a well-attended meeting with the Gold Star Mothers, so different from her presentation to the Gold Star Wives three weeks before. Then to the American Legion in Bridgeport, Connecticut. A girls' school in Waterbury, Connecticut. Chicopee, Massachusetts, where she met Leo Senecal's mother, the original Mary Victoria. A firehouse in Belchertown, Massachusetts, where several firefighters had been lost in the war, and where a shift change at a nearby factory brought an unexpected crowd.

Extraordinary events, hard to believe outside the subtle hand of Bonus Simplicitas, came at her with increasing frequency. A young boy handed her his only bag of marbles, saying, "For a little boy in Holland." A man told her of his sister's son buried at Margraten, only for Emilie to realize she had been searching for that very sister. Someone in the Netherlands had found a recording the young man made shortly before his death, and Emilie desperately wanted his mother to hear it.

"Ma'am, do you realize that there are 140 million Americans," the man said in awe, "and you spotted just the one you were looking for?"

A worker hot off his shift at a textile mill wanted to know if she knew the Dutch woman who had sent him a letter about his son, but he couldn't pronounce her last name. "No matter," he said, reaching into his breast pocket, "I always carry the letter she wrote me."

"I recognized my own signature," Emilie wrote in her diary.

Everywhere she went, she did publicity. Local newspapers. Radio stations. A second interview with *Life*. She lost her voice. She suffered from exhaustion. She nearly collapsed. When she read a speech she had written for *We The People*, a live Sunday night radio program with 35 million listeners, she had a metal shaving embedded in her eye that should have sent her to the emergency room. But she had no time for doctors, and she had two good friends to comfort her through the pain: Mabel Feil, who had traveled to New York to help her, and Leo Senecal. On the twenty-sixth day of her trip, she learned that little Mary Victoria's dangerous fever had finally broken.

She never received the register from General Larkin and the U.S. Army, but she met more than a thousand grieving relatives and recorded their names and contact information for the adoption committee. Her message reached millions through *Life*, *We The People*, and a hundred local radio programs and publications. For twenty straight days, starting with her evening with Bill Feil and his wife, she slept in the homes of strangers, not hotels, comforting them, absorbing their grief. She was bone-tired. She was emotionally drained. But her journey, despite a slow start in New York City and frustration in Washington, D.C., was a triumph. Emilie Michiels van Kessenich had done everything a human being could do, and more, to comfort the grieving families of America and promote the Civilian Committee Margraten's adoption program. She had earned her plane trip home.

A small crowd gathered on the tarmac at LaGuardia Field in the July heat to see her off, just as a crowd had gathered for her arrival five weeks before. This gathering, though, was more intimate. Both of Warren's brothers brought their wives and two children, who gathered around Emilie at the foot of the stairs to her plane. Nearby was an older woman, elegantly dressed in a dark suit and hat. She was Ida Huchthausen, Walter's mother. With her was Martha, Walter's sister. Emilie had met with them after a presentation in Stratford, Connecticut. She presented Mrs. Huchthausen with the miniature cross and a color photograph of Walter's grave. It was a gift from Engineer van Schaïk, Emilie said, the man who had drawn the map of Margraten's cemetery and was taking care of her son's grave. When Martha wrote a letter of thanks, however, it was not to Engineer van Schaïk, but to Frieda.

The two had been writing since Frieda sent the last photographs of Walter taken before he was killed. Martha knew who was really looking after his grave.

The meeting, the thoughtfulness of the gesture, clearly made an impression. They had driven from Connecticut, much as the Feils had driven from New Jersey, to see Emilie off, and thank her for her kindness and care.

A photograph was taken. Not for the newspapers, but for Emilie's Memory Book. It was, in many ways, a perfect snapshot of her trip: no dignitaries or government officials, no reporters or crowds of grieving strangers, just friends. Connected through tragedy, living half a world apart, but bound by respect and love.

Emilie hugged them, thanked them, then boarded her plane. There had been one last complication at the airport. She was taking home hundreds of telegrams and letters, along with gifts for her children, a box of chewing gum, and a bag of marbles. Her belongings exceeded the baggage allowance. This time, it was KLM that kindly waived the fee.

The flight home was uneventful.

# CHAPTER 80

# A SPECIAL GOOD-BYE

— ★ —

*Frieda van Schaïk*
July 1946

On July 20, 1946, Gordon and Frieda Gumn, newly married for the second time, stepped out of Sint Jans Church on the Vrijthof Square in the center of Maastricht. The sun was shining. Gordon was smiling, handsome in his dress uniform, his Bible clutched in his hand. Frieda wore a dark suit and a large-brim hat with a ribbon for a sash. She had a blossom in her lapel, a bundle of snow-white flowers in her arms. Rebirth and hope, beauty and joy. Flowers were everywhere that summer. They might as well have been the symbol of Limburg.

"You look lovely," Moekie whispered, straightening Frieda's lapel. Her mother was greatly diminished by her strokes, but she had "pulled up her socks" and helped her daughter plan this perfect day. Now, as she stepped away, Frieda saw that she was crying. Even during the occupation, she had only once seen her mother cry, when Moekie sent her away to Arnhem to escape the Nazis.

"We did it," Frieda said, and her mother wiped away her tears, as if only then realizing they were there.

"Yes, we did," Moekie said. "We have all made it through."

The party, as always when Pappie was holding court, went late, but with Gordon's blessing, Frieda left before the sun went down. She took the hired wedding car, telling the driver to take her to Margraten. She walked the rows, now grown with beautiful grass, where once there had been only mud.

At that most familiar of graves, she stopped. She laid her bridal bouquet on the grass. She put her hand on the cross. "I'm happy," she told Walter. "Happier than I ever thought I could be."

# CHAPTER 81

# CLOSURE

— ★ —

September 1946

The woman, lean but determined, stepped off the ocean liner *Queen Mary II*. It was September 1946. In spring 1944, the U.S. Army Air Forces had informed her that her only son was missing. Eighteen months later, in November 1945, they declared him dead. Seven months after that, in June 1946, the Army wrote to say they had not been able to locate his grave. About a week later, Helen Moore stood up at the end of a presentation by a Dutch woman in Atlanta and told the crowd that she appreciated the dedication of the Dutch to the boys at Margraten, but she was going to the Netherlands, she was finding her son, and she was bringing him home to Georgia.

Bill Moore was not her biological child. Helen and her husband, John, had fostered him, starting when he was a few months old. He was a bright boy, finishing high school early and enrolling at the University of Georgia at seventeen. But then, somehow, the young man discovered he had been living under a lie, that he had not been born Bill Moore and his biological parents were not the couple who had raised him. His life began to spin and tear apart. The next year, in spring 1939, he dropped out of college. He tried to enlist in the Army, but was rejected because of his poor eyesight. He moved out of his childhood home, listing himself as a boarder in the home of John and Helen's next-door neighbors. The following month, he was arrested on a petty charge.

He was inducted into the U.S. Army Air Forces seven months later, on December 26, 1941, three weeks after Pearl Harbor. The nation needed men, thousands and thousands of men, so the standard on physicals had been lowered. Perhaps unsurprisingly, given his early promise, Bill Moore turned his life around as an officer in the military. He was a natural leader, a fast learner, calm under pressure. He was one of the talented few chosen to be a pilot, to lead a ten-man crew into battle and make life-or-death decisions for them all. He was loved by his men. In the two years since their bomber crashed, Helen and John Moore had received several letters from his surviving crew, telling them about Bill's courage and dedication, his kindness and calm.

Perhaps that's why John took Bill's death so hard, suffering a stroke when he received the Western Union telegram, followed by a depression so severe he couldn't get out of bed. Or perhaps it was because the young man he loved as a son had stopped loving him as a father. On his induction form, under "Nearest relative," Bill Moore listed "none." He was twenty when he filled out that form. Twenty-three when he died. He had been hurt by a lie, or more accurately, a hidden truth. He was a good kid, and John a good man; they would have gotten past it. Probably. Almost surely. Now, father and son would never have that chance to reconcile.

So Helen's trip was not just for Bill, whom she loved as a son. It was for John too. It was her attempt to bring their fragmented family back together, and in doing so, save her husband's life.

She knew quite a bit about Bill's last months from the letters his crew sent her and from Chaplain McGee, who was held captive with him. The crash near the Dutch city of Apeldoorn. The months of hiding. She knew Bill had been captured and that the chaplain called her son a hero for the way he endured torture without giving away the Dutch who sheltered him. It was more than she had ever heard from the War Department, who had only sent three boilerplate telegrams in the two years and five months since Bill's plane went down.

It didn't take her long to discover the rest of the story. Soon after arriving in Apeldoorn, she connected with local resistance fighters. She met Jaap, Aart, Mother, and the other brave local citizens who had known Bill Moore and risked their lives for him. Several local resistance fighters had survived imprisonment. The Dutch authorities, they told her, had managed to take a photograph of Bill's body, as proof of the crime. The photo was gruesome, but Helen steeled herself. She needed to know. They told her about the mass execution, and how Bill Moore's last words, shouted into that dark cold morning, had been, "You can't do this to me. I'm an American officer!"

They took her to his grave, a short distance from Apeldoorn. The Resistance had buried him with a simple headstone.

Helen planned a memorial service. She wanted to honor her son before returning home. The day before the service, she published a notice in the local newspaper, inviting the public to attend. The morning broke cold and rainy, not a ray of sun in the sky, and as she walked to the grave, Helen Moore assumed a handful of people, at best, would be there, perhaps only three or four.

She found 1,200 Dutch mourners gathered in the drizzling rain at her son's side. So many, she marveled, from so far away, caring so much. As the minister closed the service, Helen Moore fell to her knees, there in the rain and the mud. She reached into her purse for a jar of red Georgia clay. She had been planning to put it in the coffin for Bill Moore's journey home. Now, she emptied the jar on his grave in Ugchelen. She spread the clay gently, passing her hand back and forth, as she had rubbed Bill's back so many nights when he lay afraid or feverish as a child.

She was leaving him, she had decided, here among the Dutch. Here among the people who appreciated his sacrifice, and honored him, and cared for him as well as any mother could.

# EPILOGUE

— ★ —

*Eighty Years*

*Time will not dim the glory of their deeds.*
General John J. Pershing
General of the Armies

The grounds I have walked on my thirteen trips to Margraten are quite different from the cemetery where Emilie, Frieda, and thousands of Dutch citizens paid their respects in the aftermath of World War II. It is an established cemetery now, settled comfortably into the rolling hills of Limburg, where before it was a fresh wound in farmland filled with Americans, not crops. Then, it was busy, bursting with painful memories. Today, it is welcoming, comforting, and quiet. Time has worn away the harsh edge of the pain, leaving respect and admiration in its place.

At the same time, it is chiseled and sharp, as precise as the snap of a military salute. The formal rows, the polished crosses and Stars of David, the thick green grass: Everything is crisp. Everything is straight. Everything is immaculately maintained. *Permanent* is a word that comes to mind. *Timeless. Unchanging.* The horror of war refined to its essence: 10,000 troops sacrificed, with every loss eternal, every person equal. Come back in fifty years, or 100, or next week, and these sixty-five-and-a-half acres of heroes will still be there, just as they are today. And yet, when I kneel at the grave of Walter Huchthausen, or Paschal Fowlkes, or Robert Cole, the stories of their lives come rushing back to me, the beautiful complexity that made them not just troops who died young, but brothers, fathers, husbands, sons, and friends.

So many layers, so many thoughts and emotions, in such a simple plot of land.

This is an effect not only of time but of design. In April 1947, the U.S. secretary of war announced that ten of the thirty-six World War II U.S. military cemeteries in the European Theater—not the two cemeteries originally assumed—would be designated "permanent." The rest would be closed, their fallen disinterred and consolidated in the cemeteries that remained. The cemetery overlooking Omaha Beach in Normandy made the list. So did Henri-Chapelle in Belgium. So did Margraten. It would become the only American military cemetery in the Netherlands.

Following the Memorial Day ceremony in 1948, the Army closed the Margraten burial grounds to the public and began construction of the permanent cemetery. This mass of graves, wrested from the elements in the midst of war by Shomon, Wiggins, and so many hundreds of others, had become a dignified burial ground. Now, the Army would make it a picture-perfect memorial.

Local Dutch laborers opened each grave using shovels. As soon as they struck bone or cloth, an American GRS soldier was called to scrape away the dirt by hand and carry the remains to the onsite morgue for confirmation of identification. Technicians removed mattress covers and uniforms, as long as this could be done without damaging the body, and a Dutch teenager burned the material in an incinerator. The technicians then sprayed the remains with deodorant and a hardening compound to dehydrate any remaining tissue. They tightly wrapped the remains in a sheet, then a blanket, and placed them inside a metal casket. One dog tag was pinned to the blanket, over the head of the soldier; the other was wired to the head end of the casket. Soldiers placed the casket inside a wooden shipping case and secured it to eliminate any chance of movement.

The fallen from other Allied nations, including the United Kingdom, the Soviet Union, Poland, and Canada, were taken to their respective national cemeteries. The remains of enemy soldiers were transported to the war cemetery near the Dutch village of Ysselsteyn, where 31,000 Wehrmacht soldiers and civilians from World War II (and a few from World War I) are buried. It is a somber and austere experience seeing a field of more than 30,000 gray granite crosses filling a nearly identical number of acres as the 8,200 Americans buried at Margraten.

At the end of 1947, the Department of Defense had begun offering next of kin the option to bring their loved ones home for reburial at the government's expense. About 39 percent of the more than 280,000 grieving families elected to leave their loved ones buried alongside their brothers in arms overseas. At Margraten, that number was higher than the average—46 percent—perhaps influenced by the adoption program and Emilie's appeals to American families to entrust their boys to the Dutch. For those families who elected to repatriate their loved ones' remains, the caskets were secured inside shipping cases, loaded onto barges, and floated to ports on the North Sea. They were taken by ship to America and interred with honors at national cemeteries, local cemeteries, and family plots across the United States.

The caskets of those remaining at Margraten were placed along the edge of the cemetery grounds, inside their protective wooden boxes. This process of disinterring, analyzing, boxing, and sorting took the entire spring and into the summer. By August, the number of Americans awaiting reburial had grown into the thousands, the wooden boxes protecting the caskets that contained their bodies stacked in enormous, orderly piles.

During this time, the cemetery was redesigned by Coolidge, Shepley, Bulfinch, and Abbott, an architecture firm in Boston that envisioned a gently sloping burial ground with curving rows of headstones spreading out from a central walkway. As the burial elections were finalized, the design coalesced around a layout of 8,200 gravesites: the approximate number of men and women whose loved ones had chosen to leave them at Margraten.

In September 1948, the grading operations began. It took two months to turn the hilly countryside into a gentle, almost imperceptible slope from the entrance to the top. Then the bulldozers and dragline excavators removed the top six feet of soil. Concrete railings were poured in concentric arches. Every six-and-a-half feet, a bracket was attached to the railings. There was no ceremony. No mourners or next of kin. A crane lifted each wooden box and centered it—not just the coffin, but the shipping case as well—in front of each bracket. Then the bulldozers replaced the dirt. A white marble headstone from Italy, carved with the name, rank, unit, state from where the person had entered the service, and date of death was screwed into each bracket. This system guaranteed the crosses and Stars of David would never move or tilt, and never fall out of line.

Forty pairs of brothers were buried side by side, and a few men were buried beside those with whom they served. For example, six of Robert Cole's men were buried near him on a single row, some side by side. But for the most part, the order of reburial at Margraten was random. There was no special treatment. Democracy in its purest form prevailed. Generals lay next to privates. Infantry next to airmen. Black soldiers next to white. Men next to women. The white Italian marble crosses and Stars of David are all exactly the same. Almost. There are six distinct graves scattered throughout the cemetery. These are six Medal of Honor recipients, awarded America's highest decoration for valor. Their headstones are exactly like the others, except for an inverted star, the words "Medal of Honor," and all the carvings, including the name, rank, and unit information, in gold leaf.

This process of planning, disinterring, sorting, preserving, reburying, and landscaping took twelve years. Some parents and loved ones were allowed to visit by special approval, but the newly named Netherlands American Cemetery did not reopen to the public until July 7, 1960. The Queen of the Netherlands was in attendance. U.S. secretary of the Army, Wilber M. Brucker, delivered remarks both poignant and prophetic: "Those who seek some easy escape from the burden of defense jeopardize everything for which so many brave men have laid down their lives. This is a form of appeasement that could destroy us."

Despite the twelve-year gap, the more than 8,200 who were buried remained adopted. The Dutch had waited through the rain and the snow, through more than a decade of growth and rebirth, eager for the day they could walk the grounds and greet their boys again. Certain individuals and groups in Europe went to great lengths to honor American soldiers who returned freedom to their respective countries. Of note was a remarkable French woman, also the wife of a mayor, Madame Simone Renaud, who dedicated her life to honoring hundreds of American soldiers who died liberating her hometown of Sainte-Mère-Église and her country in general. But no other effort equals that of the Dutch in Limburg in creating and sustaining the adoption program from a period during the war to present day without interruption.

The reason for this is obvious: those original adopters, almost 18,000 of them, now down to 10,000 (including the names on the Walls of the Missing, which received adopters beginning in 2008), loved their liberators. They cared for their soldier not as an obligation, not even as a thank-you, but as an honor. Many of them, including the Van Kliest family, had a photograph of their soldier in their living room, a treasured possession given by a grieving mother or wife, or by the soldier himself, because the Dutch in Limburg knew the Americans. They shared their homes and rations and hopes with American troops for five long months—if not with the particular young dead soldier they adopted, then with others like him. That's what made the difference.

And when those adopters grew too old, the next generation, steeped in their parents' gratitude, took over and hung those same photographs on their living room walls. Families are now in their third generation, or fourth, and they still display those photographs. Eighty years later, they write to the children, grandchildren, and extended family members of the fallen. One woman, ninety-four years old and childless, recently traveled one last time to Margraten to turn in her adoption papers. She was heartbroken, but she could no longer regularly journey the two hours from her home in The Hague to lay flowers and say a prayer on the grave she had cared for most of her life.

"Please pass this to the next family," she asked. It was a file of correspondence two inches thick going back seventy years. There are hundreds of adopters with files of correspondence two inches thick.

That's why, in 2017, the Foundation for Adopting Graves American

Cemetery Margraten and its grave adoption program was designated under UNESCO guidelines as a part of the Dutch National Inventory of Immaterial Cultural Inheritance, to be safeguarded in the same way as historic buildings and cultural sites. It is those personal connections that make the grave adoption program unique, perhaps never to be replicated. Because not once over the decades have the Dutch adopters lost their gratitude. They have never forgotten that the Netherlands was liberated by an army, but that army was made up of young men and women, scared but determined, exhausted and far from home.

Sadly, Father Heuschen did not remain with the Civilian Committee Margraten as it became a national treasure and institution. Emilie's publicity efforts on behalf of the program never sat comfortably with him and some citizens of Margraten. He resented that journalists preferred to interview a woman and mother, and that many articles mentioned (superfluously, the villagers of Margraten believed) that she had led her own push to create a grave adoption program before joining with the committee. Father Heuschen was furious when Emilie's relationship with Ambassador Hornbeck granted her access to an exclusive area at the Memorial Day 1946 ceremony. The final straw occurred during her trip to the United States, when the popular Dutch women's magazine *Libelle* published an article that, in its second half, focused on Emilie's family life, seeming to give her much of the credit for the Margraten adoption program while relegating the committee's work to the handling of technical details.

If Father Heuschen had seen some of the news reports from her time in America, where Emilie frequently corrected interviewers to give the priest credit—"It's all due to the initiative [of] a young Dutch priest, Father Heuschen," she told *Catholic Advance,* for instance—he might have thought differently. But he'd made up his mind. Like many in Margraten, he believed Emilie was trying to steal *their* adoption program.

So Father Heuschen traveled to the American Graves Registration Command headquarters at Liège to discourage the Americans from working with Emilie, falsely stating that she planned to turn grave adoptions into a "racket . . . to obtain money and parcels from the next of kin." Already, he said, Emilie had received clothes for her children, large volumes of "parcels" from America, and "thirteen gold fountain pens."

The clothes turned out to be for the needy in Maastricht; the "parcels" were food sent by the people of Waterbury, Connecticut, where Emilie had held a well-attended gathering, to help feed ill and malnourished children. Mention of pens was simply petty.

Emilie had, in fact, received one material thing of value in America. On her flight from Atlanta to New York, she happened to sit next to an agent for the hearing aid company Sonotone. Emilie's twelve-year-old son, George, needed just such a hearing aid, but the family was unable to obtain one in the war-torn Netherlands. When she returned home, Emilie learned the Sonotone company was providing George with a hearing aid. It wasn't opportunism; she paid for it. But to her, it was a miracle, a gift from Bonus Simplicitas.

In late August, U.S. Senator L.L. Biggle and a small crowd of emissaries sent by President Truman met with Father Heuschen to personally thank him for his service to America's fallen heroes. "America will never forget what you and the people of Limburg do for our dead. . . . You see all this simply as a duty of gratitude, let me assure you on behalf of our President that Americans will always be grateful." But this praise from the highest official in the United States did not quell Father Heuschen's anger or soothe his wounded ego. The following month, he resigned from the Civilian Committee Margraten. He then arranged for a library-catalog-style bureau to be built for the rolls of soldiers, graves, and adopters, meticulously compiled on index cards by his volunteers. He had the bureau placed in the Margraten town hall, where no one from Maastricht could remove it.

Father Heuschen remained a chaplain in Margraten until 1953, when he transferred to Sint Theresia Church in Maastricht, less than one mile from Emilie's home. He died in 1961, only forty-eight years old.

Emilie continued her work at Margraten for another seventeen years, officially through the Civilian Committee Margraten and the Netherlands War Graves Committee, as an adopter, and as the point of contact for next of kin who needed help making arrangements to visit the grave of their loved one. In the early 1950s, she returned to America, where she visited Pat Fowlkes's loved ones, among others. In 1960, Lib Fowlkes and her daughter Rives, now sixteen, visited Margraten. Emilie hosted them for lunch and arranged for white flowers to be placed on Pat's grave. In 2003, when Rives returned to the cemetery for her sixtieth birthday, Emilie's son George took over the honor of hosting her for lunch. The Fowlkes family was just one of many whom Emilie and her children treated so kindly.

Mary Broun, Pat's official adopter, was another dedicated friend to the Fowlkes family. She gave Rives and her older brother Frank a pair of red klompen and two hand-painted silk handkerchiefs, and she signed at least one letter to Rives as "your big sister." Rives met with Mary's niece and nephew, who had taken over as Pat's adopters, when she returned to Margraten in 2014.

Sadly, the system did not work that well for every family. At one point, Emilie guessed the Civilian Committee Margraten had next-of-kin information for about 20 percent of those buried at the cemetery. Today, that number may only be as high as 25 percent. Jacob Herman's niece, as I learned in my research, had never heard of the adoption program. She was in tears when she learned that, for all these years, a Dutch adopter had been caring for her uncle's grave. When asked if she was interested in hearing from them, she immediately replied, "Yes. Absolutely."

The miracle of the committee's work, its love and support, grows on. It is my hope that this story—and the Forever Promise Project described at the end of this book—will result in every family having the opportunity to be in contact with their adopter.

In 1963, deteriorating health forced Emilie to resign her official positions. She never recovered, really, from the hardships of the occupation, when she neglected her own health for that of her children. On Easter Sunday 1970, a few weeks after her sixty-third birthday, Willem sent a notice informing their fourteen children—in 1947, the Michiels van Kessenichs had adopted two Hungarian sisters whose parents were murdered by Soviet Red Army soldiers, and they had their last child, Beatrix, in 1948—that Mutti was seriously ill with colitis.

On April 17, Emilie underwent emergency surgery. "With this bulletin," Willem wrote the children, "I do not want you to worry unnecessarily, but I do ask all of you who can still pray that you join me in prayer. I myself experience it as a great grace and completely peaceful acceptance of all circumstances that arise."

On May 7, her lungs filled with fluid, but she managed to signal Willem closer and, with great pain, wrapped him in her arms. As Willem wrote: "Her father, when she was still a little girl, [had] said to her, 'I hope you get a husband who is kind to you when you are sick.' And then she added, with that sweet smile, 'and that's what I got.'"

Emilie Michiels van Kessenich died in the hospital on June 5, 1970. "Mother is no longer visibly with us," Willem wrote the children. She has "transitioned to eternity."

"The last weeks it was mainly the flowers in our garden that made her happy. Each time [I visited the hospital] I brought one or two to her and held them close to her face. She then visibly said, 'beautiful.' If anything will be hard for me in the future, it's that we won't be able to say 'beautiful' together anymore."

Emilie Michiels van Kessenich was buried at Tongerseweg Cemetery in Maastricht. Beside her headstone is a small sculpture of her guardian angel, Bonus Simplicitas, carved by a friend. Some might judge it amateurish and crude. But those who knew Emilie appreciate it as she would have, for its simplicity. That was Emilie: She did not care about monuments. Hers was a life of service; to her God, her family, and her friends.

On June 10, five days after her passing, the *Maaspost* commemorated Emilie, the kippenburgemeestress of Maastricht, this way:

*She was a wonderful woman for her husband, for her household and for the whole city of Maastricht. She stretched out her hand to the needy and helped people in trouble with advice and action, and all this happened in a way that testified of true secular and spiritual nobility. But we need not dwell on that. In all this sadness I must tell you of a moving incident. . . . I was stopped in*

*the street by an elderly mother, completely unknown to me, who apparently
knew me. In typical Maastricht fashion she said:*

*Sir, surely you write in the Maaspost about the wife of our former mayor,
but don't write above that article: "In memoriam." I know, said the woman, a
completely different caption and it should read: "Now the angel of Maastricht
has become a real angel." The deceased now rests in peace. We wish Baron
Michiels, his children and other relatives much strength and courage in these
trying and difficult days. But know that Lady van Meeuwen has lived a fine
and beautiful life. And that Maastricht will remain very grateful to her forever.*

A stirring sentiment, but one that proved unequivocally false.

In the earliest stages of my research, the mention of Emilie Michiels
van Kessenich resulted in more than one person in Margraten telling me,
"She tried to steal the adoption program from us!" A prominent citizen of
Maastricht used my questions about Emilie to segue into criticisms of her
husband. The most benign comment came from someone who suggested I
avoid mentioning Willem and the hostage crisis altogether, adding, "Today,
no one even thinks about Willem Michiels van Kessenich and his wife."

Rather than relying on the opinions of others, I dug into the historical record, beginning with a well-regarded history of the cemetery, *The
Margraten Boys*. This otherwise excellent book repeatedly attributed
Emilie's acts of kindness to a desire to rehabilitate her husband's career
and reputation. Even here, Emilie Michiels van Kessenich had become the
villain of a story that should have been positive and wonderful, and had no
need for villains.

Initially, I had no reason to doubt this interpretation, and no intention
of trying to rehabilitate the reputation of a woman I had never heard of. But
the Emilie Michiels van Kessenich that emerged from the historical record
was nothing like a villain. My team translated from Dutch to English
Emilie's Memory Books covering the period 1938–1946, which her children had placed with the Historisch Centrum Limburg (Limburg History
Center) in Maastricht. I wanted to learn about this woman and understand
her life and her longings. My focus was less on what she did than why. I also
befriended Jenneke and spent many hours listening to stories about their
family life, her memories of her father and mother, and what it was like
having the innocence of your childhood snatched away by war.

I discovered that Emilie never believed her husband's reputation needed rehabilitation. Instead, what I found in her Memory Books— documents never meant to be seen by anyone other than her children and grandchildren—was pride for the courage and character Willem had displayed under difficult circumstances. Rather than finding examples of Emilie trying to curry favor with American military leaders, I found repeated expressions of *their* gratitude for her grace, courteousness, and willingness to provide a respite from war by inviting them into her home. The affection she felt for Mabel, Lib, and so many others was clearly genuine, and genuinely returned.

Seven years of research and analysis of Emilie distilled down to this: she was a virtuous woman, part traditionalist—a very religious wife and mother dedicated to providing for her family—and part pioneer—a talented and driven organizer with a gift of knowing how to get things done. When opportunities arose to be something more than just Mrs. Mayor's Wife, Emilie fearlessly seized them, and *that*—an assertive woman with her own passions, and her own ideas and opinions—ruffled many feathers in that place and time. She was a woman living in a society dominated at every level, including the Civilian Committee Margraten, by men.

There was certainly an easy "villain/victim" narrative to paint. Small town defending itself from big city. Salt-of-the-earth folks fighting off a well-to-do, politically connected woman. And a point I don't think can be overstated: those who started the adoption program and quietly did the work versus an outspoken personality with ambition (a word used several times both contemporaneously and currently).

Did Emilie have a "tendency toward self-glorification," as her critics claimed during the tempest of fall 1946? It is true that she pursued publicity, but her primary motivation was to do good for those in need. She cultivated contacts with powerful people, but she also had the gift of connecting with those who weren't powerful at all. She was not a vain or boastful woman. There is no indication that she intended to slight Father Heuschen, Joseph van Laar, Emil Ronckers, or any of the wonderful people of Margraten. In fact, Emilie gave them credit constantly and almost always referred to her role as patroness or helper.

With the benefit of eighty years of hindsight, it is now clear that there were two inflection points in the growth of the adoption program that fueled suspicions toward Emilie and sowed the seeds of discord. The first occurred in September 1945, when Father Heuschen pulled that trunk full of letters out from under his bed, a moment when Heuschen's local program manageable by a few people was becoming something much larger. Where Emilie saw opportunity, Father Heuschen saw change. News that Emilie would be traveling to the United States in June 1946 marked the second inflection point. Both she and Mayor Ronckers realized that for the program to achieve its most noble purpose and live on forever, they had to engage the American families whose sons and daughters they had adopted. Father Heuschen took the news of her trip as a personal affront.

Within the Limburg community, much has been said and written about who is responsible for the success of the grave adoption program at Margraten. Is it Joseph van Laar, who aided Captain Shomon and made a promise to Captain Lane? Burgemeester Ronckers, who took Van Laar's suggestion to heart and made grave adoption the focus of the Civilian Committee Margraten? Father Heuschen, who turned the plans into reality? Or the people of Margraten, who answered the call by grabbing their shovels? Or Else Hanöver and other volunteers, mostly women, who gave hundreds of hours to the cause? And let's not forget Lies Köster and Felix Prevoo, who spent years of their lives sustaining the adoption program foundation when there was little to no funding.

The answer is simple: it was *everyone*, including all the villagers in Margraten and all nearly 18,000 adopters—and all those who have become adopters since. Everyone should feel proud.

The refusal of some in Limburg Province to acknowledge the hard work and contributions of Emilie Michiels van Kessenich reflects an unwillingness or failure to see her as a whole person, a woman with her own motivations and desires.

But what of Emilie's husband, Willem Michiels van Kessenich, who remained the burgemeester of Maastricht until his retirement in 1967, when Emilie's health began its serious decline? Jenneke insisted in our conversations that her father told her he had offered to put his name on the hostage list, but the German Feldkommandant replied: "You don't have to put your name on the list because we will get you first." Whether this happened or not, one thing is certain: this one decision, made quickly in the first hours of a devastating invasion, continues to reverberate in Limburg, and in the Michels van Kessenich family, eight decades later.

In 2023, a report commissioned by the Maastricht municipality, *Unfinished Past*, caused quite a stir in Maastricht while I was there doing research. The authors relitigated several incidents involving Willem, including the hostages and the removal of Dr. Mendes de Leon as director of the Calvariënberg Hospital because he was of "Jewish blood." They suggested the antisemitic ordinances presented to Willem for signature by the Germans, for which he was investigated and exonerated in 1945, were not dealt with seriously enough in the postwar years.

Willem was not antisemitic or a Nazi sympathizer. Historians, even those with harsh assessments of his actions, agree on that. *Unfinished Past* did not claim he was. He was mentioned on fewer than ten pages of the 319-page report. And yet, he was singled out and denounced in local news stories in the days that followed, including a rush to judgment that the city should rename a street that bore his name.

In January 2025, the Netherlands announced that they were making the Dutch Central Archive of Special Jurisdiction (CABR) available online. These archives contain the names and files of approximately 425,000 individuals investigated for "collaboration with the German occupiers, such as NSB membership, treason, or joining the German army. Not everyone appeared before a judge, was convicted, or was rightly accused." One of the names that appears is that of Willem Michiels van Kessenich. The appearance of Willem's name on two files in the archive may serve to embolden his critics, but the information that we examined in one of the two files on record (the other was in the process of being digitized and unavailable) includes documentation that the Maastricht Tribunal, a special court established after World War II to investigate individuals suspected of collaboration, "unconditionally acquitted [Willem] of prosecution." It is our understanding that the second file contains a cover note stating that Willem was suspected of helping to identify hostages and that a non-prosecution order was issued.

In the end, I find most commentators' appraisal of this "wartime mayor" incomplete and too harsh, rendered from the safety of our current times, but let each judge for themself. For my part, I embrace the truth spoken by Diego Mendes de Leon, son of the very doctor Willem was accused of removing from his position:

*When we think back now to the war years, we see them as a closed period:*
*1939–1945. But ... on May 10, 1940, when the Germans invaded our coun-*
*try, no one knew how long it would last and what would happen. It wasn't*
*even certain which side would emerge victorious in the end. The only thing*
*that was certain was that everything would change.*

Couple that with the wise words of the Dutch minister of the interior,
Mr. Jaap Burger, who in early 1945 noted: "The greater part of our nation,
of any nation, is not made up of heroes and saints."

Who are we to assume, in that same situation, we would have been
a saint?

Willem Michiels van Kessenich died in 1992, at the age of ninety. He
was buried next to Emilie, the love of his life and his most trusted counselor
and friend.

As for the others whose stories make up this book:

Margareta "Moekie" van Schaïk died of a stroke in 1947. Like Emilie
Michiels van Kessenich, her health never recovered from the war.

Dave "Pappie" van Schaïk died in 1972, at eighty-three. Only in
the decades after his death was his dedication to Sint Pietersberg truly
acknowledged by the people of Limburg. In the late 1980s, his likeness
was carved into the wall at an entrance to the caves, and a road atop the
mountain renamed Dave van Schaïk Way. Unfortunately, by then, the
cement companies had mined much of the mountain, destroying many of
the ancient passageways. Today, Dave van Schaïk Way and the roads atop
Sint Pietersberg are walking paths, closed to traffic. Tour groups regularly
walk through the remaining passages of the mine, as mesmerized today as
they were in Dave and Frieda's time. There is a magnificent view into the
open-pit mine at the center of the mountain, with sharp-cut passageways
visible in the walls. Schark Cave is open to the public, and the restaurant
where Frieda ate her first meal with Gordon is a tourist attraction.

The families of most of the soldiers in this book rarely visited
Margraten. In the decades after the war, overseas travel was much harder
and rarer than today. Stephen "Moose" Mosbacher's parents were among
the most frequent visitors. They spent time every summer with family and
friends in their old hometown of Fürth, Germany—the few, that is, who
survived the Holocaust. Most of Stephen's relatives were murdered during

the war. Every trip, if the cemetery was open, they drove to Margraten and shared a picnic lunch with their son beside his grave. They never considered repatriating Stephen to the United States or moving back to Germany. They were proud to be Americans, the country their boy had died defending.

Dr. James Norton and Miss Ed requested permission from the U.S. government to visit their son's grave in October 1946. That's when they discovered James had been reinterred at Margraten. They visited him there in summer 1947. Months later, when the burial requests were sent to next of kin, Dr. Norton was one of the first to respond.

> As I have so often said before, this boy is one of twins, the other now lying at the bottom of the North Sea not far off the coast of Holland . . . and never having been separated in life, they are as close as they can ever be just where they are, and so I wish this boy to stay exactly where he is, not only at the moment but for evermore.

James rests in Plot B, Row 16, Grave 5. Edward is listed with 1,721 other soldiers and airmen on the Walls of the Missing. One can almost be seen, while standing in front of the other.

Dr. James and Miss Ed were never again able to visit their sons. They died in 1950 and 1955, respectively. But The Twins are far from forgotten. Their nephew, Dr. James Norton Spivey, idolized them growing up. They once took him for a ride in their plane, a sacred memory. He was ten years old when Hoggy and Wack died. He made his career in the U.S. Air Force, including as a flight surgeon at MacDill Air Force Base, and retired as a full colonel around 1990. He is still angry that The Boys, as he calls them, died on "a suicide mission so stupid it never should have been flown."

In 2010, the general aviation terminal at the Myrtle Beach International Airport was dedicated to James and Edward Norton. Their hometown of Conway, South Carolina, once small and isolated, sits just inland from that vacation mecca.

"It means a lot they're not forgotten," Lieutenant Colonel Larkin Spivey, a brother of Dr. Spivey and a retired Marine officer who served in the Vietnam War, told the local paper. "There are a lot of great young men that we should not forget. But of course, I'm partial to those two."

Of all the soldiers in this book, Robert Cole is by far the most well known.

He was a legend, even in his day. Today, he is one of the most revered combat soldiers of World War II. Even members of the 82nd Airborne bragged (in their humble way) that they had fought beside Lieutenant Colonel Robert Cole and the 101st Airborne on D-Day. The road to Carentan, where Robert Cole led the charge, is known as Purple Heart Lane because of the extraordinary number of medals awarded for actions there. The Battle of Carentan has been mythologized not so much for its planning or even execution but for the sheer courage and tenacity of the men who fought and died there.

Robert Cole received his nation's highest recognition for valor, the Medal of Honor. He was the first member of the 101st Airborne, and the first airborne officer in the Army, to receive this great honor. He knew that he had been put in for the medal before his death in Operation Market Garden, though the confirmation had not yet come through. In his September 1944 eve-of-battle letter to Allie Mae, written in the last two or three days of his life, he had hurriedly scribbled: "Darling.... If anything happens to me, I want the medal to go to Mother."

And it did. Clara Cole accepted the Medal of Honor on her son's behalf at Fort Sam Houston on October 30, 1944. Allie Mae and her son, Robert Bruce Cole, barely three, were present at the ceremony. It was as close as the little boy would ever come to knowing his father.

The option for reburial went to Clara, since Allie Mae remarried in 1946. Widows who remarried were removed from the chain of rights regarding their husbands. Clara died before making a choice; Robert's brother chose to leave him at Margraten. Allie Mae visited her husband's grave for the first time in 1976. As she walked toward his row, she noticed the headstone of Robert Cole's radioman, Technician Fifth Grade Robert Doran, who had been killed just minutes before him. A few graves over were the names of two other men in her husband's battalion. "This is where Robert would want to be," she said. "With his men."

Allie Mae died in 2000. Though she was happily married for more than forty years (her second husband died in 1991), her headstone reads:

*Duty Honor Country*
*Widow of Robert G. Cole*
*LTC USA*
*Medal of Honor*

Robert's son Bruce visited his father's grave in 2009 with his stepsister Cindy. Ten years later, on Veterans Day, Bruce donated Cole's Purple Heart Medal to the Robert G. Cole High School in San Antonio, Texas, where it is displayed in a glass cabinet inside the front door. The school's name and the medal are constant reminders to the students of the values Cole stood for: Respect. Duty. Loyalty. Courage. And the understanding that to truly lead, you must put others first.

In the words of West Point's Final Salute to those in the long gray line: "Well done, be thou at rest."

Lib Fowlkes likewise remarried a few years after her husband's death. Allie Mae married an Army officer, like Robert. Lib married a minister, like Pat. She didn't talk much about Pat, either in public or to her children. Ralph (the "little frog") and Elizabeth, born Betsy but known as Rives, were raised in a happy home. They called Lib's husband "father," and they meant it. Only as an adult did Rives, born less than two years before Pat's death, decide she wanted to know her biological dad. She discovered that her mother had kept the letters he had written home from the war. Only one letter from her mother to her father, however, survived: the letter announcing her own birth.

In 2018, Rives compiled all those letters, and a few others, into a book titled *Chaplain: The World War II Letters of Army Air Corps Chaplain*

*Paschal Dupuy Fowlkes*. The letters in this book come from that labor of love for a father she had come to know, finally, by the beautiful and often inspirational words he had written more than seventy years ago.

Bill Moore was among the last Americans interred at Margraten. Helen wrote to the Office of the Quartermaster General in both 1946 and 1948, saying she did not want Bill's grave "moved or disturbed in any way." She wanted her son left right there, in Apeldoorn, with the Dutch who had known and cared for him. For years, she refused to answer any correspondence from the U.S. Army, but finally agreed to meet with an officer from the Quartermaster's Memorial Division who visited their home in June 1952. During that meeting, Helen told the officer she had withheld all mail concerning Bill from her husband, John, who had a severe heart condition doctors attributed to the loss of their son. Helen explained that the doctors expected her husband to die from his broken heart, and that the shock of news about Bill's remains might be the trigger. But the meeting had the desired effect: Helen relented and authorized relocation of Bill's remains to Margraten.

John and Helen died with no known relatives to mourn the boy they had loved as their son. But Bill Moore's men remembered him. John Low began but never completed a manuscript about his escape and evasion, "The Brave Dutch," in which he wrote in detail about his time with Moore. During his almost nine months in hiding, his parents and all of his friends had given up hope of ever seeing him alive again. All except the wife he talked about so often in the attic, Josephine. Everyone pleaded with her to give up false hope, to accept reality and begin to heal, but Jo never lost faith that one day her husband was going to walk back through her door. Love carried them—the two of them—through the months of trial.

Low was an engineer by training. He became a successful inventor. He and Jo had four children. The two lived a wild and wonderful life together, the perpetual joy of any party. But eventually, Low's drinking began to catch up with him. He died at fifty-eight. Officially, he slipped while climbing over a fence with his shotgun. His family knew otherwise. Beneath his fun-loving exterior, his war experience, especially survivor's guilt, had eaten him up. He often told his children how his friend Bill Moore had sacrificed his life so that their father and the other Underwater Boys could live.

Today, a stone memorial marks the site where Bill Moore and the twelve Dutch Resistance fighters were executed. Adolf Glück, who shot Bill in the back, was convicted of murder in 1950, based on the testimony of German troops who witnessed the thirteen executions. He was sentenced to three years in a Dutch prison but was deported to Germany after only one.

Narda "Mary" van Terwisga, who led the resistance cell that rescued Moore and Low, survived the war. But she had been tortured. She never recovered. Her testimony helped convict the man, William l'Ecluse, who had betrayed her group to the SD. He was sentenced to death but released after thirteen years in prison.

Else Hanöver, Willem's assistant, married and moved to Florida. As promised, she named her son Ralph, in honor of the young soldier whose grave she adopted. Decades later, after her husband died, she reconnected with Wilson White, the staff sergeant she met the day after Maastricht was liberated. White had recently lost his spouse too. They married and spent three happy years together before White succumbed to cancer.

Bill Hughes stayed in Europe when the 784th returned to the United States. The Army paid for him to study communications in England, then sent him to Belgium, where he spent his nights listening to American jazz at The Blue Note. He returned to Indianapolis, then California, but when he saw how Black veterans were treated in America, he wanted nothing to do with it. He took a job with the U.S. Department of Defense in Germany. To his surprise, he had become fond of the German people during his time with the occupation forces after the country's surrender. He married a German woman in 1953, divorced, and married another German woman in 1963. They had five children, one of whom died in infancy; they raised the other four in Heidelberg.

Only in 2005 did Bill realize that Curley Ausmer, the nineteen-year-old killed in a friendly-fire bombing incident before they reached the battlefield, was buried at the Netherlands American Cemetery. Bill thought Curley's death had been covered up by the military. But there he was, buried with full honors. Bill visited the cemetery in July 2005 to pay his respects to Curley and seventeen others from the 784th. He said a silent prayer at each grave. He wondered what their lives would have been like had they lived.

Bill Hughes was a practical man. He understood change was hard, and the journey long. "Be prepared," he always told his children. "Don't count on someone coming to save you." More than anything, he believed in self-reliance. He worked his whole career for the United States government, in the Department of Defense's Commercial Communications Department, never returning home for more than a few weeks at a time.

He told his children not to worry about his burial; he had chosen a place and made all the arrangements. "You know where," he told his son Max.

"No, Dad, I don't."

The old tanker smiled. "Indianapolis."

Bill Hughes is buried in his hometown, next to his infant son.

Jefferson Wiggins had a similar experience. He returned home to Alabama to find the state unchanged. Segregation was law. Racial hatred was entrenched. The freedom Black men like Jeff had died for in Europe was denied them at home. They could not live where they wanted, walk where they wanted, talk to whom they wanted. They were kept out of good jobs. They could not vote. They were refused admittance to schools, restaurants, bathrooms, and parks. German prisoners of war, sentenced to hard labor in Jeff's corner of Alabama, rode in the front of the bus; the Black Americans who had fought them, like Jeff Wiggins, were forced to ride in the back.

Orval Faubus, the infantryman who wrote of his appreciation for Bill Hughes and the other Black tankers who fought alongside him, became one of the most famous racists of the twentieth century. As governor of Arkansas, he refused to follow the ruling in *Brown v. Board of Education*, defying the federal order to desegregate schools. That showdown with his former supreme commander, President Dwight D. Eisenhower, led to the Little Rock Crisis of 1957. That's how quickly freedom slipped through the fingers of Black soldiers. That's how thoroughly America—not just the country, but some of the white soldiers who had seen the true mettle of their fellow Americans—turned its back on its Black heroes.

With the help of the formidable women in his life, his grandmother—Grandma Dawson—his mother, Essie Mae, and Mrs. Merrill, the white librarian from Staten Island who befriended him, Jeff Wiggins rose above the hate. At the insistence of Mrs. Merrill, Jeff convinced an all-white local school board that repeatedly called him "boy" to grant him a high school diploma based on his war service. He enrolled at Tennessee State, a historically Black college. He earned a history degree. He returned to Alabama to teach veterans English and math. He re-enlisted in the Army for the Korean War and served with distinction, then settled in New Jersey. He earned a teaching degree from Trenton State College and then later a PhD. For thirty years, he was a teacher, tutor, school administrator, and college professor in New Jersey. He spent his life as an educator.

In 2008, when he was eighty-three, Wiggins was contacted by a Dutch historian for an oral history of the Netherlands American Cemetery. As soon as he heard the word Margraten, his adrenaline flowed, and he became angry.

*How dare she ask me about that,* Jeff thought. As politely as he could, he told her no.

Afterward, he was agitated, withdrawn. He had never spoken of his war service. He did not stay in touch with any of the men of the 960th. He was frustrated by the role the United States had selected for him, a young Black American volunteer eager to prove his worth in the fight. And he was traumatized by his experience. He had buried deep within himself memories of the burials he had performed and witnessed at Margraten.

His wife, Janice, provided reassurance and convinced him it was time to speak. He was one of only three members of the 960th, and the only Black soldier from the unit (the other two were white officers), to participate in that oral history project, Akkers van Margraten (Fields of Margraten).

But he was never the same after reliving his time in the war, his wife told me. Quieter, less spontaneous. Sadder, perhaps. But he felt that he had to tell the story. Not his story, *their* story: the 200 Black gravediggers of the 960th Quartermaster Service Company, and all the Black soldiers who served faithfully and honorably in World War II, and whose contribution to the war effort was too often belittled or overlooked.

In 2009, Jefferson Wiggins, his wife, and two of his grandchildren attended the sixty-fifth anniversary of the founding of the Netherlands American Cemetery. There, in place of what had been a muddy, horrible ground, was an orderly field of graves, white stones against green grass.

In his speech, Jeff recounted his experience at Saint-Lô and the French woman who was standing among the ruins.

*She said to me, and I remember that clearly, "Soldier, you don't understand how it is to have your freedom, to lose it and then to regain it. . . ." I wanted to say to her, but I didn't because there wasn't time, but I wanted to say to her, "Madam, you don't understand how it is never to have had your freedom, and here you are in the middle of a country that you have never been to before, marching through a town which you know nothing about, risking your life to free someone that you will probably never meet again, and knowing that the freedom that you deserve at home, you won't have."*

The wounds were deep—from Alabama, from Margraten—but the lasting message from Jeff Wiggins rang clear.

> *During the war, we [Black soldiers] didn't often discuss our civil rights. But we certainly did realize that if we as a group were good enough to be sent to France, Belgium, and the Netherlands, to liberate the people living there, we also were able to liberate ourselves at home, in the United States.*

His parents, Grandma Dawson, so many thousands of others—Jeff never forgot that their courage and sacrifice gave him the opportunity to serve, and that his service gave him a pathway to a better life. He always believed it was his responsibility to pass that hope and promise on to the next generation.

Jefferson Wiggins did exactly that by being an educator, a mentor, a father, and a friend. He died in 2013.

And then there is Frieda. Wonderful, indomitable Frieda. She was, of course, the older woman who asked me back in 2016 if I had heard of the Margraten adoption program. That question charted the course of the next eight years (and counting) of my life. Frieda introduced me to Dutch loyalty, to the depth of the appreciation the people of Limburg felt for the Americans buried at Margraten. Like Walter Huchthausen had for her, like Mabel Feil and Lib Fowlkes had for Emilie Michiels van Kessenich, Frieda impacted my life in a profound way.

It started innocently enough. Walter Huchthausen's nephew and his wife, who I knew through my book on the Monuments Men and the work of the Monuments Men and Women Foundation, sent me a photograph: the two of them with another couple, who the back of the photo identified as Gordon and Frieda Gumn. Frieda had never, as she promised in 1945, forgotten about Walter. Even seventy years later, she was friends with his extended family. She and Gordon named their first child Esther, after Walter's sister. Their second child Paul, after Walter's brother. Their third child Martha, after Walter's other sister. Their fourth child, Francesca—that was Gordon's choice. Walter had no other sisters.

Frieda loved Walter, that was clear. But Gordon Gumn was the love of Frieda's life. Together, they raised their four children. They ran a printing business. Frieda became an expert bookbinder. Never one to shy away from trying something new, in 1976 she drove a British Chieftain tank. She gave joy to hundreds, especially a deaf man with severe learning disabilities named Jimmy, who Frieda saw when no one else in the community did. Their friendship, and Frieda's work with the National Deaf-Blind Helper's League, resulted in an invitation to Buckingham Palace to attend one of the Queen's garden parties, where she met the Duke and Duchess of Kent. She did all of it with Gordon at her side. During the sixty-eight years of their marriage—he died in 2019—Gordon never questioned her loyalty to Walter. He had been through the war too. He loved her. He understood.

In 2018, I returned to Over Wallop, in Hampshire, England, about an hour-and-a-half drive southwest of London, where Frieda and Gordon had lived since their marriage. The following day, Frieda and I traveled together to the Netherlands American Cemetery, six miles from where she was raised. By then, I was consumed by Margraten and its adoption program, determined to bring this beautiful, inspiring story to the world. I had asked all the questions I could think to ask, plumbing her memory for hours. At ninety-three, it was difficult for her to travel. She had not been back home in years. No words were spoken, but we both knew this trip would be her farewell.

It was a crisp May day, exceptionally sunny and bright, when we pulled off the Rijksweg into the cemetery at Margraten. It was impossible, on a morning like that, to picture fall 1944, with unrelenting rain, stacks of dead bodies, and the Black gravediggers slamming their shovels in frustration against the frozen ground. The American Battle Monuments Commission, which administers and maintains the twenty-six permanent American military cemeteries and thirty-two federal memorials, monuments, and markers overseas, has done remarkable work at Margraten. The solemnity, the care, the dedication to every detail is matched at the other ABMC cemeteries, but each has a defining characteristic. At Normandy, it is the beauty of the setting above the landing beaches where so many boys lost their lives. At the Sicily-Rome American Cemetery, it is the serenity of the majestic Mediterranean pines that shelter the young Americans who defeated enemy forces in Sicily, Salerno, Anzio, and Nettuno. At Margraten, it is the way the cemetery melts into the subtle beauty of countryside that appeared so familiar to American boys it reminded them of home—and for 10,000 of them, it would become just that. Every detail of the Netherlands American Cemetery has been thoughtfully crafted, but it is not the foreign park Dave van Schaïk feared. In some way, somehow, it is profoundly Dutch. It belongs here and only here. It feels as if the Lord, the U.S. Armed Forces, the Dutch people, are holding this small, sacred place in their embrace.

The entrance is wide and welcoming, bounded by the Walls of the Missing, where rosettes mark the names of those whose remains have been found in the intervening decades. Japanese cherry trees front the walls. A reflecting pool runs down the center. These elements work together, putting you at ease with their beauty, compelling you forward up an incline toward the 101-foot-tall memorial tower. The rise is mild, with occasional low steps that even a ninety-three-year-old could navigate, with a caring hand on her elbow.

We stopped at the tower, which houses a chapel. An altar is at the front. The edges are lined with flags. Frieda bowed her head, and we prayed.

Beyond the tower lay the white marble headstones, rising from a thick blanket of green grass. There is no mud. Tree-lined walkways on either side of the grass median separate the two sections of the cemetery. The grass is mowed every week. The marble headstones are constantly cleaned, no speck of imperfection visible, beyond a few delicate strands of spiderweb. If you inform the ABMC you are coming to visit a family member, they will take sand from the Normandy beaches and fill in the carvings on the headstone you are visiting, so that the words glow golden in the light. They will inform the Foundation for Adopting Graves so your grave's adopter is there to greet you.

Frieda and I did not inform the cemetery of our coming. We sought no recognition or company, only peace. We walked slowly, but with purpose, from the chapel to the memorial field. Frieda's memories came flooding back as we passed among the headstones, that joyous young woman alive in her eyes. She was thinking, perhaps, of the liberation, of the young soldiers who stopped for comfort on the road outside her home, of Walter stepping across the floor to ask her to dance, of the quiet of the caves, her family, her friends, her children, and Gordon, her life's great love. She stopped delicately, carefully in front of a grave she knew too well. The grave she promised never to forget. The grave where, on the night of her wedding, the happiest girl in Limburg had left her bridal bouquet.

Physically, this place was not the same. Walter's grave had been moved, the grounds remade. But what did that matter? This cemetery is far more than headstones. It is the 10,000 men and women who placed the needs of their nation ahead of their own and paid the highest price for doing so. It is the Dutch citizens who continue to honor them.

Too rheumatic to kneel at Walter's graveside, Frieda bowed her head and cried.

"I'm sorry," she said. "My father was so taciturn, so determined to not show emotion, that I lived that way most of my life. Now, it's like all those things I felt, the emotions of a lifetime, are bursting out, and I find myself in tears."

Oh Frieda, don't apologize. Don't you know that throughout this journey, I've been crying too?

In April 1946, General Eisenhower provided perspective on the unimaginable, a war that had claimed the lives of 70 million people, including 405,000 Americans. He said: "For a democracy at least, there always stands beyond the materialism and destructiveness of war those ideals for which it is fought."

No ideal can be more meaningful than freedom. The heroes of Margraten remind us how beautiful and meaningful that freedom is, especially for those of us who, because we haven't done anything to earn it, take our freedom for granted. They are a reminder of how horrible it is to lose your freedom, and how difficult it is to get it back once lost.

And what do you do if you're fortunate enough to get your freedom back, and the people who got it back for you aren't there to thank?

The people of the Netherlands, of Limburg, continue to inspire us with their answer, because they know what we all know deep in our hearts: each of us hopes to be remembered, somehow, some way, by someone.

Wilhelmina Frederika Elisabeth Gumn, née van Schaïk, died at home on July 17, 2023. She was ninety-eight. She was the last of our major characters to leave us. Three weeks later, I walked with her family—they were partly mine now too—behind the hearse to St. Peter's Church, where we delivered our eulogies, and said our good-byes. Frieda rests there now, through the rain and the sun, with Gordon at her side.

I am here to tell her that, like Walter Huchthausen and all the men and women buried at the Netherlands American Cemetery, *she is and always will be remembered.*

*Robert M. Edsel*
*Dallas, Texas*
*April 2024*

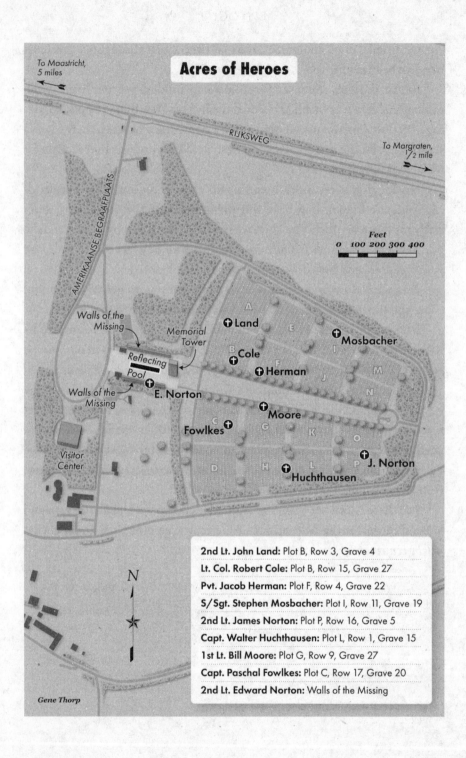

# Acres of Heroes

To Maastricht, 5 miles

RIJKSWEG

To Margraten, 1/2 mile

AMERIKAANSE BEGRAAFPLAATS

Walls of the Missing

Memorial Tower

Reflecting Pool

Walls of the Missing

Visitor Center

Feet
0  100  200  300  400

✝ Land
✝ Mosbacher
✝ Cole
✝ Herman
✝ E. Norton
✝ Moore
✝ Fowlkes
✝ Huchthausen
✝ J. Norton

A  E  I
B  F  J  M
N
C  G  K  O
D  H  P

N

**2nd Lt. John Land:** Plot B, Row 3, Grave 4

**Lt. Col. Robert Cole:** Plot B, Row 15, Grave 27

**Pvt. Jacob Herman:** Plot F, Row 4, Grave 22

**S/Sgt. Stephen Mosbacher:** Plot I, Row 11, Grave 19

**2nd Lt. James Norton:** Plot P, Row 16, Grave 5

**Capt. Walter Huchthausen:** Plot L, Row 1, Grave 15

**1st Lt. Bill Moore:** Plot G, Row 9, Grave 27

**Capt. Paschal Fowlkes:** Plot C, Row 17, Grave 20

**2nd Lt. Edward Norton:** Walls of the Missing

*Gene Thorp*

# THE FOREVER
# PROMISE PROJECT

The **Forever Promise Project** is a partnership between two non-profit organizations: the American **Monuments Men and Women Foundation** and the Dutch **Foundation for Adopting Graves American Cemetery Margraten**. The objective is to realize the founders' objective by connecting the Dutch grave adopters with 100 percent of the next of kin of all 10,000 American heroes buried or honored on the Walls of the Missing at the Netherlands American Cemetery.

The **Foundation for Adopting Graves American Cemetery Margraten (Stichting Adoptie Graven Amerikaanse Begraafplaats Margraten)** was created in February 1945 to encourage Dutch citizens to express gratitude for American liberators by adopting their graves. To qualify, volunteers agreed to regularly visit the adopted grave *and* remain in touch with the soldier's next of kin in the United States where next of kin information was available. The campaign gained massive support. By the second postwar Memorial Day in 1946, 100 percent of the nearly 18,000 graves had been adopted, but next of kin information was not available for 80 percent of those buried. To this day, very few Americans know about the Dutch grave adoption program. Some are not even aware that a family member is buried at the Netherlands American Cemetery.

The **Monuments Men and Women Foundation** was founded in 2007 to recognize and honor the work of the soldier-scholars who, during World War II, protected and safeguarded Western civilization's most important cultural treasures from armed conflict. It continues these heroes' mission restituting missing works of art and educating the public on the importance of preserving our shared cultural heritage. The Foundation is the recipient of the National Humanities Medal, America's highest honor for work in the humanities.

We invite all family members who have a loved one buried at the Netherlands American Cemetery or listed on the Walls of the Missing, and those wishing to confirm that they do, to contact the Monuments Men and Women Foundation at info@foreverpromise.org for further information about the Forever Promise Project.

# ACKNOWLEDGMENTS

It took me five years to figure out how to tell this story, and almost eight years of research to fully understand it. My gratitude to all those who helped in ways large and small is boundless.

Bret Witter had primary responsibility for shaping and writing the story, a project that consumed two years of his life. The seventeen intervening years since our work together on *The Monuments Men* provided a level of maturity and knowledge that enabled us to understand the timeless value of this story and why it was so important that it be told. Our partnership has been one of the most rewarding experiences of my professional life.

Dr. Seth Givens used his extraordinary knowledge of military history and remarkable research skills to identify most of the key characters of this book, but only after having examined the backgrounds of most of the nearly 10,000 men and women buried at Margraten. Seth was fully committed to this project from the moment I told him about it eight years ago. Even during our darkest moments of frustration and rejection, he never wavered, all the while working a forty-hour-plus-per-week, full-time job. I couldn't have written this book without him. What's more: I wouldn't have wanted to. Special thanks to his wife, Sarah, for sharing him with me during so many nights and weekends, and to Seth's twin brother, Dr. Adam Givens, whose parallel knowledge of military history provided us with a fresh set of eyes on the manuscript and some valuable improvements.

Dorothee Schneider has helped research four of the five books I have written. Her knowledge of art, culture, history, and languages are only exceeded by her understanding of and insights into people. Those gifts proved essential to understanding this story's two most important characters. Her perspective as a woman added a critical voice that made this book better. Casey Shelton, another valued member of our research team, added to that perspective along with always finding the unfindable, especially people we needed to interview. Thanks also to two newer members of our team, Shelby Landgraf and Beth Santos.

I want to extend thanks to my longtime attorney and dear friend, Michael Friedman, whose wise counsel has served me well for more than twenty years. To Daniel Greenberg with Levine Greenberg Rostan Literary Agency, thank you for your patience with my passion for this story, and for your seasoned advice on how to bring it to market.

Sometimes publishers focus on the written page of a book proposal so intensely that it blinds them to an author's vision, ability, and determination. How else to explain thirty-one out of thirty-one rejections of my first book proposal in 2018, and thirty-two out of thirty-four of the second? But Matt Baugher and his team at HarperCollins Focus believed in the story and my ability to tell it from the outset. He was always available to us, always open to our ideas. What I appreciated most, though, was Matt's gentle touch in expressing a strongly held opinion which made embracing it easy to do, even for a stubborn author. Similarly, our editor, Austin Ross, supported our approach to telling the story and exhibited a discerning eye about what not to change. There is a whole team at HarperCollins Focus committed to the success of this book; my thanks go out to all with special mention of Sicily Axton, head of marketing and Hannah Harless, marketing manager, for their steady hands throughout the process; Kevin Smith, head of publicity, along with the wonderful Lauren Kingsley; Belinda Bass, whose work on the book cover speaks for itself; Janna Walkup, our copy editor; Heather Howell, our production manager; and of course, the all-important sales team led by Doug Lockhart.

Researching this sweeping story was an immense undertaking. No matter the skill of the researcher, we depend on help from others, especially when working in foreign lands and languages. In Limburg, we benefited early on from the expertise and passion for this subject of Frans Roebroeks, an archivist specializing in the history of World War II at the Historical Center Limburg in Maastricht until his retirement in 2023. In addition to serving as one of our two early readers, Frans also deserves credit for finding the dramatic cover image of this book. At the Netherlands American Cemetery, Frenk Lahaye was an invaluable resource. Frans and Frenk's dedication to the memory of the Americans buried and remembered at Margraten is as heartwarming as it is inspiring. Historian and author, the late Dr. Paul Bronzwaer, a dear friend to all who knew him, shared with us decades of research and his personal knowledge of these wartime events. Each time Paul recounted the story of seeing the first American tanks appear on his street on September 13, 1944, we watched the elder scholar time-travel back to the amazement of an eight-year-old boy. His gratitude to Americans knew no limit. Our team grew very fond of this gentle man. We so lament his passing.

Thanks also to Fleur van Tongeren at the Historisch Centrum Limburg in Maastricht, and Tim Sijbers before her; Lars Dijkstra, Sylvia Rinsma, and Mathijs Smith at the Nationaal Archief in The Hague; Perry Schrier of the Ministry of Education, Culture, and Science's Rijksdienst voor het Cultureel Erfgoed; Michael Simonson at the Leo Baeck Institute; Rense Havinga at the Freedom Museum Groesbeek; Henk Trapman and Paul van der Flier at the Regionaal Archief Nijmegen; and authors Dr. Peter Schrijvers, Mieke Kirkels, and Sebastiaan Vonk.

To Ton Hermes, Fien Opreij-Bendermacher, and the other trustees of the Foundation for Adopting Graves American Cemetery Margraten (Stichting Adoptie Graven Amerikaanse Begraafplaats Margraten), past and present, we extend our utmost admiration and thanks.

No research involving World War II would be possible without the immense resources of the United States' National Archives and Records Administration. NARA is our nation's treasure house of history and documents, available to all. (I encourage anyone with a spare day and a little curiosity to make a trip to the National Mall or College Park, Maryland, to spend a moment holding a letter written by President Lincoln, or an original order issued by General Eisenhower, in their hand.) To the leadership and staff of the Archives, in particular those who kindly guided us to some documents and images that proved difficult to find, I want to extend our profound thanks.

This book benefited from the expertise of two men deserving special mention: Dr. John C. McManus, one of our nation's most distinguished military historians and a prolific author on World War II, and the second of our two early readers of the manuscript; and Joe Wilson, the leading expert and author of books on the Black tankers of the 758th, 761st, and 784th. Joe spent many hours interviewing Bill Hughes and generously shared his notes and recollections of those conversations with us. To both historians, our thanks.

# ACKNOWLEDGMENTS

I want to express my gratitude to the leadership, and all the dedicated employees of the Defense POW/MIA Accounting Agency and the American Battle Monuments Commission, in particular cemetery superintendents Jason Bordelon, Keith Stadler, and Carly Mathieu.

Arlette Quervel and Jasper Verschoor assisted us with translations. Elizabeth Butler-Witter, Tom Mullen, and Dale Rose provided valuable comments to the manuscript as outside readers. Bruna Bottinelli provided a fresh set of expert copy-editor eyes that found what others had missed. Geoff Gentilini at Golden Arrow Research helped during our busiest moments. Gene Thorp, mapmaker extraordinaire, did a fantastic job creating maps that merged military history with the specifics of our story.

This book benefited from the added visibility readers of the final manuscript provided, each distinguished in their own right. Admiral James G. Stavridis, Supreme Allied Commander at NATO, 2009–2013, and Donald L. Miller, one of our nation's great educators, are each *New York Times* bestselling authors. Bonnie Carroll, recipient of the Presidential Medal of Freedom in recognition for her work founding the Tragedy Assistance Program for Survivors, is a force of nature. TAPS.org is a nonprofit organization that provides compassionate care and comprehensive resources to all those grieving a death in the military or veteran community. As a widow of a U.S. Army officer, she had an acute appreciation for this story and the extraordinary efforts of the Dutch grave adopters. Finally, Major General Jeffrey Phillips, Executive Director of the Reserve Organization of America, was so moved by *Remember Us* that he contacted many of his peers to make them aware of this story and its importance. To each of them, I extend my most sincere thanks.

Without the trust and assistance of the families of Emilie, Frieda, and our key characters, the telling of this story would not have been possible. Emilie's oldest daughter, Jenneke Meyer Viol-Michiels van Kessenich, invited us into her home and spent hours sharing personal stories involving her parents and siblings. She also provided context to portions of her mother's all-important Memory Books, information only she possessed. Her son, Raymond Gijsen, not only donated his time translating many of Emilie's Memory Books, he also introduced us to the writings of Hette de Jong and Diego Mendes de Leon. Yolande and Ferdinand Michiels van Kessenich kindly provided us with access to the Memory Books and other archival information about their family.

## ACKNOWLEDGMENTS

Much of the time I spent with Frieda occurred at her home in the village of Over Wallop. Sitting at her breakfast room table, we flipped through her photo albums as she recounted experiences from the war years. From the moment of that first meeting in 2016, I knew that this seemingly ordinary woman had led an extraordinary life. And like Emilie, Frieda had done a great service to history documenting it with her letters and photograph albums. So much information left me with so many questions. Esther, the oldest of Frieda and Gordon's four children, had some answers, but not until I met Frieda's niece, Camilla Zéguers, who was also the family historian, did the significance of the Dave van Schaïk family fully emerge. Camilla shared her research with us freely. We gained further insights from Jacob Carrière and Kees Rauh, two of Frieda's nephews.

Family members of our key characters almost uniformly helped. Jim Huchthausen and his wife, Thelma, who have been friends for many years, continued to share details about Uncle Walt. Most recently, we laid a wreath in Walter's honor at the Tomb of the Unknown Soldier at Arlington National Cemetery. Bruce Cole has spent his entire life getting to know the father he never knew, gathering records that he generously shared with me. No son I have ever met has demonstrated a greater love and veneration for his father. Cindy Beall-Suich put me in touch with Bruce, her stepbrother, and shared additional family details. Dr. James Norton Spivey and Larkin Spivey still miss the Norton twins all these years later. The love and respect I heard in Dr. Spivey's childhood recollections of his two uncles is a memory I will always cherish. Lucy Low Helveston and Tineke Low Kermicle, daughters of John and Josephine, and their nephew and niece, Rhes and Jodie Low, provided important information about John Low's wife, Jo, and emphasized the gratitude—and sense of guilt—that John carried for the sacrifice Bill Moore made to save him and others. Max Hughes, who lives in Germany just as his father did, fondly recalled examples of his father's wise counsel to him as a young man, and the pride he felt having served a nation that fell far short of the equality he longed for during his youth in Indianapolis.

Janice Wiggins invited me into her home for an intimate discussion about her husband and the pain he tried every possible way to compartmentalize. I will remember always her gracious gesture allowing me to sit in the rocking chair on the front porch of their home, where Jeff spent many an hour enjoying the peaceful solitude that eluded him for much of his life.

Rives Carroll provided me with some important details about her father, in emails and conversation, but the most valuable contribution came in the form of her father's wartime letters which she published in her book. Lily Debie, granddaughter of the first adopter of Stephen Mosbacher's grave, shared vital details about Stephen's days stationed in Margraten that helped us understand the bond between those living in Limburg and American soldiers that they knew. Karen Pickering provided us with a copy of her family history, a lasting gift from her mother, Else Hanöver, filled with images and a diary of her amazing life.

A handful of people, including several dear friends, made specific contributions to this book. I want to thank Christy Fox, Dr. Nick Mueller, Johnny Van Haeften, Randy Deaton, Lynn Metzger, Tom Mayer, Gretchen Young, and Giovana De La Rosa. You each know what you did to help, and you know why it mattered. I also want to express my appreciation for the enthusiasm Christine Sullivan, Merrie Spaeth, and especially Lisette Mondello have shown for this book. Special thanks to Jim and Nancy, Ross and Sarah, Berry and Jeanne, John and Stephanie, Will and Kit, and Randy and Nancy for their early support of the Forever Promise Project.

The people of South Limburg have been gracious hosts. Maastricht and Margraten are lovely communities where Americans are warmly welcomed. My thanks to the staff of Mediterraneo and Petit Bonheur, two fabulous restaurants in Wyck and Maastricht, respectively, that sustained us on research trips. No visit to Maastricht would be complete without stopping by the shop of Adriaan de Smaakmaker to sample James and Angeliek's homemade jams and condiments. Simone Mourmans with Maastricht Underground provided an informative and fun tour of the caves of Sint Pietersberg, a wonderful opportunity for us to retrace Frieda and Dave's footsteps. And as has been the case with all my books, Badrutt's Palace Hotel in St. Moritz, Switzerland, and its remarkable staff once again provided a sanctuary for me—to read, to think, to recharge.

In his book *The Prophet*, poet Kahlil Gibran wrote about the sweetness of friendship. I have known that sweetness, and to those friends who have encouraged and sustained me during the challenges of the past eight years, in particular Robert Decherd, Mike Bylen, Bobby Zorn, Boyd Lyles, Mike Madigan, Fabrizio Parrulli, Roman Herzig, Dale Smith, Jim Sterling, Maude Cejudo, Andrea Viacava, Carmelo Carluzzo, and all my tennis buddies—Alan, Fons, Edgar, Pietro, Massimo, Flavio, Drew, Maria Laura, Gonzalo, and Rod—my profound thanks.

Last on my list but first in importance is my family. My dear parents are now gone, but my Italian family—Andrea, Bruna, and Alberto—has filled some of that void, providing one of the great blessings of my life. Children are the ultimate markers of time. When I began this project, my wife, Anna, was pregnant with our first son, Francesco. Rodney would follow two years later. Time spent researching and writing this book was time away from three of the four people in the world who matter most to me. "Daddy is working on his book," Anna would tell them, and somehow, they understood. She did too. She believed in me. She supported me. She covered for me. No one could ever hope for a more loving partner.

This book proved to be the greatest challenge of my career as a storyteller and author due largely to the pressure I felt to pay proper tribute to the Americans buried and remembered at the Netherlands American Cemetery. Getting the story right was the first step, a priority that never diminished in importance. In writing *The Monuments Men,* I hoped that that book would result in the men and women who saved much of civilization's most-valued cultural treasures from the destruction of World War II being honored. I also believed the book could be a catalyst to raise global awareness of the importance of preserving our shared cultural heritage. Fifteen years later, through the work of the Monuments Men and Women Foundation, those goals have been realized, and so much more.

I have no less hope for *Remember Us.* To raise awareness, especially in the United States, of our nation's overseas military cemeteries and memorials and the more than 218,000 Americans who are buried and remembered there? Yes, of course. To visit this special place, the Netherlands American Cemetery, where the Dutch continue to watch over and honor their American liberators? Certainly. But wouldn't it be wonderful if on this Memorial Day, and all those in the future, rather than just thinking about what we lost—U.S. military personnel who died while serving in the United States Armed Forces—we also spend time thinking about what we gained in return: our freedom. Wouldn't it be wonderful if we Americans made time to do what Limburgers have been doing for eighty years and pay a visit to a cemetery in our community and place a flag on the grave of another American who sacrificed their freedom to protect our own?

# WHAT'S IN YOUR ATTIC?

The Monuments Men and Women Foundation is a 501(c)(3) nonprofit organization dedicated to raising global awareness about the importance of respecting and preserving the world's shared cultural heritage. In addition to honoring the service of the World War II veterans known as the Monuments Men and Women, the Foundation continues their mission by working with military veterans, their family members, and others to locate and return some of the hundreds of thousands of still missing works of art and cultural objects to the rightful owners.

The Foundation uses its impartial role to act on behalf of the work of art or cultural object in question, without favoritism or agenda. For its work honoring the historic achievements of the Monuments Men and Women, the Foundation has received numerous awards, including the National Humanities Medal, the highest honor in the United States for work in the humanities.

If you or someone you know has a work of art, cultural object, or historical document taken during the World War II era, or information about such an object, and you wish to follow in the footsteps of the Monuments Men and Women, please contact the Foundation at wwiiart@mmwf.org. The Foundation accepts and maintains confidentiality for those wishing to remain anonymous.

To learn more about the Monuments Men and Women Foundation, please visit us at www.mmwf.org.

# ENDNOTES

## Epigraph

xii  Paschal Fowlkes to men of the 17th Airborne Division, March 23, 1945, in *Chaplain: The World War II Letters of Army Air Corps Chaplain Paschal Depuy Fowlkes*, ed. Rives Fowlkes Carroll (Washington, D.C.: Opus Self Publishing, 2018), p. 272.

## Epigraph

xvii  Archibald MacLeish, "The Young Soldiers Do Not Speak," folder 44, portfolio 242, Rare Book and Special Collections Division, Library of Congress, Washington, D.C.

## Prologue

xix  **Every graveyard tells a story**: Eudora Ramsay Richardson and Sherman Allan, *Quartermaster Supply in the European Theater of Operations in World War II, Volume VII: Graves Registration* (Camp Lee, VA: Quartermaster School, 1948), p. 57. Margraten had 17,742 graves by May 1946. The second largest was Henri-Chapelle American Cemetery, Belgium, with 17,320.

xx  **Beginning in 1947**: Next of kin received a pamphlet from the War Department called *Disposition of World War II Armed Forces Dead*. For repatriation and overseas burial data, see Edward Steere and Thayer M. Boardman, *Final Disposition of World War II Dead, 1945–51* (Washington, D.C.: Historical Branch, Office of the Quartermaster General, 1957), p. 365.

xx  **They include Major General Maurice Rose**: The other five Medal of Honor recipients buried at the Netherlands American Cemetery are Lieutenant Colonel Robert G. Cole; Private First Class Willy F. James Jr.; Private George J. Peters; Private First Class Walter C. Wetzel; and First Lieutenant Walter J. Will.

xx  **The American service members chosen**: The members of Company E, 2nd Battalion, 506th Parachute Infantry, 101st Airborne Division, buried at the Netherlands American Cemetery are: Second Lieutenant James L. Diel; Corporal William H. Dukeman Jr.; First Lieutenant James H. Moore; Private First Class Eugene C. Roman; First Lieutenant Raymond G. Schmitz; and Private First Class Robert Van Klinken.

xxi  **Eighty years later**: Dwight D. Eisenhower interview with Walter Cronkite, CBS television special, "Eisenhower and D-Day," June 1964.

xxiii  **"He is buried"**: Letter, Frieda van Schaïk to Harvard University, October 16,

432

1945, Frieda van Schaïk-Gumn Personal Papers (hereafter Van Schaïk-Gumn Papers).

## Part I: Freedom Lost

1 **In the future days**: Franklin D. Roosevelt, Annual Message to the Congress, January 6, 1941, in *The Public Papers and Addresses of Franklin D. Roosevelt, 1940 Volume: War—and Aid to Democracies*, ed. Samuel I. Rosenman (New York: MacMillan, 1941), p. 672.

## Chapter 1: "It's War!"

3 **Emilie Michiels van Kessenich snapped awake**: See May 10, 1940, entry, pp. 61–62, in the Michiels van Kessenich family's 1939–1940 scrapbook (hereafter MvK Memory Book), located in 22.082, Kroniek Burgemeester Michiels van Kessenich, inv. no. 5; Historisch Centrum Limburg, Maastricht, NL (hereafter HCL); Jenneke Meyer Viol-Michiels van Kessenich interview with Robert M. Edsel, Lanaken, BE, April 26, 2023.

3 **By then, Willem was dressed**: MvK Memory Book, 1939–1940, p. 62.

3 **The German warplanes**: Walter B. Maass, *The Netherlands at War, 1940–1945* (New York: Abelard-Schuman, 1970), pp. 30–31. Quote appears in Louis de Jong, *Het Koninkrijk der Nederlanden in de Tweede Wereldoorlog, Deel 3: Mei '40* (The Hague: Martinus Nijhoff, 1970), pp. 70–72.

4 **The Netherlands had declared neutrality in 1939**: E.H. Brongers, *Oorlog in Zuid-Limburg, 10 mei 1940* (Soesterberg, NL: Uitgeverij Aspekt, 2005), pp. 114–37. A.H. Paape, *Donkere jaren: Episoden uit de geschiedenis van Limburg 1933–1945* (Assen, NL: Van Gorcum & Co., 1969), pp. 14–15.

4 **Last spring**: May 3, May 10, and June 1939 entries in MvK Memory Book, 1939–1940, pp. 17, 25–29, and 61 (reverse side).

4 **"The Prussians!"**: Diary, Hette de Jong, May 10, 1940, entry, 22.001 A, inv. no. 543a, Handschriftencollectie (voormalig) Gemeentearchief Maastricht, HCL (hereafter De Jong Diary).

5 **On Akerstraat**: Brongers, *Oorlog in Zuid-Limburg*, pp. 137–46.

5 **In the basement of the hospital**: As quoted in Diego Mendes de Leon, *Mémoires: Mes mémoires ne sont pas mes confessions*, Vol. 1 (Lanaken, BE: P. Bijnens Drukkerijen b.v.b.a., 1995), no page number, ch. 3.

6 **It was too little resistance**: Brongers, *Oorlog in Zuid-Limburg*, pp. 157–58.

6 **"The same fate"**: De Jong Diary, May 10, 1940, entry.

6 **"Remarkable"**: As quoted in De Jong, *Het Koninkrijk der Nederlanden in de Tweede Wereldoorlog*, pp. 73–74.

6 **Emilie knelt at the makeshift altar**: May 9, 1940, entry in MvK Memory Book, 1939–1940, p. 61 (reverse side).

6 **The next morning**: Frieda Gumn interview with Robert M. Edsel, Over Wallop, UK, May 30, 2016.

6 **"We'll get you for this!"**: Willem C.L. van Schaïk, *Maastricht in Wartime: Resistance Underground* (Utrecht, NL: De Banier, undated), p. 25.

## Chapter 2: Rising Stars

8 **"I've been with this regiment"**: As quoted in Jean Edward Smith, *Eisenhower in War and Peace* (New York: Random House, 2013), pp. 152–53.

8 **Ike had reported to the 15th Infantry**: Smith, *Eisenhower in War and Peace*, pp. 151-53; Carlo D'Este, *Eisenhower: A Soldier's Life* (New York: Henry Holt and Company, 2002), p. 262.

8 **There was plenty of work**: Dwight D. Eisenhower, *Crusade in Europe* (New York: Doubleday & Company, 1948), p. 10.

9 **Eisenhower made things clear**: As quoted in Merle Miller, *Ike the Soldier: As They Knew Him* (New York: G.P. Putnam's Sons, 1987), p. 310.

9 **The 15th Infantry**: D'Este, *Eisenhower*, p. 264. Quote appears in Dwight D. Eisenhower, *At Ease: Stories I Tell to Friends* (Garden City, NY: Doubleday & Company, 1967), p. 237.

10 **He could be harsh**: Bernard L. Larkin, questionnaire, folder 57, box 97, Cornelius Ryan WWII Papers, Ohio University Mahn Center for Archives and Special Collections, Athens, OH (hereafter Ryan Collection). D'Este, *Eisenhower*, pp. 262–63.

10 **In response**: James W. Kenney, "Robert George Cole," attached to Robert G. Cole Official Military Personnel File (hereafter OMPF), National Personnel Records Center, St. Louis, MO (hereafter NPRC).

10 **On May 10, 1940**: Eisenhower, *At Ease*, pp. 237–38; D'Este, *Eisenhower*, pp. 263–65.

11 **The Soviet Red Army**: Lieutenant Colonel David M. Glantz, *The Soviet Airborne Experience*, Research Survey No. 4 (Fort Leavenworth, KS: Combat Studies Institute, 1984), pp. 1–24. Department of the Army Pamphlet No. 20-232: *Airborne Operations: A German Appraisal* (Washington, D.C.: Center of Military History, United States Army, 1982), pp. 1–5.

11 **The most successful drop**: Col. James E. Mrazek, USA (Ret.), *The Fall of Eben Emael: Prelude to Dunkerque* (Novato, CA: Presidio Press, 1991), pp. 135–66.

12 **Soon after, Robert Cole began considering a transfer**: Jeanne Douglas, "It Took Real Courage and Guts to Fight On!" *Austin American-Statesman*, August 8, 1945, p. 2.

## Chapter 3: Mr. and Mrs. Kippenburgemeester

14 **The Michiels van Kessenich family**: See MvK Memory Book, 1939–1940, p. 62.

14 **At first, Emilie and her eight children slept**: Paul Bronzwaer, *Maastricht en Luik bezet: Een comparatief onderzoek naar vijf aspecten van de Duitse bezetting van Maastricht en Luik tijdens de Tweede Wereldoorlog* (Hilversum, NL: Uitgeverij Verloren BV, 2010), p. 73.

15 **"Don't bother your father"**: MvK Memory Book, 1939–1940, p. 67 (reverse side).

15 **In the end**: "Slachtoffers van den oorlog. Vijftien burgers gedood door granaatscherven of door schrik tengevolge van den oorlogstoestand overladen," May 14, 1940, located in MvK Memory Book, 1939–1940, p. 65 (reverse side).

15 **The news was relentlessly awful**: May 18, 1940, entry, MvK Memory Book, 1939–1940, p. 67. See also "De verwoesting te Rotterdam. Oude stad tussen rivier en singels bestaat niet meer," on p. 68 (reverse side) and "Op 46-jarigem leeftijd is overleden prof. mr. dr. R.H.W. Regout S.J.," p. 115 (reverse side), both in MvK Memory Book, 1941–1943, 22.082, Kroniek Burgemeester Michiels van Kessenich, inv. no. 6, HCL. The Catholic Church canonized Father Brandsma as a saint in 2022.

16 **On July 6**: July 6, 1940, entry, MvK Memory Book, 1939–1940, p. 78 (reverse side).

16 **Emilie and Willem had met in college**: Meyer Viol-Michiels van Kessenich, interview.

16 **"I want to be an ambassador"**: Bronzwaer, *Maastricht en Luik bezet*, p. 114.

16 **Emilie smiled**: Meyer Viol-Michiels van Kessenich, interview.

17 **"I've changed my mind"**: Meyer Viol-Michiels van Kessenich, interview.

17 **They were married in 1929**: Trouwboekje, (Wedding book) 16.0674, Familie Michiels van Kessenich Papers (hereafter MvK Papers), inv. no. 473, HCL. Meyer Viol-Michiels van Kessenich, interview.

17 **Later that year**: Trouwboekje, HCL.

17 **By then, Queen Wilhelmina**: F.A. Brunklaus, "Meneer de Burgemeester," in *Meneer de Burgemeester*, eds. Theodorus Arnoldus van Oort et al. (Maastricht: N.V. Leiter-Nypels, 1967), pp. 12–15.

17 **"Being born into a noble family"**: Jenneke Meyer Viol-Michiels van Kessenich, email message to Robert M. Edsel, March 31, 2023.

17 **"Your father may seem important to the city"**: Meyer Viol-Michiels van Kessenich, interview and email message.

18 **Duty. Service. Love and charity**: Meyer Viol-Michiels van Kessenich, interview.

18 **After his return**: On p. 22 of Else Hanöver unpublished memoir, titled "For My Kids, Christmas 2000," in possession of Robert M. Edsel.

18 **Emilie worked to keep her family safe**: Meyer Viol-Michiels van Kessenich, interview.

19 **Her mornings were devoted**: See Caty Verbeek, "Ambassadrice van Margraten, op vleugelwiek naar de Nieuwe Wereld," *Libelle*, no. 9 (June 28, 1946), 16.0674, MvK Papers, inv. no. 657, HCL.

19 **By then, the sale of tea and coffee had been prohibited**: See "Distributie van thee en koffie: Met ingang van heden is het verkoopen dezer artikelen aan den consument verboden," attached to the May 30, 1940, entry, MvK Memory Book, 1939–1940, p. 72 (reverse side).

19 **In November, the Nazis confiscated**: November 13, 1940, entry, MvK Memory Book, 1939–1940, p. 96 (reverse side).

19 **The same month**: Mendes de Leon, *Mémoires*, no page number, chapter 9.

20 **The husband of a friend**: René and Erik van Rijselt and Marjolein Vlieks, *Onvoltooid verleden – Ontrechting en rechtsherstel van Joodse inwoners in de gemeenten Maastricht, Amby en Heer* (Maastricht: Municipality of Maastricht, 2023), p. 83.

20  **In February 1941**: J. Presser, *Ashes in the Wind: The Destruction of Dutch Jewry*, trans. Arnold Pomerans (Detroit: Wayne State University Press, 1988), pp. 45–57.

20  **But what was the man supposed to do?**: Bronzwaer, *Maastricht en Luik bezet*, pp. 303–08.

21  **They listened to Radio Orange**: November 11, 1940, entry, MvK Memory Book, 1939–1940, p. 69.

21  **Bicycle tires were rationed**: See "Distributie van rijwielbanden," attached to March 1, 1941, entry in MvK Memory Book, 1939–1940, p. 105.

21  **Signs appeared in city parks**: Meyer Viol-Michiels van Kessenich, interview.

21  **In August 1941**: August 20, 1941, entry in MvK Memory Book, 1941–1943, p. 31.

22  **They were not doing their duty**: Bronzwaer, *Maastricht en Luik bezet*, pp. 112–17.

22  **Emilie-Hélène, their ninth child**: August 20, 1941, entry, MvK Memory Book, 1941–1943, p. 31; NL-HaNA 2.04.87, inventory number, 4791 Benoeming in Beek, Maastricht, ontslag tijdens bezetting, zuivering, herbenoeming na de bevrijding, rechtsherstel, onderscheidingen, ontslag en krantenknipsels, 1933–1967, document 0061, Nationaal Archief, Den Haag. For information on the Limburg mayors resigning, including Willem, see Paape, *Donkere jaren*, pp. 26–27, and Peter Romijn, *Burgemeesters in oorlogstijd: Besturen onder Duitse bezetting* (Amsterdam: Uitgeverij Balans, Kindle Edition, 2012).

22  **"We'll have no money"**: See Resignation letter, Willem Michiels van Kessenich, in NL-HaNA 2.04.87, inventory number, 4791 Benoeming in Beek, Maastricht, ontslag tijdens bezetting, zuivering, herbenoeming na de bevrijding, rechtsherstel, onderscheidingen, ontslag en krantenknipsels, 1933–1967, document 0061, Nationaal Archief, Den Haag.

22  **The next morning**: Meyer Viol-Michiels van Kessenich, interview.

## Chapter 4: A Way Out

23  **Jefferson Wiggins was born**: In Wiggins's Army personnel file, he lists his birthday as February 22, 1923, in places and February 22, 1925, in others. His mother signed Wiggins's enlistment papers attesting that his birth year was 1923. After the Army discovered that he was underage when he enlisted, however, his mother revealed that his birth year was in fact 1925. See Jefferson Wiggins OMPF, NPRC.

23  **Jefferson's parents**: Mieke Kirkels, *Van Alabama naar Margraten: Herinneringen van grafdelver Jefferson Wiggins* (Maastricht: Drukkerij Walters, 2014), pp. 16, 19.

24  **You never know who *they* are**: Jefferson Wiggins, *Another Generation Almost Forgotten* (Bloomington, IN: Xlibris Corporation, 2003), pp. 20–23; Kirkels, *Van Alabama naar Margraten*, p. 19.

24  **When he was nine**: Jefferson Wiggins interview with Mieke Kirkels, March 2010, transcript, pt. 3, p. 6; Kirkels, *Van Alabama naar Margraten*, p. 55;

Certificate of death, Othel Wiggins, 9 June 1934, Alabama Center for Health Statistics.

24 **A few months after the funeral**: Asterisks have been added, but dialogue is quoted as it appears in Wiggins's autobiography, *Another Generation Almost Forgotten*, pp. 26–27, 185.

25 **"If you ever get a chance to get away from here"**: Based on information in Wiggins, *Another Generation Almost Forgotten*, pp. 20–21.

25 **"How much is it, boy?"**: Exchange based on Wiggins, *Another Generation Almost Forgotten*, pp. 17–18.

26 **The encounter stayed in Jefferson's mind**: Wiggins, *Another Generation Almost Forgotten*, p. 36; Kirkels, *Van Alabama naar Margraten*, p. 16.

27 *Never lie*: Jefferson Wiggins interview with Mieke Kirkels, March 2010, transcript, pt. 1, p. 8; Kirkels, *Van Alabama naar Margraten*, p. 16.

27 **The next day, January 13, 1942**: Jefferson Wiggins interview with Mieke Kirkels, March 2010, transcript, pt. 1, p. 8; Kirkels, *Van Alabama naar Margraten*, p. 17.

27 *At least I'll know my enemy*: Based on information in Wiggins, *Another Generation Almost Forgotten*, p. 46.

## Chapter 5: "Willie"

28 **Bill Hughes shook his head**: Joe Wilson Jr., *The 784th Tank Battalion in World War II: History of an African American Armored Unit in Europe* (Jefferson, NC: McFarland & Company, 2007), p. 12.

28 **His first love was music**: Wilson, *The 784th Tank Battalion in World War II*, p. 12. Family information from birth certificate, William Max Hughes, May 15, 1923, Indianapolis, Indiana; "Court House," *Noblesville Ledger*, June 8, 1939, p. 6.

29 **It hadn't always been that way**: Family information from draft registration, Twidell W. Hughes, June 5, 1917; Obituary, William A. Hazlewood, *Indianapolis News*, March 5, 1946, p. 7.

29 **Then, in the 1920s**: Leonard J. Moore, *Citizen Klansmen: The Ku Klux Klan in Indiana, 1921–1928* (Chapel Hill, NC: University of North Carolina Press, 1991), pp. 6–9, 184–85.

29 **Bill Hughes was one year old**: Wilson, *The 784th Tank Battalion in World War II*, p. 12; Suzette Hackney, "The Story of Attucks—The Shame and the Glory," *Indianapolis Star*, May 15, 2016.

30 **The Black community pooled its pennies**: Wilson, *The 784th Tank Battalion in World War II*, p. 12.

30 **He had taken the civil service examination**: Wilson, *The 784th Tank Battalion in World War II*, p. 12.

30 **He arrived to find**: Wilson, *The 784th Tank Battalion in World War II*, pp. 12–13.

31 **Three days passed**: See Martin Blumenson, ed., *The Patton Papers, 1940–1945* (New York: Da Capo Press, 1974), pp. 50–51.

31 **"This is Billy"**: Wilson, *The 784th Tank Battalion in World War II*, pp. 12–13.

## Chapter 6: The Caves

32 **David "Dave" van Schaïk was an electrical engineer**: Lucie Bastiaens, "'Hij, die zijn naam voor eeuwig verbond aan de Sint-Pietersberg'. Ir. David Cornelis van Schaïk (1888–1972) en de wording van een natuurmonument," in *Studies over de sociaal-economische geschiedenis van Limburg*, eds. Ad Knotter en Willibrord Rutten. (Maastricht: Sociaal Historisch Centrum voor Limburg, 2013), pp. 112–13.

32 **In 1930, Van Schaïk moved his wife and children**: Jacob Carrière and Kees Rauh interview with Robert M. Edsel, Maastricht, September 27, 2023. Frieda van Schaïk-Gumn, *Double Dutch*, –?, p. 20, self-published family history, in Van Schaïk-Gumn Papers.

32 **Pappie lost his heart to the caves**: Gumn, *Double Dutch*, p. 20; Camilla Zéguers, "A Brief Biography of Ir. David Cornelis van Schaïk (Rotterdam 1888–Maastricht 1972): Pioneer of the Sint Pietersberg Caves, Maastricht, South Limburg" (2018), p. 13, in Van Schaïk-Gumn Papers.

33 **Frieda was the youngest of his six children**: Gumn, *Double Dutch*, pp. 11, 20.

33 **It was a peculiar darkness**: Frieda Gumn interview with Robert M. Edsel, Valkenburg, NL, May 1, 2018.

33 **Mostly, though, she was excited**: Gumn, interview, 2016.

34 **That work was why Frieda**: Van Schaïk, *Maastricht in Wartime*, p. 81; Gumn, *Double Dutch*, pp. 23, 41.

37 **Frieda had rebelled**: Gumn, *Double Dutch*, p. 25; Gumn, interview, 2016.

## Chapter 7: Hostages

38 **One of the first things the Germans did**: Meyer Viol-Michiels van Kessenich, interview. Bronzwaer, *Maastricht en Luik bezet*, pp. 112–17. April 8, 1941, entry in MvK Memory Book, 1941–1943, p. 1.

38 **Those in Maastricht were released**: Bronzwaer, *Maastricht en Luik bezet*, p. 309.

38 *Mevrouw: Het wordt laat*: MvK Memory Book, 1939–1940, p. 67 (reverse side).

39 **The Germans continued to take hostages**: Hanöver, "For My Kids," p. 25. P. van Gestel, De laatste Nederlandsche priester die te Dachau stierf. Professor Robert Regout S.J. (Maastricht, publisher unknown, 1947).

39 **Lhoest was among the fortunate**: See p. 125 of MvK Memory Book, 1941–1943.

39 **"Give you a ride?"**: Meyer Viol-Michiels van Kessenich, email message.

39 **A year later**: Bronzwaer, *Maastricht en Luik bezet*, pp. 112–17.

40 **Since the "No Jews" signs**: Meyer Viol-Michiels van Kessenich, interview.

40 **The truth was**: Meyer Viol-Michiels van Kessenich, interview.

40 **Even after D'Ansembourg moved on**: Meyer Viol-Michiels van Kessenich, email message.

41 **"I do not know if my dear children"**: December 1941 entry in MvK Memory Book, 1941–1943, pp. 59 (reverse side)–60.

41 **"A difficult year lies behind us"**: January 1, 1942, entry in MvK Memory Book, 1941–1943, p. 60.

41 **Finally, in March, Manka found a job**: March 7, 1942, entry in MvK Memory Book, 1941–1943, p. 68.

41 **"Jhr. Mr. W. Michiels van Kessenich"**: April 16, 1942, entry in MvK Memory Book, 1941–1943, p. 73.

41 **It had been nine brutal months**: June 30, 1942, entry in MvK Memory Book, 1941–1943, p. 79 (reverse side). Meyer Viol-Michiels van Kessenich, interview.

41 **The big day**: June 30, 1942, entry in MvK Memory Book, 1941–1943, pp. 80–84.

43 *What will life be like*: June 30, 1942, entry in MvK Memory Book, 1941–1943, p. 81 (reverse side).

43 **On July 13**: July 13, 1942, and July 23, 1942, entries in MvK Memory Book, 1941–1943, pp. 87 (reverse side), 89.

43 **Soon after, an article appeared**: July 13, 1942, entry in MvK Memory Book, 1941–1943, p. 87 (reverse side).

## Chapter 8: Pig Paths

44 **Virginia was rich with such old hills**: Rives Fowlkes Carroll telephone interview with Robert M. Edsel, May 12, 2023.

45 **It unsettled him**: Carroll, telephone interview. Classification Questionnaire of Reserve Officers, Paschal D. Fowlkes, June 13, 1942, attached to Fowlkes Chaplain File, Record Group 338, NPRC.

45 **He considered journalism**: Carroll, telephone interview. Carroll, *Chaplain*, p. 1.

45 **He married Elizabeth Rives Williams**: "Miss Williams Becomes Bride of Mr. Fowlkes," *Richmond News Leader*, June 22, 1940, p. 4. Letter from Adrien Busick, May 26, 1942, as quoted in Carroll, *Chaplain*, p. 6.

46 **By then, Pat was ministering to a second congregation**: Carroll, *Chaplain*, p. 6. "Capt. Fowlkes is Killed in Germany," *Richmond Times-Dispatch*, April 9, 1945, p. 7.

46 **He was careful with his parents**: Letter from R.W. Wood, as quoted in Carroll, *Chaplain*, p. 6.

46 **But Nazi Germany's invasion of Western Europe**: As quoted in Carroll, *Chaplain*, p. 6.

46 **A few weeks later**: Letter, Henry K. Sherril, Army and Navy Commission of the Episcopal Church, to the Third Corps Area Chaplain, June 16, 1942, attached to Fowlkes Chaplain File, NPRC.

46 **July 1942 was the month of the first American air raid**: Arthur B. Ferguson, "Rouen-Sotteville No. 1, 17 August 1942," in *The Army Air Forces in World War II, Vol. I: Plans and Early Operations, January 1939 to August 1942*, eds. Wesley Frank Craven and James Lea Cate (Washington, D.C.: Office of Air Force History, 1989), pp. 658–59.

47 **A daylight raid**: James R. Warren, "Fifty Years Ago This Month—In Mid-1942, The Allies Are 'In the Shadows of a Very Black Hour,'" *Seattle Times*, July 5, 1992.

47 **Eisenhower—now Lieutenant General Eisenhower**: DeWitt S. Copp, *Forged in Fire: Strategy and Decisions in the Air War over Europe, 1940–45* (New York: Doubleday, 1982), p. 269.

47 **Soon after, Pat Fowlkes wrote**: Letter, Paschal Fowlkes to Elizabeth Fowlkes, July 26, 1942, as quoted in Carroll, *Chaplain*, p. 9.

48 **In December 1941**: Robert L. Gushwa, *The Best and Worst of Times: The United States Army Chaplaincy, 1920–1945, Volume IV* (Washington, D.C.: Office of the Chief of Chaplains, Department of the Army, 1977), p. 96. Letter, Paschal Fowlkes to Elizabeth Fowlkes, July 28, 1942, as quoted in Carroll, *Chaplain*, p. 11.

48 **"I do not need to tell you"**: Letter, Paschal Fowlkes July 26, 1942, in Carroll, *Chaplain*, p. 10.

## Chapter 9: Risks

49 **When it came to parenting**: Gumn, interview, 2016.

49 **Discipline. Lessons. Sacrifice**: Gumn, *Double Dutch*, p. 14.

49 **If you wanted to talk about nature and science**: Gumn, *Double Dutch*, p. 16.

50 **"We were never entirely sure"**: Zéguers, "A Brief Biography," p. 14.

50 **And there was nothing better**: Gumn, interview, 2016.

50 **It started in 1937**: Camilla Zéguers comments on manuscript, May 5, 2024. Bastiaens, "'Hij, die zijn naam voor eeuwig verbond aan de Sint-Pietersberg,'" p. 115.

50 **"Oh yes"**: Gumn, interview, 2016.

50 **In fact, as the student discovered**: Gumn, *Double Dutch*, p. 20; Gumn, interview, 2016.

51 **To her great disappointment**: Gumn, *Double Dutch*, p. 24; Gumn, interview, 2016.

51 **"If you ever see your father"**: Gumn, *Double Dutch*, p. 23; Gumn, interview, 2016.

52 **The problem, as clearly shown**: Gumn, *Double Dutch*, p. 24.

53 **Frieda never knew if her mother had agreed**: Gumn, interview, 2016.

53 **And Frieda?**: Gumn, interview, 2016; Zéguers comments.

## Chapter 10: Most Popular Boy

54 **Dr. Jamie and his wife**: Catherine H. Lewis, *Horry County, South Carolina, 1730–1993* (Columbia, SC: University of South Carolina Press, 1998), p. 134.

54 **The Nortons had five children**: "Dr. Norton's Rites Today at Conway," *Columbia Record*, July 22, 1950, p. 6.

55 **The boys were six**: "Double Trouble for the Axis: Conway's 'Flying Twins' Soon to Receive Air Force 'Wings,'" *The State*, August 9, 1942, p. 36.

55 **Dr. Jamie bought a piece of sandy scrubland**: Dr. James Norton Spivey telephone interview with Robert M. Edsel, September 18, 2023.

55 **They were chosen "Most Popular Boy"**: Ashley Talley, "'They never spent a night apart:' Conway twins remembered as heroes 75 years after their death in WWII," *WMBF News* (Myrtle Beach), May 17, 2018.

55 **They were roommates**: Kelly Durham, "Side by Side," *The Echo*, Clemson Alumni Association newsletter. Talley, "'They never spent a night apart.'"

56 **When they withdrew**: Lewis, *Horry County*, p. 134.

57 **Or, in the Norton twins' case**: "Double Trouble for the Axis," p. 36.

57 **"Double trouble is in store"**: "Double Trouble for the Axis," p. 36.

58 **"That's stupid, sir"**: Geoffrey Perret, *Winged Victory: The Army Air Forces in World War II* (New York: Random House, 1993), p. 251.

58 **The wing commander**: Carl H. Moore, *Flying the B-26 Marauder Over Europe: Memoir of a World War II Navigator* (Jefferson, NC: McFarland & Company, 2013), p. 49.

58 **Late that night**: Major James N. Openshaw, "The IJmuiden Power Plant Raids of WWII: Airpower Misapplied" (MA thesis, Air Command Staff College, 1987), p. 11.

59 **Stillman watched them depart**: Martin W. Bowman, *U.S. 9th Air Force Bases in Essex, 1943–44* (Barnsley, UK: Pen & Sword, 2010), p. 9.

60 **Forty minutes after takeoff**: Bowman, *U.S. 9th Air Force Bases in Essex*, p. 11; Moore, *Flying the B-26 Marauder Over Europe*, pp. 50–51.

60 **And then the sky exploded**: Moore, *Flying the B-26 Marauder Over Europe*, p. 51.

61 **There was a sudden flash**: Bowman, *U.S. 9th Air Force Bases in Essex*, p. 10.

61 **"Hold it a minute"**: As quoted in Openshaw, "The IJmuiden Power Plant Raids of WWII," p. 11.

61 **They were losing speed**: Bennett W. Longworth to Quartermaster General, U.S. Army, May 22, 1950, attached to Edward R. Norton Individual Deceased Personnel File (hereafter IDPF), NPRC.

62 **Two days later**: Catherine Lewis, "Conway WWII loss included twin brothers," *Sun News*, January 26, 1991.

## Part II: To the Wall

63 *Freedom*: As quoted in the front matter of Omar N. Bradley, *A Soldier's Story* (New York: Random House, 1999), p. i.

## Chapter 11: Hardships and Happier Times

65 **The Americans entered ground combat**: George F. Howe, *The Mediterranean Theater of Operations: Northwest Africa: Seizing the Initiative in the West*, United States Army in World War II series (Washington, D.C.: Center of Military History, United States Army, 1993), pp. 39–53, 679. Charles A. Anderson, *The U.S. Army Campaigns of World War II: Algeria-French Morrocco* (Washington, D.C.: Center of Military History, United States Army, 1993), p. 23. Major General I.S.O. Playfair et al., *The Mediterranean and Middle East, Vol. IV: The Destruction of the Axis Forces in Africa* (London: Her Majesty's Stationary Office, 1966), p. 320.

65 **Around the same time**: Craven and Cate, *Torch to Pointblank*, pp. 224–25.

66 **The biggest battles**: David M. Glantz and Jonathan M. House, *When Titans Clashed: How the Red Army Stopped Hitler* (Lawrence, KS: University

Press of Kansas, 1995), pp. 129–47. Paul Carrell and Günter Böddeker, *Die Gefangenen: Leben und Überleben Deutscher Soldaten hinter Stacheldraht* (Frankfurt am Main: Ullstein, 1996), pp. 240–41.

66 **On February 5, on Hitler's orders**: William L. Shirer, *The Rise and Fall of the Third Reich: A History of Nazi Germany* (New York: Simon and Schuster, 1960), p. 933.

66 **The Germans had assumed**: Louis P. Lochner, ed. and trans., *The Goebbels Diaries, 1942–1943* (New York: Doubleday & Company, 1948), p. 434.

67 **By spring 1943**: P.M.M.A. Bronzwaer, *Maastricht bevrijd! En toen?*, Deel 1 (Assen, NL: Van Gorcum, 1989), p. 26.

67 **They looted houses**: Hanöver, "For My Kids," p. 32.

67 **On April 30**: B.A. Sijes, *De Arbeidsinzet: De gedwongen arbeid van Nederlanders in Duitsland, 1940–1945* (The Hague: SDU Uitgeverij, 1990), pp. 672–73.

67 **Again, as with the Amsterdam ghetto uprisings in early 1941**: Zéguers, "A Brief Biography," p. 20.

67 **By the time the strike was suppressed**: Gumn, *Double Dutch*, pp. 17, 20.

68 **Frieda's mother**: Gumn, interview, 2016; Gumn, *Double Dutch*, p. 14. Zéguers comments.

68 **"Pull up your socks"**: Gumn, *Double Dutch*, p. 40.

68 **In Arnhem**: Gumn, interview, 2018; Gumn, *Double Dutch*, pp. 35, 91; Zéguers comments.

69 **Peter assumed they would marry**: Gumn, interview, 2016; Gumn, *Double Dutch*, p. 35.

69 **A month later, Moekie had a stroke**: Gumn, *Double Dutch*, p. 40.

69 **It was summer**: Gumn, interview, 2018

70 **Before the occupation**: Gumn, *Double Dutch*, pp. 16–17.

71 **Late summer meant apples in the orchards**: Bronzwaer, *Maastricht bevrijd*, Deel 1, p. 40.

71 **At night, she climbed to the attic window**: Gumn, interview, 2016. For descriptions of Limburgers experiencing Royal Air Force missions against Aachen, see Paape, *Donkere jaren*, pp. 30–32.

72 **"They got him"**: Van Schaïk, *Maastricht in Wartime*, p. 47.

## Chapter 12: A New Arrival

74 **"I know how hard your lot is"**: Letter, Paschal Fowlkes to Elizabeth Fowlkes, March 29, 1943, in Carroll, *Chaplain*, p. 45.

74 **"All I think about now"**: Letter, Paschal Fowlkes to Elizabeth Fowlkes, April 24, 1943, in Carroll, *Chaplain*, p. 51.

## Chapter 13: Basic

75 **Bill Hughes's draft number**: Wilson, *The 784th Tank Battalion in World War II*, p. 13.

75 **While the U.S. Army**: George S. Patton Jr., *War As I Knew It* (Boston: Houghton Mifflin Company, 1947), p. 160. Ulysses Lee, *Special Studies: The Employment*

*of Negro Troops*, United States Army in World War II series (Washington, D.C.: Center of Military History, United States Army, 2001), p. 675.

76 **The 758th was the first**: Dale E. Wilson, "The Army's Segregated Tank Battalions in World War II," *Army History*, no. 32 (Fall 1994): 14.

76 **"I haven't been trained to wear a uniform"**: As quoted in Wilson, *The 784th Tank Battalion in World War II*, p. 21.

76 **A mistake had been made**: Wilson, *The 784th Tank Battalion in World War II*, p. 21.

76 **Life in the Jim Crow Deep South**: Wilson, *The 784th Tank Battalion in World War II*, p. 22.

77 **The nearby town of Alexandria**: William M. Simpson, "A Tale Untold? The Alexandria, Louisiana, Lee Street Riot (January 10, 1942)," *Louisiana History* 35, no. 2 (Spring 1994): 133–49.

78 **The report only heightened**: As quoted in Wilson, *The 784th Tank Battalion in World War II*, p. 22.

78 **Many refused to take their leave**: Wilson, *The 784th Tank Battalion in World War II*, p. 22.

## Chapter 14: The Library

80 **In summer 1943**: Wiggins, *Another Generation Almost Forgotten*, pp. 40–41.

80 **He sensed, though**: Wiggins, *Another Generation Almost Forgotten*, p. 42.

81 **Eventually, a woman stopped him**: Based on information in Wiggins, *Another Generation Almost Forgotten*, p. 43.

81 **It wouldn't have mattered what she recommended**: Jefferson Wiggins interview with Mieke Kirkels, March 2010, transcript, pt. 1, p. 9; Wiggins, *Another Generation Almost Forgotten*, p. 43.

81 **Whenever Sergeant Wiggins thought of his schooling**: Jefferson Wiggins interview with Mieke Kirkels, March 2010, transcript, pt. 1, p. 9; Kirkels, *Van Alabama naar Margraten*, p. 22.

## Chapter 15: Floating Objects

83 **On July 26, 1943**: James A. Norton IDPF, NPRC.

## Chapter 16: A Welcome Surprise

84 **Chaplain Paschal Fowlkes arrived**: Colonel Mark C. Vlahos, *"Men Will Come": A History of the 314th Troop Carrier Group, 1942–1945* (Hoosick Falls, NY: Merriam Press, 2019), pp. 51–54.

84 **"We have to stand in line"**: Letter, Paschal Fowlkes to Lucy Fowlkes, May 23, 1943, in Carroll, *Chaplain*, p. 63.

84 **He traveled to hospitals**: Letter, Paschal Fowlkes to Lucy Fowlkes, May 25, 1943, and Paschal Fowlkes to Elizabeth Fowlkes, May 26, 1943, both in Carroll, *Chaplain*, pp. 64–66.

84 **They were training**: Vlahos, *"Men Will Come,"* pp. 54, 56–58.

85 **And then, suddenly**: Letter, Paschal Fowlkes to Elizabeth Fowlkes, August 10, 1943, in Carroll, *Chaplain*, p. 98.

85  **After his prayer**: Letter, Paschal Fowlkes to Elizabeth Fowlkes, August 10, 1943, in Carroll, *Chaplain*, pp. 98–99.

86  **"We were the first craft"**: Letter, Paschal Fowlkes to Elizabeth Fowlkes, August 10, 1943, in Carroll, *Chaplain*, p. 98.

86  **His heart, though**: Letter, Paschal Fowlkes to Elizabeth Fowlkes, August 10, 1943, in Carroll, *Chaplain*, p. 99.

86  **"That is the easiest part"**: Letter, Paschal Fowlkes to Elizabeth Fowlkes, August 10, 1943, in Carroll, *Chaplain*, p. 99.

86  **The paratroopers did their job**: Vlahos, *"Men Will Come,"* pp. 64–69.

86  **Two days later**: Lieutenant Colonel Albert N. Garland and Howard McGaw Smyth, *The Mediterranean Theater of Operations: Sicily and the Surrender of Italy*, United States Army in World War II series (Washington, D.C.: Center of Military History, United States Army, 1993), pp. 177, 181–82. For the Axis evacuation, see Carlo D'Este, *Bitter Victory: The Battle for Sicily, 1943* (New York: Harper, 2008), pp. 503–22.

87  **On September 1**: Letter, Paschal Fowlkes to Lucy Fowlkes, September 4, 1943, in Carroll, *Chaplain*, p. 109. For the Salerno anecdote, see War Department Historical Division, *Salerno: American Operations from the Beaches to the Volturno, 9 September–6 October 1943* (Washington, D.C.: Center of Military History, United States Army, 1990), p. 19.

87  **It was at some point**: Letter, Elizabeth Fowlkes to Paschal Fowlkes, August 24, 1943, in Carroll, *Chaplain*, p. 106.

## Chapter 17: Memory Books

88  **On May 13, 1943**: Bronzwaer, *Maastricht bevrijd*, Deel 1, p. 26. June 19, 1943, entry in MvK Memory Book, 1941–1943, p. 134 (reverse side).

88  **They also received a secret written report**: MvK Memory Book, 1943–1945, p. 63, in 22.082, Kroniek Burgemeester Michiels van Kessenich, inv. no. 7, HCL.

88  **She had always kept a pile**: Bronzwaer, *Maastricht bevrijd*, Deel 1, p. 123.

89  **She went down to the first floor**: MvK Memory Book, 1943–1945, pp. 62–63. Meyer Viol-Michiels van Kessenich, interview.

89  **She tipped the report on Sicily into her latest book**: Emilie placed the news about Sicily into her memory book in September 1944. See MvK Memory Book, 1943–1945, p. 63.

## Chapter 18: Hope Overhead

90  **The first major daylight raid**: Craven and Cate, *Torch to Pointblank*, p. 682. Missing Air Crew Report 265, First Lieutenant Arthur Sugas, August 18, 1943, Entry A1 2109B, Record Group 92, National Archives and Records Administration, College Park, MD (hereafter NARA).

90  **An hour later**: Craven and Cate, *Torch to Pointblank*, p. 682.

91  **Two months later**: Craven and Cate, *Torch to Pointblank*, p. 699. Gumn, interview, 2016.

92  **Ten miles away**: Eduard Foitzik interview with Wim Slangen, February 16, 2017, "Eyewitnesses Then and Now," accessed April 9, 2018, http://home .planet.nl/~slang075/Wim-Slangen/Breeden-eye-witnesses.html.

92  **Heinz Michels**: "Eyewitnesses Then and Now," accessed April 9, 2018, http:// home.planet.nl/~slang075/Wim-Slangen/Breeden-eye-witnesses.html.

92  **Klara Wauters**: "Eyewitnesses Then and Now," accessed April 9, 2018, http:// home.planet.nl/~slang075/Wim-Slangen/Breeden-eye-witnesses.html.

93  **"Ride?" a Dutch coal dealer asked the pilot**: George C. Kuhl, *Wrong Place! Wrong Time! The 305th Bomb Group & the 2nd Schweinfurt Raid, October 14, 1943* (Atglen, PA: Schiffer Publishing, Ltd., 1993), p. 148.

93  **He was tail gunner Dominic Lepore**: Missing Air Crew Report 1034, McDarby crew, October 16, 1943, Entry A1 2109B, Record Group 92, NARA. Kuhl, *Wrong Place! Wrong Time!*, p. 148.

93  **The next morning**: Kuhl, *Wrong Place! Wrong Time!*, p. 148.

94  **A few weeks later**: "Robert G. Wells," *American Air Museum in Britain*, accessed May 6, 2018, https://www.americanairmuseum.com/archive/person /robert-g-wells.

## Chapter 19: The Message

95  **The plane piloted by The Twins' commander**: Marilyn Jeffers Walton and Michael C. Eberhardt, *From Interrogation to Liberation: A Photographic Journey Stalag Luft III—the Road to Freedom* (Bloomington, IN: AuthorHouse, 2014), p. 158; Moore, *Flying the B-26 Marauder Over Europe*, p. 51.

96  *Report received*: Telegram attached to James A. Norton IDPF, NPRC.

## Chapter 20: Peasants and the Powerful

97  **In late October**: Letter, Paschal Fowlkes to family, October 29, 1943, in Carroll, *Chaplain*, p. 123.

97  **He was frustrated**: Letter, Paschal Fowlkes to Elizabeth Fowlkes, October 16, 1943, in Carroll, *Chaplain*, p. 117.

97  **The Soviets**: Letter, Paschal Fowlkes to Elizabeth Fowlkes, October 16, 1943, in Carroll, *Chaplain*, p. 118.

98  **"I am afraid that all my life"**: Letter, Paschal Fowlkes to Elizabeth Fowlkes, October 16, 1943, in Carroll, *Chaplain*, p. 118.

98  **In late November**: Letter, Paschal Fowlkes to Elizabeth Fowlkes, November 26, 1943, in Carroll, *Chaplain*, p. 130.

99  **A few weeks before**: Letter, Paschal Fowlkes to Elizabeth Fowlkes, November 26, 1943, in Carroll, *Chaplain*, p. 130.

99  **On December 8**: Letter, Paschal Fowlkes to Elizabeth Fowlkes, undated, in Carroll, *Chaplain*, pp. 132–35.

100  **As always, though**: Letter, Paschal Fowlkes to Elizabeth Fowlkes, November 15, 1943, in Carroll, *Chaplain*, pp. 128–29.

100  *Betsy arrived at 2 a.m.*: Letter, Elizabeth Fowlkes to Paschal Fowlkes, August 24, 1943, in Carroll, *Chaplain*, p. 106.

## Chapter 21: An Egg

101 **Jenneke stood in the doorway**: Meyer Viol-Michiels van Kessenich, interview, and Meyer Viol-Michiels van Kessenich email message to Robert M. Edsel, August 5, 2023. See also the article "Opening Centrale Keuken. Een sociaal, uit den nood der tijden geboren werk," in MvK Memory Book, 1941–1943, p. 11 (reverse side).

101 **"I got one!"**: Meyer Viol-Michiels van Kessenich, August 5, 2023, email.

102 **But at the market**: Jenneke Meyer Viol-Michiels van Kessenich email message to Robert M. Edsel, September 25, 2018.

102 **"We should play a game then"**: Based on information from Meyer Viol-Michiels van Kessenich, August 5, 2023, email.

## Chapter 22: A Miracle

104 **At 7:14 a.m. on April 29, 1944**: Missing Air Crew Report 4944, First Lieutenant Bill F. Moore crew, May 3, 1944, Entry A1 2109B, Record Group 92, NARA.

104 **The Luftwaffe was hunting that morning**: John L. Low Jr., "The Brave Dutch," unpublished manuscript in possession of Robert M. Edsel, p. 4. Wolter Noordman, *Luchtalarm op de Veluwe* (Amsterdam: VBK Media, 2002), pp. 15–16.

104 **But then another engine blew**: Low, "The Brave Dutch," p. 3; Missing Air Crew Report 4944.

105 **The ship had dropped**: Low, "The Brave Dutch," pp. 3–4.

106 **It was gone**: Low, "The Brave Dutch," p. 4.

106 **He breathed a sigh of relief**: Low, "The Brave Dutch," p. 4.

106 **By early evening**: Low, "The Brave Dutch," pp. 4–5.

107 **Low reached for his language card**: Low, "The Brave Dutch," pp. 5–8.

107 **Low thought of his wife and parents**: Low, "The Brave Dutch," pp. 8–10.

108 **"If you tell me your wife's name and address"**: Low, "The Brave Dutch," pp. 12–13.

108 **"English?" the man whispered**: Low, "The Brave Dutch," p. 14.

109 **"Where did you learn to speak English?"**: Low, "The Brave Dutch," pp. 14–15.

109 **"One more question"**: Low, "The Brave Dutch," p. 16.

## Chapter 24: Mother

111 **Shortly after the crash**: Low, "The Brave Dutch," pp. 18–19.

112 **The two men talked over their situation**: Low, "The Brave Dutch," p. 19.

112 **"I hate to think"**: Low, "The Brave Dutch," p. 7.

112 **Bill Moore didn't talk much**: Enlisted Record, Bill F. Moore, December 20, 1941, attached to Bill F. Moore IDPF.

113 **"I wish I was a soldier"**: Low, "The Brave Dutch," p. 20.

113 **"Now," she said**: Low, "The Brave Dutch," pp. 20–21, 23.

113 **They arrived at the safe house**: Low, "The Brave Dutch," pp. 22–23.

113 **Aart took them to the attic**: Low, "The Brave Dutch," pp. 24–26, 29.

114 **"Coffee?"**: Low, "The Brave Dutch," pp. 29–30.

114 **When Dick finally returned**: Low, "The Brave Dutch," p. 31.

115 **John Low was energetic**: Jodie and Rhes Low telephone interview with Robert M. Edsel, June 8, 2023.

115 **"The invasion"**: Based on information in Low, "The Brave Dutch," p. 31.

## Chapter 25: Pain

116 **He had written the Army Quartermaster Corps**: Letter, James A. Norton to Senator Burnet A. Maybank, February 29, 1944, attached to James A. Norton IDPF.

116 **He was not naive**: Letter, James A. Norton to Lieutenant Colonel John R. Murphy, n.d., attached to James A. Norton IDPF.

117 **By April 1944, Dr. Jamie's pain had turned to anger**: Letter, James A. Norton to Quartermaster General, April 18, 1944, attached to James A. Norton IDPF.

117 **Finally, on April 15, 1944**: Letter, Effects Quartermaster, ETOUSA, to Mrs. James A. Norton, March 21, 1944, attached to James A. Norton IDPF.

118 **In the middle of the night**: April 16, 1944, entry in MvK Memory Book, 1943–1945, p. 25.

## Chapter 26: D-Day

119 **"You are going to command Overlord"**: As quoted in Smith, *Eisenhower in War and Peace*, p. 318.

119 **Overlord, designed by a joint Anglo-American military staff**: Samuel Eliot Morrison, *History of United States Naval Operations in World War II, Vol. XI: The Invasion of France and Germany, 1944–1945* (Boston: Little, Brown and Company, 1957), pp. 27–32. Gordon A. Harrison, *The European Theater of Operations: Cross-Channel Attack*, United States Army in World War II series (Washington, D.C.: Center of Military History, United States Army, 1993), pp. 158–97. Headquarters, United States European Command fact sheet, "D-Day: The Beaches," accessed August 29, 2022, https://dod.defense.gov /Portals/1/features/2016/0516_dday/docs/d-day-fact-sheet-the-beaches.pdf.

120 **"Is there any reason"**: Tim Rives, "'Ok, We'll go': Just What Did Ike Say When He Launched the D-Day Invasion 70 Years Ago?" *Prologue* 46, no. 1 (Spring 2014): 37–43.

120 **He shook their hands**: Kay Summersby Morgan, *Past Forgetting: My Love Affair with Dwight D. Eisenhower* (New York: Simon and Schuster, 1976), pp. 190–91.

120 **He was surprised**: Biographic file, Lieutenant Colonel Robert G. Cole, Don F. Pratt Museum, U.S. Army Center of Military History, Fort Campbell, KY.

120 **Ike, in his crisp service uniform**: In the fleeting moment caught on film, Cole says to Eisenhower: "The men did all the tasks, sir," and "There's a lot of men up there."

121 **"They say you never"**: Letter, Paschal Fowlkes to family, September 25, 1944, in Carrol, *Chaplain*, pp. 192–94.

121 **"Full victory"**: Order of the Day, Supreme Headquarters, Allied Expeditionary

Force, June 6, 1944, reproduced in Forrest C. Pogue, *The European Theater of Operations: The Supreme Command*, United States Army in World War II series (Washington, D.C.: Office of the Chief of Military History, Department of the Army, 1954), p. 545.

122 **"Well," he said**: Morgan, *Past Forgetting*, p. 191.

122 **He went back to his cottage**: As quoted in D'Este, *Eisenhower*, p. 527.

123 **Cole chuckled**: Wright Bryan, NBC Radio, D-Day broadcast, June 6, 1944, folder 2, box 37, William Wright Bryan Papers, Clemson University Libraries Special Collections and Archives, Clemson, SC.

123 **"All set?"**: Bryan broadcast.

124 **The 3rd Battalion was supposed to parachute into Drop Zone A**: War Department Historical Division, *Utah Beach to Cherbourg, 6–27 June 1944* (Washington, D.C.: Center of Military History, United States Army, 1990), p. 17; Carl Shilleto, *Utah Beach – St. Mere Eglise: VII Corps, 82nd and 101st Airborne Divisions* (Barnsley, UK: Leo Cooper, 2001), p. 129.

124 **Cole knocked on a farmhouse door**: S.L.A. Marshall, *Night Drop: The American Airborne Invasion of Normandy* (Boston: Little, Brown and Company, 1962), p. 213.

124 **It was some time after 2:00 a.m.**: Marshall, *Night Drop*, pp. 213–14.

124 **Around 4:00 a.m.**: Marshall, *Night Drop*, pp. 213–14; Harrison, *Cross-Channel Attack*, pp. 280-81.

## Chapter 27: News

126 **In Maastricht, the local collaborationist newspaper**: June 7, 1944, entry in MvK Memory Book, 1943–1945, p. 36.

126 **"Where did you get this?"**: Based on information from Gumn, interview, 2016.

## Chapter 28: Purple Heart Lane

127 **Robert George Cole was born into a military family**: Obituary, Clarence Cole, *Marysville Advocate*, August 22, 1918, pg. 1; Clarence Cole to Dr. C.E. Yount, n.d., published in *The Military Surgeon: Journal of the Association of Military Surgeons of the United States* 33, no. 1 (July 1913): 545.

127 **Clarence Cole died when Robert was three**: Douglas, "It Took Real Courage," *Austin American Statesmen*, August 8, 1945, pg. 1. Clarence Cole death certificate, August 8, 1918, entry in *Directory of Deceased American Physicians, 1804–1929*, ed. Arthur W. Hafner (Chicago: American Medical Association, 1993).

129 **"Don't cry"**: Joseph L. Galloway and Douglas Pasternak, "The Warrior Class," *U.S. News and World Report* 127, no. 1 (July 5, 1999): 26–32.

129 **The operation began at 3:00 p.m.**: Harrison, *Cross-Channel Attack*, pp. 357–59.

130 **"We're going"**: John C. McManus, *The Americans at Normandy: The Summer of 1944—From the Normandy Beaches to Falaise* (New York: Forge, 2004), p. 111.

131 **"What's wrong, fellas?"**: Mark Bando, *101st Airborne: The Screaming Eagles at Normandy* (Minneapolis: Zenith Press, 2007), p. 85.

131 **"Reload rifles and fix bayonets"**: Joseph L. Lofthouse interview with Wayne Gilchrest et al. (AFC/2001/001/60439), Veterans History Project, American Folklife Center, Library of Congress, Washington, D.C.

131 **"We were scared to death"**: Lofthouse, interview.

## Chapter 29: Homecoming

132 **In the heat of summer**: Van Schaïk, *Maastricht in Wartime*, p. 90.

132 **Since the D-Day landings**: Gumn, *Double Dutch*, p. 26.

133 **The Americans and their allies**: Casualty figures based on the most authoritative research to date, the Necrology Project Database, National D-Day Memorial, https://www.dday.org/learn/necrology-project/#database.

133 **The trip through the caves**: Van Schaïk, *Maastricht in Wartime*, pp. 90–91.

134 **The house was full of visitors**: Zéguers comments.

134 **He was in Maastricht**: Van Schaïk, *Maastricht in Wartime*, p. 94.

134 **Wim heard the carillon of the bells**: Van Schaïk, *Maastricht in Wartime*, p. 97.

135 **And then one evening**: Van Schaïk, *Maastricht in Wartime*, pp. 104–05.

## Chapter 30: Trust

136 **"We gotta go"**: Based on information in Low, "The Brave Dutch," pp. 34–35.

## Chapter 31: Exodus

139 **On August 18**: See the article "Anglo-Amerikaanse luchtaanval op Maastricht, Reeds 84 dooden geborgen en meer dan 150 gewonden," August 18, 1944, entry in MvK Memory Book, 1943–1945, p. 49.

139 **Emilie's son Eduard was slightly wounded**: MvK Memory Book, 1943–1945, p. 49.

139 **Ninety-two people were dead**: Bronzwaer, *Maastricht bevrijd*, Deel 1, p. 32. See also the misdated August 21, 1944, entry in De Jong Diary, pp. 63–65.

139 **"A fearful smell"**: De Jong Diary, August 21, 1944, entry.

140 **A few days later, the leading edge of the German exodus**: Bronzwaer, *Maastricht bevrijd*, Deel 1, p. 34.

141 **"Aachen!"**: De Jong Diary, September 3, 1944, entry.

141 **"What is the matter, Oma?"**: Mieke Kirkels, ed., *Else Hanöver: Oorlogsjaren in Maastricht—War Years in Maastricht* (Maastricht: Stichting Akkers van Margraten, 2009), pp. 17, 40.

142 **By the evening of September 7**: De Jong Diary, September 5, 1944, entry.

142 **That evening**: De Jong Diary, September 7, 1944, entry.

## Chapter 32: Liberation

144 **For four days, an eerie quiet enveloped Maastricht**: Gumn, interview, 2016.

144 **"Get the flag"**: Gumn, interview, 2016.

145 **"So ein Witz"**: Van Schaïk, *Maastricht in Wartime*, p. 25.

145 **The next day, a Belgian Resistance fighter**: September 13, 1944, entry in MvK Memory Book, 1943–1945, p. 58.

145 **A few hours later, out of a second-floor window**: September 13, 1944, entry in MvK Memory Book, 1943–1945, p. 57 (reverse side).

146 **Dave van Schaïk snapped awake**: This vignette is attributed to Wim, but he was in Rotterdam during the German retreat from Limburg. It stands to reason that it was a family story he inadvertently misremembered fifty years after the event took place. For that anecdote, see Van Schaïk, *Maastricht in Wartime*, p. 35.

146 **The morning of September 13**: Bronzwaer, *Maastricht bevrijd*, Deel 1, pp. 44–46.

147 **And then a shaking**: Bronzwaer, *Maastricht bevrijd*, Deel 1, p. 48.

147 **Down the block, an eight-year-old boy was swept up**: Paul Bronzwaer interview with Robert M. Edsel, January 31, 2023.

148 **Dave van Schaïk sent Frieda down the road**: Gumn, interview, 2016.

149 **"Look!" Frieda yelled**: Gumn, *Double Dutch*, p. 28.

149 **Along the road, the Dutch stepped from their doors**: Henk Boersma et al., *De Bevrijding van Eijsden-Margraten in September 1944* (Gemeente Eijsden-Margraten, 2015), p. 121.

150 **"Can we hold the baby?"**: Gumn, interview, 2016.

151 **At 10:00 a.m., the Michiels van Kessenich family raised the Dutch flag**: September 14, 1944, entry in MvK Memory Book, 1943–1945, p. 59.

151 **A crash from the white house**: September 14, 1944, entry in MvK Memory Book, 1943–1945, p. 64 (reserve side).

## Chapter 33: Hell's Highway

153 **Jacob Herman Sr.**: Application for Enrollment in a Nonreservation School, Jacob Herman, folder 5155, box 130, entry 1327, Record Group 75, NARA. "Jake Herman, Colorful Indian Clown at Rodeos, Will Retire," *Argus-Leader*, August 14, 1944, p. 3.

153 **Then, in late summer 1942**: Jori Videc, Sebastiaan Vonk, and Arie-Jan van Hees, *De Gezichten van Margraten: Zij bleven voor altijd jong* (Zutphen, NL: Walburg Pers, 2020), p. 85.

154 **A few weeks later**: Patrick Lee, *Tribal Laws, Treaties, and Government: A Lakota Perspective* (Bloomington, IN: iUniverse, 2013), pp. 46–47. Kimberly Greager, "A Lakota Patriot: Rex Leo Herman," *Native Sun News*, November 7, 2018, https://www.nativesunnews.today/articles/a-lakota-patriot-rex-leo-herman-2/.

154 **Jacob enlisted the next summer**: "Service Shorts," *Rapid City Journal*, May 11, 1944, p. 6. "Colorful Indian Clown at Rodeos, Will Retire," p. 3.

154 **His mother didn't want him to go**: Lee, *Tribal Laws, Treaties, and Government*, p. 46.

154 **"Don't do it"**: Based on information in Lee, *Tribal Laws, Treaties, and Government*, p. 46.

155 **The Westwall**: Charles B. MacDonald, *The European Theater of Operations: The Siegfried Line Campaign*, United States Army in World War II series (Washington, D.C.: Center of Military History, United States Army, 1993), pp. 30–31.

156 **When Lieutenant Colonel Robert Cole**: Bruce Cole telephone interview with Robert M. Edsel, November 29, 2023.

156 **Operation Market Garden**: MacDonald, *Siegfried Line Campaign*, p. 132.

156 **And so, at 1:00 p.m.**: MacDonald, *Siegfried Line Campaign*, pp. 145–47.

157 **Cole's plane flew into ground fire**: Bruce Cole comments on manuscript, April 29, 2024. MacDonald, *Siegfried Line Campaign*, pp. 146–47. S.L.A. Marshall, *Battle at Best* (New York: William Morrow and Company, 1963), pp. 13–14. John C. McManus, *September Hope: The American Side of a Bridge Too Far* (New York: NAL Caliber, 2012), pp. 155–56.

159 **He called for air support**: Marshall, *Battle at Best*, pp. 24–25. Letter, John E. Fitzgerald to P.M. Pulles, November 17, 1988, in Robert G. Cole OMPF, NPRC.

159 **His men were stunned**: McManus, *September Hope*, pp. 189–91. George E. Koskimaki, *Hell's Highway: Chronicle of the 101st Airborne Division in the Holland Campaign, September–November 1944* (Havertown, PA: Casemate, 2003), pp. 146–47. John Fitzgerald, questionnaire, folder 44, box 97, Ryan Collection.

160 **The next day**: Phil Nordyke, *All American, All the Way: From Market Garden to Berlin, The Combat History of the 82nd Airborne Division in World War II* (Beverly, MA: Voyageur Press, 2010), pp. 88–89.

161 **It was a coldness shared by Allie Mae Cole**: Cole, telephone interview.

162 **Jacob "Sonny" Herman died a twentieth-century death**: Lee, *Tribal Laws, Treaties, and Government*, p. 47. Marla Herman telephone interview with Casey Shelton, June 15, 2024.

## Part III: Homefront Limburg

163 *The soldier is the Army*: Patton, *War as I Knew It*, p. 335.

## Chapter 34: The Process

165 **And that's before considering**: Stetson Conn, "Highlights of Mobilization, World War II, 1938–1942," file number 2-3.7 AF.B, March 10, 1959, Historical Manuscripts Collection, Center of Military History, United States Army; Mark Skinner Watson, *The War Department: Chief of Staff: Prewar Plans and Preparations*, United States Army in World War II series (Washington, D.C.: Center of Military History, United States Army, 1991), p. 127; Naval History and Heritage Command, "US Ship Force Levels, 1898–present," last modified November 17, 2017, https://www.history.navy.mil/research/histories/ship -histories/us-ship-force-levels.html#1938; Harry C. Thomson and Lida Mayo, *The Ordnance Department: Procurement and Supply*, United States Army in World War II series (Washington, D.C.: Center of Military History, United States Army, 1991), pp. 224–25.

165 **Less than five years later**: Morrison, *Invasion of France and Germany*, p. 77. Wesley Frank Craven and James Lea Cate, eds., *The Army Air Forces in World War II, Vol. III: Europe: Argument to V-E Day, January 1944 to May*

*1945* (Washington, D.C.: Office of Air Force History, 1983), p. 185. U.S. Department of Labor, Bureau of Labor Statistics, October 1944.

165 **And planes and boats were only the biggest**: Peter Caddick-Adams, *Sand and Steel: The D-Day Invasion and the Liberation of France* (Oxford: Oxford University Press, 2019), p. xli.

166 **And this doesn't include**: Caddick-Adams, *Sand and Steel*, p. xli. For casualty figures, see Department of the Army, *American Battle Casualties and Nonbattle Deaths in World War II, Final Report, 7 December 1941 – 31 December 1946.*

166 **This emphasis on respectful burial**: See Drew Gilpin Faust, *This Republic of Suffering: Death and the American Civil War* (New York: Alfred A. Knopf, 2008), pp. 61–101.

167 **President Abraham Lincoln's Gettysburg Address:** Don E. Fehrenbacher, ed., *Lincoln: Selected Speeches and Writings* (New York: Vintage Books, 1992), p. 405.

168 **In practice**: Michael Sledge, *Soldier Dead: How We Recover, Identify, Bury, & Honor Our Military Fallen* (New York: Columbia University Press, 2005), p. 34.

168 **Most countries developed**: Leo P. Hirrel, "The Beginnings of the Quartermaster Graves Registration Service," *Army Sustainment Magazine* 46, no. 4 (July–August, 2014): 64–67. Jeroen Geurst, *Cemeteries of the Great War by Sir Edwin Lutyens* (Rotterdam: 010 Publishers, 2010), p. 289.

169 **On September 11, 1943**: Edward Steere, *The Graves Registration Service in World War II*, QMC Historical Studies series, no. 21 (Washington, D.C.: Historical Section, Office of the Quartermaster General, 1951), pp. 71–72.

169 **The process began**: War Department Field Manual 10-63: *Graves Registration* (Washington, D.C.: United States Government Printing Office, 1945), p. 19.

170 **Once the pace of operations**: FM 10-63, p. 20.

170 **In the heat of summer**: See p. 3 of Charles D. Butte, "Graves Registration During World War II in Europe: 603 Quartermaster Graves Registration Company," box 1, folder 6, Charles D. Butte Collection, Betsey B. Creekmore Special Collections and University Archives, University of Tennessee, Knoxville, TN.

170 **"As gruesome as it may sound"**: Butte, "Graves Registration During World War II," p. 3.

170 **At the collecting point**: FM 10-63, p. 19.

171 **Initially, the Wehrmacht**: Col. Theodore W. Parker et al., *Conquer: The Story of Ninth Army, 1944–1945* (Washington, D.C.: Infantry Journal Press, 1947), pp. 102–03; William F. Ross and Charles F. Romanus, *The Technical Services: The Quartermaster Corps: Operations in the War against Germany*, United States Army in World War II series (Washington, D.C.: Center of Military History, United States Army, 1991), pp. 689–90.

171 **Of course, it was impossible**: British Army burial report, n.d., attached to Robert G. Cole IDPF.

172 **Lieutenant General William Hood Simpson**: Letter, Eisenhower to George C. Marshall, January 14, 1945, in *The Papers of Dwight David Eisenhower,*

*Volume IV: The War Years*, eds. Louis Galambos and Daun van Ee (Baltimore: The Johns Hopkins Press, 1970), document 2238.

172 **General Simpson made a promise**: Parker et al., *Conquer*, pp. 102–03.

173 **And so, in the first week of October 1944**: Joseph James Shomon, *Crosses in the Wind: Graves Registration Service in the Second World War* (New York: Stratford House, Inc., 1947), pp. 61–63.

174 **When Van Laar**: Jan Hendriks and Hans Koenen, *D-Day in South Limburg: Diary of the Liberation* (Landgraaf, NL: Hoppers Uitgeverijen, 1994), p. 70.

## Chapter 35: Lending a Hand

175 **"I am not looking forward to their visit"**: October 1, 1944, entry in MvK Memory Book, 1943–1945, p. 90 (reverse side).

175 **Not that the Dutch were quiet**: September 14, 1944, entry in MvK Memory Book, 1943–1945, p. 64 (reverse side).

176 **When little Hubert Michiels van Kessenich**: September 15, 1944, entry in MvK Memory Book, 1943–1945, p. 69 (reverse side); Jenneke Meyer Viol-Michiels van Kessenich email message to Robert M. Edsel, March 19, 2024.

176 **"Did you know?"**: September 18, 1944, entry in MvK Memory Book, 1943–1945, p. 77.

176 **Willem had been reinstated as mayor**: September 14, 1944, and undated entries in MvK Memory Book, 1943–1945, pp. 66 (reverse side), 73.

176 **Then she remembered the note**: September 18, 1944, entry in MvK Memory Book, 1943–1945, pp. 78-79.

177 **On September 20, a local paper admonished**: See the article "De straat op?," attached to September 20, 1944, entry in MvK Memory Book, 1943–1945, p. 82.

178 **The day after liberation**: September 13, 1944, entry in MvK Memory Book, 1943–1945, p. 57 (reverse side).

178 **"I am not looking forward to their visit"**: October 1, 1944, entry in MvK Memory Book, 1943–1945, p. 90 (reverse side).

178 **The next day, Emilie rode her bicycle**: October 2, 1944, entry in MvK Memory Book, 1943–1945, p. 91.

179 **Two days later, Emilie and Manka were summoned**: October 4, 1944, entry in MvK Memory Book, 1943–1945, p. 91 (reverse side).

179 **The liberation of Maastricht had not only released**: Bronzwaer, *Maastricht bevrijd*, Deel 1, pp. 81–83.

180 **In that scrum of accusations**: Bronzwaer, *Maastricht en Luik bezet*, p. 113; Bronzwaer, interview; F.A. Brunklaus, "Behind the Fence," in *Meneer de Burgemeester*, pp. 12–15.

180 **Emilie thought the accusation shameful**: October 4, 1944, entry in MvK Memory Book, 1943–1945, p. 91 (reverse side).

180 **About a week later**: October 15, 1944, entry in MvK Memory Book, 1943–1945, pp. 100-01.

181 **"I had an uneasy time standing at attention"**: Letter, Corlett to Eisenhower, October 16, 1944, accessed February 21, 2018, www.oldhickory30th.com.

181 **Afterward, there was a reception at city hall**: See article "Ontvangst van Amerikaanschen commandant," in MvK Memory Book, 1943–1945, p. 91 (reverse side).

181 **The XIX Corps had entered Aachen**: Walker Hancock, "Experiences of a Monuments Officer in Germany," *College Art Journal* 5, no. 4 (May 1946): 272–73.

## Chapter 36: Trouble

183 **The failure of Operation Market Garden**: John Meurs, *One Way Ticket to Berlin: A Day in the Life of the Mighty Eighth* (Brandon, MS: Quail Ridge Press, 2016), pp. 14–15.

184 **Around 3:00 p.m.**: Chapter based on information from Low, "The Brave Dutch," pp. 40–47.

## Chapter 37: Transitions

188 **On October 17**: October 17, 1944, entry in MvK Memory Book, 1943–1945, p. 105.

188 **On October 18**: October 18, 1944, entry in MvK Memory Book, 1943–1945, p. 105.

189 **"I'm entering a curious stage in my life"**: October 18, 1944, entry in MvK Memory Book, 1943–1945, p. 105.

189 **One detail, though, he did share**: Low, "The Brave Dutch," p. 43.

## Chapter 38: The Stripping Line

190 **The 117th Infantry**: After-Action Report, Headquarters, 30th Infantry Division, G-3 Section, September 1–30, 1944, Ike Skelton Combined Arms Research Library, U.S. Army Command and General Staff College, Fort Leavenworth, KS (hereafter Ike Skelton Library). Robert L. Hewitt, *Work Horse on the Western Front: The Story of the 30th Infantry Division* (Combat Books, 2020), p. 155.

191 **Almost as soon as Land fell**: Disinterment Directive, April 15, 1948, attached to John L. Land IDPF.

192 **This work was vital**: "Lt. John L. Land Killed in Action," *Montgomery Advertiser*, December 15, 1944, p. 13.

192 **At Margraten**: Inventory of Effects, November 21, 1944, attached to Land IDPF.

## Chapter 39: A Necessary Task

194 **Jefferson Wiggins, still only nineteen**: September 13, 1944, entry in 960th QSC Morning Reports, NPRC. Jefferson Wiggins interview with Mieke Kirkels, March 2010, transcript, pt. 2, p. 9; Kirkels, *Van Alabama naar Margraten*, p. 41.

194 **Wiggins was assigned to the 960th Quartermaster Service Company**: Kirkels, *Van Alabama naar Margraten*, pp. 35–37.

195 **Jeff liked the men in his unit**: Wiggins, *Another Generation Almost Forgotten*,

p. 109; Jefferson Wiggins interview with Mieke Kirkels, March 2010, transcript, pt. 2, p. 7.

195 **Now here he was**: Kirkels, *Van Alabama naar Margraten*, p. 44.

195 **By November**: There are discrepancies in individual's memories about when exactly the 960th arrived at Gronsveld, with most placing it around Thanksgiving or at the beginning of December. According to the 960th's own morning reports, the unit arrived at Gronsveld on November 17, 1944. 960th QSC Morning Reports, 17 November 1944 entry, NPRC. Dialogue from Jefferson Wiggins interview with Mieke Kirkels, March 2010, transcript, pt. 2, p. 1; Wiggins, *Another Generation Almost Forgotten*, p. 119; Kirkels, *Van Alabama naar Margraten*, p. 47.

195 **The next morning, not long after sunrise**: Ross and Romanus, *The Quartermaster Corps*, p. 692.

196 **"I know this is the most gruesome task"**: As quoted in Kirkels, *Van Alabama naar Margraten*, p. 53.

196 **Wiggins recoiled**: Based on information in Wiggins, *Another Generation Almost Forgotten*, p. 120; Jefferson Wiggins interview with Mieke Kirkels, March 2010, transcript, pt. 3, p. 5.

196 **If he had read the Quartermaster Field Manual**: Jefferson Wiggins interview with Mieke Kirkels, March 2010, transcript, pt. 3, p. 4; Quartermaster Field Manual 10-5: *Quartermaster Operations* (Washington, D.C.: War Department, 1941), p. 2.

196 **"You'll be given a pick and shovel"**: Kirkels, *Van Alabama naar Margraten*, pp. 53–54. Shomon, *Crosses in the Wind*, p. 69. George Yancho interview in *From Farmland to Soldiers Cemetery: Eyewitness Accounts of the Construction of the American Cemetery in Margraten*, eds. Mieke Kirkels, Jo Purnot, and Frans Roebroeks ('s-Hertogenbosch, NL: Heinen, 2009), p. 56.

197 **And all that time**: First U.S. Army Report of Operations, 1 August 1944 to 22 February 1945, vol. IV: 64.

197 **He walked to the nearest stack of bodies**: Kirkels, *Van Alabama naar Margraten*, pp. 53–54.

## *Chapter 40: Entertainment*

199 **Maastricht was full to bursting**: Parker et al., *Conquer*, pp. 68, 75, 107; P.M.M.A. Bronzwaer, *Maastricht bevrijd! En toen?* Deel 2, (Assen, NL: Van Gorcum, 1989), pp. 159, 165.

199 **And that was before the soldiers**: Hendriks and Koenen, *D-Day in South Limburg*, pp. 53–56; "Iris Carpenter Tells How Chicopee Mayor Foiled Plan to Dam Roads with Civilians," *Boston Globe*, October 12, 1944, pp. 1, 23.

200 **Major Senecal**: Bronzwaer, *Maastricht bevrijd*, Deel 1, p. 62; December 12, 1944, entry in MvK Memory Book, 1943–1945, p. 124 (reverse side).

201 **Conditions were far from ideal**: Bronzwaer, *Maastricht bevrijd*, Deelen 1 and 2, pp. 123, 157, 241.

201 **The most pressing need was food**: Bronzwaer, *Maastricht bevrijd*, Deel 2, p. 241.

201  **"Our distribution is miserable"**: As quoted in Bronzwaer, *Maastricht bevrijd*, Deel 1, p. 111.

201  **The daily ration had fallen to 990 calories**: Bronzwaer, *Maastricht bevrijd*, Deel 1, p. 113.

201  **And yet, Emilie Michiels van Kessenich was optimistic**: MvK Memory Book, 1943–1945, pp. 106, 124 (reverse side).

202  **And Emilie believed in her work**: Parker et al., *Conquer*, pp. 194–95.

202  **"May the diverse entertainment"**: MvK Memory Book, 1943–1945, p. 167 (reverse side).

202  **This was no debauchery district**: January 31, 1943, and August 12, 1945, entries in MvK Memory Book, 1943–1945, pp. 146 (reverse side), 243. Parker et al., *Conquer*, pp. 194–95.

203  **So she was shocked on October 31**: See the article "Aan de meisjes van Limburg; Hoe meisjes kunnen helpen de roem van ons land te handhaven en te vergrooten," in MvK Memory Book, 1943–1945, p. 106 (reverse side).

204  **She clipped the article**: October 31, 1944, entry in MvK Memory Book, 1943–1945, p. 106 (reverse side).

## Chapter 41: New Faces

205  **Like most Limburg girls**: Hanöver, "For My Kids," pp. 22, 39.

205  **The next afternoon**: Hanöver, "For My Kids," p. 39; Kirkels, *War Years in Maastricht*, p. 70; Bronzwaer, *Maastricht bevrijd*, Deel 1, p. 36.

205  **Soon, there was a knock at Else's door**: Hanöver, "For My Kids," p. 39.

206  **"It's called SPAM"**: Hanöver, "For My Kids," p. 40.

206  **Soon, he was bringing his GI friends**: Hanöver, "For My Kids," pp. 40, 42, 46.

207  **Plus, the Americans were handsome**: "Dutch Group Trying to Stop Girls Associating with G.I.'s," *Boston Globe*, December 12, 1944, pp. 1, 25.

207  **There was nothing scandalous about these encounters**: Gumn, *Double Dutch*, pp. 35, 91.

207  **By October, the weather had turned**: Gumn, *Double Dutch*, p. 41.

208  **The arrival of Captain John A. Hoadley was a blessing**: Zéguers comments.

209  **Hoadley had a habit**: Gumn, interview, 2016.

## Chapter 42: Papa

210  **Emilie Michiels van Kessenich met Major Leo Senecal**: November 8, 1944, entry in MvK Memory Book, 1943–1945, p. 117.

210  **The children loved Senecal**: Meyer Viol-Michiels van Kessenich, interview. See also p. 218 of MvK Memory Book, 1943–1945. Bronzwaer, *Maastricht bevrijd*, Deel 1, p. 109.

210  **One afternoon, he brought a tin of sardines**: Meyer Viol-Michiels van Kessenich, interview.

211  **"We do not wish that girls"**: Frans Roebroeks, "'Strijdbare Geesten' contra GI's. De Slag om de Maastrichtse meisjes 1944–1945," *De Maasgouw: tijdschrift voor Limburgse geschiedenis en oudheidkunde* 125, no. 4 (2006):

130-37. See also Claire van Dyck, "Zedenverval en geslachtsziekten: na de bevrijding begint de strijd om de Limburgse meisjes," *De Limburger,* December 27, 2019, https://www.limburger.nl/cnt/dmf20191227_00138850.

211 **The Americans responded**: Bronzwaer, *Maastricht bevrijd,* Deel 2, p. 172.

211 **On November 17, Emilie visited the U.S. Army's 91st Evacuation Hospital**: November 17, 1944, entry MvK Memory Book, 1943–1945, p. 117 (reverse side).

212 **Two days later**: November 19, 1944, entry in MvK Memory Book, 1943–1945, p. 107 (reverse side).

## Chapter 43: Courage

213 **The thirteen men were marched**: Report of Interrogation of H.A. Rauter, April 30, 1948, and Statement, Klaas Algra, June 2, 1948, both attached to Moore IDPF.

214 **"I will not"**: Based on information contained in Statement, Johaane Kleekamp, March 20, 1950, attached to Moore IDPF. Quote as appears has been adjusted to correct two German language errors in the original document.

214 **One of the visiting Nazis**: Interrogation of Eugene Dircks, October 23, 1945, attached to Moore IDPF.

## Chapter 44: The Worst Job

215 **The bugler blew reveille at 5:30 a.m.**: Kirkels, *Van Alabama naar Margraten,* p. 57.

215 *Here we go again*: Kirkels, *Van Alabama naar Margraten,* p. 55.

216 **He grabbed his pick and shovel**: Albert H. Smaha interview in *From Farmland to Soldiers Cemetery,* p. 40.

216 **At the end of his line of graves**: Kirkels, *Van Alabama naar Margraten,* p. 70.

217 **By midmorning**: Kirkels, *Van Alabama naar Margraten,* p. 70.

217 **It was Sergeant Brennan**: Shomon, *Crosses in the Wind,* p. 65.

218 **It wasn't unusual for guys to skip lunch**: Kirkels, *Van Alabama naar Margraten,* p. 57.

218 **But why them?**: Jefferson Wiggins interview with Mieke Kirkels, March 2010, transcript, pt. 1, p. 2.

218 **The sun was close to setting**: Shomon, *Crosses in the Wind,* p. 109.

218 **His man was whole**: Kirkels, *Van Alabama naar Margraten,* p. 70.

218 **They laid him on a mattress cover**: For general burial process information, see Ross and Romanus, *The Quartermaster Corps,* p. 683; Field Manual 10-63: *Graves Registration* (Washington, D.C.: War Department, 1945), p. 25. For the process at Margraten, see Shomon, *Crosses in the Wind,* pp. 70–71, 109; Kirkels, *Van Alabama naar Margraten,* pp. 59, 67, 69; Kirkels, Purnot, and Roebroeks, *From Farmland to Soldiers Cemetery,* p. 13.

220 **"We were most fortunate"**: Shomon, *Crosses in the Wind,* pp. 64–65, 75.

220 **There were no bathing facilities**: Kirkels, *Van Alabama naar Margraten,* pp. 69–70.

220 **They ate dinner in silence**: Kirkels, *Van Alabama naar Margraten*, p. 58.

220 **But Jeff Wiggins was optimistic**: Kirkels, *Van Alabama naar Margraten*, p. 72.

220 **Then, on December 17**: December 18, 1944, entry in 960th QSC Morning Reports, NPRC.

## Chapter 45: Christmas

221 **On December 20**: John M. Meeklin, "Holland Girls Urged to Shun American GIs," *Stars and Stripes*, December 20, 1944, p. 3. For Emilie's response, see p. 108 (reverse side) of MvK Memory Book, 1943–1945.

221 **An angry American private wrote**: Van Dyck, "Zedenverval en geslachtsziekten."

221 **It was a tempest in a teapot**: Bronzwaer, *Maastricht bevrijd*, Deel 2, p. 169.

222 **Jenneke Michiels van Kessenich, meanwhile, was sick**: December 12, 1944, MvK Memory Book, 1943–1945, p. 124 (reverse side).

222 **On Christmas Eve**: See December 24 and 25, 1944, entries in MvK Memory Book, 1943–1945, pp. 126, 129.

223 **Six miles away in Margraten**: Shomon, *Crosses in the Wind*, p. 86.

223 **In Maastricht**: Kevin Prenger, "Ondergrondse kerstviering tijdens WO2 in Maastricht," December 24, 2021, Historiek: https://historiek.net/55310-2 /55310/

225 **A few days later**: Peter Schrijvers, *The Margraten Boys: How a European Village Kept America's Liberators Alive* (New York: Palgrave Macmillan, 2012), pp. 7–8.

## Chapter 46: Special Friends

227 **One December, years before occupation**: Gumn, *Double Dutch*, p. 22.

228 **The next day, Hoadley dropped by again**: Gumn, interview, 2016. Robert M. Edsel with Bret Witter, *The Monuments Men: Allied Heroes, Nazi Thieves, and the Greatest Treasure Hunt in History* (New York: Center Street, 2009), p. 233.

228 **He was assigned to the Ninth Army**: Edsel, *Monuments Men*, p. 233; "Walter J. Huchthausen," Monuments Men and Women Foundation, accessed February 21, 2023, https://www.monumentsmenandwomenfnd.org /huchthausen-capt-walter-j.

228 **He had an instant connection**: Gumn, interview, 2016.

229 **She started to turn**: Gumn, interview, 2016.

229 **"It's my job"**: Based on information from Gumn, interview, 2016.

230 **"Have you seen the art vault"**: Gumn, *Double Dutch*, p. 25.

## Chapter 47: The Honeymoon Ends

231 **"Christmas Eve here"**: Letter, Paschal Fowlkes to Lucy Fowlkes, December 24, 1944, in Carroll, *Chaplain*, p. 224.

231 **Five days later, to his wife Lib**: Letter, Paschal Fowlkes to Elizabeth Fowlkes, December 29, 1944, in Carroll, *Chaplain*, p. 227.

231 **On D-Day**: Letter, Paschal Fowlkes to Lucy and Hit Fowlkes, August 7, 1944, in Carroll, *Chaplain*, p. 177.

231 **"Love, you need not to worry"**: Letter, Paschal Fowlkes to Elizabeth Fowlkes, September 1, 1944, in Carroll, *Chaplain*, p. 184.

232 **The war was**: As quoted in Carroll, *Chaplain*, p. 6.

233 **It was bitterly cold**: Letter, Paschal Fowlkes to Lucy and Elizabeth Fowlkes, January 31, 1944, in Carroll, *Chaplain*, p. 244.

233 **"I often find myself thinking"**: Letter, Paschal Fowlkes to Elizabeth and Lucy Fowlkes, January 31, 1945, in Carroll, *Chaplain*, p. 246.

234 **Five days later, on February 15**: Paschal Fowlkes, "Eulogy for Fallen Comrades," in Carroll, *Chaplain*, pp. 259–60.

235 *It is recorded that after Lee*: Robert E. Lee made this statement at the Battle of Fredericksburg, not Gettysburg.

## Part IV: Over the Rhine

237 *Volumes have been*: Eisenhower, *Crusade in Europe*, p. 467.

## Chapter 48: Curley

239 **M4 Sherman medium tanks**: Field Manual 17-67: *Crew Drill and Service of the Piece, Medium Tank M4, 5 August 1944* (Washington, D.C.: United States Government Printing Office, 1944), p. 7.

240 **The 784th spent a year at Camp Hood**: Wilson, *The 784th Tank Battalion in World War II*, pp. 25–35.

240 **The other two Black tank battalions had deployed**: Wilson, "The Army's Segregated Tank Battalions in World War II," p. 14. Department of the Army, *American Battle Casualties*, p. 92. Congressional Research Service, Report RL32492: "American War and Military Operations Casualties: Lists and Statistics," July 29, 2020, p. 2.

241 *You picture it*: Letter, Paschal Fowlkes to family, February 20, 1945, in Carroll, *Chaplain*, p. 262.

242 **Would he be ready**: Wilson, *The 784th Tank Battalion in World War II*, pp. 35–36.

242 **"What am I supposed to do?"**: As quoted in Wilson, *The 784th Tank Battalion in World War II*, p. 37.

243 **This was the front**: Butte, "Graves Registration During World War II," p. 2.

244 **"We'll get through it"**: Fowlkes, letter, February 20, 1944.

245 **It was four hours into the bombardment**: As quoted in Wilson, *The 784th Tank Battalion in World War II*, p. 43.

246 **The company clerk was told not to type the death report**: Wilson, *The 784th Tank Battalion in World War II*, p. 44.

## Chapter 49: Ritchie Boy

247 **Emil Mosbacher was the most prominent**: Biographical Note, Emil Mosbacher Family Collection, AR 25516, Leo Baeck Institute, New York, NY (hereafter Mosbacher Collection), accessed October 5, 2019, https://archives .cjh.org//repositories/5/resources/13147#a1.

247 **Sigmund was a happy, outgoing child**: Susanne Rieger and Gerhard Jochem,

"Stories of Allied Soldiers from Nuremberg-Fürth: Stephen S. Mosbacher," accessed July 6, 2019, https://rijo.hier-im-netz.de/pdf_2/EN_NU_JU _mosbacher_stephen.pdf.

249 **One had been Stephen's schoolmate**: Marianne Mosbacher Flack email message to Lily Debie, January 30, 2006, in possession of Robert M. Edsel.

249 **Stephen had hoped to become an officer**: Letter, Stephen Mosbacher to parents, January 20, 1945, folder 3, box 2, Mosbacher Collection.

250 **Eventually, the Third Army ordered him forward**: Letter, Stephen Mosbacher to parents, December 20, 1944, folder 3, box 2, Mosbacher Collection.

250 **One day, he overheard a prisoner**: Mosbacher, letter, December 20, 1944.

250 **On January 14**: Letter, Stephen Mosbacher to parents, January 14, 1945, folder 3, box 2, Mosbacher Collection.

251 **"They were friendly with the Germans"**: Letter, Stephen Mosbacher to parents, February 3, 1945, folder 3, box 2, Mosbacher Collection.

251 **Oma, the grandmother**: Letter, Stephen Mosbacher to parents, February 16, 1945, folder 3, box 2, Mosbacher Collection.

251 **There wasn't much to do**: Letter, Stephen Mosbacher to parents, January 9, 1945, folder 3, box 2, Mosbacher Collection.

252 *It's too much*: Letter, Stephen Mosbacher to parents, February 20, 1945, folder 3, box 2, Mosbacher Collection.

252 **The Vroonens' great pride was their radio**: Mosbacher, letter, February 16, 1945.

252 **The family cried**: Letter, Stephen Mosbacher to parents, February 8, 1945, folder 3, box 2, Mosbacher Collection.

253 **"IN GERMANY"**: Letter, Stephen Mosbacher to parents, February 9–10, 1945, folder 3, box 2, Mosbacher Collection.

253 **By February 14**: Letter, Stephen Mosbacher to parents, February 15, 1945, folder 3, box 2, Mosbacher Collection.

254 **"I am with you in my thoughts"**: Letter, Stephen Mosbacher to parents, January 27, 1944, folder 3, box 2, Mosbacher Collection.

## Chapter 50: The Cathedral

255 **As a Monuments Man**: Rhona Churchill, "Elderly Germans Being Used to Restore Aachen," *Journal News*, March 12, 1945, p. 2.

256 **On February 13, he visited the art vault**: Field Report, Monuments, Fine Arts, and Archives Branch, Summary for February 1–28, 1945, p. 57, Entry A1 62, MFAA Field Reports, Record Group 239, NARA.

## Chapter 51: "It Will Be Done"

257 **Lasting bonds form quickly**: Schrijvers, *Margraten Boys*, p. 201.

258 **The Allies had exploded**: After-Action Report, 784th Tank Battalion, for January–May 1945, Ike Skelton Library.

258 **A few hours later**: Medical chart and clinical history, Sergeant Charles H. Jefferson, both attached to Sergeant Charles H. Jefferson Army Personnel File, NPRC.

258 **By then, though, February was gone**: Wilson, *The 784th Tank Battalion in World War II*, p. 66.

259 **The Dutch had risen against their occupiers**: Ingrid de Zwarte, *The Hunger Winter: Fighting Famine in the Occupied Netherlands, 1940–1945* (Cambridge: Cambridge University Press, 2020), p. 2.

259 **"And we thought we had it bad"**: As quoted in Wilson, *The 784th Tank Battalion in World War II*, p. 67.

259 **"What a day this has been"**: Orval Eugene Faubus, *In This Faraway Land: A Personal Journal of Infantry Combat in World War II* (Little Rock: Pioneer Press, 1993), pp. 529–31.

260 **"Hey, white boy!"**: As quoted in Wilson, *The 784th Tank Battalion in World War II*, p. 71.

261 **"Fine," the commander said**: For detail about this engagement, see 784th AAR and Wilson, *The 784th Tank Battalion in World War II*, pp. 72–73.

262 **And then, somehow, it was done**: Wes Gallagher, "Negro Tank Battalion Fights Miniature 'Bastogne' All Alone," *Los Angeles Times*, March 5, 1945, p. 2.

262 **The "tank-riding doughboys"**: Faubus, *In This Faraway Land*, p. 534.

263 **They saw action the following day**: 784th AAR; Wilson, *The 784th Tank Battalion in World War II*, p. 82.

## Chapter 52: The Civilian Committee

264 **"I will take care of your cousin's grave"**: Schrijvers, *Margraten Boys*, pp. 7–8.

264 **On January 24, 1945**: Shomon, *Crosses in the Wind*, pp. 120–21.

265 **"We as Dutch citizens"**: As quoted in Schrijvers, *Margraten Boys*, p. 2.

265 **But the conditions weren't right**: Report of Burial, Sgt. Charles H. Jefferson, attached to Jefferson IDPF.

265 **A few weeks earlier**: Schrijvers, *Margraten Boys*, pp. 8–9.

## Chapter 53: A Ragged Bunch

267 **Combat Command B**: After Action Report, CCB, 8th Armored Division, February 1–28, 1945, "Feb 45" folder, box 12764, WWII Operations Reports: Entry 427, Record Group 407, NARA.

267 **On March 5**: After Action Report, CCB, 8th Armored Division, March 1–31, 1945, "Mar 45" folder, box 12764, WWII Operations Reports: Entry 427, Record Group 407, NARA.

267 **"We had quite an exciting trip"**: Letter, Stephen Mosbacher to parents, March 8, 1945, folder 4, box 2, Mosbacher Collection.

268 **The interrogation team set up**: Capt. Charles R. Leach, *In Tornado's Wake: A History of the 8th Armored Division* (Chicago: Argus Press, 1956), p. 130.

268 **"First customer"**: Mosbacher, letter, March 8, 1945.

268 **And yet**: Leach, *In Tornado's Wake*, p. 130.

269 **He contacted a colonel**: Mosbacher, letter, March 8, 1945.

269 **The woman was complaining**: Mosbacher, letter, March 8, 1945.

## Chapter 54: The Dance

270 **"Ik ben trots op je"**: Gumn, interview, 2018.

271 **After five months in Maastricht**: Parker et al., *Conquer*, p. 193. Gumn, interview, 2016.

271 **"You're not a coward"**: Gumn, interview, 2016.

272 **The dance was in an attic above a store**: Gumn, interview, 2016.

272 **She recognized a woman who worked at the Red Cross office**: Frieda Gumn telephone interview with Robert M. Edsel, July 21, 2018.

273 **The next morning, she grabbed her bicycle**: Gumn, telephone interview, 2018.

## Chapter 55: Promise Kept

274 **She was pregnant again**: May 6, 1945, and August 28, 1945, entries in MvK Memory Book, 1943–1945, pp. 189 (reverse side), 242 (reverse side).

274 **She had not asked for this job**: See article "Ontvangst van Amerikaanschen commandant" in MvK Memory Book, 1943–1945, p. 91 (reverse side); Willem Michiels van Kessenich, "Probeersel," pp. 13-15, 16.0674, MvK Papers, inv. no. 661, HCL.

## Chapter 56: Respite

275 **It was always the same**: Letter, Stephen Mosbacher to family, March 15, 1945, postscript to March 11, 1945, letter, folder 4, box 2, Mosbacher Collection.

275 **The third man**: Letter, Stephen Mosbacher to family, March 17, 1945, folder 4, box 2, Mosbacher Collection.

276 *It is very restful to see that landscape*: Letter, Stephen Mosbacher to family, March 11, 1945, folder 4, box 2, Mosbacher Collection.

277 **In Liège**: Letter, Stephen Mosbacher to family, March 24, 1945, folder 4, box 2, Mosbacher Collection.

278 **"Whoa, slow down, Moose"**: Based on information in Mosbacher, letter, March 24, 1945.

279 **"Real Dutch chocolate"**: Mosbacher, letter, February 16, 1945.

279 **"Stephen, was ist nicht in Ordnung?"**: Lily Debie email message to Seth Givens, May 23, 2023, in possession of Robert M. Edsel.

## Chapter 57: First Jump

280 **"What Easter signifies"**: Letter, Paschal Fowlkes to Elizabeth Fowlkes, March 20, 1945, in Carroll, *Chaplain*, pp. 270–71.

280 **Still, Montgomery waited**: Edward N. Bedessem, *Central Europe*, The U.S. Army Campaigns of World War II series (Washington, D.C.: Center of Military History, United States Army, 1995), pp. 11–12; Charles B. MacDonald, *The European Theater of Operations: The Last Offensive*, United States Army in World War II series (Washington, D.C.: Center of Military History, United States Army, 1993), pp. 296–97.

281 **The crossing would be treacherous**: Rick Atkinson, *The Guns at Last Light:*

*The War in Western Europe, 1944–1945* (New York: Henry Holt and Company, 2013), p. 562.

281 **You do not need me to tell you**: Paschal Fowlkes to men of the 17th Airborne Division, March 23, 1945, in Carroll, *Chaplain*, pp. 271–72.

282 **The next morning, March 24**: Eisenhower is clear in his memoir that he watched the river crossing operation from a church tower, but he had moved outside of town by the time of the airborne operation and watched the aircraft go overhead from a hill. See Eisenhower, *Crusade in Europe*, pp. 389–90.

282 **Chaplain Fowlkes was in the rightmost plane**: *Report by the Supreme Commander to the Combined Chiefs of Staff on the Operations in Europe of the Allied Expeditionary Force, 6 June 1944 to 8 May 1945* (Washington, D.C.: Center of Military History, United States Army, 1994), p. 100.

283 **Pat felt the familiar tug of the static line**: Letter, Estill Caudill to Elizabeth Fowlkes, June 20, 1945, in Carroll, *Chaplain*, pp. 279–80.

## Chapter 58: Frantic Days

284 **The last and heaviest bombardment**: MacDonald, *Last Offensive*, p. 305.

284 **"How are you feeling, son?"**: Eisenhower, *Crusade in Europe*, p. 389.

284 **The boats set out at 2:00 a.m.**: MacDonald, *Last Offensive*, pp. 305–06.

284 **The airborne passed over the Rhine at 10:00 a.m.**: MacDonald, *Last Offensive*, p. 309.

285 **The 960th had reached the Battle of the Bulge**: Kirkels, *Van Alabama naar Margraten*, p. 76.

285 **They returned to Margraten**: February 5, 1945, entry in 960th QSC Morning Reports, NPRC. William O. Solms interview in *From Farmland to Soldiers Cemetery*, p. 36.

285 **Now they were at the front again**: The 960th supported the 17th Airborne Division in Operation Varsity.

285 **Around 2:00 p.m., a pontoon bridge was operational**: "Historical Report for Operation Varsity," 17th Airborne Division, p. 25, Ike Skelton Library.

285 **A temporary airborne cemetery had been planned**: "Historical Report for Operation Varsity," pp. 24–25.

286 **Two days into Operations Plunder and Varsity**: Shomon, *Crosses in the Wind*, p. 107.

286 **So Shomon went to Ronckers**: Shomon, *Crosses in the Wind*, pp. 107, 109.

286 **It is impossible to say**: Report of Burial, attached to Fowlkes IDPF.

287 **Seven months later**: Effects inventory, Army Effects Bureau, October 20, 1945, attached to Fowlkes IDPF.

287 **My Darling**: Letter, Elizabeth Fowlkes to Paschal Fowlkes, August 24, 1943, in Carroll, *Chaplain*, p. 106.

## Chapter 59: River Crossing

288 **"If we go in the water"**: Based on information in Wilson, *The 784th Tank Battalion in World War II*, p. 110.

288 **Bill Hughes had never been so happy**: As quoted in Lee, *The Employment of Negro Troops*, p. 677.

## Chapter 60: Lost

290 **Shortly before 2:00 p.m.**: Robert M. Edsel, *The Greatest Treasure Hunt in History: The Story of the Monuments Men* (New York: Scholastic Focus, 2019), pp. 284–86.

291 **"They're firing at us!"**: "Statement Regarding the Incident Involving the Decease of Captain Walter J. Huchthausen, AC," MFA&A: Personnel: Officers—US.: Personal Histories, in possession of Robert M. Edsel.

## Chapter 61: Man Behind

292 **On March 26**: Letter, Major John R. Elting to Mosbacher family, June 9, 1946, attached to "Stories of Allied Soldiers from Nuremberg-Fürth: Stephen S. Mosbacher."

292 **Major Elting decided to move forward**: Elting, letter.

293 **"Get us out of here!"**: Elting, letter.

## Chapter 62: O-910847

295 **It was Captain Sully**: Gumn, interview, 2016.

## Chapter 63: The Letter

297 *My dear good one*: Letter, Emil Mosbacher to Stephen Mosbacher, April 5, 1945, folder 4, box 2, Mosbacher Collection.

## Chapter 64: Slaughter

298 **The fighting was intermittent**: 784th AAR.

299 **"Slow down!"**: Based on information quoted in Wilson, *The 784th Tank Battalion in World War II*, pp. 132–33.

299 **As the Allies advanced over the Rhine**: Daniel Blatman, *The Death Marches: The Final Phase of Nazi Genocide*, trans. Chaya Galai (Cambridge, MA: Harvard University Press, 2011), pp. 272–342.

300 **"Keep moving!"**: Based on information quoted in Wilson, *The 784th Tank Battalion in World War II*, pp. 132–33.

300 **Bill Hughes's Company D**: Wilson, *The 784th Tank Battalion in World War II*, p. 143.

302 **The 784th would never cross the Elbe**: 784th AAR.

302 **And then they had a celebration**: Wilson, *The 784th Tank Battalion in World War II*, p. 143.

## Chapter 65: The End

303 **Three weeks later**: Letter, Elizabeth Fowlkes to Quartermaster General, April 26, 1945, attached to Fowlkes IDPF.

304 **That was April 26, 1945**: Bronzwaer, *Maastricht bevrijd*, Deel 2, p. 224.

April 28, 1945, entry in MvK Memory Book, 1945–1946, p. 185, in 22.082, Kroniek Burgemeester Michiels van Kessenich, inv. no. 9, HCL.

304 **The news from Germany was coming in dribs and drabs**: See p. 182 (reverse side) and p. 286 (reverse side) of MvK Memory Book, 1945–1946.

304 **The citizens of Maastricht and Margraten learned of Hitler's death**: See the *Stars and Stripes* article "Hitler Dead," attached to May 2, 1945, entry in MvK Memory Book, 1945–1946, p. 186.

304 **On May 4, the German army in the Netherlands surrendered**: May 6, 1945, entry in MvK Memory Book, 1945–1946, p. 189 (reverse side).

305 **A few hours later**: As quoted in Pogue, *Supreme Command*, p. 490.

305 **Eisenhower knew**: Stephen E. Ambrose, *Eisenhower: Soldier and President* (New York: Simon & Schuster, 2014), p. 200.

## Chapter 66: The Photos

306 **Frieda van Schaïk snapped awake**: Gumn, interview, 2016.

306 **In one of their last conversations**: Gumn, interview, 2016.

306 **Frieda hopped on her bicycle**: Gumn, *Double Dutch*, p. 29.

307 **It was late afternoon when she finally found him**: Gumn, interview, 2016. Werner Mantz fled his native Germany after Kristallnacht in November 1938 to escape Nazi persecution. In the 1920s, he had been a prominent and influential photographer of modernist architecture in Cologne. It is unclear if it was on purpose or simply coincidence that Huchthausen, an architect, selected Mantz's studio for his portrait.

## Chapter 67: Memorial Day

309 **In 1868, three years after the Confederate surrender**: John R. Neff, *Honoring the Civil War Dead: Commemoration and the Problem of Reconciliation* (Lawrence, KS: University Press of Kansas, 2005), pp. 137–38.

309 **Captain Shomon's 611th Graves Registration Company started**: Shomon, *Crosses in the Wind*, p. 125.

309 **So the citizens of Margraten stepped in**: Shomon, *Crosses in the Wind*, pp. 121–23; Schrijvers, *Margraten Boys*, pp. 3–4.

311 **On the evening of May 29**: Math Robroek interview in *From Farmland to Soldiers Cemetery*, p. 171; Shomon, *Crosses in the Wind*, p. 127.

312 **The attendees began arriving with the sun**: Shomon, *Crosses in the Wind*, pp. 127–28; Schrijvers, *Margraten Boys*, p. 5.

312 **At 9:00 a.m., volunteers began handing out small bunches of flowers**: Program, Civilian Committee Margraten, May 24, 1945.

313 **A hush fell on the crowd**: May 30, 1945, entry in MvK Memory Book, 1945–1946, p. 205 (reverse side). For film footage of Simpson exiting his vehicle and shaking Willem's hand, see Army Signal Corps film clip, "Memorial Day Ceremony in Margraten, Holland," May 30, 1945, National Archives ID 18525, NARA.

313 **His speech was short**: As quoted in Kenneth L. Dixon, "GIs Say Goodbye to Lost Buddies," *Dayton Journal Herald*, June 2, 1945, p. 4.

314 **He stepped down from the dais**: Parker et al., *Conquer*, p. 356; Shomon, *Crosses in the Wind*, pp. 128–29.

314 **The soldiers were the first to break**: Dixon, "GIs Say Goodbye to Lost Buddies," p. 4.

314 **The Dutch didn't want to leave**: Shomon, *Crosses in the Wind*, p. 129.

314 *You, who enter this cemetery*: Prayer card attached to May 30, 1945, entry in MvK Memory Book, 1945–1946, p. 203.

## Chapter 68: A Sign

316 **Emilie's eleventh child, a girl, was born on June 4**: June 4, 1945, entry in MvK Memory Book, 1945–1946, p. 208.

317 **After the baptism**: "Probeersel," p. 14.

317 **"Rest, my love"**: Based on information in "Probeersel," pp. 13–15.

317 **So when the letter arrived soon after**: "Probeersel," pp. 13–15. Willem Michiels van Kessenich's personal papers leave no doubt that it was Fowlkes's wife who wrote the letter, not his sister who shared the same first name, because it came from "the widow of an Army chaplain." See pp. 14–15 of "Probeersel."

## Part V: Love and Remembrance

319 *With all my heart I believe*: George C. Marshall, "Our War Memorials Abroad: A Faith Kept," *National Geographic* 111, no. 6 (June 1957): 733.

## Chapter 69: Going Home

321 **Almost as soon as Hitler committed suicide**: Roland G. Ruppenthal, *The European Theater of Operations: Logistical Support of the Armies, Volume II: September 1944–May 1945* (Washington, D.C.: Center of Military History, United States Army, 1995), p. 497.

322 **There was, however, a large segment**: Steere and Boardman, *Final Disposition of World War II Dead*, pp. 37, 120–21, 307.

322 **So it was in May**: Letter, H.P. Soland to Elizabeth Fowlkes, May 9, 1945, in Carroll, *Chaplain*, p. 286.

323 **A medic from the 507th**: Caudill June 20, 1945, letter.

323 **The Army chaplain**: Aubrey Morris, "Kin of Hero Sought: Atlantian Defied Threat of Gestapo to Aid Dutch," *Atlanta Journal*, August 30, 1945, p. 5; "Journal Story Finds Captive Flier's Mother," *Atlanta Journal*, August 31, 1945, p. 1. Chaplain McGee has his own extraordinary story. He was awarded the Distinguished Service Cross for his actions in Normandy with the 506th Parachute Infantry. He then jumped in Operation Market Garden, where he was captured in the second week of fighting. It was during his captivity that he met Bill Moore in Apeldoorn.

323 **It was also in June**: Elting, letter.

324 **He then offered one more**: Elting, letter.

325 **Elting's Dutch friends**: Letter, Al Helms to Elizabeth Fowlkes, September 21, 1945, in Carroll, *Chaplain*, p. 288.

327 **Captain Shomon was determined**: Shomon, *Crosses in the Wind*, pp. 123–24.

327 **The relationship, though, was about far more than jobs**: Unpublished history of American Military Cemetery Margraten, attached to letter, A.J.N. Boosten to Henry R. Shepley, January 27, 1949, p. 4, in possession of Robert M. Edsel.

328 **But not long after Memorial Day**: Shomon, *Crosses in the Wind*, pp. 129–33.

329 **"I'll come back!"**: Bronzwaer, *Maastricht bevrijd*, Deel 2, p. 243.

329 **Before leaving**: August 12, 1945, entry in MvK Memory Book, 1945–1946, p. 243.

329 **Nazi Germany and Fascist Italy were defeated**: Radio address, Lieutenant Commander Ernest A. de Bordenave, April 16, 1945, as quoted in Carroll, *Chaplain*, p. 282.

## Chapter 70: Mail

330 **In the final days of August**: Willem Michiels van Kessenich, "Letter from the Burgomaster," *Life* 19, no. 9 (August 27, 1945): 4.

330 **Two weeks later, on September 12, a letter arrived**: Letter, Mabel Rose Feil, August 26, 1945, 16.0674, MvK Papers, inv. no. 659, HCL.

331 **Willem's secretary, Else Hanöver, read the letter**: Hanöver, "For My Kids," p. 49.

331 **Lib Fowlkes's letter**: "Probeersel," pp. 13–15.

331 **So around the time of Senecal's request**: "Probeersel," pp. 14–15. Schrijvers, *Margraten Boys*, pp. 10–11.

332 **On September 9**: See article "S-Day at Maastricht, The Netherlands. American honoured by the Dutch," in September 9, 1945, entry in MvK Memory Book, 1945–1946, p. 245 (reverse side).

332 **Emilie smiled when she saw the paragraph**: See article in MvK Memory Book, 1945–1946, p. 245 (reverse side).

332 **She was shocked by the response**: See p. 275 (reverse side) of MvK Memory Book, 1945–1946; Schrijvers, *Margraten Boys*, p. 16.

333 **After the article, Emilie met with Father Heuschen**: "Probeersel," p. 14.

333 **"I don't know what to do with all these"**: "Probeersel," p. 15.

333 **This made some sense**: Steere and Boardman, *Final Disposition of World War II Dead*, p. 130.

334 **When remains were found**: Steere and Boardman, *Final Disposition of World War II Dead*, pp. 165–272. Herbert (Herb) E. Hackett interview in *From Farmland to Soldiers Cemetery*, p. 146.

334 **This reburial effort started while Shomon was still in theater**: Shomon, *Crosses in the Wind*, p. 134. Charles (Buck) D. Butte interview in *From Farmland to Soldiers Cemetery*, p. 141.

335 **Dear Mr. President**: Letter, Emilie Michiels van Kessenich to President Harry S. Truman, September 27, 1945, folder 293: "Holland," box 189, NND-785095, General Correspondence file, Record Group 92, NARA.

336 **Then, after apologizing**: Emilie Michiels van Kessenich to Truman letter.

## Chapter 71: Tour Guide

337 **Peter had asked to see her**: Gumn, *Double Dutch*, p. 35.

338 **After liberation, Dave van Schaïk had been blackballed**: Zéguers, "A Brief Biography," p. 27.

338 **Fortunately, the Americans saw things differently**: Ir. D.C. van Schaïk, *The Old Town of Maastricht and the Caves of Mount St. Peter* (Maastricht: publisher unknown, 1945), p. 3.

339 **Each tour was a two-person job**: Gumn, interview, 2016.

339 *Royal Air Force*, **she noted**: Gumn, *Double Dutch*, p. 37.

339 **After the tour, the group had lunch**: Gumn, *Double Dutch*, p. 37.

339 **The artworks from the vault in the mountain were being sent back**: Gumn, *Double Dutch*, p. 23.

340 **"Give me your address"**: Gumn, *Double Dutch*, p. 37.

## Chapter 72: Family Affair

341 **It had been a surprisingly difficult six months**: Bronzwaer, *Maastricht en Luik bezet*, p. 310

341 **By the fall, his actions were being investigated**: Bronzwaer, *Maastricht en Luik bezet*, pp. 310–11.

341 **The commission cleared him**: "The Opinion issued by the Advisory Committee for the Purification of Mayors in Limburg regarding jhr mr W. Michiels van Kessenich, mayor of the municipality of Maastricht," January 4, 1946, document 0089, NL-HaNA 2.04.87, inventory number 4791, Nationaal Archief, Den Haag. Bronzwaer, *Maastricht en Luik bezet*, p. 311.

342 **"De beste stuurlui staan aan wal"**: Meyer Viol-Michiels van Kessenich, email message.

342 **Only Emilie, his heart's companion and confidante, knew**: June 23, 1945, entry in MvK Memory Book, 1945–1946, p. 212 (reverse side).

342 **Plus, she had her own project**: Letter, Lieutenant General Edmund B. Gregory to Emilie Michiels van Kessenich, November 6, 1945, folder 293: "Holland," box 189, NND-785095, General Correspondence file, Record Group 92, NARA.

343 **As the weather began to turn toward winter**: See p. 276 of MvK Memory Book, 1945–1946.

344 **In the coming year, she would do this many times**: See p. 276 (reverse side) of MvK Memory Book, 1945–1946.

345 **In November, Manka fell ill**: November 9, 1945, entry in MvK Memory Book, 1945–1946, p. 280 (reverse side).

345 **On January 1, 1946, Emilie's father suffered a stroke**: January 1–3, 1946, entry in MvK Memory Book, 1945–1946, p. 294.

345 **On January 10, she traveled to Utrecht**: January 10, 1946, entry in MvK Memory Book, 1945–1946, pp. 297–98.

## Chapter 73: Haarlem

346 **Frieda had arrived in Haarlem**: Gumn, *Double Dutch*, p. 38.

346  **She didn't notice him at first**: Gumn, interview, 2016.

347  **"The knowledge that someone lives so near his grave"**: Letter, Paul Huchthausen to Major John Hoadley, November 21, 1945, Van Schaïk-Gumn Papers.

348  **"I was so impressed, Frieda"**: Letter, Gordon Gumn to Frieda van Schaïk, December 6, 1945, Van Schaïk-Gumn Papers.

349  **But then came an announcement**: Gumn, *Double Dutch*, p. 40.

350  **She chose a sunny day**: Letter, Gordon Gumn to Frieda van Schaïk, February 24, 1946, Van Schaïk-Gumn Papers.

## Chapter 74: Reinforcements

351  **The letter section**: "Adopted Grave," *Life* 20, no. 6 (February 11, 1946): 6.

351  **"Dearest Mabel"**: Letter, Emilie Michiels van Kessenich to Mabel Feil, February 24, 1946, in Warren F. Feil IDPF, NPRC.

351  **There was such a movement in the Netherlands**: See pp. 297 and 297 (reverse side) of MvK Memory Book, 1945–1946.

352  **Even the Americans**: Emilie Michiels van Kessenich to Feil letter.

352  **Mabel responded with a second letter to *Life***: "Adopted Graves," *Life* 20, no. 9 (March 4, 1946): 6.

352  **Mabel's mother, Mabel Rose Levy**: Letter, Mabel Rose Levy to Congressman Frank W. Boykin, March 5, 1946, attached to Feil IDPF.

352  **Boykin passed the letter on to the military brass**: Letter, Major General Thomas B. Larkin to Congressman Frank W. Boykin, March 28, 1946, attached to Feil IDPF. For the most sensationalist reporting on the subject, see "Europe Racket Swindles Kin of Slain Yanks," *Chicago Daily Tribune*, October 18, 1946, p. 31.

353  ***Mrs. Michiels van Kessenich is a woman and a mother***: Letter, Mabel Rose Levy to Major General Thomas B. Larkin, April 1, 1946, in Feil IDPF.

354  **Emilie was wrong about a few things**: The Second Field Command was the AGRC headquarters responsible for recovering dead American service members in the Low Countries after the war. Their inactivation on July 31, 1946, accounts for the records moving. See Steere and Boardman, *Final Disposition of World War II Dead*, p. 205. For information about Heuschen, see Schrijvers, *Margraten Boys*, p. 41.

354  **In this, Else Hanöver, Willem's secretary**: Hanöver, "For My Kids," pp. 49–50.

## Chapter 75: Relocations and Beautification

356  **By April 1946**: Data comes from an undated history of Margraten cemetery, attached to letter, A.J.N. Booston to Henry R. Shepley, January 27, 1949.

357  **In Germany, the GRS had searched**: Steere and Boardman, *Final Disposition of World War II Dead*, p. 189. Moore IDPF.

357  **And all of it, at least at Margraten, was temporary**: Steere and Boardman, *Final Disposition of World War II Dead*, p. 130.

357 **The Army's Quartermaster General's plan**: Steere and Boardman, *Final Disposition of World War II Dead*, pp. 39–40, 51.

357 **"In the opinion of this office"**: As quoted in Steere and Boardman, *Final Disposition of World War II Dead*, p. 51.

358 **As a well-known amateur botanist and local flora enthusiast**: Gumn, interview, 2016.

359 **On April 8, she visited the cemetery**: Letter, Frieda van Schaïk to Gordon Gumn, April 6, 1946, Van Schaïk-Gumn Papers.

359 **"How I wish you could have been with me"**: Van Schaïk to Gumn, letter, April 6, 1946.

359 **That evening, though, her Pappie needed her**: Gumn, interview, 2016.

## Chapter 76: A New Approach

362 **In Emilie, they discovered an ideal interview**: Verbeek, "Ambassadrice van Margraten."

363 **She offered the opportunity to Father Heuschen**: Schrijvers, *Margraten Boys*, pp. 40–41.

364 **It wasn't until KLM Royal Dutch Airlines**: "Probeersel," p. 15.

## Chapter 77: Planning

365 **A friend of Frieda's from Haarlem**: Letters, Frieda van Schaïk to Gordon Gumn, April 20, 1946, and May 1, 1946, Van Schaïk-Gumn Papers.

366 **A few weeks before Memorial Day**: "Dutch Forbidden to Honor Graves," *New York Times*, May 20, 1946, p. 8. Schrijvers, *Margraten Boys*, pp. 47–48. "Army in Holland Ends Grave Floral Ban," *New York Times*, May 23, 1946, p. 7.

366 **The president of the Gold Star Wives of America**: Marie Jordan-Speer interview with Robert M. Edsel, 2016.

366 **On May 28, KLM flew Emilie to The Hague**: Letter, Frieda van Schaïk to Gordon Gumn, May 22, 1946, Van Schaïk-Gumn Papers. See also pp. 331 (reverse side) and 332 of MvK Memory Book, 1945–1946.

367 **That week, the last of May**: Gumn, interview, 2016.

367 **Again, the crowds began to arrive at dawn**: David Anderson, "Grateful Dutch Honor U.S. Heroes," *New York Times*, May 31, 1946, p. 4.

368 **Emilie's two eldest boys**: May 30, 1946, entry in MvK Memory Book, 1945–1946, p. 335.

368 **The crowd was larger than the year before**: Anderson, "Grateful Dutch Honor U.S. Heroes," p. 4.

369 **A few months later**: Shomon, *Crosses in the Wind*, pp. 188–89.

369 **Frieda was in her bedroom**: Letter, Frieda van Schaïk to Gordon Gumn, June 1, 1946, Van Schaïk-Gumn Papers.

369 **She was taking other things**: "Itinerary USA trip," 16.0674, MvK Papers, inv. no. 659, HCL.

369 **"I know someone!"**: Based on information in Van Schaïk to Gumn, letter, June 1, 1946, and Gumn, interview, 2016.

## Chapter 78: Approvals

371 **Frieda couldn't take her eyes off**: Gumn, *Double Dutch*, p. 42.

372 **But now she was free**: Gumn, *Double Dutch*, p. 41.

372 **That was a Tuesday**: Gumn, *Double Dutch*, p. 42.

372 **The officers in charge were not amused**: Gumn, *Double Dutch*, p. 43.

## Chapter 79: The Trip

374 **On the morning of June 8, 1946**: June 8, 1946, entry in MvK Memory Book, 1946, p. 4, in 22.082, Kroniek Burgemeester Michiels van Kessenich, inv. no. 8, HCL.

374 **"The flight is lovely"**: June 8, 1946, entry in MvK Memory Book, 1946, p. 4 (reverse side).

374 **In Amsterdam**: June 8, 1946, entry in MvK Memory Book, 1946, p. 5.

375 **She took notes in her diary**: June 8, 1946, entry in MvK Memory Book, 1946, p. 5 (reverse side).

375 **LaGuardia Field seemed a marvel**: June 9, 1946, entry in MvK Memory Book, 1946, p. 7 (reverse side).

375 **"Wanted to run to them"**: June 9, 1946, entry in MvK Memory Book, 1946, p. 8.

375 **The Customs inspector frowned**: June 9, 1946, entry in MvK Memory Book, 1946, p. 9 (reverse side).

376 **That afternoon, she was the guest of honor**: June 9, 1946, entry in MvK Memory Book, 1946, p. 9.

376 **The next few days**: June 10–12, 1946, entries in MvK Memory Book, 1946, pp. 10–13.

377 **She met with reporters**: "Gold Star Wife Returns," *New York Times*, June 10, 1946, p. 22.

377 **On Thursday, June 13, she boarded a train**: June 13, 1946, entry in MvK Memory Book, 1946, p. 13 (reverse side).

377 **At 5:00 p.m., a reception with members of Congress**: June 14–15, 1946, entries in MvK Memory Book, 1946, p. 17 (reverse side).

377 **On Sunday, Emilie attended Mass**: June 16, 1946, entry in MvK Memory Book, 1946, p. 22 (reverse side).

378 **Marie Jordan wanted her to tour California**: Letter, Emilie Michiels van Kessenich to Major General Thomas B. Larkin, November 6, 1946, in folder 293: "Holland," box 189, NND-785095, General Correspondence file, Record Group 92, NARA.

378 **Another option was Texas**: June 14, 1946, entry in MvK Memory Book, 1945–1946, p. 17 (reverse side) to 18.

378 **After a visit to Mount Vernon**: June 16, 1946, entry in MvK Memory Book, 1946, p. 22 (reverse side).

379 **That evening, she was on an ABC radio program**: June 17, 1946, entry in MvK Memory Book, 1946, pp. 25 (reverse side) to 26.

379 **The next day, more grieving families came to see her**: June 18, 1946, entry in MvK Memory Book, 1946, pp. 26 (reverse side) to 27.

379   **That evening, at the Feil home**: June 18, 1946, entry in MvK Memory Book, 1946, pp. 26 (reverse side) to 27.

379   **She boarded a plane for Texas**: June 20, 1946, entry in MvK Memory Book, 1946, p. 28.

380   **When she arrived at Love Field in Dallas**: June 21, 1946, entry in MvK Memory Book, 1946, p. 28 (reverse side).

380   **In Lockhart, she was greeted**: June 21, 1946, entry in MvK Memory Book, 1946, pp. 31–32.

380   **The next day, the Connollys drove her**: June 22, 1946, entry in MvK Memory Book, 1946, p. 32 (reverse side). "Abilene Couple Will Learn from Dutch Woman of Care Given to Grave of Son," *Abilene Reporter*, June 22, 1946, p. 11.

381   **The next day, Emilie spoke again to an overflowing crowd**: June 23, 1946, entry in MvK Memory Book, 1946, pp. 36–39 (reverse side).

381   **In the days that followed, she traveled from Mineral Springs**: June 24–25, 1946, entries in MvK Memory Book, 1946, pp. 39 (reverse side) to 47.

382   **Mabel's spitfire mother**: June 25, 1946, entry in MvK Memory Book, 1946, pp. 46–47.

382   **The mayor of Demopolis, Alabama, had arranged a police car**: "Netherlands Visitor Describes Plans and Development of Graves Program," *Demopolis Times*, June 27, 1946.

382   **Days before, in Birmingham**: June 25, 1946, entry in MvK Memory Book, 1946, p. 43.

382   **In Demopolis**: June 25, 1946, entry in MvK Memory Book, 1946, p. 47.

384   **She traveled from Demopolis to Atlanta**: June 27, 1946, entry in MvK Memory Book, 1946, p. 53. Katherin Barnwell, "Flowers, Trees Circle Graves of GI Heroes," *Atlanta Constitution*, June 28, 1946, p. 26.

384   **The mother from Tucker wept**: Rebecca Franklin, "Poignant Stories of War: Holland Busy 'Adopting' 19,000 Georgian Graves," *Atlanta Journal*, June 28, 1946, p. 9.

384   **From there, it was back to New York City**: June 28 and July 2, 1946, entries in MvK Memory Book, 1946, p. 62, 67 (reverse side) to 68.

384   **Extraordinary events**: June 28 and July 3, 1946, entries in MvK Memory Book, 1946, pp. 58–74.

384   **A worker hot off his shift at a textile mill**: July 4, 1946, entry in MvK Memory Book, 1946, p. 78.

385   **Everywhere she went, she did publicity**: Entries for June 29 to July 4, 1946, entries in MvK Memory Book, 1946, pp. 63–77.

385   **A small crowd gathered on the tarmac**: July 10, 1946, entry in MvK Memory Book, 1946, pp. 81 (reverse side) to 82.

386   **The flight home was uneventful**: July 10, 1946, entry in MvK Memory Book, 1946, p. 82 (reverse side).

## Chapter 80: A Special Good-bye

387   **On July 20, 1946**: Gumn, *Double Dutch*, pp. 41, 44–45.

387 **"You look lovely"**: Gumn, *Double Dutch*, p. 40.

388 **At that most familiar of graves**: Frieda Gumn interview with Casey Shelton, Over Wallop, UK, September 3, 2018.

## Chapter 81: Closure

389 **The woman, lean but determined**: Albert Riley, "Mother Reaches Goal: Finds Grave in Holland of Son Killed by Gestapo," *Atlanta Constitution*, November 24, 1946, p. 60.

389 **Bill Moore was not her biological child**: Enlistment Record, Bill F. Moore, December 20, 1941, and Fulton County, Georgia, police booking photo, May 24, 1941, both in Moore IDPF.

390 **Perhaps that's why John took Bill's death so hard**: Lieutenant Colonel E.M. Brown to Chief, Memorial Division, "Report of Official Travel," June 27, 1952, in Moore IDPF.

390 **She knew quite a bit about Bill's last months**: Morris, "Journal Story Finds Captive Flier's Mother," p. 1. Letter, Fred Patterson to John W. Moore, July 13, 1946, in Moore IDPF. Telegram, War Department to John W. Moore, May 15, 1944, in Moore IDPF.

390 **It didn't take her long**: Riley, "Mother Reaches Goal," p. 60.

391 **They took her to his grave**: Riley, "Mother Reaches Goal," p. 60.

## Epilogue

393 *Time will not dim*: John J. Pershing, "Our National War Memorials in Europe," *National Geographic* 65, no. 1 (January 1934): 36.

394 **This is an effect not only of time but of design**: Steere and Boardman, *Final Disposition of World War II Dead*, p. 319. See also American Battle Monuments Commission, *Time Will Not Dim: American Battle Monuments Commission, A Century of Service, 1923–2023* (Arlington, VA: American Battle Monuments Commission, 2023), pp. 118–19.

394 **Following the Memorial Day ceremony in 1948**: Joseph T. Layne and Glenn D. Barquest, "Margraten: US Ninth Army Military Cemetery, Margraten, Holland," 172d Engineer Combat Battalion Reunion, May 14, 1994, Greenville, SC, pp. 15–16. Harry Steijns, Sjef Duizens, and Mathieu van Loo interviews in *From Farmland to Soldiers Cemetery*, pp. 148–55, 175. Frenk Lahaye interview with Robert M. Edsel, Margraten, NL, September 26, 2023.

394 **The fallen from other Allied nations**: Layne and Barquest, "Margraten," p. 16.

395 **At the end of 1947**: Steere and Boardman, *Final Disposition of World War II Dead*, p. 365. The 46 percent comes from 8,195 of the 17,738 next of kin electing to have their loved ones buried permanently in Margraten. Note that 17,738 was the number of positively identified remains at the time of elections. Data from Frenk Lahaye email message to Robert M. Edsel, July 25, 2024.

395 **The caskets of those remaining**: Lahaye, interview. Layne and Barquest, "Margraten," pp. 17–18.

395 **Forty pairs of brothers**: Brochure, ABMC, "Netherlands American Cemetery and Memorial," December 2018: https://www.abmc.gov/sites /default/files/2020-06/Netherlands%20American%20Cemetery%20and%20 Memorial%20brochure%20%282019%29.pdf.

396 **This process of planning**: As quoted in "Juliana Helps Dedicate U.S. WWII Cemetery," *Tacoma News Tribune*, July 7, 1960.

396 **Despite the twelve-year gap**: Jeff Stoffer, *Mother of Normandy: The Story of Simone Renaud* (Los Angeles: Iron Mike Entertainment, Inc., 2010).

397 **And when those adopters grew too old**: Ton Hermes interview with Robert M. Edsel, Margraten, NL, September 28, 2023.

398 **Sadly, Father Heuschen did not remain**: Schrijvers, *Margraten Boys*, pp. 39–40.

398 **If Father Heuschen had seen**: "Dutch Town 'Adopts' Graves of 19,000 Yank Liberators," *Washington Post*, June 30, 1946, p. B2. For Emilie giving Heuschen credit, see "Netherlands Visitor Describes Plans and Development of Graves Program," *Demopolis Times*, June 27, 1946, p. 1; Katherin Barnwell, "Flowers, Trees Circle Graves of GI Heroes," *Atlanta Constitution*, June 28, 1946, p. 26; "Graves Adopted by Dutch; 20,000 GI's Cared For," *Catholic Advance*, June 28, 1946, p. 7.

398 **So Father Heuschen traveled**: Schrijvers, *Margraten Boys*, pp. 40–41.

398 **The clothes turned out to be for the needy in Maastricht**: Letter, Emilie Michiels van Kessenich to Ambassador John Loudon, November 7, 1946, 16.0674, MvK Papers, inv. no. 659, HCL.

399 **Emilie had, in fact, received**: June 28, 1946, entry in MvK Memory Book, 1946, pp. 62–62 (reverse side).

399 **In late August, U.S. Senator L.L. Biggle**: See the article, "Pres. Truman dankt kapelaan Heuschen en de bevolking van Limburg," August 20, 1946, in 16.0674, MvK Papers, inv. no. 657, HCL.

399 **Father Heuschen remained a chaplain**: Frans Roebroeks email message to Robert M. Edsel, April 4, 2024.

399 **Emilie continued her work**: Letter, Commissaris de Konigin in de Provincie Limburg, Maastricht, May 21, 1963, 16.0674, MvK Papers, inv. no. 657, HCL. Rives Fowlkes Carroll, telephone interview and email message to Robert M. Edsel, January 5, 2023.

400 **Sadly, the system did not work that well for every family**: Herman, telephone interview.

400 **On April 17, Emilie underwent emergency surgery**: Appendix to Rondschrijfbrief Serie III, No. 29, June 11, 1970, Jenneke Meyer Viol-Michiels van Kessenich Personal Papers (hereafter JMV-MvK Papers).

400 **On May 7, her lungs filled with fluid**: Appendix to Rondschrijfbrief Serie III, No. 29, June 11, 1970, JMV-MvK Papers.

401 **On June 10, five days after her passing**: Appendix to Rondschrijfbrief Serie III, No. 29, June 11, 1970, JMV-MvK Papers.

402 **Rather than relying on the opinions of others**: See Schrijvers, *Margraten Boys*, pp. 33–44.

403  **There was certainly an easy "villain/victim" narrative**: Schrijvers, *Margraten Boys*, p. 42.

404  **But what of Emilie's husband**: Meyer Viol-Michiels van Kessenich, interview.

405  **In 2023, a report commissioned by the Maastricht municipality**: René and Erik van Rijselt and Marjolein Vlieks, *Onvoltooid verleden – Ontrechting en rechtsherstel van Joodse inwoners in de gemeenten Maastricht, Amby en Heer* (Maastricht: Municipality of Maastricht, 2023).

405  **In January 2025, the Netherlands announced**: Nationaal Archief, "Centraal Archief Bijzondere Rechtspleging," accessed January 20, 2025, https://www.nationaalarchief.nl/onderzoeken/zoekhulpen/centraal -archief-bijzondere-rechtspleging-cabr#collapse-1098. Centraal Archief Bijzondere Rechtspleging (CABR), Nationaal Archief, Den Haag, inv. no. 48374 (file 365) and inv. no. 111865 (file I-38499). On the top corner of the inventory card associated with Willem's second file appears the letters "OBV" in red pencil. The initialism stands for "Onvoorwaardelijk Buiten Vervolging": unconditionally exempt from prosecution.

406  ***When we think back now***: De Leon, *Mémoires*, chapter 9.

406  **Couple that with the wise words**: As quoted in Hans Goossen, "Burgemeesters in oorlogstijd: Goed of fout blijkt niet altijd zwart-wit," *De Limburger*, April 29, 2020, https://www.limburger.nl/cnt/dmf20200428 _00158167.

406  **The families of most of the soldiers**: Debie, email message.

407  **Dr. James Norton and Miss Ed requested permission**: James A. Norton to John L. McMillan, October 4, 1946, and Request for Disposition of Remains, December 5, 1947, both attached to James A. Norton IDPF.

407  **Dr. James and Miss Ed were never again able to visit their sons**: James Norton Spivey, telephone interview.

407  **"It means a lot they're not forgotten"**: Lieutenant Colonel Larkin Spivey telephone interview with Robert M. Edsel, September 18, 2023.

408  **Robert Cole received his nation's highest recognition for valor**: Cole, telephone interview. "Slain Colonel's Mother Gets Medal of Honor," *Fort Worth Star-Telegram*, October 31, 1944, p. 16.

408  **The option for reburial went to Clara**: Cole, telephone interview.

409  **Lib Fowlkes likewise remarried**: Rives Fowlkes Carroll email message to Robert M. Edsel, June 6, 2023; Carroll, *Chaplain*, pp. 1–3.

410  **Bill Moore was among the last Americans interred**: Letter, Helen Moore to Quartermaster General, August 8, 1946, and report, Lieutenant Colonel E.M. Brown to Chief, Memorial Division, "Report of Official Travel," June 27, 1952, both attached to Moore IDPF.

410  **John and Helen died with no known relatives to mourn**: Jodie and Rhes Low telephone interview with Robert M. Edsel, June 10, 2023. "John Low III's Death Described as Accidental Shooting," *Hattiesburg American*, December 18, 1978, p. 2.

411  **Today, a stone memorial marks the site**: Meurs, *One Way Ticket to Berlin*, p. 808. "Narda van Terwisga," *Apeldoorn en de Oorlog*, https://www .apeldoornendeoorlog.nl/achtergronden/narda-van-terwisga

411  **Else Hanöver, Willem's assistant**: Kirkels, *War Years in Maastricht*, p. 112.

411  **Bill Hughes stayed in Europe**: Wilson, *The 784th Tank Battalion in World War II*, pp. 173, 183, 185–87. Max Hughes telephone interview with Robert M. Edsel, September 19, 2023.

412  **Jefferson Wiggins had a similar experience**: Wiggins, *Another Generation Almost Forgotten*, pp. 155–58.

413  **With the help of the formidable women in his life**: Wiggins, *Another Generation Almost Forgotten*, pp. 158–68.

413  **In 2008, when he was eighty-three**: Kirkels, *Van Alabama naar Margraten*, pp. 97–100. Janice Wiggins interview with Robert M. Edsel, New Fairfield, CT, October 24, 2023.

414  **In 2009, Jefferson Wiggins**: Kirkels, *Van Alabama naar Margraten*, pp. 100–03.

414  **In his speech**: Kirkels, *Van Alabama naar Margraten*, p. 95.

416  **Frieda loved Walter**: Gumn, interview.

419  **In April 1946, General Eisenhower**: Dwight D. Eisenhower, "Art in Peace and War," *Metropolitan Museum of Art Bulletin* 4, no. 9 (May 1946): 221–23.

# BIBLIOGRAPHY

## Books

Ambrose, Stephen E. *Eisenhower: Soldier and President*. New York: Simon & Schuster, 2014.

American Battle Monuments Commission. *Time Will Not Dim: American Battle Monuments Commission, A Century of Service, 1923–2023*. Arlington, VA: American Battle Monuments Commission, 2023.

Atkinson, Rick. *The Guns at Last Light: The War in Western Europe, 1944–1945*. New York: Henry Holt and Company, 2013.

Bando, Mark. *101st Airborne: The Screaming Eagles at Normandy*. Minneapolis: Zenith Press, 2007.

Blatman, Daniel. *The Death Marches: The Final Phase of Nazi Genocide*. Translated by Chaya Galai. Cambridge, MA: Harvard University Press, 2011.

Blumenson, Martin, ed. *The Patton Papers, 1940–1945*. New York: Da Capo Press, 1974.

Boersma, Henk, Sjef Kusters, Jo Purnot, and Frans Roebroeks. *De Bevrijding van Eijsden-Margraten in September 1944*. Gemeente Eijsden-Margraten, 2015.

Bowman, Martin W. *U.S. 9th Air Force Bases in Essex, 1943–44*. Barnsley, UK: Pen & Sword, 2010.

Bradley, Omar N. *A Soldier's Story*. New York: Random House, 1999.

Brongers, E.H. *Oorlog in Zuid-Limburg, 10 mei 1940*. Soesterberg, NL: Uitgeverij Aspekt, 2005.

Bronzwaer, P.M.M.A. *Maastricht bevrijd! En toen?* Deel 1. Van Gorcum, Assen/ Maastricht NL: Stichting Historische Reeks Maastricht, 1989.

Bronzwaer, P.M.M.A. *Maastricht bevrijd! En toen?* Deel 2. Van Gorcum, Assen/ Maastrich NL: Stichting Historische Reeks Maastricht, 1989.

Bronzwaer, Paul. *Maastricht en Luik bezet: Een comparatief onderzoek naar vijf aspecten van de Duitse bezetting van Maastricht en Luik tijdens de Tweede Wereldoorlog*. Hilversum, NL: Uitgeverij Verloren BV, 2010.

Caddick-Adams, Peter. *Sand and Steel: The D-Day Invasion and the Liberation of France*. Oxford: Oxford University Press, 2019.

Carrell, Paul, and Günter Böddeker. *Die Gefangenen: Leben und Überleben Deutscher Soldaten hinter Stacheldraht*. Frankfurt am Main: Ullstein, 1996.

Carroll, Rives Fowlkes, ed. *Chaplain: The World War II Letters of Army Air Corps Chaplain Paschal Dupuy Fowlkes*. Washington, D.C.: Opus Self Publishing Services, 2018.

Copp, DeWitt S. *Forged in Fire: Strategy and Decisions in the Air War over Europe, 1940–45*. New York: Doubleday, 1982.

De Jong, Louis. *Het Koninkrijk der Nederlanden in de Tweede Wereldoorlog, Deel 3: Mei '40*. The Hague: Martinus Nijhoff, 1970.

D'Este, Carlo. *Bitter Victory: The Battle for Sicily, 1943*. New York: Harper, 2008.

D'Este, Carlo. *Eisenhower: A Soldier's Life*. New York: Henry Holt and Company, 2002.

De Zwarte, Ingrid. *The Hunger Winter: Fighting Famine in the Occupied Netherlands, 1940–1945*. Cambridge: Cambridge University Press, 2020.

Edsel, Robert M. *The Greatest Treasure Hunt in History: The Story of The Monuments Men*. New York: Scholastic Focus, 2019.

Edsel, Robert M., with Bret Witter. *The Monuments Men: Allied Heroes, Nazi Thieves, and the Greatest Treasure Hunt in History*. New York: Center Street, 2009.

Eisenhower, Dwight D. *At Ease: Stories I Tell to Friends*. Garden City, NY: Doubleday & Company, 1967.

Eisenhower, Dwight D. *Crusade in Europe*. New York: Doubleday & Company, 1948.

Faubus, Orval Eugene. *In This Faraway Land: A Personal Journal of Infantry Combat in World War II*. Little Rock: Pioneer Press, 1993.

Faust, Drew Gilpin. *This Republic of Suffering: Death and the American Civil War*. New York: Alfred A. Knopf, 2008.

Feldman, Glenn. *Politics, Society, and The Klan in Alabama 1915–1949*. Tuscaloosa, Alabama: The University of Alabama Press, 1999.

Geurst, Jeroen. *Cemeteries of the Great War by Sir Edwin Lutyens*. Rotterdam: 010 Publishers, 2010.

Glantz, Lieutenant Colonel David M. *The Soviet Airborne Experience, Research Survey No. 4*. Fort Leavenworth, KS: Combat Studies Institute, 1984.

Glantz, David M., and Jonathan M. House. *When Titans Clashed: How the Red Army Stopped Hitler*. Lawrence, KS: University Press of Kansas, 1995.

Gumn, Frieda. *Double Dutch, –?*. London: LifeBook Limited, 2015.

Gushwa, Robert L. *The Best and Worst of Times: The United States Army Chaplaincy, 1920–1945, Volume IV*. Washington, D.C.: Office of the Chief of Chaplains, Department of the Army, 1977.

Hendriks, Jan, and Hans Koenen. *D-Day in South Limburg: Diary of the Liberation*. Landgraaf, NL: Hoppers Uitgeverijen, 1994.

Hewitt, Robert L. *Work Horse on the Western Front: The Story of the 30th Infantry Division*. Combat Books, 2020.

Kirkels, Mieke, ed. *Else Hanöver: Oorlogsjaren in Maastricht—War Years in Maastricht*. Maastricht: Stichting Akkers van Margraten, 2009.

Kirkels, Mieke. *Van Alabama naar Margraten: Herinneringen van grafdelver Jefferson Wiggins*. Maastricht: Drukkerij Walters, 2014.

Kirkels, Mieke, Jo Purnot, and Frans Roebroeks, eds. *From Farmland to Soldiers Cemetery: Eyewitness Accounts of the Construction of the American Cemetery in Margraten*. 's-Hertogenbosch, NL: Adr. Heinen Uitgevers, 2009.

Koskimaki, George E. *Hell's Highway: Chronicle of the 101st Airborne Division in the Holland Campaign, September–November 1944*. Havertown, PA: Casemate, 2003.

Kuhl, George C. *Wrong Place! Wrong Time! The 305th Bomb Group & the 2nd Schweinfurt Raid, October 14, 1943*. Atglen, PA: Schiffer Publishing, Ltd., 1993.

# BIBLIOGRAPHY

Leach, Capt. Charles R. *In Tornado's Wake: A History of the 8th Armored Division.* Chicago: Argus Press, 1956.

Lee, Patrick. *Tribal Laws, Treaties, and Government: A Lakota Perspective.* Bloomington, IN: iUniverse, 2013.

Lewis, Catherine H. *Horry County, South Carolina, 1730–1993.* Columbia: University of South Carolina Press, 1998.

Lochner, Louis P., ed. and trans. *The Goebbels Diaries, 1942–1943.* New York: Doubleday & Company, 1948.

Maass, Walter B. *The Netherlands at War: 1940–1945.* New York: Abelard-Schuman, 1970.

Marshall, S.L.A. *Battle at Best.* New York: William Morrow and Company, 1963.

Marshall, S.L.A. *Night Drop: The American Airborne Invasion of Normandy.* Boston: Little, Brown and Company, 1962.

McManus, John C. *The Americans at Normandy: The Summer of 1944—From the Normandy Beaches to Falaise.* New York: Forge, 2004.

McManus, John C. *September Hope: The American Side of a Bridge Too Far.* New York: NAL Caliber, 2012.

Mendes de Leon, Diego. *Mémoires: Mes mémoires ne sont pas mes confessions.* Vol. I. Lanaken, BE: P. Bijnens Drukkerijen b.v.b.a., 1995.

Meurs, John. *One Way Ticket to Berlin: A Day in the Life of the Mighty Eighth.* Brandon, MS: Quail Ridge Press, 2016.

Miller, Merle. *Ike the Soldier: As They Knew Him.* New York: G.P. Putnam's Sons, 1987.

Moore, Carl H. *Flying the B-26 Marauder Over Europe: Memoir of a World War II Navigator.* Jefferson, NC: McFarland & Company, 2013.

Moore, Leonard J. *Citizen Klansmen: The Ku Klux Klan in Indiana, 1921–1928.* Chapel Hill, NC: University of North Carolina Press, 1991.

Morrison, Samuel Eliot. *History of United States Naval Operations in World War II, Vol. XI: The Invasion of France and Germany, 1944–1945.* Boston: Little, Brown and Company, 1957.

Mrazek, Col. James E, USA (Ret.). *The Fall of Eben Emael: Prelude to Dunkerque.* Novato, CA: Presidio Press, 1991.

Neff, John R. *Honoring the Civil War Dead: Commemoration and the Problem of Reconciliation.* Lawrence, KS: University Press of Kansas, 2005.

Noordman, Wolter. *Luchtalarm op de Veluwe.* Amsterdam: VBK Media, 2002.

Nordyke, Phil. *All American, All the Way: From Market Garden to Berlin, The Combat History of the 82nd Airborne Division in World War II.* Beverly, MA: Voyageur Press, 2010.

Paape, A.H. *Donkere jaren: Episoden uit de geschiedenis van Limburg, 1933–1945.* Assen NL: Van Gorcum & Co., 1969.

Parker, Col. Theodore W., et al. *Conquer: The Story of Ninth Army, 1944–1945.* Washington D.C.: Infantry Journal Press, 1947.

Patton, George S., Jr. *War As I Knew It.* Boston: Houghton Mifflin Company, 1947.

Pejacsevich de Veröcze, Marie (Countess). *A 20th Century Odyssey: A Personal Memoir.* Edited by Lily von Blanckenstein. 's-Hertogenbosch, NL: Gopher Publishers, 2005.

# BIBLIOGRAPHY

Presser, J. *Ashes in the Wind: The Destruction of Dutch Jewry*. Translated by Arnold Pomerans. Detroit: Wayne State University Press, 1988.

Richardson, Eudora Ramsay, and Sherman Allan. *Quartermaster Supply in the European Theater of Operations in World War II, Volume VII: Graves Registration*. Camp Lee, VA: Quartermaster School, 1948.

Romijn, Peter. *Burgemeesters in oorlogstijd: Besturen onder Duitse bezetting*. Amsterdam: Uitgeverij Balans, Kindle Edition, 2012.

Rosenman, Samuel I., ed. *The Public Papers and Addresses of Franklin D. Roosevelt, 1940 Volume: War—and Aid to Democracies*. New York: MacMillan, 1941.

Schrijvers, Peter. *The Margraten Boys: How a European Village Kept America's Liberators Alive*. London: Palgrave Macmillan, 2012.

Shilleto, Carl. *Utah Beach – St. Mere Eglise: VII Corps, 82nd and 101st Airborne Divisions*. Barnsley, UK: Leo Cooper, 2001.

Shirer, William L. *The Rise and Fall of the Third Reich: A History of Nazi Germany*. New York: Simon and Schuster, 1960.

Shomon, Joseph James. *Crosses In The Wind: Graves Registration Service in the Second World War*. New York: Stratford House, Inc., 1947.

Sijes, B.A. *De Arbeidsinzet: De gedwongen arbeid van Nederlanders in Duitsland, 1940–1945*. The Hague: SDU Uitgeverij, 1990.

Sledge, Michael. *Soldier Dead: How We Recover, Identify, Bury & Honor Our Military Fallen*. New York: Columbia University Press, 2005.

Smith, Jean Edward. *Eisenhower in War and Peace*. New York: Random House, 2013.

Steere, Edward, and Thayer M. Boardman. *Final Disposition of World War II Dead, 1945–51*. Washington, D.C.: Historical Branch, Office of the Quartermaster General, 1957.

Stoffer, Jeff. *Mother of Normandy: The Story of Simone Renaud*. Los Angeles: Iron Mike Entertainment, Inc., 2010.

Summersby Morgan, Kay. *Past Forgetting: My Love Affair with Dwight D. Eisenhower*. New York: Simon and Schuster, 1976.

Van Gestel, P. *De laatste Nederlandsche priester die te Dachau stierf. Professor Robert Regout S.J.* Maastricht: publisher unknown, 1947.

Van Oort, Theodorus Arnoldus, et al., eds. *Meneer de Burgemeester*. Maastricht: Leiter-Nypels, 1967.

Van Schaïk, Ir. D.C. *The Old Town of Maastricht and the Caves of Mount St. Peter*. Maastricht: publisher unknown, 1945.

Van Schaik, Willem C.L. *Maastricht in Wartime: Resistance Underground, English Translation of "Ondergronds Verzet."* Utrecht, NL: De Banier, 1997.

Videc, Jori, Sebastiaan Vonk, and Arie-Jan van Hees. *De Gezichten van Margraten: Zij bleven voor altijd jong*. Zutphen, NL: Walburg Pers, 2020.

Vlahos, Colonel Mark C. *"Men Will Come": A History of the 314th Troop Carrier Group, 1942–1945*. Hoosick Falls, NY: Merriam Press, 2019.

Walton, Marilyn Jeffers, and Michael C. Eberhardt. *From Interrogation to Liberation: A Photographic Journey Stalag Luft III—the Road to Freedom*. Bloomington, IN: AuthorHouse, 2014.

Wiggins, Jefferson. *Another Generation Almost Forgotten*. Bloomington, IN: Xlibris Corporation, 2003.

Wilson, Joe, Jr. *The 784th Tank Battalion in World War II: History of an African American Armored Unit in Europe*. Jefferson, NC: McFarland & Company, Inc., Publishers, 2007.

## Government Publications

Anderson, Charles A. *The U.S. Army Campaigns of World War II: Algeria-French Morocco*. Washington, D.C.: Center of Military History, United States Army, 1993.

Bedessem, Edward N. *Central Europe*. The U.S. Army Campaigns of World War II series. Washington, D.C.: Center of Military History, United States Army, 1995.

Craven, Wesley Frank, and James Lea Cate, eds. *The Army Air Forces in World War II, Vol. II: Europe: Torch to Pointblank, August 1942 to December 1943*. Washington, D.C.: Office of Air Force History, 1983.

Craven, Wesley Frank, and James Lea Cate, eds. *The Army Air Forces in World War II, Vol. III: Europe: Argument to V-E Day, January 1944 to May 1945*. Washington, D.C.: Office of Air Force History, 1983.

Department of the Army Pamphlet No. 20-232: *Airborne Operations: A German Appraisal*. Washington, D.C.: Center of Military History, United States Army, 1982.

Department of the Army. *American Battle Casualties and Nonbattle Deaths in World War II, Final Report, 7 December 1941–31 December 1946*.

Garland, Lieutenant Colonel Albert N., and Howard McGaw Smyth. *The Mediterranean Theater of Operations: Sicily and the Surrender of Italy*. United States Army in World War II series. Washington, D.C.: Center of Military History, United States Army, 1993.

Harrison, Gordon A. *The European Theater of Operations: Cross-Channel Attack*. United States Army in World War II series. Washington, D.C.: Center of Military History, United States Army, 1993.

Howe, George F. *The Mediterranean Theater of Operations: Northwest Africa: Seizing the Initiative in the West*. United States Army in World War II series. Washington, D.C.: Center of Military History, United States Army, 1993.

Lee, Ulysses. *Special Studies: The Employment of Negro Troops*. United States Army in World War II series. Washington, D.C.: Center of Military History, United States Army, 2001.

MacDonald, Charles B. *The European Theater of Operations: The Siegfried Line Campaign*. United States Army in World War II series. Washington, D.C.: Center of Military History, United States Army, 1993.

MacDonald, Charles B. *The European Theater of Operations: The Last Offensive*. United States Army in World War II series. Washington, D.C.: Center of Military History, United States Army, 1993.

Perret, Geoffrey. *Winged Victory: The Army Air Forces in World War II*. New York: Random House, 1993.

Playfair, Major General I.S.O., et al. *The Mediterranean and Middle East, Vol. IV: The Destruction of the Axis Forces in Africa*. London: Her Majesty's Stationary Office, 1966.

Pogue, Forrest C. *The European Theater of Operations: The Supreme Command*. United States Army in World War II series. Washington, D.C.: Office of the Chief of Military History, Department of the Army, 1954.

Quartermaster Field Manual 10-5: *Quartermaster Operations*. Washington, D.C.: War Department, 1941.

Quartermaster Field Manual 10-63: *Graves Registration*. Washington, D.C.: War Department, 1945.

*Report by the Supreme Commander to the Combined Chiefs of Staff on the Operations in Europe of the Allied Expeditionary Force, 6 June 1944 to 8 May 1945*. Washington, D.C.: Center of Military History, United States Army, 1994.

Ross, Willam F., and Charles F. Romanus. *The Technical Services: The Quartermaster Corps: Operations in the War Against Germany*. United States Army in World War II series. Washington, D.C.: Center of Military History, United States Army, 1991.

Ruppenthal, Roland G. *The European Theater of Operations: Logistical Support of the Armies, Volume II: September 1944–May 1945*. United States Army in World War II series. Washington, D.C.: Center of Military History, United States Army, 1995.

Steere, Edward. *The Graves Registration Service in World War II*, QMC Historical Studies series, no. 21. Washington, D.C.: Historical Section, Office of the Quartermaster General, 1951.

Thomson, Harry C., and Lida Mayo. *The Ordnance Department: Procurement and Supply*. United States Army in World War II series. Washington, D.C.: Center of Military History, United States Army, 1991.

Van Rijselt, René and Erik, and Marjolein Vlieks. *Onvoltooid verleden – Ontrechting en rechtsherstel van Joodse inwoners in de gemeenten Maastricht, Amby en Heer*. Maastricht: Municipality of Maastricht, 2023.

War Department Historical Division. *Salerno: American Operations from the Beaches to the Volturno, 9 September–6 October 1943*. Washington, D.C.: Center of Military History, United States Army, 1990.

War Department Historical Division. *Utah Beach to Cherbourg, 6–27 June 1944*. Washington, D.C.: Center of Military History, United States Army, 1990.

War Department Field Manual 10-63: *Graves Registration*. Washington, D.C.: United States Government Printing Office, 1945.

War Department Field Manual 17-67: *Crew Drill and Service of the Piece, Medium Tank M4, 5 August 1944*. Washington, D.C.: United States Government Printing Office, 1944.

Watson, Mark Skinner. *The War Department: Chief of Staff: Prewar Plans and Preparations*. United States Army in World War II series. Washington, D.C.: Center of Military History, United States Army, 1991.

## Edited Volumes

Bastiaens, Lucie. "'Hij, die zijn naam voor eeuwig verbond aan de Sint-Pietersberg.' Ir. David Cornelis van Schaïk (1888–1972) en de wording van een natuurmonument." In *Studies over de sociaal-economische geschiedenis van Limburg*, edited by Ad Knotter and Willibrord Rutten. Maastricht: Sociaal Historisch Centrum voor Limburg, 2013.

Brunklaus, F.A. "Meneer de Burgemeester." In *Meneer de Burgemeester,* edited by Theodorus Arnoldus van Oort et al. Maastricht: N.V. Leiter-Nypels, 1967.

Fehrenbacher, Don E., ed. *Lincoln: Selected Speeches and Writings.* New York: Vintage Books, 1992.

Ferguson, Arthur B. "Rouen-Sotteville No. 1, 17 August 1942." In *The Army Air Forces in World War II, Vol. I: Plans and Early Operations, January 1939 to August 1942,* edited by Wesley Frank Craven and James Lea Cate. Washington, D.C.: Office of Air Force History, 1989.

Galambos, Louis, and Daun van Ee, eds. *The Papers of Dwight David Eisenhower, Volume IV: The War Years.* Baltimore: The Johns Hopkins Press, 1970.

Hafner, Arthur W., ed. *Directory of Deceased American Physicians, 1804–1929.* Chicago: American Medical Association, 1993.

## Articles

Eisenhower, Dwight D. "Art in Peace and War," *Metropolitan Museum of Art Bulletin* 4, no. 9 (May 1946): 221–23.

Galloway, Joseph L., and Douglas Pasternak. "The Warrior Class." *U.S. News and World Report* 127, no. 1 (July 5, 1999): 26–32.

Hancock, Walker. "Experiences of a Monuments Officer in Germany." *College Art Journal* 5, no. 4. (May 1946): 272–311.

Hirrel, Leo P. "The Beginnings of the Quartermaster Graves Registration Service." *Army Sustainment Magazine* 46, no. 4 (July–August 2014): 64–67.

Marshall, George C. "Our War Memorials Abroad: A Faith Kept." *National Geographic* 111, no. 6 (June 1957): 733–37.

Rives, Tim. "'Ok, We'll go': Just What Did Ike Say When He Launched the D-Day Invasion 70 Years Ago?" *Prologue* 46, no. 1 (Spring 2014): 37–43.

Roebroeks, Frans. "'Strijdbare Geesten' contra GI's. De Slag om de Maastrichtse meisjes 1944–1945." *De Maasgouw: tijdschrift voor Limburgse geschiedenis en oudheidkunde* 125, no. 4 (2006): 130-37.

Simpson, William M. "A Tale Untold? The Alexandria, Louisiana, Lee Street Riot (January 10, 1942)." *Louisiana History* 35, no. 2 (Spring 1994): 133–49.

Wilson, Dale E. "The Army's Segregated Tank Battalions in World War II." *Army History,* no. 32 (Fall 1994): 14–17.

## Dissertations and Theses

Openshaw, Major James N. "The IJmuiden Power Plant Raids of WWII: Airpower Misapplied." MA thesis, Air Command Staff College, 1987.

## Newspapers and Magazines

*Abilene Reporter,* Abilene, TX

*Argus-Leader,* Sioux Falls, SD

*Atlanta Journal,* Atlanta, GA

*Austin American-Statesman,* Austin, TX

*Boston Globe,* Boston, MA

*Catholic Advance,* Wichita, KS

*Chicago Daily Tribune,* Chicago, IL

*Columbia Record,* Columbia, SC

*Dayton Journal Herald,* Dayton, OH

*De Limburger,* Maastricht, NL

# BIBLIOGRAPHY

*Demopolis Times*, Demopolis, AL
*Fort Worth Star-Telegram*, Fort Worth, TX
*Hattiesburg American*, Hattiesburg, MS
*Horry Herald*, Conway, SC
*Indianapolis News*, Indianapolis, IN
*Indianapolis Star*, Indianapolis, IN
*Journal News*, White Plains, NY
*Libelle*, Amsterdam, NL
*Life*, New York, NY
*Los Angeles Times*, Los Angeles, CA
*Marysville Advocate*, Marysville, OH
*Montgomery Advertiser*, Montgomery, AL
*Native Sun News*, Rapid City, SD

*New York Times*, New York, NY
*Noblesville Ledger*, Noblesville, IN
*Rapid City Journal*, Rapid City, SD
*Richmond News Leader*, Richmond, VA
*Richmond Times-Dispatch*, Richmond, VA
*Seattle Times*, Seattle, WA
*Stars and Stripes*, Washington, D.C.
*Sun News*, Myrtle Beach, SC
*Tacoma News Tribune*, Tacoma, WA
*The Echo*, Clemson, SC
*The State*, Columbia, SC
*Washington Post*, Washington, D.C.
*WMBF News*, Myrtle Beach, SC

## Interviews

Jason Bordelon
Dr. Paul Bronzwaer
Jacob Carrière
Rives Fowlkes Carroll
Robert Bruce Cole
Lily Debie
Stephanie Flack
Jennifer Geduldig
Raymond Gijsen
Esther Gumn
Frieda van Schäik-Gumn
Lucy Low Helveston
Marla Herman
Ton Hermes
Jim Huchthausen
Max Hughes
Father Frits Janssen
Tineke Low Kermicle

Mieke Kirkels
Frenk Lahaye
Jodie Low
Rhes Low
Jenneke Meyer Viol-Michiels van
    Kessenich
Kees Rauh
Prof. Dr. Kees Ribbens
Frans Roebroeks
Dr. Peter Schrijvers
Marie Jordan-Speer
Dr. James Norton Spivey
Lt. Col. (Ret.) B. Larkin Spivey Jr.
Cindy Beall Suich
Sebastiaan Vonk
Janice Wiggins
Joe Wilson Jr.
Camilla Zéguers

## Archives and Personal Papers

Alabama Center for Health Statistics, Montgomery, AL.
Betsey B. Creekmore Special Collections and University Archives, University of
    Tennessee, Knoxville, TN.
    Charles D. Butte Collection
Center of Military History, Washington, D.C.
    Historical Manuscripts Collection
    Don F. Pratt Museum, Fort Campbell, KY.
Clemson University Libraries Special Collections and Archives, Clemson, SC.
    William Wright Bryan Papers

# BIBLIOGRAPHY

Else Hanöver Personal Papers
Historisch Centrum Limburg, Maastricht, NL.
    Familie Michiels van Kessenich
    Ir. D.C. van Schaïk archief
    Kroniek Burgemeester Michiels van Kessenich
    Handschriftencollectie (voormalig) Gemeentearchief Maastricht
Jenneke Meyer Viol-Michiels van Kessenich Personal Papers
Leo Baeck Institute, New York, NY.
    Emil Mosbacher Family Collection
Library of Congress, Washington, D.C.
    Rare Book and Special Collections Division
John L. Low Jr. Personal Papers
Marianne Mosbacher Flack Family Collection
Ohio University Mahn Center for Archives and Special Collections, Athens, OH.
    Cornelius Ryan Collection
National Archives and Records Administration, College Park, MD.
    Record Group 75
    Record Group 92
    Record Group 239
    Record Group 338
    Record Group 407
National Personnel Records Center, St. Louis, MO.
    Morning Reports
    Individual Deceased Personnel Files
    Official Military Personnel Files
Nationaal Archief, Den Haag, NL.
Frieda van Schaïk-Gumn Personal Papers

# PHOTO CAPTIONS AND CREDITS

The appearance of U.S. Department of Defense (DoD) visual information does not imply or constitute DoD endorsement.

*Major Characters*
**Page xiii:** Robert G. Cole (1939 Howitzer, United States Military Academy Archives)
**Page xiii:** Paschal "Pat" D. Fowlkes (Michiels van Kessenich Family Photographs)
**Page xiii:** Jacob T. Herman Jr. (Oglala Lakota College Archives, Special Collections, Oglala Lakota College)
**Page xiv:** Walter J. Huchthausen (Van Schaïk/Gumn Family Photographs)
**Page xiv:** Bill M. Hughes (Courtesy of Joe Wilson Jr.)
**Page xiv:** Emilie Michiels van Kessenich (Jenneke Meyer Viol-Michiels van Kessenich Photographs)
**Page xiv:** John L. Low Jr. (*Ondergedoken op de Veluwe*, written by Wolter Noordman and published by OMNIBOEK, Kampen, 2010.)
**Page xiv:** Bill F. Moore (*Ondergedoken op de Veluwe*, written by Wolter Noordman and published by OMNIBOEK, Kampen, 2010.)
**Page xv:** Sigmund (Stephen) Mosbacher (Marianne Mosbacher Flack Family Photographs)
**Page xv:** James A. and Edward R. Norton (Courtesy of Lt. Col. (Ret.) B. Larkin Spivey Jr.)
**Page xv:** Frieda van Schaïk (Van Schaïk/Gumn Family Photographs)
**Page xv:** Jefferson Wiggins (Courtesy of Mrs. Janice Wiggins)
**Page xvi:** Margraten (Courtesy of Frans Roebroeks)

*Images*
**Cover image:** An American paratrooper from the 82nd Airborne Division playing with two Dutch children, near the village of Malden, south of Nijmegen, the Netherlands, on September 18, 1944, the day after the commencement of Operation Market Garden. Please contact the author at info@robertedsel.com if you are able to identify the soldier or children in this photograph. (Fotocollectie Regionaal Archief Nijmegen)
**Page 5:** German soldiers near the destroyed Wilhelmina Bridge. (Bundesarchiv, Bild 146-1984-093-27 / photographer: unknown)

**Page 15:** A postcard of Villa Maya around 1930. (Historisch Centrum Limburg, unknown author, Fotocollectie GAM, 3838)

**Page 35:** Rijksmuseum officials standing next to *The Night Watch*, with its life-size figures. (National Archives (239-RC-93-1))

**Page 35:** Dutch workers moving *The Night Watch* into a bunker at Heemskerk in March 1941. The following year, it was moved to Sint Pietersberg and placed in its custom-designed storage bin. (Left image Rijksmuseum, Amsterdam, RMA-SSA-F-05307-1; right image National Archives (239-RC-93-8))

**Page 50:** Margareta and Dave—Moekie and Pappie—van Schaïk. (Van Schaïk/Gumn Family Photographs)

**Page 51:** Dave and Frieda inside the caves of Sint Pietersberg. (Van Schaïk/Gumn Family Photographs)

**Page 52:** One of Dave's maps of the tunnel system located on a wall inside Sint Pietersberg. (Roderburg, K. (Kris), Cultural Heritage Agency of the Netherlands, 345.166)

**Page 56:** Edward and James, suited up for a game. (Courtesy of Lt. Col. (Ret.) B. Larkin Spivey Jr.)

**Page 57:** Lieutenant Colonel Stillman (center, stick in hand), conducting the mission briefing for the initial raid on Velsen three days earlier. (United States Air Force, ID 050606-F-1234P-004)

**Page 59:** A B-26 Marauder and its tightly packed crew. (United States Air Force, ID 080306-F-3927A-035)

**Page 91:** American bombers and the contrails that provided hope for Frieda and her countrymen and women. (United States Air Force, ID 060517-F-1234S-001)

**Page 105:** First Lieutenant Bill Moore (back row, far left) and his crew in front of their B-24 Liberator. (USAAF image courtesy 467th BG Assn. Ltd.)

**Page 121:** General Eisenhower and Lieutenant Colonel Cole, just hours before the 101st dropped into Normandy. (National Archives (342-USAF-19674-R3))

**Page 129:** The elevated and exposed causeway that Cole and his men had to traverse. Utah Beach is visible at the top of the image. (Department of the Army Historical Division)

**Page 146:** Willem's two photos of the Germans fleeing. (Michiels van Kessenich Family Photographs)

**Page 148:** The happy moment of liberation in Wyck, September 13, 1944. (Historisch Centrum Limburg, J. Naseman, Fotocollectie GAM, 480)

**Page 149:** Sighting of the first Yanks; Frieda waving in excitement as the column passes in front of the Van Schaïk home. (Van Schaïk/Gumn Family Photographs)

**Page 150:** Frieda, her niece Ietje, and three American tankers. (Van Schaïk/Gumn Family Photographs)

**Page 155:** A portion of the Siegfried Line and its miles of anti-tank "dragon's teeth" that proved such a formidable defensive barrier. (National Archives (111-SC-194028))

**Page 157:** Just a few of the more than 34,000 men making the daylight jump into the Netherlands as part of Operation Market Garden. (National Archives (111-SC-354702))

**Page 177:** Prince Bernhard and a very gaunt Willem greet thousands of jubilant citizens from a balcony at Maastricht City Hall. (Michiels van Kessenich Family Photographs)

**Page 197:** Black soldiers of the 3136th Quartermaster Service Company were already at work by the time Jeff Wiggins and the 960th arrived. (Stichting Adoptie Graven Amerikaanse Begraafplaats Margraten; Foundation for Adopting Graves American Cemetery Margraten)

**Page 200:** U.S. Army troops created mountains of supplies along the Rijksweg. (National Archives (111-SC-415370))

**Page 203:** One of the many dances organized for American soldiers by Emilie and her committee. (Historisch Centrum Limburg, unknown author, Fotocollectie GAM, 5437)

**Page 206:** Entrance to the Victoria Inn, where a German booby trap killed one American soldier and wounded many others. (Historisch Centrum Limburg, J. Naseman, Fotocollectie GAM, 2773)

**Page 219:** Part of the task of Jeff Wiggins and his fellow quartermaster troops involved affixing one of the soldier's dog tags to the grave marker prior to placing the body inside the mattress cover. (Public domain / U.S. Army Signals Corps / Major James E. McCormick, HQ 9th Army Quartermaster Corps / courtesy Mr. Kimo McCormick III via Arie-Jan van Hees.)

**Page 225:** American soldiers celebrating Christmas Vigil Mass inside Schark cave. (Historisch Centrum Limburg, unknown author, Fotocollectie GAM, 39339)

**Page 248:** Emil and Rose Mosbacher, with their son, Sigmund, in happier times. (Courtesy of the Leo Baeck Institute.)

**Page 256:** Captain Walter Huchthausen (center) at the German border during the brutal winter of 1945. (Van Schaïk/Gumn Family Photographs)

**Page 263:** Bill Hughes (in front of the garage, looking at the camera) and Company D in Sevelen. (National Archives (111-SC-336785))

**Page 286:** Some of the townspeople of Margraten who volunteered to help dig graves. (Stichting Adoptie Graven Amerikaanse Begraafplaats Margraten; Foundation for Adopting Graves American Cemetery Margraten)

**Page 296:** Frieda's photograph of Walter's grave on the day of her visit. (Van Schaïk/ Gumn Family Photographs)

**Page 308:** Captain Walter Huchthausen as Frieda always remembered him. (Van Schaïk/Gumn Family Photographs)

**Page 310:** Graves of barren earth, mounded for the first postwar Memorial Day ceremony, May 30, 1945. (Stichting Adoptie Graven Amerikaanse Begraafplaats Margraten; Foundation for Adopting Graves American Cemetery Margraten)

**Page 312:** 30,000 Limburgers, some visible in the distance, attending the first Memorial Day ceremony. (National Archives (111-SC-207725))

**Page 313:** Willem greeting Lieutenant General Simpson shortly before the ceremony begins. (Michiels van Kessenich Family Photographs)

**Page 317:** Papa Senecal, holding Mary Victoria, and Jenneke. (Michiels van Kessenich Family Photographs)

**Page 326:** Children, three of them Emilie's, outside the GRS Information Office. Inside the tent, local girls seek information about American soldiers. (Top image

Michiels van Kessenich Family Photographs; lower image Nationaal Archief, Den Haag, CC0, Fotocollectie Anefo, Koos Raucamp (photographer) Nummer toegang 2.24.01.09, Bestanddeelnummer 900-0416)

**Page 335:** Emilie at her writing desk in the dining room of their home. (Michiels van Kessenich Family Photographs)

**Page 344:** Emilie's photograph of the grave of Private Warren Feil. (Michiels van Kessenich Family Photographs)

**Page 344:** Emilie's photograph of the grave of Chaplain Pat Fowlkes. (Michiels van Kessenich Family Photographs)

**Page 361:** Frieda translated into English the text on the map that Dave prepared. (Historisch Centrum Limburg, archief ir. D.C. van Schaïk, 1903-1972, 21.170A, map D5)

**Page 368:** Grass covered large portions of the cemetery by the second Memorial Day ceremony. (Historisch Centrum Limburg, Het Zuiden, Fotocollectie GAM, 35597)

**Page 379:** Emilie points to Dave's map during a presentation in Atlanta, a scene she repeated regularly when meeting with next of kin. (From *The Atlanta Journal-Constitution*. © 1946 *The Atlanta Journal-Constitution*. All rights reserved. Used under license. Historisch Centrum Limburg, Familie Michiels van Kessenich, 16.0674, inv. no. 659)

**Page 383:** The map on which Emilie traced the route she took during her journey across the United States. (Michiels van Kessenich Family Photographs)

**Page 386:** Departure at LaGuardia Field and good-byes to the Feil and Huchthausen families. (Michiels van Kessenich Family Photographs)

**Page 388:** Mr. and Mrs. Gordon and Frieda Gumn. (Van Schaïk/Gumn Family Photographs)

**Page 388:** Frieda laying her bridal bouquet at Walter's grave. (Van Schaïk/Gumn Family Photographs)

**Page 397:** Bill Moore's portrait sits on the Van Kliests' piano in the room where the Underwater Boys spent so much time with the family. Left to right: Mek, Jaap, Abe, Mother, and Aart. (*Ondergedoken op de Veluwe*, written by Wolter Noordman and published by OMNIBOEK, Kampen, 2010.)

**Page 401:** Emilie and Willem's family: twelve children of their own and the two girls they adopted. (Jenneke Meyer Viol-Michiels van Kessenich Photographs)

**Page 409:** Lieutenant Colonel Cole's son, Bruce, and his stepsister, Cindy, during their visit to Margraten in 2009. (Courtesy of Cindy Beall-Suich)

**Page 411:** Bill Hughes paying his respects to Curley Ausmer in 2005. (Courtesy of Joe Wilson Jr.)

**Page 414:** In 2009, Netherlands American Cemetery Superintendent Mike Yasenchak presented a flag that flew over the cemetery to Jeff Wiggins in honor of his service during World War II. (United States Army)

**Page 415:** The photograph that set in motion my desire to tell this story—Gordon and Frieda hosting Thelma and Jim Huchthausen during their trip to Over Wallop in 2015. (James Huchthausen)

**Page 418:** Frieda and Robert Edsel visiting Walter's grave, May 2, 2018. (Robert M. Edsel Collection)

**Page 431:** (Anhaltische Gemäldegalerie Dessau/Photographer: Sven Hertel)

# INDEX

**A**

Aachen, Germany, 4, 72, 141, 144, 151, 155, 161, 173, 181–82, 190–91, 197, 228, 243, 255, 265, 271, 273, 276, 310–11

Aachen Cathedral, 229, 255–56, 306

African Americans, 24–26, 28–30, 75–78, 412. *See also specific persons*

Afrika Korps, 65

Akicita Honoring song, 162

Alexandria, Louisiana, 77–78, 298

Allies
  advancement of, 136, 140, 199, 241, 257–58, 274, 298–99
  air superiority of, 178
  attack from, 86–87, 125, 160–61
  bombardment by, 139, 141, 147, 178, 245, 284, 299
  casualties of, 86–87
  on D-Day, 119
  in European Theater, 65
  failure of, 142, 155
  in France, 136
  Germans posing as, 109
  ground campaign of, 235
  landing in Sicily by, 88
  in Normandy, 132
  in Operation Market Garden, 160–61, 183
  in Operation Overlord, 129–30
  in Operation Pegasus, 189
  in Operation Plunder, 279–81, 284–85, 289
  prisoners of war, 140
  propaganda regarding, 140
  at Siegfried Line, 161
  supplies transported by, 165–66.
  *See also* British military; United States military; *specific companies and divisions*

American Battle Monuments Commission, xxii, 416–17, 426

American Graves Registration Command, 354, 398. *See also* Graves Registration Service

Antwerp, Netherlands, 160–61

Apeldoorn, Netherlands, 113, 115–16, 136–37, 183, 185, 357, 390–91, 410

Apeldoorn Resistance, 137, 183

Apostolate of the Front, 212, 274, 317, 331

Arbeitseinsatz, 67, 69, 156

Arlington National Cemetery (United States), 309, 377–78, 427

Armored Force Liaison Office (United States), 30–31, 75

Army Group B (Germany), 4, 136, 157, 281

Arnhem, Netherlands, 32, 68–69, 142, 155–56, 183, 207, 270, 337, 349, 387

Arnold, Henry H. "Hap," 47

art, protection of, 34–36, 229–30, 256, 272

*Atlanta Journal* (newspaper), 323, 355

Ausmer, Curley J., 245–46, 412

autobahn, 290–91

**B**

B-17 Flying Fortress, 65, 92, 384

B-24 Liberator, 65, 104–5, 111, 116, 284

B-26 Marauder, xv, 56, 58–62,

Band of Brothers (Easy Company, 506th Parachute Infantry), xxi, 124

Barsh, Chaplain, 271

Battle of the Bulge, xxi, 221–22, 228, 243, 249, 276, 285

Belgian Gate, 130

Belgium, 6, 11, 15, 52, 66, 68, 114, 132–33, 136, 140, 172, 188, 196, 199, 202, 208,

220–22, 228, 234, 248, 253, 276, 286, 321–22, 342, 352, 354, 357, 394, 411, 415

Bender, SS-Oberscharführer, 213

Berlin, Germany, 241, 280, 299–30, 301–2, 304

Bernhard, Prince, 176–77, 329, 368

Biggle, L.L., 399

Bitter, Joop "Joke," 111, 113, 138

Black, xxi, 23, 26, 28–31, 75–82, 171, 192, 194, 196–98, 216–18, 240, 252, 257–60, 262–265, 276–77, 286–88, 301, 314, 322, 334, 376, 383, 396, 412–16, 425. *See also specific persons*

Bongers, J.C.J., 42

Bordenave, Ernest A. de, 329

Boykin, Frank W., 352

Bradley, Omar N., 8, 63, 155, 280

Brady, Francis M., 58

Brandsma, Father Titus, 16

Brennan, Urban, 216–17, 265

British military, 15–16, 46–47, 65, 168–69. *See also* Allies; *specific companies and divisions*

Brothers of the Immaculate Conception of the Blessed Virgin Mary, 223–24

Broun, Mary, 327, 400

*Brown v. Board of Education*, 413

Brucker, Wilber M., 396

Burger, Jaap, 406

**C**

C-47 Skytrain, 122–23, 282–83

Cadier en Keer, Netherlands, 190

Camp Claiborne, 76–79

Camp Haaren, 39, 42

Camp Ritchie, 249

Carentan, France, 129, 131, 156, 158, 160, 408

Castelvetrano, Italy, 98

Catholic Church (Netherlands), 16, 20, 39, 43, 67, 202–4, 207, 211–12, 221, 224, 227

Cats, Tilly, 133

chaplain, 48, 219. *See also* Fowlkes, Paschal "Pat"

Cheves, Gilbert X., 75–76

Christiansen, Friedrich, 35–37, 338

Churchill, Winston, 47, 100, 282

cigarette camps, 321–22

Civil War, 44, 166–69, 241, 309

Civilian Committee Margraten, 264–66, 310–11, 314–15, 325, 331–32, 334, 343–45, 351–52, 366, 369, 377, 381, 385, 398–400, 403–4

Clark, Mark W., 99–100

Cocq, Frans Bannick, 35

Cole, Allie Mae, 12–13, 128–29, 161, 408, 409

Cole, Clara, 127, 161, 408

Cole, Clarence, 127

Cole, Robert
  background of, 9–10, 127
  burial of, 170–71, 357, 393
  characteristics of, 10, 120
  death of, 159–61
  Eisenhower and, 120–21, 181
  family of, 127–29
  honors to, 407–8
  leadership of, 12, 129–31
  morale of, 128
  Operation Market Garden and, 157–60
  Operation Overlord and, 120, 122–24
  overview of, xiii
  photo of, xiii, 121
  at Siegfried Line, 156
  transfer of, 13

Cole, Robert Bruce, 128, 408–9, 427

Cologne, Germany, 245

Columbia, Alabama, 23

Combat Command B, 8th Armored Division (United States), 250–51, 267, 276

Cook, Jack, xx

Coolidge, Shepley, Bulfinch, and Abbott, 395

Corlett, Charles "Cowboy Pete," 175–82, 188–89, 195, 212, 274, 329, 363

Corman, Lieutenant, 369

Crispus Attucks High School (Indianapolis, Indiana), 29–30

Crystal, Thomas, 212

Cymbalski, Charlotte, 378, 380

**D**

Daniels, George, 76, 242

D'Ansembourg, Count Max Marchant et, 21–22, 39–40, 118, 304, 341

Dawson, Grandma, 24–27, 80, 82, 413, 415

D-Day, 119–25, 128–29, 132–33, 154, 156, 165, 169, 194, 211, 228, 231, 241, 280–81, 372, 408

Decoration Day, 309

Delbrück, Germany, 293

displaced persons (DPs), 292

Donovan, Edwin J., 217, 220

Doran, Robert E., 159, 408

Dutch Resistance, 66, 69, 93, 109, 111, 137–38, 183–84, 189, 213, 323, 357, 411

**E**

Easy Company, 506th Parachute Infantry (United States), xxi, 124. *See also* Band of Brothers

8th Armored Division (United States), xv, 250, 267–68, 275, 292

8th Armoured Brigade (Britain), 260

8th Infantry (United States), 125

82nd Airborne Division (United States), xi, xiii, 85–86, 124, 154, 156, 160, 172, 408

Eindhoven, Netherlands, 156, 171, 253

Eisenhower, Dwight D.
  with 101st Airborne Division, 119
  broad-front strategy of, 155
  on casualties, xxii, 333
  correspondence, 181
  on freedom, 237
  on General Simpson, 172
  Gold Star Wives and, 366
  leadership of, 8–11, 161, 282, 284, 301
  letter to Omar N. Bradley, 8
  Little Rock Crisis of 1957 and, 413
  in Maastricht, 253
  on military cemeteries, 357
  on Captain Kegelman, 47
  Operation Overlord and, 119–25
  photo of, 121
  in Sicily, 99–100
  Siegfried Line and, 161
  victory message of, 305
  on war, 9, 419
  in Washington, 30

Elizabeth "Hit," 325, 344, 377

*Elmer's Tune* (P-47 Thunderbolt), 90

Elting, John R., 278, 292–94, 323–25, 327, 355

English Channel, 6, 119, 123, 195, 243, 359, 372

European Theater of Operations, xx, 47, 57, 65, 119, 169, 172, 322, 394

**F**

Faubourg d'Amiens Cemetery (France), 168–69

Faubus, Orval, 259–60, 262, 288, 412

Feil, Eugene, 375–77, 385

Feil, Mabel Rose, 330–33, 342, 345, 351–52, 362, 364, 381–82, 385, 403, 415

Feil, Warren F., 330–31, 343–44, 353, 375, 382

Feil, William "Bill," 375, 377, 379, 385

Fernand, 73, 132–33

15th Infantry (United States), 8–9, 13, 120

55th Anti-Aircraft Artillery Brigade (United States), 222

First Army (United States), 136, 172, 197, 255, 286

First Canadian Army (Canada), 280

1st Airborne Division (Britain), 161, 189

1st Battalion, 15th Infantry (United States), 8–9

Fitzgerald, John E., 159–60

501st Parachute Infantry Battalion (United States), 13

502nd Parachute Infantry (United States), 120, 124, 128, 131, 156–62

504th Parachute Infantry (United States), 85–86

505th Parachute Infantry (United States), xiii, 85, 156

506th Parachute Infantry (United States), xxi, 124

507th Parachute Infantry (United States), 232, 234, 281–83, 323

Foitzik, Eduard, 92–93

*Forever Promise Project*, 400, 421–22, 428

Fort Benning, 11–12, 78, 80–81

Fort Bragg, 78, 128

Fort Eben-Emael (Belgium), 11–12

Fort Lewis, xiii, 8–9, 12, 30, 120

Fort Sam Houston, 9, 127, 161, 408

Fort Wadsworth, 80

Foundation for Adopting Graves American
Cemetery Margraten, xxiii–xxiv, 397–98,
417, 421
467th Bombardment Group (United States),
xiv, 105
477th Bombardment Group (Tuskegee
Airmen) (United States), 75
4th Infantry Division (United States), 125
Fowlkes, Lib
burial information to, 325, 327, 344
explanation of Pat's service to, 322–23
family of, 45–46, 74, 87, 377, 409
grief of, 303–5
influence of, 331, 342
letter from, 317
in Margraten, 399
Pat's letter to, 47–48, 74, 85–86, 97–100,
231–34, 241–42, 280
as receiving Pat's personal effects, 287.
See also Williams, Elizabeth Rives
Fowlkes, Paschal "Pat"
background of, 44–45
burial of, 286–87, 325, 327, 344, 393, 399
in Castelvetrano, 98–99
as chaplain, 47–48, 74, 84, 86, 98–99,
231–35, 281–82
characteristics of, 44
on combat, 244
commission of, 46
on country life, 100
death of, 283, 322–23
on dignitaries, 99–100
on Easter, 280
family of, 74, 87, 100, 287, 303–5, 377
on indolence, 97–98
Lib's letter to, 87, 100, 287
marriage of, 45
in Operation Varsity, 280–83
overview of, xiii
photo of, xiii
in Sicily, 87, 97
on Siegfried Line, 241–42
in Tunisia, 84, 86–87
work of, 45–46
Fowlkes, Rives "Betsy," 87, 100, 287, 399–400,
409, 428

France, xx, 4, 6, 11, 15, 68, 114, 127, 136,
140–41, 155, 168, 178, 195–96, 220, 232,
234, 241, 243, 248–50, 276–77, 281, 305,
313, 321–22, 415
French Resistance, 232
Fürth, Germany, 249–50, 278, 406

G
Gardelegen, Germany, 299, 301
Geldern, Germany, 260
Georgi, Nephi, 250, 268–69
German military
attacks from, 104
booby traps by, 144, 205–6, 258
burial processes of, 171
casualties of, 66, 87, 136, 169
confiscation by, 140–41
defeat of, 329
exodus of, 140–42
at Fort Eben-Emael (Belgium), 11–12
hostages taken by, 38–43
invasion of the Netherlands by, 3–7
in Operation Overlord, 124–25
parachute drops of, 11
property occupation of, 14–15, 53, 67
retaliation by, 259
Siegfried Line and, 155–62
strategies of, 11
successes of, 15–16
suffering of, 301
surrender of, 262, 304.
See also specific companies and divisions
Germany, Dutch citizens in, 304
Gestapo, 53, 89, 132, 137, 186–87, 208, 337
Gettysburg Address, 167
Girardi, Albert, 151
Gluck, Adolf, 213–14, 411
Goebbels, Joseph, 67
Gold Star Mothers, 384
Gold Star Wives, 366, 375–76, 378, 384
grave markers, 166–68
Graves Registration Service (GRS)
clean up processes of, 170
in Germany, 333–34, 357
grave digging for, 196–98, 215–20
identification process of, 171–72, 191, 394

origin of, 169

processes of, 168–74, 191–93, 218–19, 244, 265, 285–86, 328

searching by, 99

transportation vehicles of, 171

Great Depression, 8, 28, 45

Greentree, William, 205

Gronsveld, Netherlands, 72, 147, 195, 202, 215, 217

Gumn, Gordon, 339–40, 347–50, 358–59, 365, 367, 371–73, 387–88, 406, 415–16, 418–19

**H**

Hall, Walter "Pop," 262

Hallum, Harvey, 377

Hallum, Hyde, 377

Hancock, Walker, 255–56

Hanöver, Else, 18–19, 39, 141, 205–7, 331, 354–55, 404, 411

Hanover, Germany, 299, 305

Harte, Frank W., 384

Heer, Netherlands, xv, 6, 32, 53, 148, 227, 257, 339, 367

Henri-Chapelle cemetery (Belgium), 172, 197, 286, 357, 394

Herman, Alice, 154, 161

Herman, Jacob, Jr., xiii, 153–54, 156–62, 249, 321, 400

Herman, Jacob (Jake), Sr., 153

Heuschen, Father Johannes, xvi, 311, 325–27, 332–35, 345, 352, 354–55, 363–64, 366, 368–69, 398–99, 403–4

Heynen, Father Pierre, xvi, 219–20, 223, 265, 311, 314, 325

Hilfarth, Germany, 258, 267

Hiroshima, Japan, 332

Hitler, Adolf, 4, 6, 22, 66, 166, 241, 247–48, 304, 321

Hitler Youth, 300

Hoadley, John A., 208–9, 228–29, 271

Hobbs, Leland S., 145

Hodges, Courtney H., 136

Hoogveld, Johannes, 43

Hornbeck, Stanley K., 345, 363, 368, 375, 398

*Horry Herald* (newspaper), 56

hostages, German actions regarding, 38–43. *See also* prisoners of war

Hôtel de Paris, 276–77

Huchthausen, Walter J. "Hutch"

Aachen Cathedral and, 255–56

on art, 228–29

burial of, 295–96, 350, 388, 393

Frieda and, 272–73, 306–8, 347–48, 350

overview of, xiv

photo of, xiv, 256, 308

at Rhine River, 290–91

Hughes, Bill M.

in 758th Tank Battalion, 76

aftermath of, 411

background of, 29–31

characteristics of, 28, 244–45, 412

in combat, 258–63, 298–302

Curley Ausmer and, 411–12

death of, 412

deployment of, 241–46

enlistment of, 28, 30–31

in Germany, 322

grief of, 246

military overview of, 75–79

overview of, xiv

photo of, xiv, 263, 411

racism and, 78–80

at Rhine River, 288–89

work of, 31, 243

Hunger Winter, 259, 346

**I**

"In Case of Failure" speech (Eisenhower), 122

Indianapolis, Indiana, xiv, 28–31, 46, 77, 79, 241, 244–45, 298, 411–12, 427

Italian military, 87

Italy, 16, 87, 97–100, 119, 240–41, 322, 329, 395

**J**

Jackson, Edward L., 29

Jackson, Robert, 46

Japanese Americans, roundup of, 249

Jefferson, Charles, 257–58, 265, 267

Jewish Committee, 253

Jews

criticism of, 275

in hiding, 52–53, 251, 253, 259, 265
restrictions to, in the Netherlands, 19–22
roundup of, in the Netherlands, 20
smuggling of, 132–34
sponsorship of, 248
Jodl, Alfred, 305
Johnson, J.J., 30
Johnson, Lyndon B., 378–80
Jones, Ralph Van Kirk, 354–55
Jong, Hette de, 139, 147, 426
Jordan, Marie, 366, 375–76, 378
Jordan, Edward, 366

**K**

Kamperbruch, Germany, 263
Keck, Sheldon W., 290–91
Kegelman, Charles C., 47
Kissinger, Henry, 249
KLM Royal Dutch Airlines, 364, 366, 375, 386
Koninklijke Houtvesterij Het Loo
    (Netherlands forest), 106
Köster, Lies, 404
Kraut girls, 140, 221
Ku Klux Klan, 24–27, 29

**L**

LaGuardia Field, 375, 383, 385
Lakota Nation, xiii, 153–54, 162
Land, Elizabeth, 192
Land, John, 191–93, 198, 226, 249, 264–66,
    321
land mine, 292
Lang, Captain, 271
Larkin, Thomas B., 352–53, 357, 363, 377–79,
    381, 385
Le Havre, France, 243, 321
l'Ecluse, William, 411
Lee, Robert E., 44, 235
Lepore, Dominic, 93
Levy, Mabel Rose, 352–53, 382
Lhoest, Léon, 39, 41, 314
*Libelle* (magazine), 398
Liège, Belgium, 133, 277, 342, 352, 354, 398
*Life* (magazine), 330–31, 351–52, 376, 385
Limburg, Netherlands
    Allied control of, 161, 172–73

American evacuation from, 322
American presence in, 199, 255, 322, 397
cemetery in, 172–73
dances in, 188, 274
defense of, 132
description of, 212, 250–51, 257
food in, 70–71, 364
grave adoption program and, 331–34,
    362–63, 396
line of advance in, 11–12
news in, 126
pernicious relations in, 207
raid over, 90–92, 94
resignations in, 39
resistance in, 67
roundups in, 43
Lincoln, Abraham, 167–68
Lindbergh, Charles, 55
Little Rock Crisis of 1957, 413
Low, John L., Jr., xiv, 105–9, 111–15, 136–38,
    184–87, 189, 410
Luftwaffe, 86, 90, 104, 144, 178, 213, 222–23,
    243
Luxembourg, 15, 66, 221, 234, 249–50, 253,
    276, 322, 354

**M**

Maas River, 4–6, 12, 16, 32–33, 73, 139–40,
    147, 151, 200, 243, 250, 310
Maastricht, Netherlands
    American presence in, 172–73, 199–204,
        223–25, 241–43, 255, 257, 271, 306, 312,
        321, 338
    bombardment in, 139, 243, 245
    business closings in, 66
    casualties in, 139–40
    celebration in, 304
    cemetery in, 173, 352, 355, 401–2
    Christmas celebration in, 223
    citizens in hiding in, 144
    combat in, 139, 142, 146–47, 178
    communications in, 304
    conditions of, 40, 142, 201
    curfew in, 142
    description of, 14, 17–18, 228
    destruction in, 67, 139–40

drinking in, 202–3, 322

fear in, 221–22

food restrictions in, 21–22, 102, 132, 201, 210

German exodus in, 140–42, 144–45

German occupation of, 11–12, 14–16, 19, 38–39, 66–68, 134, 144–45, 342

hostages in, 38, 180

liberation of, 147–49, 151, 156, 161, 177–80, 332–33, 382, 411

map of, 143

morale in, 41–42, 89, 144, 330

Nazi support in, 20, 126, 175, 405

news at, 126

previous attacks on, 4

prisoners of war in, 16

prostitution in, 202–3

railroad bridge bombing in, 142

recreation in, 202, 220

refugees in, 304

resources in, 321–22

rupture of social order in, 18

surrender of, 6

threat to, 221–22

MacLeish, Archibald, xvii, xxiii, xxiv

malnutrition, 102, 118, 188, 202, 222, 259, 317, 331

Mantz, Werner, 307–8

Margraten, Netherlands

American military presence in, 251–53, 257

attack on, 223

cemetery in, 197, 215–16, 225, 264–66, 285–87, 295, 303, 306, 324–25, 327–29, 331–35, 342–44, 348, 350–52, 354–59, 365–66, 376–78, 380–81, 384–85, 393–400, 402–4, 406–8, 410, 413, 415–17, 419

characteristics of, 220

Christmas celebration in, 223

conflict in, 190–93

description of, 174

map of, 216

Memorial Day in, 309–15, 367–69, 375

overview of, xvi, xix–xxiv

photo of, xvi

process in, 165–74

weather in, 265.

*See also* Netherlands American Cemetery

Marquez, Henry E. "Rickey," xx

Marshall, George C., 11, 30, 319

Martha, 347–48, 385–86, 416

McCroskey, Samuel L., 225

McDarby, Dennis, 93–94

McGee, Tildon S., 323, 355, 390

McNair, Lesley J., 11

Medal of Honor, xx, 47, 396, 408

Memorial Day, xx, xxiii, 309–15, 325, 327–28, 356, 363, 366–69, 375, 394, 398, 421

Mendes de Leon, Dr. Charles, 20, 405

Merrill, Mrs., 81–82, 413

Michels, Heinz, 92

Michiels van Kessenich, Eduard, 20, 139, 176, 188, 202, 222, 368, 401

Michiels van Kessenich, Emilie

beliefs of, 17–18

burial of, 401

celebration of, 42–43

criticism of, 398, 402–4

dance organization by, 188–89, 199–204, 211, 221, 274, 317

death of, 401

description of, 401–2

family of, 17–19, 21–22, 40, 88, 101–3, 110, 176, 178, 188–89, 209–10, 222, 274, 304, 316, 332, 343–45, 351, 382, 399, 401

on German exodus, 145–46

as grave caretaker, 325, 329, 331–36, 343, 351–55, 362–64, 369–70, 375, 381, 385, 399

at The Hague, 366

home of, 14–15, 17, 22, 41–42, 101–3

hostage situation and, 38–43

illness of, 118, 317, 331, 384–85, 400

Lib Fowlkes and, 325

liberation of, 151, 178

Charles "Cowboy Pete" Corlett and, 175–82

marriage of, 16–17

Memory Book of, 89, 145, 175, 179, 189, 204, 212, 329, 342, 345, 367, 386, 402–3, 426

morale of, 16, 21, 41, 181–82, 201–2, 222–23
at 91st Evacuation Hospital (United States), 211–12
overview of, xiv
photo of, xiv, 335, 379, 386
publicity of, 398
radio of, 88
refugees in home of, 304
routine of, 18–19
social activities of, 201–2
start of war and, 3–7
travels of, 374–86
on Willem, 342
work of, 19
Michiels van Kessenich, Hubert, 176, 401
Michiels van Kessenich, Jenneke, 3–4, 18, 40, 89, 101, 103, 118, 176, 222, 316–17, 401–2, 404, 426
Michiels van Kessenich, Willem
accusations to, 180, 405
celebration of, 42–43
controversy regarding, 341–42
criticism of, 405
death of, 405–6
family of, 17, 110, 145, 304, 316–17, 332, 401
home of, 14–15, 17, 41–42, 101
honor from, 329
hostage situation and, 38–43
illness of, 16, 18, 179, 345
leadership of, 15, 17–18, 20–21, 176
letter from Americans to, 145
liberation of, 151
Maastricht and, 304, 354, 402, 404–5
Major General Charles "Cowboy Pete" Corlett and, 175–82
marriage of, 16–17
at Memorial Day, 313
morale of, 222–23
photo of, 177, 313
on recreation, 202
refugees in home of, 304
request to, 330
resignation of, 22
retirement of, 404
speech of, 180–81
start of war and, 3–7

work of, 41
Michiels van Kessenich, Willem, Jr., 140, 368, 401
Miller, Doris "Dorie," 26, 81, 285
Millingen, Netherlands, 263
Mittelbau-Dora concentration camp, 299
Model, Walter, 142, 157
Montgomery, Bernard Law, 65, 120, 136, 155–62, 280–81
Montgomery, Wes, 30
Moore, Bill F.
burial of, 357, 409–10
commission of, 389–90
crash of, 104–9, 116
death of, 214, 323, 389–91, 411
escape of, 184–87
family of, 355, 389
overview of, xiv
photo of, xiv, 105, 397
rescue of, 111–15, 189
trust of, 136–38
Moore, Helen, 323, 389–91, 410
Moore, John, 389–90, 410
*Moreton Bay* (British transport), 242
Mosbacher, Emil, 247–48, 250, 253, 324, 406–7
Mosbacher, Rose, 248, 324, 406–7
Mosbacher, Sigmund (Stephen) "Moose," xv, 247–54, 267–69, 292–94, 297, 321, 323–25, 406–7

**N**

Nagasaki, Japan, 332
Nance, Otto, 380
Naples, Italy, 97
Nationaal-Socialistische Beweging in Nederland (NSB) (Dutch Nazi party), 15–16, 39, 53, 66, 126, 135, 141, 145, 178, 180, 265, 304, 341, 405
National Deaf-Blind Helper's League, 416
Nazi Party, 20, 67, 248
Nederlandse Landwacht, 126, 132
Netherlands
accusations in, 180
Arbeitseinsatz in, 67, 69, 156
Catholic Church in, 16, 221
cross-border travel to, 342–43

defense by citizens of, 259
destruction in, 232–33
food restrictions in, 19, 21, 101–3, 132
German invasion map of, 2
Jewish restrictions in, 19–20
labor conscription program in, 67
liberation of, 147–48, 175–76
map of, 174
Nazification of, 66–67
neutrality of, 4
photo of, 5
pledge of loyalty demands in, 20
public opinion of Germans in, 67
radio confiscation in, 88
restrictions in, 19–21
revenge in, 179–80
start of World War II in, 3–7
strike in, 67
surrender of, 6, 11
war reports in, 88.
*See also specific locations*
Netherlands American Cemetery
  botany at, 358–60, 365–66
  chapel at, 358
  construction of, 356, 394
  current state of, 393
  description of, 225, 393, 417
  Dutch visitors to, 325
  family burial choices in, 395
  grave adoption at, 309–15, 325–28, 332–36, 369, 396–97
  improvements to, 327–28
  map of, 361, 376, 379
  Memorial Day at, 311–15, 367–69
  overview of, xix–xxiv
  as permanent, 394
  plans for, 357
  pride in, 252–53
  processing at, 395
  reburial process at, 395–96
  records of, 352–54
  redesign of, 395
  relocations and, 356–60
  reopening of, 396
  requests regarding, 330–36
  restrictions at, 325, 366

statistics regarding, 356.
  *See also* Civilian Committee Margraten
Netherlands War Graves Committee, 345, 352, 363, 375, 399
Neuengamme concentration camp, 299
New York City, 330, 364, 376–77, 384–85
*New York Times* (newspaper), 369, 377, 426
*The Night Watch* (Rembrandt), 34–36, 230, 256, 340
Nijmegen, Netherlands, xi, 68, 71, 156, 160, 338, 357, 425
960th Quartermaster Service Company (United States), 194–96, 198, 215, 217, 220, 242, 284–87, 305, 322, 413–14
91st Evacuation Hospital (United States), 211–12, 271
92nd Infantry Division (United States), 75
Ninth Army (United States), xxi, 172–74, 181, 191, 197, 199–204, 211, 219, 228, 230, 255, 271–73, 280–81, 285–86, 290, 306, 309, 312–13, 321–22
No Flesh Creek, Kyle, South Dakota, 153–54, 162
Normandy, cemetery at, 172, 357, 394, 417
Normandy Campaign, 241
Norton, Dr. Jamie, 54–55, 62, 96, 116–17, 171, 192, 406–7
Norton, Edward "Miss Ed" Robertson, 54–55, 62, 95–96, 116–17, 171, 192, 355, 407
Norton, Edward R.
  background of, 54–56
  commission of, 56–57
  in European Theater of Operations, 60–62
  as missing in action, 95–96
  overview of, xv
  personal effects of, 116–17
  photo of, xv, 56
Norton, Eugenia, 96
Norton, James A.
  background of, 54–56
  burial of, 171, 356–57, 407
  commission of, 56–57
  discovery of, 83
  in European Theater of Operations, 60–62
  as missing in action, 95–96
  overview of, xv

personal effects of, 116–17
photo of, xv, 56
Nuremberg Laws, 247

**O**

Omaha Beach, 129, 194, 394
117th Infantry (United States), 190–91
176th Infantry Division (Germany), 144–45, 151
116th Panzer Division (Germany), 292
134th Infantry (United States), 258
137th Infantry (United States), 298
101st Airborne Division (Screaming Eagles) (United States), xiii, 119, 171–72, 408
104th Infantry Division (United States), 243
105th Evacuation Hospital (United States), 258
Operation Avalanche, 87
Operation Grenade, 257–58, 267
Operation Husky, 84–86, 169
Operation Market Garden, xi, xxi, 156–62, 171, 183–85, 189, 241, 408
Operation Overlord, 119–25, 129–30, 169
Operation Pegasus, 189
Operation Pegasus II, 189
Operation Plunder, 279–83, 286, 288–89, 310, 328
Operation Torch, 65, 84–85
Operation Varsity, 280–81, 286, 310
Ossenberg, Germany, 268–69

**P**

Pacific Theater of Operations, 60, 181, 328, 357
Panzerfaust (German), 244, 260–61
paratroopers, 11–12, 65, 74, 85–86, 120-25, 130–31, 156-62, 172, 189, 232–33, 281–84, 299–300, 356. *See also specific companies and divisions*
Paris, France, 4, 8, 136, 139, 241, 276–78, 292
Patton, George S., 11, 31, 75, 86, 99–100, 136, 163, 171, 232, 249
Pearl Harbor, 26, 30, 48, 56, 77, 389
Pershing, John J., 393
Peter, 69, 207, 337
Peterson, George, xx

Pine Ridge Reservation (South Dakota), 153–54, 156
Prevoo, Felix, 404
prisoners of war, 16, 94–95, 134, 140, 213–14, 274, 298–300, 334, 412
Prosnes Airfield A-79, 281
prostitution, 78, 202–3

**R**

racism, xiv, 24–26, 28–31, 46, 77–78, 275, 412
Radio Orange, 21, 88, 126
Recklinghausen, Germany, 290
Red Cross, 68, 72, 85, 91, 96–98, 108, 141, 201–2, 208–9, 271–72, 282
Regout, Father Robert, 16
Rembrandt, 34–35, 230
Renaud, Simone, 396
René, Father, 20
Rheinberg, Germany, 267
Rhine River, 156, 161, 183, 190, 258, 263, 268, 273, 279–82, 284–86, 288–90, 292, 299, 302
Ritchie Boys, 249
Robinson, Jackie, 240
Roer River, 243–44, 257–58, 267, 271, 304
Rommel, Erwin, 65
Ronckers, Joseph, xvi, 217, 220, 265–66, 286, 311, 328, 331–32, 334, 403–4
Roosevelt, Franklin D., 1, 99–100, 119
Roosevelt, Teddy, Jr., 12, 125
Rose, Maurice, xx
Rotterdam, Netherlands, 6, 11, 15, 208, 228, 337
Rough Feather, Mrs., 162
Ruhr Valley, 281, 289–90, 292, 298–99, 301–2, 334

**S**

Sainte-Mère-Église, France, 124, 396
Saint-Lô, France, 133, 195, 414
Saint-Martin-de-Varreville, France, 124–25
Sande, Germany, 293
Sasaoka, Itsumu, xx
Schark Cave, 223–25, 406
Schloss Neuhaus, Germany, 293–94
Schmidt, Wilhelm, 145, 179
Schutzstaffel (SS), 20, 299–300

Second Army (Britain), 281

segregation, 28–29, 31, 80, 412

Senecal, Leo P., 200–2, 210–11, 221–22, 274, 304, 316–17, 329–31, 336, 342, 375, 377, 384–85

Sevelen, Germany, 260–63, 267, 288, 302

758th Tank Battalion (United States), 75–76, 240, 425

761st Tank Battallion (United States), 76, 240, 425

784th Tank Battalion (United States), xiv, 76–77, 79, 239–46, 257–63, 265, 267, 275, 288–89, 298–302, 305, 322, 411–12, 425

17th Airborne Division (United States), 232, 281

Seventh Army (United States), 86, 99, 172

Sherman (M4), 239, 242–43

Shomon, Joseph J.

  background of, 173–74

  home of, 217

  leadership of, 218–20, 309

  in Margraten, 220, 223, 225, 335, 358, 394

  on Netherlands American Cemetery, 265, 285–86, 310–11, 325–29, 333–34, 404

  and 960th Quartermaster Service Company, 196–97

  and 611th Graves Registration Company, 313–14

  overview of, xvi

Sicherheitsdienst (SD) (Germany), 144–45, 151, 183–85, 411

Sicily, xx, 84, 86–89, 97–98, 100, 119, 169, 171, 417, 424

Sicily-Rome American Cemetery (Italy), 417

Siegfried Line, 155, 161–62, 173, 190, 228, 234, 241–42, 259, 280

Simpson, William Hood, xxii, 172, 181, 201, 222, 313–14, 378, 383

Sint Pietersberg, 33–37, 49–50, 52, 69, 132–33, 144, 209, 223, 228, 230, 256, 271, 338–39, 406, 428

Sint Servaas (church), 67, 134, 229

Sint Servaas Bridge, 4–6, 147, 201, 222, 250–51

603rd Quartermaster Graves Registration Company (United States), 333–34, 343, 358, 365

611th Quartermaster Graves Registration Company (United States), xvi, 173, 215–20, 265, 309, 313, 327, 328

6th Army (Germany), 66

Smith, David, 114

*The Snooty* (C-47), 122–23

Solms, William O., 195–96, 215

Son U.S. Military Cemetery (Netherlands), 171–72

Sonotone company, 399

Soviet Red Army, xx, 11, 66, 97, 301–2, 400

Soviet Union, 4, 66, 394

Spivey, Dr. James Norton, 407, 427

Spivey, Larkin, 407, 427

Stalag Luft III, 95

Stalin, Joseph, 11, 66, 100

Stalingrad, 66

stamppot, 101

*Stars and Stripes* (newspaper), 221–22

starvation, 259, 338

*The State* (newspaper), 57

Stillman, Robert M. "Moose," 57–60, 95

Stopka, John, 123–24, 130, 159

Stout, George, 256

Straarup, Superintendent, 358–60, 365, 367

Stuart (M5), 149, 240, 242–43

Sully, Captain, 295

Summersby, Kay, 120

**T**

3rd Battalion, 502nd Parachute Infantry (United States), 120–21, 124, 128–31, 156–62, 171, 259, 281

Third Army (United States), 136, 232, 249–50

30th Infantry Division (Old Hickory) (United States), 145, 172, 181, 190, 194, 284

35th Infantry Division (United States), 258, 267, 288–89

314th Troop Carrier Group (TCG) (United States), 74, 85–87, 98, 323

322nd Bomb Group (United States), 57–58

332nd Fighter Group (Tuskegee Airmen) (United States), 75

3136th Quartermaster Service Company (United States), 197, 217, 286, 313–14, 334

Tiger tanks (Germany), 244

Toledo, Ohio, xv, 248
trench warfare, 168
Truman, Harry S., 335–36, 342–43, 358, 363, 366, 399
Twelfth Army Group (United States), 155–62
21st Army Group (Britain), 136, 155
26th Infantry Division (United States), 240
20th Kansas Volunteers (United States), 127
286th Battery, 97th Anti-Tank Regiment, 51st Highland Division (Britain), 171

**U**

Underwater Boys, 115, 136–38, 183–87, 189, 410
Union Army (Civil War), 166–68, 309,
United States military
  in Badlands of South Dakota, 153
  bombardment by, 65–66, 90–91
  burial practices of, 169
  casualties of, 133, 166, 241, 263, 322, 380
  characteristics of, 175
  indolence in, 97
  morale of, 9
  photo of, 150
  raid by, 46–47
  redeployment to United States, 321–29
  relationships with Dutch women and, 211, 221
  segregated units in, 75–77
  statistics of, 165
  supplies transported by, 165–66.
  *See also specific divisions/regiments*
USAT *Frederick Lykes*, 194
Utah Beach, 125, 129

**V**

van Haersma Buma, Sybrand Marinus, 39
van Hövell, Jos, 304
van Kliest, Aart, 113–14, 136–37, 183–84, 390
van Laar, Joseph, xvi, 174, 217, 225–26, 264–66, 311, 403–4
van Lanschot, Maes, 304
van Manen, Erro, 304
van Royen, Anne, 20
van Schaïk, David "Dave"
  as botanist, 358–60

  bravery of, 36–37
  characteristics of, 49, 70
  Civil Affairs Officers and, 208–9, 228
  death of, 406
  family of, 49–51, 427–28
  fears of, 417
  with German soldiers, 146
  in hiding, 144–45
  home of, 32, 69, 126, 367
  liberation of, 148–51
  maps of, 52, 376, 378, 380–81
  Memorial Day actions of, 311
  network of, 51–53, 67–68
  photo of, 50
  at Sint Pietersberg, 256
  suspicions regarding, 338
  as tour guide, 338–40
  work of, 32–34, 36–37
van Schaïk, Frieda
  accusations against, 337–38
  aftermath of, 415–16
  as American soldier host, 209, 271
  on American tanks, 149–50, 165
  approvals for, 371–73
  in Arnhem, 68–69, 156
  background of, 70
  bravery of, 36–37
  characteristics of, 37, 50, 69, 207
  at Christmas, 227–28
  at the dance, 270–73
  death of, 419
  education of, 67–68
  in England, 372
  family of, 32–34, 49–53, 67–68, 70–71, 132–35, 207–9, 228, 360, 415–16
  Gordon Gumn and, 339–40, 347–50, 358–59, 365, 367, 371–73, 387–88, 406, 415–16
  as grave caretaker, 331, 365, 367, 369–70, 393
  grief of, 295–96, 306–8
  in Haarlem, 346–50
  in hiding, 144–46
  home of, 69
  illness of, 295
  in International Red Cross, 72
  liberation of, 148–51
  at Margraten cemetery, 359–60

at Netherlands American Cemetery, 416–19
overview of, xv
photo of, xv, 51, 149–50, 388, 415, 418
response of, 6–7
at Sint Pietersberg, 33–36, 50, 256
as tour guide, 338–40
Walter Huchthausen and, 229–30, 272–73, 295–96, 306–8, 325, 358–59, 385–86, 415–16
war witness of, 72–73, 90–92, 126, 173, 271
van Schaïk, Helen, 68, 71, 338–39, 350, 359–60, 365, 367
van Schaïk, Jacoba, 68, 208, 228
van Schaïk, Margaret, 68, 71, 134, 149, 229, 250
van Schaïk, Margareta "Moekie," 6, 49–53, 68–71, 132–35, 144–45, 149, 207–9, 227–28, 270, 272, 337–39, 346–47, 349–50, 373, 387, 406
van Schaïk, Thea, 338, 359, 365
van Schaïk, Wim, 33–34, 36–37, 50, 71–72, 132–35, 207–8, 228, 230, 337, 349–50, 367
van Sonsbeeck, Willem, 118
van Terwisga, Narda "Mary," 137, 183–85, 411
Venlo, Netherlands, 257–59, 262, 275, 288, 302, 304
Verdun, France, 169
Villa Maya, 14–15, 17, 42, 88
Vinsant, Wilma R. "Dolly," xx
Virginia, xiii, 44–46, 98, 232, 287, 303, 305, 329, 377
Volkssturm, 268, 299
Von Kolnitz, Colonel, 116
Vroonen family, 251–54, 269, 278–79, 325

**W**

Walloons, 222–23
Walls of the Missing, Netherlands American Cemetery, xix, xx, 396, 407, 417, 421–22
Warden, Germany, 190–91
Waters, First Lieutenant, 260–61, 300
Wauters, Klara, 92
*We The People* (radio program), 385
Wehrmacht, 11, 171, 173, 182, 190, 221, 248, 302, 394
Wells, Robert, 94

White, Wilson Clifford, 205–6, 411
Wiggins, Clemon "Clem," 23–24
Wiggins, Essie Mae, 23–25, 413
Wiggins, Jefferson
background of, 23
death of, 415
enlistment of, 26–27
grave digging mission of, 194–98, 215–20
grief of, 24
home going of, 322, 412–13
leadership of, 215
leisure time of, 217–18, 242
library and, 80–82
morale of, 220, 305
at Netherlands American Cemetery, 413–15
overview of, xv
photo of, xv, 414
at Rhine River, 284–86
on Staten Island, 80
work of, 25–26
Wiggins, Othel, 24, 198
Wijngaard, Mr., 253
Wilhelmina (Queen), 17, 21, 176, 180, 304, 329, 341
Wilhelmina Bridge, 5, 147, 200, 222
Wilhelmina Canal, 156
Wilhelmshaven, Germany, 65
Williams, Elizabeth Rives, 45. *See also* Fowlkes, Lib
Winters, Dick, 124
World War I, 4, 29, 54, 127, 154, 168–69, 188, 241, 247, 262, 309, 394
World War II, xxi, 3–7, 165, 169, 330, 393–94, 405, 408, 409, 414, 421, 424–25, 429, 431. *See also specific aspects; specific locations*
Wounded Knee Massacre, 153–54, 162
Wyck, Netherlands, 4–5, 19, 38, 147–49, 172, 194, 199, 250, 428

**X**

XIX Corps, 172, 175, 178, 181–82, 195, 290
XXXVI Corps, 181

**Y**

"The Young Dead Soldiers Do Not Speak" (MacLeish), xvii, xxiii

**ROBERT M. EDSEL** is the #1 *New York Times* bestselling author of four nonfiction books, including *Rescuing da Vinci, Saving Italy,* and *The Monuments Men* (also with Bret Witter), which served as the basis for Academy Award recipient George Clooney's 2014 film.  Mr. Edsel has been honored with the Texas Medal of Arts; the President's Call to Service Award; the Hope for Humanity Award, presented by the Dallas Holocaust and Human Rights Museum; and the National Archives Foundation's Records of Achievement Award. In 2022, the United States Army and the Smithsonian Institution made Mr. Edsel an honorary graduate of the first Army Monuments Officer Training Program, an idea for which Mr. Edsel advocated for nearly twenty years. Mr. Edsel is also the Founder and Chairman of the Monuments Men and Women Foundation, recipient of the National Humanities Medal, awarded by President George W. Bush. (www.robertedsel.com)

To inquire about a speaking engagement with Robert Edsel, please write info@robertedsel.com.


**BRET WITTER** has co-written nine *New York Times* bestsellers, including the #1 bestsellers *Dewey* and *The Monuments Men* (with Robert Edsel). He lives in Atlanta, Georgia. (www.bretwitterbooks.com)

503

# American Battle Monuments Commission
## WWI and WWII Cemeteries and Memorials
### Pacific

✝ American Cemetery
✚ American Cemetery and Memorial
◑ Memorial

RUSSIA

MONGOLIA

Beijing ✪

CHINA

N. KOREA

S. KOREA

JAPAN

East
China
Sea

Tokyo ✪

BURMA

LAOS

THAILAND

VIETNAM

CAMBODIA

Manila ✚ Clark

✚ Manila American

South
China
Sea

PHILIPPINES

North
Mariana
Islands (U.S)

Guam (U.S)

BRUNEI

MALAYSIA

PALAU

SINGAPORE

I N D O N E S I A

SOLOMON
ISLANDS

PAPUA
NEW GUINEA

EAST TIMOR

Port
Moresby ✪

Gene Thorp

AUSTRALIA